BERNARD OF CLAIRVAUX

BERNARD *of* CLAIRVAUX

Between Cult and History

Adriaan H. Bredero

WILLIAM B. EERDMANS PUBLISHING COMPANY
GRAND RAPIDS, MICHIGAN

Originally published as *Bernard van Clairvaux: tussen cultus en historie*
© 1993 Kok/Agora, Kampen, the Netherlands

English translation © 1996 Wm. B. Eerdmans Publishing Co.
255 Jefferson Ave. S.E., Grand Rapids, Michigan 49503
All rights reserved

Printed in the United States of America

01 00 99 98 97 96   7 6 5 4 3 2 1

Library of Congress Cataloging-in-Publication Data

Bredero, Adriaan Hendrik.
[Bernard van Clairvaux: tussen cultus en historie. English]
Bernard of Clairvaux: between cult and history /
Adriaan H. Bredero. — 1st English ed.
p.   cm.
Includes bibliographical references and index.
ISBN 0-8028-3796-4 (cloth: alk. paper)
1. Bernard, of Clairvaux, Saint, 1090 or 91-1153.
2. Bernard, of Clairvaux, Saint, 1090 or 91-1153 — Cult.
3. Christian saints — France — Biography. I. Title.
BX4705.B5B813 1996
271'.1202—dc20
[B]   96-14649
CIP

Contents

ᕽ   ᕽ

Preface

I MET Bernard of Clairvaux for the first time in November 1942. In a secondhand bookstore I happened to see two polemics in which Bernard in 1224/25 had attacked the overly comfortable lifestyle of the monks in Cluny. It was a Dutch translation of these writings, edited and introduced by Anton van Duinkerken and published in 1938. I bought the book more because of the translator than because of any interest in the original author, but I soon put the book in my bookcase and did not begin reading it until the spring of 1944.

In the meantime my life had changed rather drastically. I was in hiding since May 1943 because I had refused to sign the declaration of loyalty that the occupying power demanded from university students and had ignored the call to report for the *Arbeitseinsatz* (forced labor) in Germany that had been issued to all who had reacted as I had. For the time being I stayed at home and spent most of my time in my study.

I wanted to do something useful and to increase my proficiency in medieval Latin. For that reason I asked Jan Waszink to assist me. Waszink had not yet become a professor at Leyden University; he still taught at the municipal *Gymnasium* at Utrecht, where I had graduated in 1941. Thus began a series of weekly private tutorings. I always looked forward to them and have remained thankful for that privilege. Early in 1944 he suggested that we read the tract *De consideratione* by Bernard of Clairvaux. The problem we faced was to find a second copy of this text. However, a chaplain in my parish church had in his possession the *opera omnia* edition of Bernard, published by Merlo Hortius in Cologne in 1641. He gave me this impressive folio for free.

For over a year I worked on the translation of this treatise, which fascinated me more and more. I put the translation in writing and hoped I would be able to publish it at some future date. Meanwhile I heard that Anton van Duinkerken was also working on a translation of this text and of some of the other writings of Bernard at the request of an editor who was planning to begin publishing the series *Monumenta christiana* after the war ended.

In August 1945 I met Anton van Duinkerken during a meeting of the Brabant student association. We talked together, and I happily agreed to his suggestion that we continue the translation of these writings together. In the summer of 1946 we signed a contract with the publisher; however, by the time the translation was finished, the publisher had lost interest in the project. Another translation of *De consideratione* had just appeared elsewhere, and the series did not sell as well as expected. The broad interest for these classical writings that had reemerged during the war years had quickly dissipated. But Anton van Duinkerken continued to be interested in my study of Bernard.

When I finally finished my university studies in 1950, I first contemplated writing a dissertation about "Bernard as viewed by his contemporaries." For some years I collected all written statements about him that his contemporaries had left. The harvest was too limited and too diverse to serve as the basis for a doctoral dissertation; however, while collecting these statements, I became aware of the oldest hagiography of Bernard, which in part had been written while Bernard was still alive. And this did provide a topic for a dissertation.

With this in mind, I contacted Dom Jean Leclercq in 1954. At the time, this Benedictine monk, who lived in the Saint Maur abbey in Clervaux, Luxembourg, was working on a new edition of Bernard's writings. He showed an interest in my study and was immediately prepared to help me in my search for and examination of the ancient manuscripts in which this *vita* had been transmitted. He also made sure that others would not touch this same subject. He arranged for the publication of some of my preliminary findings and later also of my dissertation *"Etudes sur la vita prima de saint Bernard"* by the *Editiones cistercienses* in Rome. I worked on my dissertation under the direction of Professor R. R. Post and received my Ph.D. degree at the Catholic University of Nijmegen in 1960.

The next phase of my study of Bernard focused on the involvement of Bernard of Clairvaux with the rapid growth of the Cistercians, who were founding monasteries almost everywhere at the time. I was permitted to spend a year (1962/63) in France and Italy visiting universities, libraries, and archives for this research. This enabled me to meet others who were studying Bernard. My research did not bear too many tangible results, but it did provide me with a clearer picture of Bernard as a historic individual. It also led to a lecture, published as a small book in 1966: *Bernard von Clairvaux im Widerstreit der Historie* (translated as "Saint Bernard and the Historians," in *Saint Bernard of Clairvaux* [1977], 27-62).

In 1968/69 Rob Huygens, professor of medieval Latin at the University of Leyden, made me return to Bernard. He was working on a revised text of the *Dialogus duorum monachorum,* supposedly a dispute between a Cistercian and a Cluniac monk around 1155. Huygens asked me to write a historical introduction. I agreed to do this, but his revised text appeared without the introduction he had requested. The new insights I had gained while preparing this sketch simply proved too extensive. My research did, however, result in a series of articles, later combined in *Cluny et Cîteaux au douzième siècle* (1985).

I continued to be intrigued by the question of how Bernard must be understood as a human being. My quest for an answer again led to a few historical and historiographical articles. I was now able to give more precise information regarding a number of points that had already been touched upon in my dissertation, such as: the year of Bernard's birth and that of his entry in Cîteaux; the origin of the letter he allegedly wrote just before his death; his relationship with Peter the Venerable, the abbot of Cluny; and the events that preceded his canonization in 1174. All this resulted in some essays, published in various journals, such as often precede the writing of a book.

When in early 1988 Edo Klement of Kok/Agora Publishers (in Kampen, the Netherlands) asked me to write a new book — this time about Saint Bernard — I spontaneously promised to do so. At first I thought I would be able to provide him with a manuscript in 1990; however, the writing of this book required more time than I had foreseen. One of the reasons was the fact that the ninth centennial celebration of Bernard's birth in 1990/91 led to several fascinating congresses. Because of my involvement with some of these conventions, this book has become somewhat different from what I originally had in mind.

In this short survey of my almost fifty years of study of Bernard, I have mentioned a few individuals who have played an absolutely vital role. There are many others who have greatly contributed by their assistance and friendship; however, I can mention only a few. My contact with Giles Constable, first at Harvard and now at Princeton, dates from 1955. He asked me to write a contribution for a collection of essays at the occasion of the 800th anniversary of the death of Peter the Venerable, the most important opponent of Bernard. I first met Dom Pietro Zerbi of the Catholic University of Milan in 1962; ever since then we have learned from each other without ever fully agreeing. Last but not least, I want to mention the late Father Edmundus Mikkers of the Achel abbey, who since 1953 has often been willing and able to help me with his extensive knowledge of Bernard and the Cistercians.

I have benefited from the help of many others who have made it possible for me to publish about Bernard outside the Netherlands in four languages. They have seen to it that my work would be intelligible and would also be read. I want to thank all of them, but I will only mention Dr. Reinder Bruinsma by name. Once again he has invested much of his time in the translation of a rather substantial text. His translation gave me the additional opportunity to consider and then clarify a number of ambiguities that are found in the original Dutch version. Undoubtedly, this edition still leaves much to be desired. For this, however, the translator should in no way be held responsible. I owe it to him that worse errors have been avoided.

February 1995   ADRIAAN BREDERO

Abbreviations

🙐   🙐

ABR	*The American Benedictine Review*
AnBoll	*Analecta Bollandiana*
AnCi	*Analecta Cisterciensia*
AnnESC	*Annales: Economies, Sociétés, Civilisations*
Apo	*Apologia*
BdC	*Bernard de Clairvaux,* Paris 1953
BHL	*Bibliotheca Hagiografica Latina*
BNF	*Bibliothèque Nationale, fonds français*
BNL	*Bibliothèque nationale, fonds latin*
CC	*Corpus Christianorum*
CC, cont. med.	*Corpus Christianorum, continuatio medievalis*
CCM	*Cahiers de civilisation médiévale*
CC Mon.	*Corpus consuetudinum monasticarum*
CF	Cistercian Fathers series
C.S.S.	Cistercian Studies series
Cist. St.	*Cistercian Studies*
Cîteaux	*Cîteaux: commentarii cistercienses*
COCR	*Collectanea Cisterciensia*
D.A.	*Deutsches Archiv für die Erforschung des Mittelalters*
Ep.	*epistola*
Epp.	*epistolae*
Etudes (1960)	A. H. Bredero, *Etudes sur la "vita prima" de saint Bernard*
"Fragmenta"	Les *"Fragmenta de Vita et Miraculis S. Bernardi"*

Gesta	*Gesta, The International Center of Medieval Art*
H.J.	*Historisches Jahrbuch*
James	Bruno Scott James, *The Letters of St. Bernard of Clairvaux*
JEH	*Journal of Ecclesiastical History*
LdM	*Lexikon des Mittelalters*
Letters	G. Constable, *The Letters of Peter the Venerable*
MGH	*Monumenta Germaniae Historica*
M.I.ö.G.	*Mitteilungen des Instituts für oesterreichischen Geschichtsforschung*
M.R.S.	*Medieval and Renaissance Studies*
M.S.	*Mediaeval Studies*
NAKG	*Nederlands Archief voor Kerkgeschiedenis*
P.L.	J. P. Migne, *Patrologia Latina*
RBen.	*Revue bénédictine*
Recueil	J. Leclercq, *Recueil d'études sur saint Bernard et ses écrits*
R.H.E.	*Revue d'Histoire Ecclésiastique*
R.H.S.	*Revue d'Histoire de la Spiritualité*
RMab	*Revue Mabillon*
R.Q.H.	*Revue des Questions Historiques*
R.S.	Roll Series
SBO	*Sancti Bernardi Opera*, éd. J. Leclercq et H. Rochais, 7 tomes, Rome, 1957-1977
S.C.	*Sources chrétiennes*
SCH	*Studies in Church History*
S.M.	*Studi Medievali*
SMBO	*Studien und Mitteilungen aus den Benediktinerorden und aus den Zisterzienserorden* (from vol. 32 [NF 1], 1911: *Studien und Mitteilungen zur Geschichte des Benediktinerordens und seiner Zweige)*
SRG	*Scriptores rerum germanicarum*
SS	*Scriptores*
S.S.L.	*Spicilegium sacrum Lovaniense*, études et documents
V.M.	*Vita Malachiae*
Vp	*Vita prima*
Vs	*Vita secunda*

I

Introduction

꙼   ꙼

THERE SEEMS to be little doubt that during his lifetime the Cistercian abbot Bernard of Clairvaux (1091-1153) was an influential man. He was involved with numerous matters outside his monastery and almost to the same extent outside his order. Often these involvements went quite far. As a result, he was a controversial figure during his life, in spite of his reputation, because of his mortifications, his charisma as a spiritual writer and preacher, and his fame as a *thaumaturge* (miracle worker). However, not everyone appreciated Bernard's interventions and was prepared to recognize him forthwith as a saint.

Otto of Babenberg (1138-1158), the bishop of Freising and previously a monk and abbot in Morimond,[1] was among those who were prepared to recognize him as a saint, but who nevertheless at times voiced criticism of Bernard. This aspect of Bernard's life story was, of course, hardly highlighted in the hagiographic literature about him. Due to the veneration he had already received before his death, he was seldom publicly criticized. This condoning of his actions, at least in part caused by the substantial influence he exerted upon the world of his day, led to a distortion of his life story both at the time and later.

Nevertheless, we do have information regarding some aspects of his

---

1. *Ottonis . . . gesta Friderici imperatoris,* book I, c. XXXV-LXV (passim); Waitz and Simson, eds., in SRG B. 46, 1912, 54-93.

I

activities. We know that Bernard showed himself to be very partial in some conflicts concerning episcopal appointments — for instance, in the controversy surrounding the see of Langres in 1138, and in the appointment of William Fitzherbert as the archbishop of York against his wishes. This struggle began in 1140 and was not resolved until thirteen years later.[2] More widely known was the fierce battle that Bernard waged in 1141 against the theological writings and the person of Peter Abelard and, in 1148, against the trinitarian views of Gilbert de la Porrée. The disaster of the Second Crusade, which Bernard had promoted, must also have damaged his reputation. Finally, there are indications that Bernard's success in expanding his Cistercian Order through the founding of many new monasteries was not appreciated by all abbots.

But even in the available sources about the sometimes dubious activities of Bernard in these matters, the information is often given summarily and even in a cryptic form. As a result, we know but little about how this Cistercian abbot really operated.[3] Much has been written about his life, but we must nevertheless conclude that usually less attention has been paid to his actual accomplishments than to the sainthood he was said to have exemplified in his life, and to the extensive literary heritage in which, in particular, this sainthood was embodied.

Bernard's many literary works indeed brought him much fame. He was much interested in them and took great care in their conservation for readers in future times. In close consultation with Bernard, his secretaries prepared a register for his most important letters and made sure that his works were distributed and that his published sermons, which explained in detail his views regarding theology, spirituality, and the monastic way of life, were constantly revised. This much is clear, that he considered his writings as extremely valuable, even though he probably did not expect that they would continue to be read and reread.

In spite of the stubborn prejudice of classical scholars against Christian and medieval Latin, Bernard has maintained his fame as author through the centuries. Even today Bernard is read because of the religious-mystical content of his works as well as for his creative and literary use of language. Between 1957 and 1977 a critical edition of his complete works

2. Baker, *"Viri religiosi"*; idem, "San Bernardo e l'elezione di York." See below, p. 156.

3. Cf. "The Conflicting Interpretations" (1980).

was published.[4] Remarkably, several reprints have since appeared, as well as new translations and revised annotations in Italian, Spanish, German, and French. A Japanese translation is now being added to those that are already available. Apart from these *Gesamtausgaben,* many anthologies of his writings are regularly translated, in particular for those who appreciate Bernard as a saint and are interested in the mystical experiences he so ably described.

I. BERNARD AS PORTRAYED IN HIS OWN WRITINGS AND IN HIS HAGIOGRAPHY

BERNARD'S WRITINGS naturally contain information about his life. We know some things from what he wrote to certain people about the problems he was involved with and about the thoughts he developed about these issues. His letters further indicate who he was in regular contact with and what he wanted some of his correspondents to know at certain times.[5] But often this is far from clear. In those days there was no such thing as private correspondence, and care had to be exercised that outsiders would not learn about certain things one wanted to discuss with a correspondent. Bernard repeatedly experienced this problem. In such cases he followed the custom of his day of writing letters that testified of his friendship and goodwill toward the addressee, while the courier who delivered the letter was charged with orally transmitting or explaining the real reason that Bernard had sent this person a religious treatise.

This complication has misled many subsequent readers of his letters about the friendship that supposedly existed between the addressee and Bernard. In particular, this applies to the correspondence that Bernard carried on from 1137 onward with Peter the Venerable, who was then the

4. Leclercq and Rochais, *Sancti Bernardi Opera* (abbreviated as SBO). A significant portion of Bernard's writings have already been published in English. His *Letters,* for instance, were edited by Bruno Scott James in 1953, while a number of works were published in the Cistercian Fathers series: *On the Song of Songs* in three vols. (CF 4, 7, and 31), his *Treatises* in 2 vols. (CF 1 and 3), *The Life and Death of Saint Malachie the Irishman* (CF 10), and the *Five Books on Consideration* (CF 37). The *Apologia* was edited once more by C. Rudolph (Philadelphia, 1990), while G. R. Evans edited some *Selected Works* (New York, 1987).

5. Talbot, "San Bernardo nelle sue lettere." Also Diers (1991), 153-176. James, "The Personality," in S. Teubner-Schoebel (1993), 7-30.

abbot of Cluny. Bernard's relationship with Peter was far more cumbersome than is usually assumed. As we shall see, a close friendship between the two certainly did not exist.[6]

The precise role of his secretaries constitutes a further problem for our understanding of Bernard's letters. Sometimes Bernard did not know the exact content of letters that were sent out. There are good reasons to think that his last letter was not written until after his death; Geoffrey of Auxerre was most likely the author, and the letter was not sent by Bernard to the addressee.[7]

Even less accessible to historical research concerning Bernard's actual role were the sermons Bernard left in writing. To a greater extent even than his pamphlets, Bernard used his sermons to present his thoughts and views, or rather, his experiences and his teachings about spiritual theology and mysticism. Since Jean Leclercq's studies, it is generally assumed that Bernard's published sermons were never preached in that form. They must rather be viewed as part of his literary oeuvre, which through the centuries has fascinated and inspired its readers, regardless of whether they were able to recognize the theological teachings Bernard intended to develop in these sermons or to understand those in their historical context.

All attempts, therefore, to trace in retrospect what Bernard as a theologian wanted to say, or was able to say in his sermons *at a particular moment,* must leave several questions unanswered. The fact that he repeatedly edited and revised the texts of his writings is an extra complication. Through the years Bernard must have been involved in this process. The fact that earlier versions of his published sermons are often not extant makes it almost impossible to discover his development as a mystic and a theologian from these writings. It could therefore be greatly misleading to cite these writings or to refer to them in an attempt to sketch this development in Bernard unless one possesses external data that can situate a particular sermon in a more specific context.

It now appears to be possible to read Bernard's writings, in particular his letters, in such a way that they yield some information about the tactics of the abbot in his dealings with others: how he related to his supporters, and how he exercised his authority over them by pointing out to them his duty to defend the cause of Christ, and at the same time

---

6. Below, 227-239.

7. Cf. *Recueil* IV, 125-225: "Lettres de S. Bernard." Also: "Saint Bernard in his Relations" (1992) and "Der Brief" (1988).

stressing his own humble role and especially his personal unworthiness. This kind of information is not immediately apparent. It may be gleaned from incidental, often short passages in which he dealt with these topics; and it requires a careful comparison of all relevant statements. This textual analysis also enables us to discover what tactics Bernard used in dealing with his opponents and how he would, if things did not turn out the way he wanted, put the blame for any mishap on the ecclesiastical authorities, whose approval and support he had sought before launching his initiative.[8]

The writings that were later attributed to Bernard but were not written by him constitute an added problem for the historical accessibility of his person. This also applies to numerous statements that were ascribed to him but were not originally his. It has been shown that several texts in late medieval breviaries, which were attributed to Bernard and were highly popular in folk piety, are also merely pseudo-Bernardine. The story about a discussion between the devil and Bernard is the best-known example. Against the will of the devil, Saint Bernard is said to have discovered which six or eight verses from the Psalms would guarantee a blessed death to those who would recite them daily. An added condition for receiving this grace was the recitation of the prayer found in Psalm 39:4: "Lord, let me know my end, and what is the measure of my days; let me know how fleeting my life is."[9]

⁂   ⁂

LIKEWISE SOME of the writings of Bernard's contemporaries, in which they chronicled what they remembered about Bernard and, above all, wanted to testify to his sainthood, contain partially misleading information. In the opinion and experience of these authors, Bernard's life had been characterized by sainthood; but more than that, a special grace had predestined him for sainthood from his birth. On the basis of this view, they concluded that Bernard's actions had to be interpreted against the backdrop of his call to sainthood. His deeds were not to be criticized, since

---

8. Diers (1991), 150-269.

9. Peter Ochsenbein, "Bernard von Clairvaux im spätmittelalterlichen Gebetsbüchern," 213-219. The last line of this verse from the Psalms is found seven times in Bernard's writings. It seems that Agnes Sorel (1422-1450), the mistress of Charles VII, had written these "verses of Bernard" in her book of hours and prayed them before she died. Cf. J. Mellot, "Saint Bernard et la guérison des malades," 186.

such criticism would reduce his sainthood, which was, in fact, the determining factor in everything he did.

This corpus of hagiographic texts is quite extensive and poses many problems for those who want to distill from them information about Bernard's life. It is difficult to determine the historical value and reliability of these texts. This is also true of the influence of these writings in the period prior to the invention of printing. The main reason for this is the limited distribution of some of these texts in manuscript form; while other texts were apparently quite widely, but haphazardly, distributed. It is therefore difficult to ascertain for which specific purpose each of these texts was written.

In this respect most questions are raised by the oldest life story, known as the *Vita prima sancti Bernardi*. This treatise, which many historians have quite confidently referred to, is much more extensive than any other contemporary text that testifies to Bernard's sainthood. Yet this *vita* was more widely distributed and better known than any other. One hundred and thirty manuscripts of this text have been preserved, and many of the incidents it relates have often been depicted.[10] The extant manuscripts show some remarkable textual variants, which until recently defied any satisfactory explanation. The published editions of this treatise, on which most subsequent biographers to a considerable extent had to depend, contain such an amalgamation of these variants that they must, from a text-critical point of view, be regarded as rather unreliable.

When the text of this *vita* was first examined at the end of the previous century, the conclusions were rather positive. It was suggested that the revision of this document, which had led to many of these variants, had been undertaken by Geoffrey of Auxerre, one of the three authors of this work. His attempt to increase the credibility of this treatise was viewed as successful. This conclusion failed to consider the question of whether the authors of this *vita* in their portrayal of Bernard were not primarily interested in matters that we would have labeled as the salvific aspects of the life of a saint, rather than in the actual events of his earthly existence.

At the time when it was formulated, this conclusion about Bernard's sainthood was also seen as confirming the historical accuracy of the various biographies that had been published during the nineteenth century; for

---

10. For these manuscripts, see *Etudes* (1960), 15-23. For the pictures, see *Vita et miracula divi Bernardi Clarevallensis abbatis,* Rome, 1587; reprinted, Florence, 1987. Also Dal Prà, *Iconografia,* II, 1, La Vita, Rome, 1991.

these closely paralleled — both in content and in import — the information this *vita* at first view seemed to offer. This credibility was in particular ascribed to the *Vie de saint Bernard,* published by Elphège Vacandard in 1895, and reprinted and translated until 1927. Vacandard's extensive work is now regarded as the classic biography of Bernard. The many biographies that appeared in the first decades of the twentieth century were usually merely excerpts from this two-volume book. This once led a reviewer to lament: "It is, so to speak, too easy to always call upon Vacandard."[11]

Even later some authors leaned, at times uncritically, to a large extent, on this book. To give an example: On Vacandard's authority, many still mention 1090 as the year of Bernard's birth, even though he did not enter this world until 1091, as had earlier been generally and correctly assumed.[12] Likewise Vacandard's positive evaluation of the factual credibility and historical accuracy of the *prima vita* was quite generally accepted, and few saw the need for a closer examination of his statement. More than half a century later, Vacandard's judgment of Bernard's saintly life could still be uncritically repeated in a study of hagiography.[13]

The problem is that in evaluating this treatise, until recently no attention was given to the fact that it had originally been written to promote Bernard's canonization, that is — literally — to write him heavenward. If by comparing various manuscript texts this aspect had been detected earlier, the present impasse in the historical research of Bernard's life would have occurred long ago. The problem we face now is that we really do not know what to do with this extensive and reputable life story. And without denying the relationship that has been established between the writing of the *vita* and Bernard's canonization, some still support the literal and historical reliability of this treatise on the basis that the historical criticism against it has been too negative.[14]

As a result of this impasse, no new approach in the historical research regarding Bernard has emerged. And the historians have failed to see how this cultic treatise presented a theological rather than a history-based plea for Bernard's sainthood,[15] and how this has served as a surrep-

---

11. See Hugo Lang in SMBO 47 (1929), 400 ("Es ist so einfach, Vacandard sozusagen auf Flaschen zu ziehen").

12. "Saint Bernard, fut il né en 1090?" (1994).

13. Below, 170, note 70.

14. Leclercq (1976), 10-14. Goodrich, "The Reliability."

15. This is in particular true of the first book of this pamphlet. See Paul, "Les débuts de Clairvaux."

titious defense of this abbot against a number of objections from his contemporaries, called forth by his often too compelling dealings in church and society. Due to this veiled defense, a close reading of this *vita* appears to offer a remarkable mirror image of the controversial person Bernard must have been during his life in the eyes of many. More recently, the penetrating study of Bernard by Michaela Diers has shown that this methodology may also be applied to shorter text passages, and even to incidental phrases in Bernard's own writings.[16]

It is also important to note that in the course of this century, a closer study has been made of medieval canonization procedures.[17] That led to the discovery of how this oldest life story of Saint Bernard was written with the primary purpose of supporting the request for his canonization. Until then, how this treatise gave information about that aspect had not been recognized, since this is provided only indirectly. On the contrary, the historicity of the standard accounts — the so-called *topoi* of the hagiography, of which this *vita* contains several — was trusted almost unconditionally.

In this saint's *vita* attention is also paid to the many ways in which Bernard interacted with the world outside the monastery without, however, providing much detail about these involvements. This attention led later biographers in their paraphrases of this cultic treatise to deal extensively with Bernard's role in the church and the society of his day. It was generally assumed that this had put him in a position of leadership in the world of his time. But their approach usually remained uncritical. And so it went unnoticed that the ample attention given in this *vita* to Bernard's involvement with matters outside the monastery resulted at least partly from a desire to defend him against the criticisms he had to face regarding these matters. One of these criticisms was that he involved himself in many issues without being prepared to assume any official responsibility for these interventions: he repeatedly refused the episcopal office, which would have enabled him to assume official responsibility for certain involvements.

The fact that this veiled apologetic, which is repeatedly present in this *vita,* has been overlooked may to some extent explain why in later historical writings Bernard's leading role in the church and the world of his day has been somewhat exaggerated. This situation inspired the French

16. Diers (1991).
17. Kemp (1948); Vauchez (1981).

historian Achille Luchaire at the beginning of this century to make this rather exaggerated statement:

> Saint Bernard, who through the fame of his eloquence and sainthood directed Latin Christendom from 1125 to 1153, presents a synthesis of his times. He personified the entire political and religious system of an era of the Middle Ages that was dominated by the church's moral authority. To write his life story is to write a history of the monastic orders, of the (Gregorian) Reformation, of orthodox theology and the teachings of the heretics, of the Second Crusade and the events in France, Germany and Italy during a period of almost forty years. It is therefore hardly surprising that the biographers hesitated when faced with such a tremendous task.[18]

In the last sentence of this quasi-serious remark, which betrays a measure of French chauvinism, the "university professor" Luchaire attempted — at least for insiders — to discredit the scholarly value of the work of "abbé" Vacandard.[19] But ever since, it has been repeated and thereby confirmed.

2. THE CONTEXT OF THE TWELFTH CENTURY

IN OUR PRESENT VIEW of the significance of the twelfth century in the development of the society of medieval Western Europe, the leadership role of Bernard appears to have been of less direct importance than was often assumed on the basis of his cultic reputation. The structural changes that took place at that time were totally ignored in that earlier assessment. The fact that the twelfth century followed a period in which a series of significant developments had taken place was disregarded.

Eleventh-century Europe, which since the mass migrations had been fully controlled by a military elite (resulting in an economy of plunder), began to pay more attention to agriculture. A new technology for working the soil had sharply increased the yields, which in turn made the strong population growth less threatening. No longer were all the peasants needed in the agricultural production process, and progress in the cultivation of forests and swamps created a larger acreage for agriculture.

During the twelfth century this development further stimulated the

18. *Les premiers Capétiens*, 279.
19. "Conflicting Interpretations" (1980), 71. Below, 184, note 99.

continuous growth of a monetary and market economy. This in turn favored the rise of towns, several of which had by then already become trade centers of more than local importance. The development of urban centers also had definite spiritual and intellectual consequences, even though these affected only a minority of the population. Cathedral and chapter schools were established in a number of towns. These were frequented by boys of noble birth, who preferred the estate of the clergy and decided against the military profession or, at times, also the risky existence of commerce. These "city-schools" soon eclipsed the convent schools to which parents used to send one or more of their sons. In these monasteries boys would take their vows as oblates at a very young age; however, upon reaching adulthood many of these boys regretted having taken such vows. As a result, the preference for the new type of schools rapidly increased.[20]

The new monastic orders, the Cistercians in particular, exploited these developments. They required a minimum age of sixteen for entry into the monastery. Thus any intellectual training these monks may have received was acquired prior to their entry into the monastery at such schools. They therefore knew a little more of the outside world than previously had often been the case. This trend also caused a change in the understanding and portrayal of the love toward God, which now more closely reflected the love between men and women.[21]

From the beginning, the Cistercians realized the importance of the new agricultural production process that had been recently introduced. Since the ninth century, the Benedictine Rule concerning obligatory manual labor had been relegated to the background in many monasteries, while choral prayer and liturgical celebrations occupied an ever larger portion of daily life. Private masses became much more frequent; consequently, the number of priest-monks sharply increased, while lay brethren or *conversi* declined, not only numerically, but also in social status. These changes resulted from the close ties between the monasteries and the nobility — the military elite. Their monks were usually recruited from this class, and they in turn supported the military exploits with their prayers and penances.

The eleventh century, however, saw the establishment of monasteries that more strictly followed the Rule of St. Benedict. Manual labor

20. Cf. De Jong (1996).
21. Leclercq (1979), 15-16.

was reinstated, and more lay brothers were admitted. These were in particular occupied with the cultivation and exploitation of the land. The orders that originated in these monasteries — among which the Order of Cîteaux soon was the most important — adjusted in their lifestyle and social orientation to the agrarian and economic changes of that time. This largely explains the formidable number of monasteries founded or otherwise acquired by this order between 1112 and 1153. Its rapid growth also shows the interest in this order from elsewhere, because this extension was not limited to monasteries in France. Often the founding of new monasteries was not due to any initiative of the Cistercians themselves, but rather to requests from feudal lords who wanted to profit from the skills of these monks in the cultivation of their land.[22]

A second aspect that has often been overlooked by those who have attempted to explain the success of the Cistercian Order is the religious renewal that had already been realized elsewhere. The subsequent incorporation of a single monastery or group of monasteries in that order facilitated the smooth merger of such religious initiatives with the direct contribution of this religious order, and of Bernard in particular, to the religious renewal of that time. The takeover of the Order of Savigny, which in 1147 already counted seventeen monasteries, may serve as a clear example. This group of monasteries admittedly suffered from internal problems at the time of the takeover; nevertheless, it constituted an important and valuable extension of the Cistercian Order. Thus other monasteries that had been founded in the transition between the eleventh and the twelfth centuries significantly contributed to the new situation in which a personal and free choice for the monastic life had become rather common.[23] This is another aspect that should not be forgotten if one is to explain Bernard's success in attracting so many to life in the monastery.

BERNARD'S PERSONALITY fits well in this new context, in particular during the first half of his life. There is likewise no doubt about his ability to

---

22. For the relationship between these two aspects in earlier times, see Rosenwein (1982), 30-56.

23. Lackner (1972), 131-216. The share of the monasteries in social development since the sixth century gradually made monastic life, which because of its escape from the world could be viewed as a form of anti-culture, a basic cultural element in the medieval world. Prinz (1980).

make good use of these new circumstances, in which monastic spirituality also had to find a new form. But this fact in itself does not confirm the quite general notion that the renewed vigor of this order was largely due to his input, recruiting success, and initiatives.

In contrast to his five brothers, Bernard had been predestined by his mother for the clergy from his birth. For that reason he was, from around 1098, when he was about seven years old, educated at the chapter school of Saint-Vorles, also known as the Notre Dame de Châtillon. Bernard's stay at this chapter school must have been preceded by a parental decision to educate him for a spiritual position. This was not without precedent in his family; however, this decision, which must also have been a motivating factor for Bernard himself, coincided with a significant event in the region where Bernard lived. This was the founding of the monastery of Cîteaux, which initially was referred to as the *novum monasterium*. This founding was especially remarkable in view of the fact that it was the home of monks who intended to break a number of the rules that were current in the Benedictine monasteries of the time. They opted rather for a stricter way of life. No doubt the young Bernard had heard about this, the more so since these monks were supported by the Duke of Burgundy and the nobility related to him. This convergence between the already predestined future of Bernard as a member of the clergy and the founding of Cîteaux may therefore provide an answer to the question of why he chose to enter Cîteaux rather than Cluny. Cîteaux, which must already have been well established when he entered there in 1113, was not, however, to be the final destination for Bernard and his friends. It was rather a temporary home, from where this group itself founded a *novum monasterium* two years later. Whoever studies the relationship between Cîteaux and Clairvaux during Bernard's lifetime more closely must conclude that Cîteaux and the monasteries that were founded from there gradually adapted themselves more toward Clairvaux than vice versa.

A second remarkable event from roughly the same time that must have influenced Bernard's later actions was no doubt the conquest (or the deliverance, as it was rather called in his circles) of Jerusalem in 1099. This feat must have made a considerable impression, in particular from a religious point of view, upon the milieu of the military nobility, to which Bernard's family belonged. The fact that these two youth experiences of Bernard almost coincided may well explain why Bernard was always opposed to monks who wanted to make a pilgrimage to the terrestrial city, rather than discover the heavenly city in the monastery;

but at the same time, he was always prepared to help gather a crusader army in order to reach the heavenly Jerusalem through this terrestrial city. His willingness in this respect was already apparent in 1128, when he attended the Council of Troyes, which discussed the issues of the Templars, and in 1130, when he wrote his *Laudatio de novae* on behalf of this order of knights. Thus his choice for a new monastery that distanced itself from old customs did not signal a spiritual break from the circles of military nobility from which he had come. And it would also explain why this contradiction, which many subsequently believed to have existed between, on the one hand, Bernard's choice for the monastery, and on the other hand, his willingness to preach a crusade, was not experienced as such by Bernard himself.

Bernard's writings repeatedly refer to this noble milieu from which many of his metaphors were derived. The common prejudice of the dominating, noble minority against the serfs, who formed the majority of the population, at times shows through. Bernard manifested this bias in one of his literary sermons on the Song of Songs, which he wrote around 1145, when he had already been abbot for thirty years. Attempting to counter popular heresies, he pictured the followers of these heretical preachers as "a low and crude kind of people, illiterate, and as cowardly as one could possibly imagine."[24]

But more recently it has been argued that the way in which Bernard elsewhere typified the difference in the human experience before and after the Fall — based on the contemporary contrast between the nobility and the peasants[25] — should not lead us to conclude that he accepted this difference in status as inevitable. For in his "Letter in the Rain," written about 1124, in which he compared the Cluniac monks with their Cistercian counterparts, he described the voluntary lifestyle of the Cistercian monk as closely resembling the utter poverty of the peasants. This description almost seems a statement of Bernard's solidarity with this segment of the population.[26] But linking two texts that were written far apart in time and in totally different contexts can only lead to questionable conclusions. The identification of such solidarity on Bernard's part would seem to be based mainly on a projection of contemporary social thinking into the twelfth century.

24. *Sermo* 65, c. 8; SBO II, 177, lines 15-16.
25. *De diversis*, sermo 2, c. 6-7; SBO V, 83-84.
26. *Ep.* 1, 12; SBO VII, 9-10. Van Hecke (1990), 44-45.

This is another cultic way of understanding Bernard: to ascribe to him social virtues that are current in the classless society we now want to create and, at least in principle, attempt to disavow all forms of discrimination. It cannot be denied that Bernard very ably appealed to the status and codes of honor of the important personalities with whom he interacted.[27] Moreover, Bernard's ability to approach each social class according to its specific nature and status constituted an important aspect of his charisma. Geoffrey of Auxerre was eager to emphasize this particular quality:

> Often, when a good opportunity presented itself, he preached to all kinds of people, anxious as he was for the salvation of their souls. He adapted himself to each particular audience, on the basis of what he knew about their understanding, their customs, and their interests: for peasants, as if he had also grown up in the country-side. In a similar way he addressed any other group, if he had been able to get acquainted with their occupations: with the learned as a well-educated man, with the simple in all simplicity, and when speaking to spiritual persons with ample provision of subject matter about perfection and wisdom. In his desire to win all for Christ, he adapted himself to all.[28]

But there was another side to this coin. Bernard tended to mistrust those who did not share or support his views. He saw them as people who refused to be won for Christ; and he suspected them, often without solid reason, of promoting heresy, or accused them of a desire to sow disunity in the church. He launched fierce and far-fetched accusations against them in sermons and letters, the content of which was soon public knowledge. These were often based on a contemporary, collective prejudice that he was prepared to share, without any effort to verify the biased information he had received. He would simply assume it to be right. In his opinions about his opponents, he shared the stereotypical judgments that were current in his day; he adopted the general views regarding the usually discriminated category to which he assigned his opponent on the basis of his feelings. How unfounded his view could be is clear from his totally incorrect evaluation of Henry of Lausanne in a letter he wrote in 1144 to the count of Saint-Gilles.[29]

---

27. Diers (1991), 239-243.
28. Vp III, c. III, 6; P.L., CLXXXV, 306.
29. *Ep.* 241; SBO VIII, 125-127. Cf. *Christendom* (1994), 219-220. Grundmann, "Der Typus des Ketzers," 311-327. Riché, "La connaisance concrète de la chrétienté," 383-400.

꙳   ꙳

MOST PROBABLY Bernard's literary education prior to his entry in Cîteaux was not sufficient to make him conversant with all the different aspects of the intellectual renewal of that time that, since around 1928, have led historians to consider the twelfth century as a period of renaissance.[30] For Bernard "knowledge" equaled "spiritual experience"; the one was in any case linked to the other. But he had no affinity with Scholasticism, which was then on the rise, since this based knowledge too much on rational thinking (dialectics). Likewise, the intellectual renewal in legal matters that found expression in the rebirth of Roman law did not really appeal to Bernard, in spite of the realignment of canonical law brought about by the completion of Gratian's *Decretum* in 1143. On the contrary, he showed but little appreciation for the influence of Roman jurisprudence. Thus in his treatise *De consideratione,* he directed a sophisticated accusation to Eugenius III, a former Cistercian monk, claiming that in the papal palace more attention was given to the laws of Justinian than to the prescripts of the Lord.[31]

His objections against the role of Roman law at the papal court, which he also stated in this same treatise, coincided with his negative feelings regarding the ways in which justice was there dispensed. He scolded the abuses of lawyers, justices, and prosecutors, and reminded the pope that doing justice required strict impartiality. He also dealt extensively with the abuses that were common, and tolerated, when appeals were made to the Roman court.[32] These chapters clearly indicate that Bernard was well acquainted with canon law and with the dealings of this court, to which he must have repeatedly appealed, as in the case of the dispute regarding the see of Langres.

It remains difficult to know exactly how Bernard related to the theology of his day. His fondness for the patristic tradition that until then had fully determined theological practice is apparent from his efforts to have Abelard and Gilbert de la Porrée condemned for their teachings. His objections to the introduction of the Feast of Mary's Immaculate

---

30. Haskins (1927). Benson and Constable (1982) and Packard (1973), 150-222.
31. Book I, c. IV, 5; SBO III, 399, line 4. Jacqueline (1975), 39, with note 91.
32. *De consideratione,* book I, c. X, 13; SBO III, 408; II, XIV, 23; 430; III, c. II, 6-12.

Conception, voiced in a letter he wrote to the canons of Lyon, points in that same direction. This happened when the see of Lyon was vacant. Bernard argued that the canons went beyond the limits positioned by the Fathers regarding Mary's part in man's redemption through the Incarnation.[33]

This total reliance on tradition must not, however, be regarded as the only criterion of Bernard's theology. In the course of this century, Bernard's personal spirituality, as well as the particular nature of monastic theology in the eleventh and twelfth century, has become better understood; and the way in which Bernard practiced this theology has received special emphasis. Etienne Gilson's study *La théologie mystique de saint Bernard,* published in 1934, and also *The Love of Learning and the Desire of God* by Dom Jean Leclercq were crucial for this new understanding of his theology.[34] Both publications were appreciated by a somewhat broader readership and saw reprints and translations. Moreover, they were followed by further research into Bernard's religious experience and mysticism. This has left no doubt that his theological ideas were primarily determined by his religious experience and also, to some extent, by his mystic contemplation. He clearly gave priority to the affective element in knowledge over the rational element, to the extent that by that time these had already become separate categories.[35]

3. THE DISTORTED VIEW OF BERNARD IN OUR TIME AND THE PURPOSE OF THIS STUDY

PREVIOUS STUDIES of Bernard's theology have been very illuminating, but may have too easily ignored its historical context, as was evident during the 1990 official congress organized by the Cistercians at the occasion of the ninth centennial of Bernard's birth.[36] The structure of Bernard's writings was mostly overlooked, and no *close reading* was applied to the texts. As indicated above, a useful method for this approach was introduced only recently.

---

33. *Ep.* 174; SBO VII, 388-392.
34. Originally "L'amour des lettres et le désir de Dieu," New York, 1961 (1962); Paris, 1957; 2nd ed. 1963.
35. Verdeyen, "Un théologie de l'expérience," 551-557. Pranger, "The Virgin Mary and the Complexities of Love-Language in the works of Bernard of Clairvaux," 112-137. Also Köpf (1980), Van Hecke (1990), and de la Torre, "Experiencia Cristiana."
36. *La dottrina della vita spirituale nelle opere di san Bernardo.*

Bernard's formulation of his theological and spiritual ideas was in part shaped by his relationship with those he wanted to reach. Yet it remains almost impossible to establish any direct link between his statements and his actual involvements in the affairs and problems of the church. This makes it extremely difficult to determine with any precision what influence Bernard's charisma exerted on society. But this influence must have enabled him to transmit firmly established religious norms and images as renewed values to the next generation, which was confronted with serious cultural changes.

Bernard's charisma also influenced his writings. On the other hand, it may also have determined, to a considerable extent, the success of his public and political activities. But as was stated above, those who studied Bernard's theology and his approach to and interpretation of the Bible failed in their analysis of his sermons and treatises to give ample attention to the actual context of his statements. This even seemed superfluous as long as the historical and the cultic approaches were seen as indistinguishable. Any understanding of his historical significance was reached on the basis of an a priori recognition of Bernard's sainthood.

Moreover, such an approach ignores yet another aspect of both Bernard's personality and his writings. Since he was often involved in political affairs, these also influenced and to some extent determined his approach to life. As is commonly known, these experiences at times led him to different choices in his dealings with church and society.[37] For instance, his ever-changing argumentation regarding the acceptance of monks who came to Clairvaux from elsewhere is noteworthy. His interpretation of the precepts of the Rule that were relevant to this matter also clearly changed with the circumstances.[38] Likewise, in his theology he emphasized an ad hoc synthesis rather than a methodical structure.[39] He wanted latitude in his expositions. This is evident from his love for comparisons in his explanations and from his literary preference for using alternating terms with approximately the same meaning and words that showed some similarity in tone and form.[40]

His style of writing can form another hindrance for a historical understanding of Bernard. In any case, it may mislead the reader with

---

37. Grotz, "Kriterien auf dem Prüfstand."
38. Diers (1991), 20-27.
39. Köpf (1980), 224-226 and 234-237.
40. Timmermann (1983).

respect to the reasons why he wrote and why he wrote as he did. His ability to play with words and to rephrase his arguments in such a way that they did not appear repetitious not only convinced his contemporary readers, but continues to be felt in later interpretations of his writings. As a result, intentions were at times ascribed to him that to some extent place him outside his own time. A study of the last chapters of the *Apology*, written by Bernard in 1125 about the situation in Cluny, is a recent example of this phenomenon. These chapters deal with the extravagance in redecorating the abbey churches and the monasteries to the glory of God. Since Bernard referred to this as the most important problem in this treatise, it is argued that the whole document should not be viewed as a polemic against the lifestyle of the Cluniacs, but rather as his authoritative contribution to the ongoing discussion about whether artistic embellishments of church buildings are acceptable. Thus "research" may again lead to cult.[41]

A one-sided, predominantly cultic evaluation of Bernard, which has often been defended even to the present,[42] carries yet another objection. This concerns the distance in time that separates us from Bernard. This approach to Bernard, which in fact fuses a cultic view of his person with a historical portrayal, does not fit our present view of culture, developed in particular in the Western world. In this new context, completely different premises serve as a point of departure. No longer do cult and history together constitute the basis for such an evaluation. Our present judgment of a historical person depends to a considerable extent on a view of culture that incorporates opinions about the experience of earthly reality that are totally different from those that were current in Western European society of the twelfth century.

This dissimilarity in approach is especially obvious in historiography. Historians tend to confirm their own culture because their views tend to fit within that culture and are in fact part of it. For that reason, modern historiography cannot conform to a medieval understanding of reality, in spite of its awareness of that particular worldview. A modern historian cannot adopt the medieval approach to reality and then present it as still valid in our time. Any attempt to do so leads to an anachronistic approach that ignores the fact that cult and history, which were intertwined at the

---

41. Rudolph (1990); cf. below 73, note 23.

42. "Conflicting Interpretations" (1980), 59-61, with the references given. *Christendom* (1994), 186-188.

time, are separate concepts in our day. This is a very essential difference between medieval and modern historiography. Mixing cult and history results in a portrayal that many fail to understand and cannot accept as credible.

In the modern context of the secularized experience of reality, a historian is first of all interested in determining and evaluating what Bernard was like in everyday life, before attempting to conclude how this human being could develop into a saint. There is no a priori assumption that the historical Bernard corresponds fully, or even to a considerable degree, to the reputation he acquired as a cultic figure during his life and after his death. The stories that undergird this cultic prestige in his hagiography either defy credibility or are conceptually so inaccessible that the identity of Bernard as a historical person remains obscure.

Theoretically, this secular approach seems a logical point of departure for a story of Bernard in his historic dimensions. The question is, however, whether this will also permit us to recognize his sainthood. This inquiry should, of course, avoid the criteria that were used when Bernard was canonized in 1174. We should rather base our judgment on the biblical concept of sanctity. But all this in no way means that we should totally overlook the way in which the Cistercians developed their view of Bernard's sainthood.

It is worth noting that initially not all members of the order held the same view. This difference, which is not immediately apparent, results from the fact that the way in which Bernard was remembered by those who had known him primarily as abbot did not fully coincide with the manner in which he was pictured by those who were involved in efforts to have him canonized. These very differences are important for a correct understanding of the development of the cult and thus for the historical understanding of this saint.

❦   ❦

I HOPE THAT this explication also clarifies the fact that this book about Bernard of Clairvaux does not pretend to offer yet another biography. It rather intends to pave the way for some future biographer who would want to break through the current impasse in the historiography of Bernard. Such an historian must be made aware of the many problems that beset this field of inquiry. Concerning the impasse itself, it has already been stated that one of the requirements for such a breakthrough would be a more precise delineation of the value of the contemporary hagiographical writings about Bernard as a source for a history of his person. This would apply to the *vita prima* in particular.[43] Justifiably, this extensive document his been valued highly. But so far there have been no guidelines as to how this treatise exactly helps us to understand Bernard historically. For that reason, this study will time and again refer to this *vita*.

This book is, of course, also intended for all those who continue to manifest an interest in Bernard. Since, however, with regard to a number of issues dealt with in this book, it would be insufficient to refer to research findings that have been published elsewhere, it is at times necessary to relate such findings here. Wherever possible this is done in footnotes or in paragraphs set in smaller type. These passages need not be read by everyone. Thus the book remains readable for those who want to skip such details.

This study — or rather this final report of a long investigation — deals with three separate aspects, which, however, complement each other and are interrelated. The first aspect concerns the textual problems surrounding the earliest hagiography of Bernard, in particular the *vita prima* and the relationship between the authors of this work and Bernard. A second aspect follows closely: the evaluation of Bernard in historiography and literature. The third aspect deals with the question of how Bernard ought to be viewed in his own historical context, and this will explore his actions during his "earthly" life.

For a long time scholars have been aware that the textual problems of the *vita prima* are far more complicated than is the case with many other lives of saints. This explains why so far nobody has ventured to provide a responsible text edition. And so far, no adequate inventory of these problems has been made, even though for centuries it has been known that two totally different redactions have been transmitted. Moreover, we are now aware that these textual differences have to do, to a considerable extent, with the rewriting of this *vita* after the first request for Bernard's canonization had been rejected.

However, it has remained largely unnoticed that both editions contain different strands of tradition. The reason for these differences is the same in both cases. One version was intended for wider distribution, the other exclusively for the codex to be handed to the pope with the canonization request. These specific versions, which only in exceptional

43. "La vie et la *Vita prima*" (1992), 53-81.

cases are mentioned in the textual tradition and are only referred to in critical editions as secondary variants, are nonetheless important if one wants to determine how the text and the concept of Bernard's sainthood, as it is found in twelfth-century Cistercian hagiography, developed.

The authors of the *vita prima*, of course, played an important role in the evolution of Bernard's reputation as a saint. Therefore, we must deal with the relationship between Bernard and each of these authors at some length, as well as with the protest within the order against this notion of sainthood. That leads us to the second aspect of our research report. Historians have based their writing about Bernard mainly on the work of these hagiographers. Thus their historiography has been and has remained, through the centuries, completely cultic in nature. Consequently, the way Bernard was portrayed was also determined by the times in which the various authors lived and was therefore subject to constant change. We will, in particular, focus on the association between cult and history, even though time-related aspects that had a bearing on these shifting evaluations also receive attention.

The third aspect of this study concerns the problem of whether our modern criteria of historical criticism enable us to understand Bernard as an historical person. Here we will present only some preliminary suggestions. A significant part of our presentation will, of course, be based on earlier research undertaken in different contexts, or build on the work of others, which to some extent already provided a breakthrough in a modern understanding of this abbot. We now know more about Bernard's role within his own order, about his relationship with Cluny, and about the famous friendship that supposedly existed between Bernard and Peter the Venerable. The traditional views on these matters have had a cultic rather than a historical background.

This also applies to the familiar explanation for why Bernard was entrusted in 1130 with the task of determining, on behalf of the French king, that Innocent III was to be recognized as the legitimate pope, while Anacletus II was to be viewed as merely a detestable anti-pope. The customary allusion to his sainthood does not provide an adequate explanation. Nor does this satisfactorily explain the various conflicts concerning episcopal elections in which Bernard intervened, or his role in the condemnation of the writings of Peter Abelard and Gilbert de la Porrée.

We will not deal with all of these subjects explicitly. We will largely ignore Bernard's controversies with Abelard and Gilbert de la Porrée, and also his often quarrelsome interventions in episcopal elections. These topics have been dealt with adequately elsewhere. Likewise, we will only cursorily deal with Bernard's preaching of the Second Crusade and the consequences he suffered when this expedition faltered. On the other hand, a major chapter is devoted to Bernard in his monastic *Umwelt*. In spite of his many escapades into the world, he was part of this milieu. For there, after all, he became a saint.

In this chapter due attention is given to his relationship with Cîteaux, Cluny, and Clairvaux. Since he was fond of referring metaphorically to his own abbey and even to all Cistercian monasteries as the Jerusalem of the monks, this imagery will also be dealt with in that chapter. Its title — "Jerusalem in the light of the lamps" — is taken from Bernard's commentary, in one of his sermons on the Song of Songs, on a text of the prophet Zephaniah.[44]

The information we can gather about his role in the peculiar monastic *Umwelt* perhaps enables us to sketch a more reliable historical portrait of Bernard, one which is acceptable to people living in the last decade of the twentieth century: a portrait that does not reduce the many contradictions in his life story to corollaries of the role divinely attributed to him as a saint even before his birth, to a fashionable story about his ambivalent character, or to an alleged internal dichotomy of his personality, based on the fact that he once called himself the chimera; that is, the monstrous dual being of his time.

But in spite of all its demythologizing of the history of Bernard, which in fact was more cult than history, we did not write this book to prove that Bernard has no right whatsoever to the predication of sainthood that the church officially conferred upon him. Any attempt to picture him as an historical person must recognize Bernard's ability to share his authentic religious experiences and mystic encounters with the Divine with others. For that reason, we will in this study not approach the abbot of Clairvaux from an exclusively secular point of view. On the contrary, an historian who deals with Bernard must also give due attention to the religious significance of his writings and incorporate this significance in his or her evaluation of the kind of man Bernard must have been.

44. See below, 191, with note 112.

II

Saint Bernard:
The Origin of His Cult in the
Cistercian Order and His Canonization

⅛   ⅛

THE FEAST DAY of a saint usually coincided with the calendar day on which his earthly life ended. That day is regarded as the beginning of the heavenly continuation of his earthly existence. As a result of the time-consuming character of the canonization process that the ecclesiastical authorities had developed over time, canonization was effected retroactively as a canonization applied to someone who had lived as a saint. The person who was regarded as a saint was usually already venerated as such during his lifetime. Since the ninth century, continuation of this cult after the saint's death required approval of the local bishop. From the eleventh century onward, this endorsement was gradually replaced by papal approval.

Chronological complications connected with these procedures usually defy any later reconstruction of the precise origin of the veneration of a saint. Such a reconstruction, however, is an inescapable task for the scholar who stresses the importance of distinguishing the historical person of the saint from the cultic portrait that resulted from his veneration. With respect to Bernard of Clairvaux, this task is indeed inescapable if we want to understand this monk in the historical context in which he lived. But this enterprise is far from simple. If we are to believe his oldest *vita,* he came sanctified from his mother's womb, and his cult began when his mother dedicated him to God immediately after his birth, just as Hannah had committed her son Samuel to God.

Yet, this *vita* shows a remarkable interest in the activities of this saint outside his monastery. This is perhaps more readily understood if one realizes that the first book of the *vita* was already written in 1147, five years before Bernard died. In the period 1146-47, Bernard was heavily involved with political matters, as, for example, his preaching of the Second Crusade indicates. He was instrumental in leading, among others, Emperor Conrad III to his decision to join this expedition. But when the enterprise totally collapsed in 1148, and many participants did not survive, Bernard was held accountable. This was one of the reasons that he began the second book of his treatise *De consideratione,* which he was in the process of dictating at that time, with an explicit defense concerning this matter.[1]

William of Saint-Thierry, the author of the first book of the *vita prima,* wrote before the failure had become fully apparent. Yet he must already have sensed the necessity of providing protection against criticism. He did not mention Bernard's preaching of the crusade, nor did he deal in any concrete way with the various matters in which Bernard had become involved in the world outside his monastery. William simply wrote about Bernard's religious calling, which had been announced even before his birth. He characterized it as a divinely ordained task of preaching to the world, of defending the church and the faith against external enemies and heretics.

William also linked Bernard's sainthood to the religiosity and the ascetic lifestyle that Bernard was said to have followed, according to the gospel prescripts, with his monks. Thus the historical person of Bernard was, already in this first book of the *vita,* pushed aside in favor of a portrait that was determined by his cult and theologically influenced by biblical examples and associations, and could therefore be defended against the criticism of contemporaries.

Remarkably enough, after Bernard's death not all within the Cistercian Order agreed about what in particular made him a saint. The monks, who had known Bernard primarily as their abbot, mainly emphasized what he had meant to them in that role; while the authors of the *vita prima,* without ignoring this aspect, also stressed the accomplishments of this (at the time not yet canonized) saint in his activities and writings for church and Christendom.

An extra complication is found in the fact that in spite of the many miracles Bernard allegedly performed during his lifetime, this miraculous

---

1. C. 1, 1-4; SBO III, 410-413.

activity found no continuation at his tomb. Likewise, his official cult did not recognize him as a thaumaturge, even though this aspect confirmed his sainthood during his life in the minds of the common people.

I. BERNARD'S CONTEMPORARY HAGIOGRAPHY

THE COMPLICATED GENESIS of this cultic portrait of Bernard can be followed in detail from what we know about the origin and spread of the various hagiographical texts that provide a contemporary testimony about him. The majority of these texts were written prior to his canonization in 1174. The rest date from no later than the twelfth century. The total of sixteen texts[2] can be categorized in four different genres. In part they consist of writings about particular incidents — for instance, the lamentation written by Odo of Morimond at Bernard's death and several sermons in which his former secretary, Geoffrey of Auxerre, commemorated his abbot.[3] Another part consists of three hagiographical *lives*. Among these the *Vita prima sancti Bernardi*, already mentioned above, deserves most attention. This *vita* is the oldest, the most important, and the most extensive description of Bernard's life that has been preserved in many manuscripts. Both other *lives* are significantly less comprehensive and, to a large extent, depend for their content on this *vita prima*.[4]

A third group consists of four texts that were written to facilitate the first redaction of the *vita prima*. Three were written when a *vita Bernardi* was being planned. In 1145 Geoffrey of Auxerre, who for some years had already worked for Bernard as one of his secretaries, began to make notes that could be of use in such an endeavor. He wrote, for instance, a letter to Archenfridus, an unknown magister who probably worked in a collegiate chapter. In this letter he gives an eyewitness report of a preaching tour of Bernard to Languedoc, where he visited, among other places, Toulouse and Albi, with the purpose of combatting the heretical itinerant preacher Henry of Lausanne.[5]

---

2. BHL, nos. 1207-1238.

3. BHL, 1210, and BHL, 1230a, 1230b, 1230c.

4. BHL, 1212-1220 (Vp), 1232 (Vs, auctore Alano) and 1234 (*vita quarta*, auctore Johanne eremita). For the *vita tertia*, see below, note 9. For the *vita quarta*, which we will not discuss, see Hüffer (1886), 153-157. Text in P.L., CLXXXV, 531-550.

5. BHL, 1228. *Epistula Gaufridi de miraculis in Aquitania patratis*, P.L., CLXXXV, 410-416. Cf. "Henri de Lausanne" (1983), 108-123. *Christendom* (1994), 211-224.

Lastly, Geoffrey oversaw the final editing of a three-volume report of the miracles Bernard performed in Rhineland when he preached the crusade there in 1146-47. Fellow travelers helped with the creation of this treatise. Each night they made a report of what they knew about the miracles performed by Bernard during the day. Some they had witnessed themselves; while other miraculous events had been related to them.[6] After a revision by Geoffrey, the full text of this report was later added, probably around 1190, as a sixth book of this description of Bernard's life in some manuscripts of the *prima vita*. [7]

One of the other two texts utilized in the writing of the *prima vita* dates from 1153. Around that time, Geoffrey wrote an account of the last year of Bernard's life and of his death.[8] We will return to the relationship between this work and, in particular, the fifth book of this *vita*. The so-called *Fragmenta Gaufridi* constitutes the fourth work that belongs to this subgroup of texts. It was written around 1145. The text has been incompletely transmitted in various manuscripts. The oldest and least incomplete manuscript at our disposal is the *Codex Aureavallensis* (from Orval), which was recovered in 1929.[9]

It has long been assumed that Geoffrey collected these biographical fragments to provide William of Saint-Thierry with material for the first book of the *vita prima*.[10] The relationship between these *Fragmenta* and the first book of this *vita* has, however, proven to be somewhat more complicated. William did indeed use some of the data these *Fragmenta* provided. Recent textual analysis, however, has shown that Geoffrey, who collected most of these *Fragmenta*, initially wrote these notes to assist Rainald, the former abbot of Foigny. This Rainald returned to Clairvaux in 1131 in order to accompany Bernard as secretary during his many travels. Rainald must have sent a report of some of these journeys to Clairvaux, but no manuscript of these is extant.[11]

6. BHL., 1222-1227. *Miracula in itinere Germanico patratis*, P.L., CLXXXV, 349-416. Cf. "Studien zu den Kreuzzugsbriefen" (1958).

7. For the extant manucripts of this text, cf. *Etudes* (1960), 78-79.

8. "Un Brouillon" (1959).

9. BHL, 1207. Lechat, *"Fragmenta."* Presse, "Un manuscrit des *Fragmenta Gaufridi.*" In the editions of J. Mabillon these *"Fragmenta"* are regarded as the *vita tertia*.

10. *Etudes* (1960), 77.

11. Gastaldelli, "Le piu antiche testimonianze." The *Exordium magnum*, dist. II, c. 16, mentions a travel report of Rainald; ed. Griessen, 110.

It seems likely that initially Geoffrey requested Abbot Rainald to write a *vita Bernardi*. Whatever he wrote as part of such a work has been lost almost completely. Only the first section has been preserved, as part of the *Fragmenta Gaufridi*. The first six short chapters simply repeat a number of things that are related in the subsequent chapters of the *Fragmenta*. This would indicate that originally Geoffrey wrote these notes about Bernard's life not to assist William of Saint-Thierry, but for someone else. This other person may be identified as Rainald. Since the first section of the *Fragmenta* repeats some matters that were also related by Geoffrey, it may be assumed that these first short chapters were written by Rainald.

We do not know whether the texts of these chapters were completely identical to what Rainald himself is supposed to have written. But as noted above, William of Saint-Thierry did consult these *Fragmenta* when he wrote his part in the *vita prima*. It remains unclear, however, whether he had access to other notes of Rainald, which have not been preserved. This seems unlikely, since it would be improbable that precisely this *vita,* written by one of Bernard's secretaries, would have been almost completely lost, while so much more of other texts is rather abundantly extant.

We therefore have reason to assume that Rainald soon discontinued his attempt to write a *vita Bernardi*. The reason he decided not to pursue this project may have been that he felt too close to Bernard. In his daily, confidential contacts with Bernard as his abbot, he had been associated with him for much longer than Geoffrey. This closeness is also reflected in his return from Foigny to Clairvaux.[12] Another possibility is that Rainald may not have fully agreed with Geoffrey's plans regarding a *vita Bernardi*. For in this treatise, Bernard's activities outside his monastery and order are accentuated, while this emphasis on Bernard's involvements met with considerable resistance among the Cistercians.

Geoffrey, however, must soon have approached William of Saint-Thierry with these notes. This Benedictine abbot had long been a friend of Bernard, but he knew the abbot of Clairvaux in a different way than Rainald — from close by as well as from afar. He was also older. When William, at a more advanced age, became a Cistercian monk, he opted — whether or not he was encouraged to do so by Bernard is unknown — for another monastery. That is where he lived when Geoffrey handed him his handwritten chapters of the *Fragmenta*, possibly together with their partial repetition by Rainald. After William's death, Geoffrey sought, for the

---

12. Rainald's dependence on Bernard becomes apparent in three of the letters, which Bernard received from him while he was abbot at Foigny. *Epp.* 72, 73, and 74; SBO VII, 175-181.

writing of the second book, the assistance of Arnold of Bonnevaux, a Benedictine abbot from the Chartres region. He also gave the *Fragmenta* to him. It remains difficult to ascertain whether Geoffrey's choice of these two Benedictine authors had anything to do with the nature and intended structure of the *vita prima*. The fact that both came from outside the Cistercian Order must be of some significance: they were not accountable to the general chapter for what they wrote.

The fourth category of texts, which completes our list of hagiographic writings devoted to Bernard, has but little in common with the previously mentioned texts. It consists of three treatises from Clairvaux, for the most part written between 1170 and 1180. Best known are the *Exordium magnum,* written by Conrad of Eberbach while still a monk at Clairvaux, and *De miraculis* by Herbert of Torres, from which Conrad borrowed many of his stories.[13] Without much system, these writings incorporated a number of anecdotal stories about Bernard, in particular focusing on his relationship with his fellow monks — a direct witness to the great esteem in which these monks held their former abbot, who after his death lived on in their midst as a saint.[14]

These last-mentioned texts thus differ significantly from the proper *lives* of saints, and in particular from the *vita prima.* For this *vita* is equally interested in Bernard's involvement in the affairs of the church and the world, as in his significance for monasticism. This dual role of monk and politician, which Bernard was apparently able to fulfill, made him in many ways a paradoxical figure. This further poses the question of to what extent the paradoxical evaluations of Bernard in later centuries were directly based on the way in which Bernard was seen in his own day, or rather based on later reconstructions by historians.

Could it be that these historians were too heavily influenced by the portrait this abbot once painted of himself in a letter to the Carthusian Bernard, the prior of the monastery of Portes, in which he called himself the chimera of his time?[15] Is their portrayal of Bernard not too much a projection from a different time and a different culture, as, for instance, when Bernard is pictured as a sexually frustrated person? Some scholars

13. BHL, 1235. Grieser, ed., *Exordium magnum Cisterciense.* BHL, 1231. *Miracula auctore Herberto,* libri tres. P.L., CLXXXV, 1273-1384.

14. McGuire, "The First Cistercian Renewal." This source mentions a third, anonymous document, which remained unpublished. Idem, "A lost Clairvaux *exemplum* found."

15. *Ep.* 250, c. 4. SBO VIII, 147. Cf. "De toegankelijkheid" (1987-1988), 308-312.

maintain that this picture arises from Bernard's sermons on the Song of Songs, in which he speaks of a mystical union.[16] Here we clearly detect a projection originating in a culture in which many have no use for or understanding of any form of mysticism.

2. THE NIGHT VISION OF MOTHER ALETH

WITHIN THE SOCIETY in which Bernard participated, the criteria that served to evaluate him during his earthly existence changed as his life progressed and his reputation among his contemporaries developed. As a result of this shift, more attention was given to the way in which his sainthood was perceived, to his involvement in matters that usually fell outside the sphere of a monk. This is quite clear from the first book of the *prima vita*, written when he was still alive, in particular in the story of the prophetic dream that Aleth, the mother of Bernard, was reported to have had:

> While she was still carrying her third son, Bernard, within her womb, Aleth had a dream which portended things to come. She dreamed that she had within her a barking dog, which had a white coat and a tawny back. This dream made her very frightened, and so she went to ask a certain holy man about it. When she spoke to him, he was immediately filled with the same spirit of prophecy which had enabled David to say of the Lord's forerunners that the tongues of their dogs would be red with enemy blood (Psalms 67:24). And the holy man answered the trembling and worried woman: "There is no need to be afraid, because this dream foretells nothing but good. You are to be the mother of a wonderful dog who is destined to be the guardian of the Lord's house. You have heard him barking, because soon now he will rush out against the enemies of the faith. He is to be a marvellous preacher, and as a dog will lick its master's wounds clean of all that may poison them, so the words that his tongue speaks will heal and cure many of the evils that disease men's souls."[17]

In many *lives* of saints we find similar prophetic announcements of a

---

16. Philipps, "The Plight of the Song" and Leclercq, "Agressivité et répression chez Bernard" (1976).

17. Vp, b. I, c. I, 2; P.L., CLXXXV, 227-228. Transl. Webb and Walker, 14, 15.

special divine grace by which a yet unborn person would distinguish himself in his earthly life. They follow, in fact, the pattern of the New Testament stories that precede the birth of John and the birth of Jesus. Such stories belong to the hagiographic genre and usually derive their meaning from a text of Scripture. Examples are Jeremiah 1:5 — "Before you were born, I consecrated you" — or Luke 1:41, 42, which relates the encounter of Mary with her cousin Elizabeth.[18]

The Psalm verse cited in the text just quoted appears nowhere in the writings of Bernard, and thus it did not yet carry a special meaning in connection with him. The interpretation here given of that Psalm verse attempts to represent Bernard as preacher and thereby to justify his actions in church and world. For that reason this text was chosen. Not once, but even twice, we also find the story about the dream of Bernard's mother that she carried a barking dog in her womb in the *Fragmenta Gaufridi.*[19] Geoffrey mentions it briefly, but Rainald of Foigny adds the comment that this child will not be like "dumb dogs" that cannot bark (Isaiah 56:10).

To a large extent the story of this dream is based on the explanation Gregory the Great gave to this verse from Isaiah as early as the sixth century. He also included a reference to the verse from the Psalms that was quoted in the *vita prima,* "The tongues of your dogs may have their portion from the foe" (67:24, Vulgate). In his explanation, Gregory remarks that this verse refers to the tongue of holy preachers. Amid the (infidel) Jews they had already been chosen to bark loudly for the Lord, so that they might confirm his truth against thieves and robbers. With their dog-tongues these holy *doctores* healed wounds. This they did by teaching the confession of sins. With their tongues, in a sense, they licked the wounds of the soul, and with their words, which tore the people loose from their sins and returned them to salvation, they, in a sense, touched their wounds.[20]

The metaphor of the barking dog, incorporated by Geoffrey in the *Fragmenta* as the more or less obligatory dream vision that a *vita* was expected to contain, was — as already mentioned — borrowed by Rainald of

18. Following a prediction concerning the yet unborn saint, the oldest *vita* of St. Dunstan (†988, as archbishop of Canterbury) refers to both texts. A further comment reads, "Thus we have a new John from a new Elizabeth; we have the Jeremiah of our days. The one was announced by God Himself as being consecrated from the womb, while the other was heralded as such by God's archangel." P.L., CXXXVII, 416.

19. C. 2 and 6; ed. Lechat, 90 and 91.

20. *Homiliarium in Evangeliis,* II, homilia 40, c. 2; P.L., LXXVI, 1302-1303. For the story about the dream of Bernard's mother prior to his birth as being a topos, cf. Gastaldelli, "I primi venti anni," III-116.

Foigny and William of Saint-Thierry. This showed some originality, since the allegorical interpretation of these Bible texts, although constantly repeated in later exegesis,[21] had previously not been common in hagiographic stories about dreams.[22] It was quite applicable to Bernard, in particular, in the functional elaboration by William of Saint-Thierry. Since 1140 Bernard, in his role as a preacher, had increasingly defended the interests of the church in society, and had acted like a barking dog against those who, in his opinion, were a menace to the church, the faith, and monastic life.

This enables us to understand why at the time Bernard was perhaps compared to a barking dog by some who had been approached with this fierceness and had been irritated by it. We no longer have any direct proof for this supposition. We do know, however, that Berengard the Scholastic, a pupil of Abelard and the author of a satirical apology, sharply criticized Bernard and accused him, among other things, of abusing his gifts of oratory against Abelard. The abbot allegedly used his oratorical talents to purposely mislead the participants of the Council of Sens, so that they no longer could differentiate between truth and error.[23]

It has also been suggested that some of his contemporaries facetiously called Bernard the *summus magister hiandi,* that is to say, the best teacher in widely opening his jaws.[24] In any case, a passage from the beast epic *Ysengrimus,* written in Latin around 1150, refers to such a characterization of Bernard's eloquence. Its imagery is not found with other authors,

21. It is known that in a letter to Cuthbert, the archbishop of Canterbury, the holy Boniface compared himself with "a dog that starts barking when it sees how robbers break into the house of the Lord, and undermine and destroy it. But since it finds no helpers to assist in the defense, it can eventually only moan softly." Cf. A. Jelsma (1973), 145. The quotation is from R. Rau (1968), 244-245, *Ep.* 78.

22. It is also found in the oldest hagiography of St. Dominicus. Vicaire (1982), 75-76: "Les premiers hagiographes . . . ont réceuili sur la naissance de saint Dominique plusieurs traits édifiants, qui ont le seul inconvenient d'avoir déja servi pour d'autres saints." [The earliest hagiographical writings . . . contain several instructive treatises concerning the birth of St. Dominic. Unfortunately, however, they have already served other saints.] In a footnote Vicaire refers to the *vita sancti Gregorii* and to the *vita secunda sancti Bernardi.* The first reference, however, is incorrect. The *Legenda aurea,* an anthology of *lives* of saints composed (before 1260) by the Dominican Jaques de Voragine, in which Bernard received ample attention, also uses this dream vision for the life story of Dominic. See McGuire, "A Saint's Afterlife."

23. Thomson, "The Satirical Works of Berengar of Poitiers," M.S. 42 (1980), 121-124. Luscombe (1970), 29-49. Cf. below, 79, with note 36.

24. Van Mierlo (1943), 49-50. Cf. also A. Schönfelder (1955), 125, note 3.

but is, nonetheless, remarkable. Magister Nivardus from Ghent, the author of this epic, who elsewhere also wrote critically about Bernard, dared to compare the wolf Ysengrim with Bernard, because of its wide-open jaws.[25]

This almost inevitably leads to the supposition that the dream experience of Aleth, first introduced by Geoffrey, was turned by William of Saint-Thierry in the *vita prima* into a sacral argument in order to answer the often sharp disapproval for some of Bernard's involvements with affairs outside the monastery. Unlike Geoffrey of Auxerre and Rainald of Foigny, William extended this dream story into a consistent defense of Bernard against such criticism. As indicated in the *vita prima,* this story of the dream also constituted a veiled apology, which was, as much as possible, based on Bible texts, and was woven into this saint's *life.*

The reason that Bernard needed to be defended against the criticism of contemporaries had to do with the nature of this writing as well as the moment when it was composed. Earlier research has shown that this *vita* was written in support of a request for Bernard's canonization. An important requirement for canonization was the presentation of a written *vita* of the person whose liturgical veneration was desired.[26]

In his later years, Bernard was frequently involved with many affairs outside his monastery, and his many interventions landed him in many conflicts. These matters could not be ignored in a *vita* written during his lifetime. This treatise, in fact, was intended to illustrate Bernard's sainthood even when involved in such controversial actions. This task forced the authors to present Bernard's activities in a suitable biblical and cultic setting. Performing this task must also have been a matter of honor to them. Their acceptance of this assignment already shows that they were convinced of Bernard's sainthood. Moreover, two of them were intimately acquainted with Bernard.

By means of this cultic and biblical setting in which these authors placed Bernard's often controversial actions, they were able to put a positive spin on his interventions without being untruthful. Those who venerated Bernard as a saint saw no problem in fusing the cultic and historical approach to his person. But as we have already mentioned, this *vita*-image

25. *Ysengrimus*, Liber Sextus, lines 87-89; ed. Jill Mann (1989), 492: "Inde michi tota protende voragine fauces — Quam late valeas pandere labra, vide! Rumor ubique refert, quam sis Bernardus hiandi"; 493: "Then stretch open your jaws for me to the full extent of their chasm. See how wide you can open your mouth! Rumour everywhere relates that your jaws gape as wide as Bernard's."

26. *Etudes* (1960), 147-161.

of Bernard differs significantly from recollections afterward recorded at Clairvaux, originating with monks who had known him as their abbot. These had continued to venerate him as their holy abbot after Bernard's death, but prior to his canonization. The request of this monastic community for permission to venerate him as such in their daily choral prayers had already been approved by the general chapter of this order in 1159.[27] Thus developed a cult of Bernard, in which he was above all remembered as abbot, rather than as a popular preacher involved with all kinds of matters in the outside world. In these anecdotal accounts, which, as we saw, were recorded in Clairvaux without much system or order and without any further pretence, the image of Bernard as a saintly abbot who cared for his monks played a central role.

The words used in this cult of Bernard were simple and contrasted sharply with the care exercised in designing the cultic portrait that the authors of the *vita prima* have transmitted. Remarkably enough, this carefully constructed image of Bernard's holiness was initially much less popular within the Cistercian Order than the more traditional representation of his sainthood, which the monks of Clairvaux apparently preferred. The fact that they only recorded their recollections of Bernard after 1170, when the *vita prima* had already been written and revised, points in the same direction. But in the long run, this rather unpretentious portrayal had to give way to the far more comprehensive image of Bernard as saint, as presented in his official *vita*.

3. THE EARLIEST VERSION OF THE *VITA PRIMA*: PREPARATION AND WRITING

How THIS SHIFT occurred can now be reconstructed, to a considerable extent, on the basis of what has been discovered about the origin of this document and the manner in which it subsequently had to be revised when a first request for Bernard's canonization in 1163 had been refused by Pope Alexander III. This reconstruction includes the slow start of the manuscript distribution of this *vita*. Thus it became possible not only to reconstruct the blending of cult and history in this *vita*, but also to analyze the background of its presentation of Bernard's sainthood. This analysis will concern us in the next chapter. But before we can identify the two

27. Canivez (1932), I, 70, art. 7.

options that presented themselves with regard to Bernard's cult within the Cistercian Order, we must first occupy ourselves with the origin of his first *vita*, then with the revision of that text, and finally with the history of the attempts to have this abbot canonized.

As indicated above, the preparations for the writing of the *vita prima sancti Bernardi* already started in 1145.

After a first attempt to create a *life* by Rainald of Foigny, William of Saint-Thierry began in 1147 with the writing of the *vita prima*. After his death, the work was continued by Arnold, the abbot of the Benedictine abbey of Bonnevaux, which was situated near Chartres. His assignment was to describe Bernard's life during the period 1130 to 1145. Arnold particularly emphasized Bernard's efforts within the church at large to find recognition for Pope Innocent II. Innocent had been forced to leave Rome after two popes had been simultaneously elected in 1130. The other candidate, Anacletus II, regarded as anti-pope by the supporters of Innocent II, first gained the upper hand. Bernard soon became one of the main champions of Innocent and spent much energy to combat the claims of Anacletus, as well as Anacletus himself and his supporters.

Remarkably enough, the preparations for the writing of a *vita* began in the context of the election of Pope Eugenius III in the early part of 1145. The new pope belonged to the Cistercian Order. As monk he had been educated in Clairvaux and had subsequently, since 1139/1140, served as the abbot of the Tre Fontane monastery near Rome. Tre Fontane was an already existing Benedictine abbey, whose remaining monks had been expelled by Innocent II, after they had (during the schism) recognized Anacletus as the legitimate pope. Thereupon Innocent had offered the monastery to the Cistercians, or especially to Bernard.[28]

Bernard's poor health around 1145 raised the expectation that he would die during the pontificate of this new pope. It is clear from a letter sent by Bernard to Eugenius after the latter had been elected pope that he believed he would not live very much longer.[29] If this expectation were indeed to come true, a request for Bernard's canonization, provided it was supported by a *vita*, would have more chance of being approved during this pontificate than when Eugenius would have been succeeded by a

28. "St. Bernard and the Historians" (1977) 58, note 120.
29. *Ep.* 238, c. 6: "Who will grant me, before I die, to see the church as she was in the days of old?"; SBO VIII, 118. James, 279.

non-Cistercian. For that reason, it seems, immediately after the election of Pope Eugenius, preparations began for the writing of this *vita*.

Here we should also pay attention to the manner in which Peter the Venerable, the abbot of Cluny, reacted to the election of Pope Eugenius III. Cluniac tradition involved that he should have prepared the canonization of his predecessor, Pons of Melgueil. But Pons was no candidate for canonization since he had been deposed as unworthy in 1122; and he had also caused a schism in Cluny by returning to that abbey in 1125, only to die, finally, in a papal prison in Rome.[30] Peter the Venerable therefore began to prepare the way for the canonization of Matthew, the cardinal of Albano, who had bitterly opposed Pons and had strongly defended the Cluniac traditions. After Matthew's death in 1136, Peter wrote a *vita* in which he portrayed him as a saint. But in 1146 Peter refrained from further attempts to push for Matthew's canonization. He then included this *vita* in his *Liber de miraculis*, apparently convinced that Matthew's chances for sainthood had evaporated under the pontificate of an ex-Cistercian.[31]

It is impossible to determine to what degree Geoffrey of Auxerre, in his plans for Bernard's canonization, was influenced by this older Cluniac tradition to have the abbots-general of their order canonized after their death. It is conceivable, however, that the coincidence between these two events was more than simply a matter of accident. It would rather appear that, because of the election of Eugenius III, Geoffrey believed the Cistercians ought to seize this former Cluniac prerogative — the more so since it concerned Bernard, who as abbot had been such a strong factor in the shaping of his order.

As long as Bernard was alive, care had to be exercised to keep him in the dark about the preparations for his *vita*. But he may have known something about Geoffrey's plans. A statement by Bernard in the *vita Malachiae* perhaps points in that direction. He indicated that this abbot-bishop had begun his ecclesiastical career when he was still below the age required by canon law. This, however, also applied to himself — something he avoided mentioning. But with regard to Malachias, Bernard believed this noncompliance to be justified since he regarded Malachias as a recognized saint.

Bernard must have been aware of his saintly reputation among his contemporaries. Thus it becomes plausible that in this comment regarding

---

30. *Christendom* (1994), 140-146.

31. D. Bouthillier (1988), 72*-76*, who prepared a critical edition of the *Liber de miraculis*, maintains that Peter incorporated the *vita* of Matthew of Albano in this work between the summer of 1144 and November 1145. Why he did this remains unknown. Cf. "La canonisation de saint Hugues" (1990), 166-167.

Malachias's early consecration as abbot — which he mentioned around 1150 in the hagiography of a friend — Bernard also was reminded of his own disregard for ecclesiastical law. He himself had also been consecrated abbot at an early age. For that reason his remark about the youthfulness of Malachias at the time of his consecration may indicate that Bernard was not totally ignorant about the hagiographic activities of his secretary, to whom he addressed these remarks.[32]

During those years Geoffrey, of course, could not go beyond the preparatory work. Apart from the required approval of the general chapter of his order, as a monk he needed the endorsement of his own abbot or a bishop for the writing and distribution of a text. To acquire such approval, the author usually had to write an introductory letter addressed to the person who was to endorse the publication with his authority. In this case it was impossible as long as Bernard was alive, the more so since Geoffrey as the author of this *vita* could hardly have approached the bishop of Langres, in whose diocese the monastery of Clairvaux was situated.

Godefroy de la Roche Vanneau, the bishop of Langres and a cousin of Bernard, had served as prior of Clairvaux and had thus for many years been the right hand of Bernard, who had often asked Godefroy to be his caretaker during his frequent absences. Even later Godefroy continued to be heavily involved with the affairs of the monastery; while Bernard also meddled in the affairs of the diocese. For instance, when in 1147 Godefroy departed for the crusade, he left the diocese in the care of Bernard during his absence. If Geoffrey of Auxerre had told bishop Godefroy about this *vita,* there would have been a risk that Bernard would also have been informed. Otherwise he would have created the possibility that the bishop would have taken the matter in his own hands, as he did afterward with the *vita secunda.*

His age — he was at the most thirty years old at the time — was another reason why Geoffrey was not acceptable as author. Therefore, he had to

---

32. Bernard wrote in 1150 in c. III, 6 of the V.M.: "He (Malachias) was about twenty-five years of age when he was ordained as priest. Both ordinations (as deacon and as priest) were not completely conformed to canon law. Because he received the office of a deacon (levite) before he was twenty-five, and that of a priest before his thirtieth. . . . As far as I am concerned, I do not feel this is wrong when the person is a saint, but it should not be done when the person is not saintly" (SBO III, 314-315). Bernard's statement is remarkable in that he himself was consecrated as abbot when he was twenty-four years old. He must therefore have received his ordinations as deacon and priest long before the prescribed age.

find a potential author who, because of his abbatial authority, would have some freedom in writing, and yet was not in any way part of the "abbatial establishment" in the Cistercian Order.[33] After the cooperation with Rainald, the former abbot of Foigny, had failed, he chose — as already mentioned — William, the former abbot of the Benedictine monastery of Saint-Thierry. In 1136 this monk had entered the recently established filiation of Clairvaux in Signy, near Reims. As titular abbot, his position there allowed him much more freedom than an ordinary monk would have had. From then on he published widely and was involved in monastic affairs outside the Cistercian Order.

This last aspect is evident in his contribution to the *prima vita*. During the final years of his life, William had a close relationship with the Carthusians of the "Mountain of God," to whom he also addressed his Golden Letter.[34] His contacts with this monastery help explain why in the first book of the *prima vita* he compared Clairvaux with the Subiaco cave in which Bernard had lived as a recluse, while subsequently indicating that the monks in this monastery, supposedly established by Bernard in this forlorn and forsaken area, were living as spiritual recluses.[35] But the real reason that Geoffrey wanted the assistance of William was rather obvious. He had been a longtime friend of Bernard and was an author of some reputation.

On the other hand, it may be that William first suggested to Geoffrey that preparations might be undertaken for the writing of a *vita*. In his preface to the first book, worded in a conventional style, he indicated how he had earlier contemplated bearing witness to Bernard's sainthood, but had, out of respect for him, decided to wait until after his death. As his own health deteriorated, while Bernard regained his strength, he had changed his mind. He added that his

33. It was decided in 1137 that Cistercian abbots, monks, or novices were not allowed to publish without the approval of the general chapter. Canivez, I, 23: "Statutorum annorum precendentium collectio," c. LVIII (1137): "Si liceat alicui novos libros dictare." It seems, however, that this rule was not strictly enforced. Cf. de Lubac, *L'exégèse médiévale*, seconde partie, I, 275. This decision by the general chapter could not have been made without Bernard's knowledge; possibly he even took the initiative. In any case, he sent a messenger to this chapter from Italy, who carried a letter that was less than businesslike. *Ep.* 145; SBO VII, 347.

34. A Middle-Dutch translation of this letter was published by J. M. Willeumier-Schalij (1950). It begins as follows: "Hier beghint Sunte bernardus epistel die hi schreef totten breuderen vanden berghe godes" [Here begins the letter of St. Bernard, which he wrote to the brethren on the mountain of God].

35. Vp I, c. VII, 34-35; P.L., CLXXXV, 247-248. Cf. J. Paul, "Les débuts de Clairvaux." See also below, 265, with note 138.

decision to write the *vita* after all was taken at the instigation of some brothers who were in daily contact with the "man of God" and had conscientiously provided him with facts, which they in part had witnessed in person.[36] This encouragement supposedly came from Geoffrey, although we cannot exclude the possibility that Geoffrey's plan to have a *vita* produced resulted from a suggestion from William to Geoffrey.

As indicated above, the author of the second book, Arnold of Bonneval, also came from outside the Cistercian Order. His personal relationship with Bernard remains utterly unclear. We will return to this problem in the fourth chapter, where we will also look at his relationship with Geoffrey of Auxerre. The factual content of the second book would lead the casual observer to the conclusion that Arnold must have written, or at least completed, this work around 1153. For although he deals primarily with Bernard's activities during the 1130-1145 period, attention has also been given in this second book to Bernard's treatise *De consideratione,* written for Pope Eugenius III.[37] Bernard began its writing around 1147; the fifth book of this extensive and important document dates from as late as 1152 or early 1153.

The introduction that Arnold wrote for the second book of the *vita* indicated that he was approached with the request to be the author soon after the death of William of Saint-Thierry, possibly already in 1148. Most likely he wrote this second book as early as 1148/49. The passage about *De consideratione* was probably added at a later time. A more specific look at the Latin text of this *vita* leads to the conclusion that the two chapters about this treatise by Bernard constitute a later insertion, for the paragraphs immediately preceding and following these two short chapters seem to fit together perfectly. Since Geoffrey, as Bernard's secretary, was closely involved with the writing of this treatise, it seems probable that at some later date he himself inserted these chapters about the *De consideratione.*[38]

36. *Praefatio;* P.L., CLXXXV, 225.

37. SBO III, 393-493.

38. Vp II, c. VIII, 51-52. Cf. "Der Brief . . . auf dem Sterbebett" (1988), 213, with note 35. Our conjecture regarding this (inserted) passage implies that in that same chapter, Geoffrey added at least some names of Cistercians, referred to by Arnold as cardinal or bishop, to this list, since they received their office only after 1151/52. On the other hand, if Arnold had continued to work on this book after Bernard's death in 1153, we would expect that he would have indicated that Eugenius III had died in the meantime. Vp II, c. VIII; P.L., CLXXXV, 297. A further indication that Arnold completed the second book in 1149/1150 is found in the fact that no reference is made to the V.M., which Bernard wrote in 1149/1150.

Most probably, Geoffrey made these additions only after Bernard's death, when he completed this *vita* by writing the last three books, either on his own initiative or at the request of others. At first Geoffrey limited himself to the composition of an account of Bernard's final years, his death, and his funeral; later he revised his text as the fifth book of this *Life* of Bernard. The prologue that introduces his account indicates that Eskil, the archbishop of Lund, who had been one of Bernard's closest friends, had authorized the publication of Geoffrey's account. Eskil visited Clairvaux in 1152,[39] and on that occasion they may already have agreed that Geoffrey would write such an account and would send it to him after Bernard's death.

Several factors help us to understand why Geoffrey did not address the introductory letter to Robert, until then abbot of Ter Duinen, whom Bernard, before his death, had designated as his successor. This Robert — inducted through the intervention of Godefroy de la Roche into his new function in late October 1153, two months after Bernard's death — was only grudgingly accepted by many Cistercians as Bernard's successor. Probably they would have raised objections against anyone appointed to continue Bernard's work. This fact already explains why Geoffrey did not write this account of the last period of Bernard's life under the patronage of Robert.

However, in his report to Eskil, Geoffrey showed himself to be loyal toward Robert. He did this in a subtle way by telling about a vision that a monk, who in the meantime had died, had supposedly seen seven years earlier. In that dream, we are told, the succession by Robert had already been announced.[40] This story in support of Robert, who in a later text revision was even mentioned by name, seems to indicate that Robert's controversial position was not the only reason that he refrained from introducing the last three books of the *vita prima* with a prologue addressed to this abbot. He even refrained, possibly at the instigation of others, from writing the prologue under his own name. The original prologue suggests that a group of Cistercian abbots and bishops had met to write this introduction as well as the three books following. The bishops who were part of this writers' collective had earlier, of course, been Cistercians, or had been friends of Bernard.[41]

By the time Geoffrey wrote these three books, it was no longer necessary to make haste with the completion of this *vita*. Pope Eugenius III had

39. Schonsgaard, "Un ami de saint Bernard, l'archevêque Eskil."
40. Vp V, c. III, 17; P.L., CLXXXV, 361.
41. The text is found in *Etudes* (1960), 40.

died July 13, 1153, before Bernard's life ended. An important aspect in the preparation of the *vita* was the restructuring of this report for Eskil into the fifth book. Later research has enabled scholars to establish roughly how Geoffrey incorporated this account into this *vita*. A comparison between the original and the revised text shows how this revision must have been executed at the scriptorium of Clairvaux. In addition to an early copy of the original version of Eskil's account, the draft of the revision has been preserved.[42] Although the condition of this draft is rather poor, it enables us to conclude that Geoffrey at first planned to keep the introductory letter to Eskil as part of this revised account, even though he preceded it with a fourth and fifth book.

In the third book of the *vita prima,* in which Geoffrey discusses Bernard's virtues at a more mature age, he also mentions a few delicate events in his life: the failure of the Second Crusade, his opposition against the philosopher Peter Abelard and the theologian Gilbert de la Porrée, as well as against the popular heretical preacher Henry of Lausanne. The fourth book also emphasizes the miracles Bernard is reported to have performed in his later years — an element that had to be included in this *vita*. Since at the time when he completed this part Geoffrey still had the status of only an ordinary monk, his contribution to the *vita* had to be endorsed by the authority of at least an abbot or a bishop.

But a decision of the general chapter of the order in 1137 stipulated that the publication of a text by a Cistercian monk required the approval of this council. When asked for approval in this particular case, the chapter probably delegated the decision to the abbots and bishops referred to above. According to the prologue of these books, this group probably met some time during 1155 or 1156, no more than two or three years after Bernard's death, to write it together. In actual fact, it was rather an approval of what had already been written. Nevertheless, these judges referred to themselves in their prologue, which also must have been written by Geoffrey, as the authors of these books. Their intention was to give greater authority to his contribution than he would have been able to furnish himself through an introductory letter, the more so since he otherwise would have been forced to contact the still controversial successor of Bernard in Clairvaux.

This somewhat strange and misleading presentation of those books of the *prima vita* that were written by Geoffrey was primarily caused by

42. BN, lat. 7561. Cf. "Un Brouillon" (1959).

the intervention of the general chapter, which had to give formal approval of the publication of the sections written by him.[43] For the first version of the fifth book, Geoffrey had dodged this disagreeable requirement by dedicating this treatise to archbishop Eskil. This had been agreed, probably already in 1152, as the archbishop visited Clairvaux, while Bernard was still alive. When Geoffrey, however, had to complete the work of the other two authors, his publication no longer required such a solution, the more so since Eskil was part of the group entrusted by the general chapter with an evaluation of his work. By so doing, this college encouraged the rather unconventional presentation of these last three books as written by an authors' collective. Thus it was possible to endow this *vita*, which had to be deposited with the canonization request, with greater authority than it would have possessed if Geoffrey had introduced it himself with a letter, which he then would have had to address to the successor of Bernard in Clairvaux.

The decision of this meeting of abbots and bishops to present itself as an authors' collective may also have been prompted by the fact that because of the death of Eugenius III, the circumstances had become less favorable for Bernard's canonization than they had been when the project was in its initial stages. This may well have been the reason why these abbots and bishops thought it important to present this *vita*, which had to be handed to the pope when the request for canonization was made, as a treatise with greater authority. For in this prologue, this reputable group guaranteed the truth of what was affirmed about Bernard. Moreover, from the transmission of the manuscript of the prologue, it appears that this group presented itself as a writers' collective only in the codex that was submitted to the pope when the first canonization request was made.

But the abbots and bishops also dealt with the content of these books. In any case, they added four miracle stories to the fourth book. These were contributed by some of the participants who knew about them, either through information from others or through personal experience. It may be that they also decided to discard the postscript to the first book of William of Saint-Thierry, written by Burchard, the abbot of Balerne. However, it is not impossible that this postscript had been dropped by Geoffrey himself from the manuscript he had submitted to the abbots and bishops for evaluation and that served as the original text from which the

43. Cf. above, 37, note 33.

codex, to be delivered to the pope with the canonization request, was copied. When he later revised the text of the *vita*, Geoffrey felt somewhat unhappy with the postscript. In any case, he deemed it necessary to delete the clichéd story about Bernard's modesty as a baby when drinking from his mother's breast.[44]

The "esteemed authors' collective" also seems to have preserved a passage in the fifth book that Geoffrey had earlier eliminated. This concerned a healing miracle that supposedly happened shortly before Bernard's death.[45] The decision to maintain this passage in the revised text of the fifth book must have been made at the instigation of Bishop Eskil, who knew it from the earlier version of this book that Geoffrey had sent him at the time. We will deal extensively with the nature and content of this passage in the next chapter. Eskil, who himself also contributed a healing miracle, must, through his personal authority, have played a major role at this meeting. For the letter to him by which Geoffrey had introduced the oldest version of the fifth book remained in the text that was then agreed upon, even though it did not correspond to the suggestion that the last three books were written by an author's collective.

As mentioned above, the prologue, in which the abbots and bishops present themselves as the authors' collective of the last three books, is found in only one of the circa 130 manuscripts that are extant. This is also true of two other variants, mentioned above, which these abbots and bishops introduced into the text. However, the miracle stories that they added do occur in all other manuscripts as far as these contain the full text of this *vita*. Since the prologue and the other textual variants are found only in the manuscript that was produced between 1163 and 1165 in the scriptorium of the Benedictine monastery of Anchin, it seems likely that this manuscript largely depended on the codex that had been submitted to the pope when Bernard's canonization was requested in 1163.[46] As we shall see below in section 5, this manuscript contains further important data concerning the textual development of the *vita*.

---

44. Vp I, *Subscriptio Buchardi; Etudes*, 34-35. For the translation, see below, 139-140, with note 111.

45. Vp V, c. II, 15; *Etudes*, 54, with note 2.

46. Reference is to ms Douai, 372, vol. II. Cf. below, 43-49, with notes 61 and 62.

4. THE FIRST REQUEST FOR CANONIZATION

THE PROSPECT FOR a speedy canonization of Bernard diminished after the death of Eugenius III in 1153. Pope Anastasius IV, the immediate successor of Eugenius III, did not support the Cistercians in the protracted conflict between the Cluniac abbey of Gigny and the Cistercian monastery Le Miroir.[47] Anastasius's demise in 1154 did not offer any new perspective, since his successor, Adrian IV, appears to have been very restrained in his canonization strategies.

Nor could, at that moment, any new initiative be expected from members of the Cistercian Order. Abbot Gosvinus of Cîteaux, who succeeded Rainald of Bar-sur-Aube in that position in 1151, died four years later. And as far as his successor Lambert (1155-1162) is concerned, no remarkable deeds are recorded. From Clairvaux itself, very little could be expected for a while. Until his death in 1157, Abbot Robert was too busy with the opposition of those who found it difficult to accept him as Bernard's successor. Robert's successor, Fastredus, was a stronger leader, which perhaps explains why he was elected abbot of Cîteaux in 1162. He was the one who in 1159 requested the general chapter to allow Bernard's veneration as saint during the daily choral prayers at Clairvaux.

At first the death of Pope Adrian IV in that same year seemed to lessen the chances for a canonization of Bernard. The newly elected pope, Alexander III, was too occupied with the general acceptance of his election. An anti-pope, who soon acquired the support of Emperor Frederick Barbarossa, contested its legitimacy. Likewise, the Cistercians were faced with a formal complication. In 1159 Geoffrey of Auxerre had been elected as abbot of Igny. As a result, he was no longer able to support directly possible initiatives that had to come from Clairvaux.

Yet this papal schism offered the Cistercians new opportunities to put Bernard's canonization on the agenda. Inspired by the memory of Bernard's role in the struggle for Innocent II's recognition as legitimate pope during the schism of 1130-1138, the Cistercians — in contrast with Cluny — immediately sided with Alexander III and gave him tangible support.[48] As a result, the Cistercians could expect more cooperation from this pope than from his immediate predecessors. The first opportunity to focus anew on Bernard's canonization occurred in 1162. After Abbot Lam-

---

47. *Cluny et Cîteaux* (1985), 238-239.
48. Preiss (1934), 27-59.

bert's death, Fastredus became the abbot of Cîteaux; in Clairvaux he was succeeded as abbot by Geoffrey of Auxerre.

At about the same time, in 1163, Alexander III decided to come to France and to call a church council in Tours. For Clairvaux, this council appeared to offer a perfect opportunity for a canonization request, the more so since this abbey now had one of the most qualified supporters of the idea within its walls. Naturally, Abbot Geoffrey utilized this chance; when, shortly before the council, he met the pope in Paris, he initiated the request of Bernard's canonization. This request implied, among other things, the submission of a copy of the *vita*. Prepared in Clairvaux's scriptorium, it conformed to the version that had been agreed upon at an earlier date during a meeting of abbots and bishops.

As was indicated earlier, Geoffrey must have had another version of this *vita* that differed somewhat from this canonization file: it lacked the prologue of the abbots and bishops to the last three books and Geoffrey's letter to Archbishop Eskil as introduction to the fifth book, while this fifth book missed the healing miracle that had occurred after Bernard's death when his body lay in state. In this particular version of the *vita*, which Geoffrey had in his possession, the epilogue (added by Abbot Burchard of Balerne) following the first book, which was written by William of Saint-Thierry, was maintained. This somewhat different version of the text of the *vita prima* apparently was considered more suitable for readers, or possibly listeners, who above all wanted to be edified.

It was, of course, extremely important that the official version of this *vita* would edify the reader. For a canonization made no sense if subsequently no cult of the newly proclaimed saint were to evolve. This, therefore, was an aspect to be reckoned with in the evaluation of a *vita*. The spread of the extant manuscripts does not suggest, however, that this *vita* was quickly disseminated in the Cistercian monasteries. With the exception of Clairvaux, we also fail to discover a cult of Bernard in these monasteries. Only during the meeting of the general chapter of 1175, after Bernard's canonization, was it officially decided to introduce his feast in all monasteries.

Returning to the canonization request of 1163, we must conclude that Alexander III must have told Geoffrey in Tours that he found it impossible to put this request on the council's agenda. According to one of the letters from this pope at the occasion of Bernard's canonization in 1174, the official reason was the flood of canonization requests at that time.[49] Since he could not approve all of these requests, the pope must have preferred to postpone all decisions. Although this aspect was most likely one of the real reasons, it probably played only a minor role in the pope's decision to delay all discussion of current canonization requests. The fact that he did not strictly adhere to his decision adds further support to this supposition.[50] Alexander's wish to adhere to the new procedures for papal canonizations as developed by his immediate predecessors must have been the main reason. One of the changes was that canonization requests could no longer be submitted during a synod or council.[51]

The earliest papal canonizations date from the end of the tenth century. They were requested when a local bishop had refused to become involved or when the petitioner came under direct papal authority, as was the case in Cluny.[52] Initially, the procedure was limited to a consultation, usually during a synod chaired by the pope. This, in any case, was common when the request had been submitted by one or more participants at the synod. The discussion centered mainly on the information given by the petitioner to all the synod delegates. Often this meant the reading of the written *vita*, if this was already available. The discussion ended with a decision. In case of a positive decision, the petitioner could, after the synod had ended, and usually with episcopal assistance, begin with the exhumation and reburial of the remains of this saint, that is, with his solemn elevation and translation. These were from time immemorial the main aspects of an episcopal canonization.

During the first half of the twelfth century, this type of procedure was in principle still followed by papal canonizations, even though normally a request had to be accompanied by a written *vita*. But by this time the desire had grown on the part of those who were to make the evaluations to verify the facts that the petitioners had affirmed about the life of the candidate-saint and about his heroic manifestations of virtue. They also wanted to check the miracles he was said to have performed and those which supposedly had occurred at his tomb or elsewhere as a result of his intervention. This wish for verification, which fits to some extent with the rise of Scholasticism, was, in fact, foreign to the other requirement of a *vita* when a canonization was requested. This requirement implied that the stories in a *vita* about virtuous deeds and miracles were to fit the more or less stereotypical scheme that corresponded with the position of the candidate-saint in the world of church and society during his life.

---

49. P.L., CLXXXV, 622. Somerville (1977), 59-60.
50. "The Canonization" (1977), 86.
51. Ibid., 70-74.
52. "La canonisation de Saint Hughes" (1990), 156.

As a result of these changes in procedure, a *vita* now had to satisfy paradoxical requirements. On the one hand, a stereotypical *Life* of the saint, characterized by piety, was required; on the other hand, information was to be provided with regard to authentic facts. This paradox forced the hagiographer to select and disguise his facts in such a way that verification would be difficult, if not impossible. Such selectivity was of special importance when the candidate-saint had been a well-known figure during his lifetime, or, at least, while it was still possible to hear people tell about the reported miracles. If Geoffrey of Auxerre was aware of these changes in procedure, this may have prompted him, as the only author who was still able to do so, to change the text of the *vita prima* accordingly.

We have evidence that he indeed knew of these changes. From a sermon Geoffrey preached to the participants of the council in Tours, we may infer that he himself also took part in its discussions.[53] It therefore stands to reason that he learned the real reason why no canonization request was dealt with at this council. And this fact then explains why after the council he completely revised the text of this *vita*. For this new procedure, intended to make a verification of miracles and visions possible, allowed for spending more time in dealing with canonization requests than had formerly been the case. Earlier the decision regarding such a request usually took no longer than most other agenda items of a synod, which was normally of limited duration. But now the desired verification required much more time.

5. GODFRIED'S TEXT REVISION OF THE *VITA PRIMA*

GEOFFREY'S REVISION of this *vita* after the council of Tours concerns mainly abridgments or elimination of passages, as well as some stylistic and factual improvements. For example, in the first chapter of book I by William of Saint-Thierry, the statement that Bernard was born in *Castellione oppido Burgundie* (in Châtillon-sur-Seine in Burgundy) was replaced by *Burgundie partibus, Fontanis oppido* (in Burgundy, in Fontaines-lès-Dijon).[54] The miracle stories, which had been added to book

---

53. *Recueil* I, 43.

54. The main textual differences between the two redactions are listed in *Etudes* (1960), 27-57. In this particular case one incorrectness was replaced by another. Cf. Gastaldelli, "Le piu testimonianze," 11-12.

IV by the meeting of abbots and bishops at Clairvaux, were also better incorporated in the text. But this hardly informs us about the more fundamental reasons why Geoffrey began this textual revision after the Council of Tours. Other textual variants provide more insight into that matter.

A remarkable example is provided by a miracle story that was incorporated in book IV during the meeting of bishops and abbots who had to approve this text. According to the first version of this *vita*, it was contributed by Bishop Eskil himself. The second version mentions that it was reported by some godly persons who were associated with the archbishop but remain unidentified.[55] Two other names of persons who were still alive and who had been mentioned in stories of miracles and visions were eliminated in this revision.[56] These were names of people of noble birth. Well-known as they were, they could easily have been questioned about the miracles; and for that reason, it seems, their names were no longer mentioned in the revision. Miracle stories about peculiar healings and answers to prayer concerning members of the nobility who were still alive were therefore completely omitted.[57] On the other hand, two additional stories about visions in which Bernard had appeared to Cistercian monks after his death were incorporated into the revision of book V. One of the monks, William of Montpellier, from the monastery of Grandselve, is mentioned by name. From the cartulary of that monastery it is clear, however, that this William must have died around 1162, so that he could no longer have been called as witness.[58]

We are thus confronted with textual revisions that were intended to avert or avoid further questioning and research. We also find in the second version of this *vita* a softening of conclusions and statements, indicating an awareness of a somewhat changed political climate in Rome. The appreciation expressed in the first version for the work of Pope Honorius, who died in 1130, was now eliminated. Likewise, the second version no longer referred to Abelard as a heretic; and the accusation of the Jews in Rome because of their role in the schism of Anecletus also appears to be softened.[59] In addition, some healings that

55. C. IV, 26. *Etudes*, 48.

56. Vp III, c. VI, 19 and VP IV, c. VIII; *Etudes*, 42, 50, and 145, with note 4.

57. Vp IV, c. I, 6; c. II, 11; c. III, and c. VII, 37; *Etudes*, 45-47.

58. C. III, 22 and 23; *Etudes*, 55-56. For the story about William of Montpellier, see "St. Bernard and the Historians" (1977), 51, with note 95.

59. *Etudes* (1960), 146.

had apparently occurred through Bernard's intervention were now described as having occurred at a much faster pace and thus appear to be more miraculous. In some instances the name of the church where a miracle had occurred, or that of the saint who was there venerated, was no longer mentioned.[60] The reason for these deletions may have been to prevent the attribution of the particular miracle to the intervention of the local saint. But this type of textual adaptation was not executed systematically.

We know where, how, and when these revisions were made. The changes were applied in the scriptorium of Clairvaux. One of the manuscripts that was utilized for this purpose had before, in 1163, been presented to the pope, when Bernard's canonization had been requested. He probably returned this manuscript after his decision not to deal with the request at that time. Thus the manuscript must have become available for the execution of the text revision. It may have been particularly suited for that purpose; it had been produced with great care because of its special function. It was probably a codex of a larger format, with ample margins on each page around the areas with the writing. However, this is mere conjecture since, unlike the manuscript in which the report to Archbishop Eskil about the last year and death of Bernard had been recast as the fifth book, this codex of the *vita prima* has not been preserved.

But we have reason to think that a careful copy of this "working document" has been preserved. When the work on this second version of this *prima* was well advanced, Geoffrey entrusted the scriptorium of the Benedictine monastery of Anchin with the manuscript that contained the suggested changes. At the time Clairvaux had close ties with this scriptorium, which enjoyed great fame. Monk Siger, later the abbot, was in charge. Shortly after 1163, Siger had begun to copy Bernard's writings. In the three-volume codex in which these writings were copied, Siger also included the text of the *vita* and the account of Bernard's preaching of the crusade in Germany. On the basis of the peculiarities in the copies of these two texts in this codex of Anchin,[61] we may assume that Geoffrey, at Siger's

---

60. Vp II, c. IV, 22 and Vp IV, c. VII, 43; *Etudes*, 37 and 50.
61. Douai, Bibliothèque municipale, ms 372. Concerning this manuscript and the relationship between the two monasteries, see Dom Séjourne, "Les inédits bernardins du manuscrit d'Anchin." In this manuscript (fol. 169, recto), Siger emphasizes the nature of the remarks in the third book of the *vita* about Bernard's preaching of the crusade: "De expeditione Ierysolamitana quomodo abbas Clarevallis excusatur."

request, made this version of both writings, which is unique on account of its alternative readings and improvements, available to him.

This manuscript from Anchin is therefore of extreme importance for our understanding of the textual development of the *vita prima,* the more so since this three-volume codex can be dated rather precisely. The volume of the manuscript in which this *vita* was copied is listed in the catalogue of the municipal library of Douai as the second volume of the codex; however, in fact, it is the third volume. Both other volumes are said to have been produced when Geoffrey was still the abbot of Clairvaux, but in the volume with the *vita,* he is referred to as "the former abbot of Clairvaux."[62] These clues enable us to date this manuscript rather accurately. We know that Geoffrey abdicated from his post as abbot of Clairvaux in 1165. Thus the conclusion may be drawn that the volume the Douai catalogue lists as II was written after Geoffrey's abdication, while volumes I and III must have been created earlier, but not earlier than 1163. We shall return to this manuscript in chapter III.

In 1165 the discussion within the Cistercian Order concerning the canonization of Bernard came to an impasse after the involuntary abdication of Geoffrey as abbot of Clairvaux. His resignation had been insisted upon by King Louis VII, as well as by Pope Alexander III. Their indignation about the abbot had been caused by his hesitance to take sides in favor of Thomas Becket, the archbishop of Canterbury, in his conflict with King Henry II of England. When Thomas fled to France in 1164 and found refuge in the Cistercian abbey of Pontigny, Geoffrey had strongly insisted that his stay be terminated. He believed it could harm the Cistercian monasteries in England, which were threatened with reprisals by Henry II because they lent support to Thomas Becket. Almost all these monasteries were under the jurisdiction of Clairvaux, which had either established them or assumed responsibility for them. Contrary to the opinion of many Cistercians, Geoffrey did not see any immediate relationship between the conflict between Becket and the English king and the papal schism. This schism continued as long as Frederick Barbarossa supported the antipope.[63]

Geoffrey's impartiality in the conflict between Thomas and Henry II not only irritated the pope and the French king, but also many within his own order, in particular in Clairvaux. One of the reasons for their displeasure was the damage Geoffrey's attitude could cause to the

---

62. *Etudes,* 118, note 1.
63. Cf. "Thomas Becket" (1975), 55-62.

good relationship with Pontigny, which dated from Bernard's days. At the time, Godefroy de la Roche Vanneau was Geoffrey's most prominent opponent in Clairvaux. As was mentioned above, this Godefroy had for many years been Bernard's right hand, at first as prior of Clairvaux, and subsequently as bishop of Langres. In the meantime, between 1162 and 1164, Godefroy had returned to Clairvaux. There he organized the opposition against Abbot Geoffrey, even though Gilbert, abbot of Cîteaux since 1163, subscribed to Geoffrey's view. In line with the wish of Louis VII and Alexander III, Godefroy did his part to bring about Geoffrey's abdication as abbot.[64]

Godefroy's objections against Geoffrey not only concerned the Becket affair and the fact that, as a result, Clairvaux's relationship with Pontigny had been disturbed, but also the *vita prima*. The bishop-emeritus was of the opinion that this document failed to do justice to the memory of Bernard; therefore, it had to be replaced by another *vita*, and Godefroy planned to do the writing himself. But as a result of his death around 1165, this remained an attempt that, in fact, was no more than a repetition of some sections from the *vita prima* in other words.[65]

After his involuntary abdication, Geoffrey of Auxerre found refuge in Cîteaux. Most likely he brought with him a codex that contained a copy of the revised version of the *vita prima*. Until around 1170 he refrained from working on this almost completed revision. As a result, the manuscript, which had been intended for the canonization request of 1163, and which, in a sense, had deteriorated into a "working copy," was now available for the scriptorium in Anchin. As already indicated, some texts that are missing elsewhere occur only in this manuscript.[66] On the other hand, a number of less important stylistic changes, which are present in other manuscripts and which Geoffrey incorporated in his text revision at a later date, are absent.

The fact that these stylistic corrections are missing from the manuscript of Anchin leads to the conclusion that this type of minor change was not the ground for the revision of the *vita*. They were not absolutely necessary. Considering the enormous amount of work these corrections on parchment required, it stands to reason that nonessential modifications were made at a later time. Possibly, Geoffrey

64. Ibid., 59-60.
65. Cf. the prologue to the Vs; P.L., CLXXXV, 469.
66. The healing miracle recorded in this manuscript, which happened shortly after Bernard's death in Clairvaux and is absent from most manuscripts, is found in precisely those manuscripts of redaction A which in some places in the fifth book make use — in an artificial archaizing fashion — of the text of the report to Eskil. *Etudes*, 54, with note 2.

made these corrections himself at a later date in the codex of the *vita prima,* which at his departure he brought along to Cîteaux. This manuscript also includes the epilogue of Burchard of Balerne, though in a more modest version. In a similar way, Geoffrey censored, in this second version, the three temptations of chastity, which, according to the author of the first book, Bernard had experienced in his youth. Geoffrey eliminated the most provocative temptation and expurgated the two other incidents by a slight abbreviation of the text.[67]

It turns out that about the same number of manuscripts of both editions of this *vita,* which were completed in 1156 and 1163 respectively, and are now commonly referred to as redactions A and B, have been preserved. It is also noteworthy that besides the manuscript that Geoffrey of Auxerre used in 1153 for the first revision of the fifth book, and the similarly unique manuscript of Anchin, no *vita* manuscript is extant from the time when these two manuscripts were produced. Finally, it appears from the available data that only twelve of the one hundred and thirty manuscripts in which this *vita* has been preserved in full or in part existed already between 1175 and 1200. Only four of these originated in Cistercian monasteries. Of these two are based on redaction A, and the two other manuscripts on redaction B.

One of these redaction B manuscripts, originating from Clairvaux, cannot have been written before 1190, since it already includes a sixth book: the account of Bernard's preaching of the crusade in Germany, which was composed in 1146.[68] Considering the attempt in the third book of the *vita prima* to clear Bernard of all blame for the failure of this expedition, it would seem likely that this account, which clearly mentions his role in this venture, was not added to this *vita* until around the time when preachers once again called Christendom to participate in a crusade. At that time, around 1190, it had been largely forgotten that Bernard, who at one time preached the Second Crusade, had by some, if not by many of his contemporaries, been blamed for its unfortunate result. Moreover, the failure of the Second Crusade appeared less significant after 1190, since the Third Crusade had not fared much better.

Together these various data indicate that the text of the *vita prima* did not receive any wide distribution until later. A few other, indirect clues suggest that this distribution at first remained rather limited. These data

67. Above, 42, with note 44, and Vp I, c. III, 6-7, *Etudes,* 28-29.
68. Troyes, bibliothèque municipale, ms 888. For a full list of all the mss of the Vp, see *Etudes,* 15-23.

are, however, somewhat confusing. It appears that Clairvaux must still have disposed of a copy of the second redaction of this *vita* after Geoffrey had left for Cîteaux. And it has also been found that precisely the first redaction of this *vita* was used in the many Cistercian monasteries that were established by the Morimond monastery or had a close tie with it.

This latter fact may be related to the rivalry in the Cistercian Order between Morimond and Clairvaux. Both monasteries had simultaneously, in 1115, been founded by Cîteaux, but for a long time Morimond received less attention than Clairvaux. Considering the subsequent feelings of rivalry in Morimond, the exclusive use of the first redaction of the *vita prima* by this group of monasteries is more than coincidence; it is rather an expression of the preference of the monasteries that were under Morimond's umbrella to cling to the oldest textual tradition concerning Bernard.

This was the main reason that the monasteries that were associated with Morimond later manifested little interest in the new redaction of this document, which Geoffrey of Auxerre had produced in Clairvaux between 1163 and 1165, and which subsequently, from about 1180, was distributed from there. Thus, the rejection of the new edition by these monasteries had nothing to do with the resistance against the *vita prima* that can be detected around 1165 in the Cistercian Order. At that time Clairvaux itself was one of the centers of this opposition, which was related to the resistance against the uncooperative attitude of Geoffrey of Auxerre in the affair of Thomas Becket — the reason why Geoffrey had to leave Pontigny.

Remarkably, these monasteries associated with Morimond also preferred the older version of Bernard's own writings. This version was older than the archetypes that were produced at Clairvaux after Bernard's death and were distributed from there.[69] They wanted to read Bernard's writings in their most authentic version. This was also the case with the text of the *vita prima*. For in several manuscripts from the Morimond monasteries, some passages in the fifth book manifest an artificial archaizing, apparently based on the older version of this text; that is, on the account of Bernard's last year and death which Geoffrey of Auxerre had already sent to Archbishop Eskil, before he wrote the fifth book of this *vita*.[70]

69. For the sermons on the Song of Songs, see *Receuil* I, 245-274; for the treatises: *Recueil* II, 35-40 and 104-116; for the liturgical sermons: *Receuil* II, 233-238; and for the letters: *Receuil* III, 310-315.

70. *Études* (1960), 64 and 95.

6. THE *VITA SECUNDA* AND ITS RELATIONSHIP TO THE *VITA PRIMA*

WE RETURN to the fact that initially the *vita prima* was not distributed very widely. There are several reasons for this. The main cause, no doubt, was the attempt at Clairvaux between 1165 and 1170 to replace this document, which was so closely tied to the person of Geoffrey of Auxerre, with another *Life*. This attempt resulted in a *vita secunda*. From the preface to this document, we learn that after his return to Clairvaux, Godefroy de la Roche Vanneau felt it to be his task to rewrite the *vita prima*. Before he died, he transferred this uncompleted assignment to Alain of Auxerre, who has since been recognized as the author of the *vita secunda*.

Alain came from Flanders. He studied in Lille and, encouraged by Bernard, had entered Clairvaux in 1131. In 1140 he became the abbot of the newly founded monastery of Arrivour; and later, in 1152, he was elected as bishop of Auxerre. Alain resigned from this post in 1167 and returned to the area of Clairvaux, where, upon the request of Pontius, the abbot of Clairvaux who had succeeded Geoffrey in 1165, he began writing a second *vita*.

Pons of Auvergne, known — among other things — for his excellent relationship with Thomas Becket, the archbishop of Canterbury who had fled to France, did not consider himself a friend of his predecessor, Abbot Godefroy.[71] Remarkably enough, Pons, in his function of abbot of Clairvaux, did not submit a new request for Bernard's canonization, even though he had direct ties with Alexander III. The pope had ordered Pons also to look after the papal interests in his contacts with the court of Frederick Barbarossa (a situation Pons utilized mostly for the benefit of the Cistercian monasteries in the German Empire). Nevertheless, Pons may have decided to wait with a new request for Bernard's canonization because this was, in his opinion, only feasible on the basis of a new *vita*. This may be inferred from his involvement with the completion of the *vita secunda*.

Alain of Auxerre, who wrote this *vita secunda*, deemed it advantageous to address this work to Abbot Pons. Among other things, he mentioned in his prologue the objections Godefroy de la Roche Vanneau felt against the *vita prima*. These objections, which he himself shared, concerned some stern expressions in the *vita prima* regarding ecclesiastical and worldly authorities. Godefroy had reacted against these assertions,

---

71. "Thomas Becket" (1975), 62.

since, in his opinion, Bernard had always acted gently.[72] In reality this seems to have been a minor problem, since the *vita secunda* repeated many passages from the first *Life* almost verbatim. This leads us to conclude that the disapproval of the *vita prima* was primarily based on Geoffrey's involvement with it, and much less on its content; and secondly, that the first *vita* was considered too lengthy.

However, if we focus not only on the texts from the *vita prima* that were maintained in this process of abbreviation, but also on what was eliminated in those abridgments, we notice how all passages that in any way criticized Bernard's actions were consistently eliminated. In the *vita prima* this criticism was usually expressed in mild terms, to be subsequently rebuffed or transformed into an argument in favor of Bernard's sainthood. In other words: the *vita secunda* no longer alludes to the fact that at least some of his contemporaries were at times somewhat critical regarding Bernard's actions outside his monastery.

Thus the *vita secunda* became little more than a rather colorless excerpt of the first biography, written because the authors of the first version lacked in reverence for Bernard. A remarkable *novum* in this second *vita*, however, is the account of Bernard's death, which cites statements that Bernard is reported to have made in the presence of his fellow brethren. Since he believed he was unable to leave them (as inheritance) outstanding examples of religiosity, he admonished those who were present to practice the virtues of humility, patience, and neighborly love. This admonition was worded in such a way that it implicitly testified to what the pursuit of these virtues had meant for himself in his association with others.[73]

This account of Bernard's death may first have been written down by Godefroy de la Roche Vanneau, the bishop of Langres, the only one of those who witnessed Bernard's death who was mentioned by name. Alain's retelling of Godefroy's report shows such detachment that it is unlikely that he himself was present at the occasion. On the other hand, a close study of this *vita* nowhere shows that kind of personal involvement which is found in the *vita prima*, in particular with William of Saint-Thierry and Geoffrey of Auxerre. That such personal involvement seems lacking on the part of Alain may largely have resulted from the fact that he never himself assumed the role of a spokesperson.

Finally, it should be noted that this rewriting of the *vita prima* was primarily based on the second redaction of this document. This version must therefore have been available at Clairvaux after 1165. Nevertheless, considering the low esteem

---

72. P.L., CLXXXV, 469.
73. Vs, c. XXX, 81-82; P.L., CLXXXV, 520.

in which this treatise was held, we can hardly assume that the text of this *vita* was further distributed from the monastery during the abbatiate of Pons.

The *vita prima* and the *vita secunda* do, however, have one important aspect in common: they place much more emphasis on Bernard's actions outside his monastery than is the case in the other hagiographic writings which originated in Clairvaux between 1170 and 1180. As already mentioned, these later texts reported a number of anecdotes that were intended to illustrate the special relationship between Bernard and his monks. The special attention for this aspect of Bernard's life may indicate that even after 1170, when Pons's abbatiate had ended, the *vita prima* continued to be of less interest to the older Cistercian monks.

The reason for this situation is obvious. Much of what this *vita* reported about Bernard did not directly confirm the recollection these monks had of Bernard as their abbot and leader. Apparently the *vita prima* would have little chance for wider distribution until Bernard would have been canonized and a new generation of monks, which had not known Bernard personally, had come on the scene. Another reason for the limited spread of this *vita* within their own order is no doubt the length of the document. Many monasteries did not have the material facilities and the accommodations required for the copying of such long texts.

A third reason for the slow distribution was the initial lack of interest in the veneration of Bernard outside the Cistercian Order. Only after Alexander III had canonized Bernard in 1174 were other monasteries prepared to include his feast in their own liturgical calendar. We know when some orders and dioceses made that decision: the Carthusians as early as 1174; the diocese of Paris in 1207; and Cluny not until 1321, after an agreement concerning this matter was reached with the Cistercians.[74]

7. THE CANONIZATION IN 1174

GEOFFREY'S SUCCESSOR at Clairvaux apparently was unable to clear the deadlock within the Cistercian Order with regard to Bernard's canoniza-

---

74. "San Bernardo: Correlazione" (1975), 38. In this accord with Cluny, the Cistercians promised to celebrate the feast of Abbot Hugh of Cluny. Cluny and its affiliated monasteries, on their part, would celebrate the feast of Bernard and regard it as on the same level as the liturgical feasts of the other founders of monasticism.

tion, which ensued in 1165, after Geoffrey's forced abdication. For that reason he did not submit a new canonization request. The possibility exists, however, that after the *vita secunda* had been completed, Abbot Pons also found this document unsuitable to support such a request. But it may also be that the general chapter did not allow the distribution of this work, and that it failed to receive the required expression of adhesion from Cîteaux. This may have been in reaction to the standpoint of the abbot of Clairvaux, who had found the *vita prima* unsuitable for that purpose.

Concrete facts are not available, but we know that Geoffrey of Auxerre, who still resided in Cîteaux, must have understood by around 1169 or 1170 that the *vita secunda* was regarded as unfit to support such a request. For at that time he resumed in Cîteaux his work of revising the *vita prima*. The scriptorium of this monastery most likely offered him the facilities to produce another codex to be presented to the pope in support of a new canonization request.

If at that time Abbot Pons had wanted to begin preparations for a new request, he found few opportunities to do so. For in 1170 or 1171 Alexander III appointed him as bishop of Clermont. The appointment was intended to get this abbot out of the way. The pope had been discontent with Pons's role in the continuing papal schism. Pons seemed to pay more attention to the interests of the Cistercian Order in the German Empire than to those of the pope. Hence Alexander III chose this method to end Pons's involvement with the indirect negotiations between Rome and Frederick Barbarossa about a possible end of the schism.[75]

Indirectly, the abdication of Pons of Auxerre was to the advantage of Geoffrey of Auxerre's position in the Cistercian Order. In a sense he had already been rehabilitated prior to this, for already in 1169 he had been asked to mediate in the conflict between Thomas Becket and King Henry II. The archbishop had no choice but to accept this arbitration,[76] which resulted in a temporary reconciliation between Thomas and the king, followed by Thomas Becket's return to Canterbury. Subsequently, a new conflict between the two erupted, with the murder of the archbishop as the final result. Geoffrey received no blame for this unfortunate outcome, at least not from the pope, who in 1170 agreed to his appointment as abbot, now of the abbey of Fossa Nova. Since this monastery was situated outside France, his election did not require the approval of

75. Preiss (1934), 126.
76. "Thomas Becket" (1975), 61, with note 50.

Louis VII. In Fossa Nova Geoffrey succeeded Abbot Girald, who in the meantime had been transferred to Clairvaux.

During his abbacy in Clairvaux, Girald had apparently invested new energy in a request for Bernard's canonization. The canonization letters, which Alexander circulated in January 1174, indicate that the request submitted to the pope by Girald and his community had received explicit support from all the Cistercian abbots, the French bishops, and the king of France. At that time such evidences of support were already considered as extremely important because they reflected the chances of a wide dissemination of the cult of the candidate-saint. No direct information is available concerning any efforts by Abbot Girald in soliciting this support.

We do know, however, that the preparations for this request were completed in less than two years. For already in January 1174 the canonization process, which could begin only after the request and evidences of support had been submitted, resulted in Bernard's canonization. This was almost a year after Becket's canonization, but there is no indication that the recognition of his sainthood prepared the way for Bernard's canonization. We have reason to suppose, however, that the request for Bernard's canonization was not submitted before February 1173, when Thomas Becket's canonization was finalized. That there is no direct relationship between the two canonizations is even more clear, since the confirmation of the sainthood of this martyr-bishop can hardly be compared with that of Bernard.

We possess some detailed information about the process of Bernard's canonization, for the report of one of the champions, which was subsequently sent to Abbot Girald, has been preserved.[77] The champion in question, the monk Tromund from Chiaravalle, near Milan, probably played an important role. It seems that at the time, this monk had some relationship to the papal chancellery.[78] This allowed him to exert a personal influence on the redaction of the four letters, addressed to the petitioner and those who had officially supported the request, in which the pope announced his decision to recognize the liturgical veneration of Bernard. This personal influence is clearly visible, for, remarkably, the explanation of the papal decision does not refer to any of the miracles Bernard allegedly performed during his lifetime. When compared with papal letters concerning other canonizations, this appears to be quite unusual. This disregard for Bernard's posthumous miraculous deeds fits, however, with the intentions of the Cistercians themselves to prevent in

77. P.L., CLXXXV, 626-627.
78. *Receuil* I, 268, note 2. *Etudes*, 154.

St. Bernard's cult his veneration as a thaumaturge. It is clear from these letters that they succeeded in their intentions. We shall return to this aspect in the next chapter.

Tromund's account of the canonization process mentions a few things that deserve our attention in this context. First, there is his remark that Bernard was not added to the community of the saints as a novice, but that his inclusion with them was due to the fact that, as is often the case with saints, he had shared their fate from his mother's womb, while, on the other hand, he had received the recognition of his sainthood through the benevolence of the church. Apparently, people at that time already realized that the beginning of someone's sainthood did not coincide with the time of his canonization. But it is nevertheless remarkable that, according to Tromund's account, the moment of Bernard's birth was to be viewed as the point in time from which Bernard was to be regarded a saint. It remains difficult to determine whether this remark reflects a commonly held opinion or must be interpreted as a direct reference to the dream of Bernard's mother, which is reported in the *vita prima*. Whatever the case, it is clear that in the canonization process, the petitioners deliberately emphasized the image of Bernard's absolute sainthood as presented in the *vita prima*. This image precluded any essential development in his sainthood; in contemporary opinion this grace was manifested in Bernard from the moment of his birth.

Next, there is the statement by Tromund about his decision, taken after consultations with the pope, to withdraw the canonization request for Bishop Malachias, which had been submitted together with that for Bernard. Insisting on this double request for canonization would also have resulted in the rejection by the pope of Bernard's canonization. This double canonization request indicates that the Cistercians, when requesting Bernard's canonization, had assumed that a recognition of Bernard's sainthood would automatically imply papal approval for the liturgical veneration of Archbishop Malachias, since Bernard in his *vita Malachiae* had portrayed this bishop as a saint and had, according to the *vita prima*, venerated him as such.[79] But the pope did not accept Bernard's statements to that effect, in spite of his intention to have the abbot canonized.

Tromund further mentioned in his account the difficulties he and those who had assisted him had experienced. Among other things, he complained about the "Roman greediness," which they had been forced to

---

79. Vp III, c. I, 1; IV, c. IV, 21; V, c. III, 23-24; P.L., CLXXXV, 303, 333, and 364-365. Cf. *Etudes* (1960), 159, note 2.

answer with "Gallic liberality." The petitioners supposedly met with greater opposition than usual. It is not clear whether this refers to any opposition among the Curia because of activities of Bernard that continued to stir negative recollections. Tromund's appreciation for the counsel that some had provided as he worked for Bernard's canonization may point in that direction. He applauded their input and mentioned some of these advisors by name and function. In this connection he also referred to the abbot of Fossa Nova, that is, to Geoffrey of Auxerre, who apparently had supported him during the proceedings, together with the abbot of Casamari and the bishop of Verulana.

These words of appreciation are not the only evidence that Geoffrey of Auxerre was directly concerned with the canonization process. As mentioned above, his involvement had already begun during his stay in Cîteaux. One of the manuscripts of the *vita prima* (redaction B), which originated in that monastery, includes a passage that he must have inserted between 1169 and no later than 1171. In this paragraph Geoffrey refers to a vision in which Bernard, sixteen years after his death, belatedly appeared to a Cistercian monk.[80] The manuscript dates from the end of the twelfth century, but must have been based on a manuscript prepared by Geoffrey during the last years of his stay in Cîteaux, in support of the new request for canonization that followed shortly afterward. How else can it be explained that he included an additional passage about yet another vision? For this passage occurs only in three manuscripts and thus was not incorporated into the text of the *vita* to give it as yet a wide circulation.[81]

These facts also imply that hagiographic support for this new request was sought in the *vita prima,* as is also clear from the letters in which the pope explains his decision to recognize Bernard's sainthood. It is also evident that Bernard's canonization contributed to the fact that among the various hagiographic texts that in the meantime had become available, the *vita prima* eventually emerged as the most authoritative and most informative. This conclusion is confirmed by the existence of so

---

80. Vp V, c. III, 23. Text in *Etudes,* 56. Since Bernard died in 1153, the date *post quem* must be 1169, while the date *ante quem* is fixed by Geoffrey's appointment as abbot of Fossa Nova, which took place after the abdication of Abbot Pons in Clairvaux in 1170/71.

81. Dijon, Bibliothèque municipale, ms 659, provenance: Cîteaux, end of twelfth century. Chalon-sur-Saône, Bibl. mun., ms 6, prov.: Clairvaux and written in 1290. Genua, Bibl. dell Università, ms A IV 33, prov.: Saint Bénigne in Genua (O.S.B.), beginning of fourteenth century.

many manuscripts in which this *vita* has been preserved since the end of the twelfth century.

Even more important than these conclusions, however, is the fact that we are now able, on the basis of what has been discovered regarding the origin of this document and its significance for Bernard's canonization, to locate in this *vita* a number of elements that embody historically important information about this saint as a human being — information that until now was hidden under the cloak of his cult.

III

Bernard as Saint in the Cistercian Hagiography of the Twelfth Century

꙰   ꙰

IN THE MIDDLE AGES the physical death of a saint was not viewed as
the end of his history, in any case not of his blessed work on earth. He
continued to exist in a more miraculous mode than before, as was evident,
in particular, in his further involvement with mortal beings and this-
worldly matters. Consequently, his *vita* also listed the posthumous miracles
that had occurred through his intervention, as well as the visions in which
he had appeared, though not corporeally, to different people. His *vita*, of
course, also described how he had lived as a saint in pursuit of heroic
virtues, inspired by the special grace God had bestowed upon him.

As mentioned earlier, the life story of a saint usually includes a
dream or vision in which, prior to his birth, his predestination to sainthood
was announced. Thus, a sanctity was ascribed to him that as an absolute
fact would determine the further course of his life, regardless of any
incidental human mistakes. For that reason, a hagiographer usually compared events in the life of a saint with the experiences of Old Testament
prophets. This model was also used in the portrayal of Bernard's life, so
that in different contexts some of his actions were compared with those
of Moses, Samuel, and David.

In the depiction of absolute sainthood that the hagiographer would
inevitably create of his hero, he was compelled to make ample mention
of the miracles the saint had performed during his lifetime. In that respect,
the saint also followed in Christ's footsteps. The pattern for these stories

was suggested by the miracle stories in the Synoptic Gospels. Any borrowing was mostly indirect, through older *Lives* of saints — in particular the *vita* of St. Benedict written by Pope Gregory the Great, and that of St. Martin by Sulpicius Severus — which were viewed as normative.

That the saint lived on was evident from the miracles that occurred near his tomb or elsewhere where his relics were preserved and venerated. Through his emphasis on these things, a hagiographer attempted to promote the cult of a saint. In the course of the twelfth century, however, the veneration of new saints usually became dependent on papal approval in the form of a canonization. Since that time, this type of written *Life*, as here described in general terms, counted as the prescribed model for a papal canonization, including posthumously performed miracles and appearances. This requirement developed over time. At first such a life story was submitted with the request for canonization as a sort of information file offering the desired evidence and statements from witnesses. But soon, with some exceptions, Rome required the submission of a more extensive hagiographic *vita*.

1. THE CRITERIA FOR SAINTHOOD IN THE *VITA PRIMA*

TO A LARGE DEGREE this model was followed in the hagiographic writings on Bernard of Clairvaux's life. Strangely enough, however, they contain hardly any accounts of his posthumous miracles. This is true of the *vita prima*, in particular, even though it was written and submitted with the express purpose of supporting the request for Bernard's canonization. One notable exception to this silence about posthumously performed miracles appears in the redaction of the document as found in the manuscript of Anchin, which in many ways must be viewed as an atypical version of this *vita*.

This particular version mentions a miraculous healing that is said to have occurred after Bernard's death near his bier. In addition, there is the account of an answer to prayer allegedly given to a monk who was close to the bier, which may also be classified as a miraculous healing.[1]

---

1. Vp V, c. II, 15; *Etudes* (1960). For the second healing miracle, recorded in Douai, Bibl. munic., 372, vol. II, originating in Anchin and in the deliberately archaized text of the fifth book, followed by a few chapters from the Morimond sphere of influence, cf. *Etudes*, 54 with note 2, and "Un Brouillon" (1959), 56, line 432.

This exception is quite remarkable, the more so since all these writings give ample attention to the miracles performed by Bernard during his life. These miracles even exceed in number those recorded in other contemporary hagiographic writings.[2]

Since this silence regarding posthumously performed miracles is rather exceptional, any analysis of the portrayal of Bernard as saint, as found in twelfth-century Cistercian hagiography, must deal with this phenomenon. It may betray some resistance, which probably existed within the order, against a portrayal of Bernard's sainthood in full accordance with the criteria required of a *vita* that was submitted when a canonization was requested. These criteria not only applied to the miracles performed by the candidate-saint, but also to the manner in which he pursued a virtuous life. And his hagiographers may have found it difficult to make Bernard as saint fit these latter criteria.

The way in which the virtues of a saint were to be described in his *vita*, in accordance with these criteria, was in part dependent upon the role the candidate-saint had played during his life in church and society: a different kind of virtue was expected from a bishop than from a monk or abbot. Bernard had applied these norms quite strictly in his own hagiographic work. Thus he mentioned, in the *vita* that he wrote around 1150 for his deceased friend Malachias (who had died in Clairvaux in 1148), that Malachias had persisted — as was considered appropriate for a saintly bishop — in his resistance against his election as archbishop of Armagh in Ireland. In this *vita* the miracles Malachias allegedly performed after his death were also left out, with only one exception.[3]

As far as these criteria of virtuous conduct were concerned, the hagiographers who wrote Bernard's official *Life* in order to advance his canonization had to contend with a far greater problem than Bernard had to face in his *vita Malachiae*. For Bernard had been involved in a great variety of matters and had been associated with or been entrusted with many tasks and assignments that normally lay well beyond the scope of a Cistercian abbot. Consequently, the hagiographer, who in the *vita* also wanted to pay attention to Bernard's place in contemporary society, was confronted with some special problems. For Bernard's position was so unique and so comprehensive that actions which could be interpreted as virtuous from

2. Sigal (1985), 18-20.
3. V.M., c. III, 16; SBO III, 325. For those criteria, cf. L. Delehaye (1955), 92. Also V.M., c. XXXI, 75; III, 378.

one perspective, could also be interpreted as negative. As we shall see, this situation caused some problems, in particular with regard to the image of Bernard's absolute sainthood that was to be portrayed in this *Life*, if it were to be in harmony with the pattern of an abbatial *vita*.

That Geoffrey of Auxerre clearly recognized this problem is evident from the manner in which he initially attempted to solve it in the third book of the *vita prima*. In this chapter Geoffrey commented briefly on the "variety of spiritual gifts" mentioned by the apostle Paul (1 Corinthians 12). He more or less tried to present a typology of holy men, and he differentiated between those who had excelled through miracles, through the spirit of prophecy, or through mortification or preaching. He continued with these words:

> Others again have given all their strength in the building of monasteries, thus propagating the fame of their saintliness. Or they successfully attempted to suppress the annoyances and tempests of this world and have looked after the interests of the church, and in so doing were useful through their activities. Or they enjoyed a spiritual rest in holy meditation and thus reached the summits of contemplation.
>
> What of all this lacked in Bernard? Indeed, which of these things was not already so splendid, that there would have been ample reason to praise him, even if something of the rest had been missing. For while the church in its distress . . . experienced the advantage of his activity, he also excelled in the gift of contemplation. . . .[4]

In redaction B of the *vita prima*, Geoffrey later eliminated this passage. But this quotation, nevertheless, expressed a view that he continued to find appealing and later repeated. For in his last revision, Geoffrey inserted in the fifth book a passage in which, though admittedly in a more abbreviated form, he once again referred to the plurality of spiritual gifts that the Holy Spirit had bestowed on Bernard. This can be found in the manuscript of the *vita prima* that he produced between 1169 and 1171 in Cîteaux, in the preparation of a new canonization request. (A codex is not extant; it follows redaction B, but inserts some passages that are not found elsewhere.) As already indicated in the previous chapter, the moment of this insertion can be precisely dated, since this same addition mentions how a Cistercian monk had experienced a vision of Bernard about sixteen years after his death.[5]

4. Vp III, c. VIII, 31; P.L., CLXXXV, 321-322. *Etudes*, 43-44.
5. Cf. above, 59, and note 80. *Etudes*, 56, and note 1.

Since this addition begins with a reference to the remark about the variety of spiritual gifts, which Geoffrey had earlier eliminated when he revised redaction A, it clearly indicates that Geoffrey himself was responsible for this later insertion. Who else would still have known that this passage had been part of redaction A? Who else, except the author, had any reason to insert it once more in the *vita?* Only someone who was thoroughly conversant with this document, which had not yet been circulated (and was even considered taboo in Clairvaux between 1165 and 1171), can have deemed it desirable to focus once again, by means of this word from Paul, on this, from a hagiographic perspective, confusingly wide range of Bernard's talents, and to highlight this attribute as evidence of his sainthood. This particular comment also emphasized that Bernard's multifaceted nature enabled him to lead many to bliss.

2. THE SILENCE REGARDING POSTHUMOUSLY PERFORMED MIRACLES

LET US RETURN NOW to the extraordinary fact that the hagiographic writings about Bernard hardly mention any miracles that he supposedly did after his death. In a number of cases this peculiarity can easily be explained; for, as we mentioned earlier, some of these texts were already written when Bernard was still alive, in preparation of the *vita prima.* The first and the second book of this document were completed some years before Bernard died. Moreover, the other three books were composed, at least in outline, quite soon after his death.

With respect to the last three books, however, this explanation is inadequate. For in the oldest version of the fifth book — the account of Bernard's last year and of his death that Geoffrey sent to Archbishop Eskil, of which both the original text and the first textual revision have been preserved in manuscript form — we find a report of a healing miracle *post mortem.*[6] But in the manuscript, in which this account was recast as the fifth book, this miracle story eventually was eliminated.

This miracle occurred in Clairvaux when Bernard's corpse had not yet been buried. A withered arm of a boy was healed after contact with Bernard's hand. In his account of this miracle, Geoffrey also referred to a healing miracle reported by Bernard himself in his *vita Malachiae.* This miracle occurred under similar circumstances; that is, it also occurred in Clairvaux, after the death of the bishop, while his corpse had not yet been

6. "Un Brouillon" (1959), 42, lines 432-447.

buried. Bernard himself was involved in the event; for during Malachias's funeral, he had noticed a boy with a withered hand in the crowd. He had brought him to the body of the bishop lying in state. When the boy touched the hand of the deceased, his own hand was suddenly healed.[7]

It is evident from this manuscript with the textual modification of Eskil's account, that only at a later stage did Geoffrey decide not to include this passage in the fifth book; for he made a few corrections in this passage before he finally eliminated it.[8] But there is yet another indication that this passage was deleted at a late stage: it also appears in the manuscript from Anchin, which we discussed earlier,[9] together with the correction Geoffrey initially had ordered. In the manuscript of Anchin, this miracle story is accompanied by a shorter text that is missing both in the report to Eskil and in the working copy of this report that Geoffrey used as the basis for the fifth book. This short passage, therefore, was only later incorporated into redaction A of the *vita*.

This section, which at a later stage was added to redaction A, deals with an answer to prayer received by an epileptic monk after he had fervently, and with great faith, prayed for healing near the body of Bernard on the bier. Subsequently, when he experienced no further attacks, it became clear that his prayer had been answered. This explains why the story was added to the fifth book at some later time. But when preparing redaction B, Geoffrey decided to delete this addition. Apparently this miracle story — a miraculous answer to prayer — was deemed unsuitable, just as were the accounts of the other healing miracles that were reported to have occurred near the biers of both Bernard and Malachias.[10] These two stories had already been deleted in redaction A.

A further addition in the fifth book (in the manuscript from Anchin that records this subsequently established answer to prayer) is the account of the two other healing miracles from the report to Eskil, which was eventually eliminated from the working copy of the fifth book and also, for that reason, does not occur in redaction A, with a few exceptions.[11]

7. V.M., c. XXXI, 75; SBO III, 378, lines 13-19.

8. This ms is: Paris, BNL ms 7561, 82.

9. Cf. above, 48, and note 61.

10. For the text of these miracle stories, which are part of Vp V, c. II, 15, see *Etudes* (1960), 54.

11. This miracle story is also found in four manuscripts (redaction A) from the Morimond sphere of influence. These present the text of the fifth book in a deliberately archaized form. Cf. "Un Brouillon" (1959), 29-30.

No doubt the explanation for these textual complications in the Anchin manuscript must be sought in the direct relationship between this manuscript and the codex that was prepared for the first canonization request. As we already saw, this codex differs in some instances from the text of the *vita*, redaction A, as it occurs in other manuscripts.

During the meeting of abbots and bishops in 1155 or 1156, the text changes that were then incorporated into or maintained in this codex must have been discussed and approved. This grand assembly — which, as mentioned earlier, probably met at the initiative of the general chapter — apparently agreed that the *vita prima* would not include any of Bernard's posthumous miracles, but was willing to make one exception: for the codex to be submitted together with the canonization request of this abbot. With regard to this special codex, the assembled abbots and bishops apparently were inclined to follow the common practice of including such miracles in an official *vita*.

This fact provides further proof that the manuscript from Anchin was copied from this special codex, which is not extant. After his decision in 1163 not to proceed with the request for Bernard's canonization, Pope Alexander must have returned to the petitioner the codex that had been submitted to him. Subsequently, Geoffrey of Auxerre utilized this codex, which, in view of the new canonization procedures, he considered unsuitable for a renewed request, in his work on redaction B. He made the necessary corrections in this codex. From this "working copy," which has not been preserved, the text of the *vita prima* in the Anchin manuscript must have been copied. This explains why the Anchin manuscript includes a number of passages that are missing in almost all other manuscripts of both redactions.

On the basis of this presupposition, it also becomes clear why the text of the *vita prima* in this manuscript follows in part redaction B, but in part also redaction A. It was copied from the canonization codex of 1163, in which subsequently some of the modifications of redaction B were incorporated. All this, however, does not explain why almost none of the manuscripts of redaction A mention the miracle at the bier of Bernard, while the story does occur in the report to Eskil, in the Anchin manuscript, and in the four manuscripts from the Morimond region, which contain an archaized version of the fifth book of the *vita*. This textual difference in the fifth book, redaction A, is related to the absence of *post mortem* miracle stories elsewhere in almost all of Bernard's hagiography.

For a better understanding of these stories, we must look more closely at the complete text of which the story of the miracle at Bernard's bier was initially a part. For the text also relates how, during the period that Bernard's corpse was still lying in state, a multitude of people of noble and of common descent from the surroundings of the abbey came to touch Bernard's feet, to kiss his hands, or to touch with all kinds of objects the priestly robes that had once belonged to Bishop Malachias and now covered the body of Bernard. While these visitors succeeded in entering the monastery even at improper times and thus disturbed the daily routine of the monks, the gatekeeper outside was confronted with the bitter lamentations of the many weeping women who, without exception, were refused entry into the monastery.[12]

This account indicates that in the days prior to Bernard's funeral, the situation at Clairvaux must have been rather tumultuous, requiring measures to be taken to prevent further chaos. Geoffrey repeated the information about these disturbances that he reported to Eskil almost verbatim — with the exception of the story of the miraculous healing of the boy with the withered hand, which was eliminated — in the *vita prima*, redaction A. He left these remarks unchanged in redaction B; later they were also incorporated word for word in the *vita secunda*.[13] The events in Clairvaux were also reported by Conrad of Eberbach in the *Exordium magnum*. At the time Conrad was still a monk in Clairvaux, where these events apparently were remembered in more detail than Geoffrey's record suggests. Conrad's account indicates that after Bernard's death, healing miracles did take place at Clairvaux.

But these healing miracles are not mentioned in the *De miraculis* by Herbert of Clairvaux, a treatise dating from the 1170s that served as an important source for Conrad's *Exordium magnum*.[14] Conrad probably depended for his posthumous healing miracles on oral tradition. In any case, he mentions only four. Three occurred prior to Bernard's funeral. The first story, concerning an epileptic, may have developed from the account of an answer to a prayer said near Bernard's bier by someone who suffered from this illness. The second story is about the healing of a boy with a withered hand. As indicated earlier, this also features in the report to Eskil and in the Anchin manuscript. The third of these healing miracles occurred to a person who was unable to walk.

---

12. Vp V, c. II, 14; P.L., CLXXXV, 360.

13. Vs, c. XXXI, 87; P.L., CLXXXV, 523.

14. *De Miraculis*, libri tres; P.L., CLXXXV, 1273-1384. Excerpts from this source concerning Bernard (Vp I, c. 5-7; II, c. 12-14 and 25) are found together in P.L., CLXXXV, 453-466. Hüffer (1886), 158-171.

All these miracles happened after someone touched Bernard's corpse. Geoffrey apparently knew about two of these stories already in 1153; but in his version, one of these miraculous healings is reported as an answer to prayer that only in retrospect was viewed as miraculous. This different report, which occurs in the *Exordium magnum,* may depend on an oral tradition of this story in Clairvaux. Conrad probably also resorted to oral tradition in Clairvaux for his account of the third healing miracle. This seems to be indicated by the context within which Conrad placed the third miracle. It occurred during the night office, the day before Bernard was to be buried. While the monks sang their psalms from the choir benches, a physically weakened man used the opportunity to crawl to the bier. As he arrived there, he was suddenly able to stand erect and was taken to the altar. We can only guess how the service proceeded. However, with this disturbance the limit of tolerance was reached, at least on the part of the abbot of Cîteaux, who had come with other Cistercian abbots to attend the services for the mourning and burial of Bernard.

The *Exordium magnum* presents a rather peculiar account of Geoffrey's subsequent intervention:

> Seeing the enormous problem caused by the swelling crowds and surmising from what was happening what might occur in the future, he (the abbot of Cîteaux) began to worry greatly. For if, due to an increase in miracles, an intolerably large multitude would continue to gather, monastic discipline would be destroyed by the unruly nature of such crowds, and this place would slacken in the zeal of its holy piety. After consultations, he reverently approached (the dead body) and forbade it on the basis of the virtue of obdience to perform any further miracles.

Conrad of Eberbach's comment on this story is — if possible — even more striking:

> However, while the apostle Paul says about our Lord Jesus Christ that He was obedient to the Father until death, and while our lawgiver, the holy Benedict, following that example, requires from us also obedience until death, the holy and truly humble soul of our father continued his obedience to a mortal human being even after his physical death. For the signs of emanation, which had already begun, stopped, and thus there was never any further indication of public

miracles, even though until today there have been many believers, in particular brothers in his order, who have called upon him [Bernard] when suffering [physical] distress. Because it is clear that the abbot of Cîteaux only objected to those miracles that would endanger the discipline in the monastery, as a result of the chaos caused by the gathering of multitudes.[15]

This remark, which concludes Conrad's comment regarding the intervention by the abbot of Cîteaux, is further confirmed in his fourth account of a posthumous miracle by Bernard, which concerns an exorcism performed a few years later by a Cistercian abbot through the intervention of Bernard. The abbot succeeded in chasing the devil by means of a few hairs of Bernard's beard; he always carried this relic with him in order to drive out evil. The evil spirit was powerless against this relic, in spite of his mockery that this saintly little fellow — this *Bernardulum* — had been forbidden to perform any miracles after his death.[16]

ই৽   ই৽

IT HAS AT TIMES been suggested that in his account of Bernard's posthumous interventions, Conrad von Eberbach wanted to provide an excuse for the absence of miracles at Bernard's tomb. In so doing, he allegedly wanted to prevent the idea that after his death Bernard no longer possessed the miracle power he had so amply manifested during his life.[17] This doubt had to be prevented, since it would have been detrimental to the acceptance of Bernard's sainthood. The tomb of a saint held a central place in his cult. There his sainthood was to be confirmed through signs and wonders.

This explanation fails to convince, since the leaders of the Cistercian Order, as far as we know, were not inclined to promote Bernard's veneration as a miracle worker, and tried, in any case, to prevent the development of a cult at his tomb. Remarkably enough, these attempts to hinder the development of such a cult do not seem to have caused much protest among the Cistercians. Conrad of Eberbach, who showed some interest in this aspect of Bernard, knew of only four healing miracles that had occurred after Bernard's death, while among all the hagiographic texts

15. Griesser, ed., *Exordium magnum* (1961), distinctio secunda, c. XX, 116-117.
16. Ibid., 117.
17. Ward (1982), 180.

written about Bernard after his death, this particular chapter from the *Exordium magnum* remains an exceptional phenomenon.

There is reason to think, however, that the absence of more posthumous healing miracles in the *Exordium magnum* was somewhat compensated for by stories of visions in which Bernard is said to have appeared after his death to individual monks. These reports were largely borrowed from the treatise *De miraculis*, written by Herbert of Clairvaux. But this is no more than conjecture. Such visions are found in many *vitae*, and it is thus far from certain that in this case the miracles *post mortem*, which Bernard failed to perform, were deliberately replaced by the accounts of these visions. It is also true that the *vita prima* mentions only a few visions in which Bernard is said to have appeared to his brethren. Moreover, not all reports of visions in this document are reliable.

The theory that Conrad's story of how Bernard had been forbidden to perform any miracles after his death had its origin in the embarrassment about the absence of such miracles can also be refuted in another way: by means of the letters circulated by Alexander III in January 1174, in which he announced his decision to allow the liturgical veneration of Bernard.[18] Alexander's arguments as to why the abbot was worthy of this honor also completely ignored the many healing miracles which Bernard, according to the *prima vita*, had performed during his life. Apparently, the pope found it totally unnecessary even to mention the miraculous powers of Bernard as proof of his sainthood.

This was very extraordinary, however. For in earlier canonization letters that Alexander had issued — on behalf of Edward the Confessor in 1161, Canut Laward in 1169, and Thomas Becket in 1173 — the miracles performed by these saints during their life, and even more the miracles that had subsequently occurred at their tombs, had been presented as the most important argument for their canonization.[19] This twofold argumentation had also been used by his predecessor, Pope Eugenius III, in his only canonization letter.[20] Likewise, in the five canonization decrees issued by the chancelleries of the second and third successor of Alex-

18. P.L., CLXXXV, 622-625.

19. For the respective canonization bulls, see P.L., CC, 106, 608, and 901. Kemp (1948), 82-87.

20. This bull concerned Emperor Henry II, who died in 1024 and was canonized by Eugenius III in 1146; P.L., CLXXX, 1118. Klauser (1957). About the canonization, see below, 147.

ander III — Pope Clemens III (1187-1191) and Celestine III (1191-1198) — these two classes of miracles formed a definite and important argument for the respective canonizations.[21]

There is thus a remarkable difference between all these bulls and the letters that Alexander III issued to announce Bernard's canonization. As has already been mentioned, this may well be attributed to the monk Tromund from the Cistercian abbey Chiaravalle, near Milan, who, at least in the earlier phase, as an employee in the papal chancellery, had been responsible for the redaction of these letters.[22] He may have been the reason why nothing about the miracles of Bernard was mentioned in these canonization decrees. If so, Conrad's story that Bernard was forbidden to do any *post mortem* miracles cannot be pushed aside as a simple excuse for the absence of these. For this Tromund must have been acquainted with the customs of the papal chancellery, as well as with the ideas among the Cistercians concerning Bernard's cult. Apparently he gave these Cistercian ideas more weight when he worked on the redaction of these bulls.

All things considered, Conrad's story is best explained as a translation of the express wish of the leadership of the order that no miracle cult was to develop at Bernard's tomb. This wish was quite understandable. In the first place, Bernard himself had not promoted such a cult for Archbishop Malachias, next to whom he was buried in the church of the Clairvaux monastery. Secondly, it would have been harmful for monastic life in Clairvaux for the required rest to be disturbed by a flood of pilgrims. An additional argument may have been that the healing miracles at Bernard's tomb were essentially different from the miracles he had performed during his life. When he was alive, his miracles had primarily served to safeguard the spiritual well-being of those involved. The miracles *post mortem*, however, favored first of all the temporal well-being of those who were healed. Moreover, these miracles inevitably would have added a commercial dimension to the sanctuary where Bernard's mortal remains were preserved and venerated. Finally, tolerating financial profit-making at the tomb of this abbot would have been in total contradiction of Bernard's criticism, in his widely read *Apology*, directed against the commercial intentions that, through a display of riches, enticed pilgrims

---

21. P.L., CCIV, 1426 and 1436: for Stephen of Grandmont and Otto, bishop of Bamberg (both in 1189). P.L., CCVI, 869-871, 918, and 970: for Peter, bishop of Tarentaise (1191), for Ubald of Gubbio (1192), and for Bernward, bishop of Hildesheim (1193). Kemp (1948), 94-98.

22. *Receuil* I, 268, note 2. Heathcote, "The Letter Collections attributed to Master Trasmundus," 86-89. Cf. above, 57-59.

to visit the recently built abbey church of Cluny and other sanctuaries where saints had been buried.[23]

3. FROM ABBOT TO TEACHER: A SHIFTING IDEAL OF SAINTHOOD

ONE OF THE LETTERS issued by Alexander to announce the canonization of Bernard was addressed to the French bishops. In this letter the pope explained at length the criteria he had used for this canonization. These criteria had not been mentioned anywhere in connection with the canonizations referred to above, and they were most likely never utilized in any of these canonization procedures. In his letter to the episcopacy, the pope praised Bernard's special accomplishments for the church in the areas of religious experience and doctrine.

The *prima vita* repeatedly pointed to these accomplishments. In this connection Geoffrey of Auxerre even quoted a passage from a privilege accorded to Clairvaux when Pope Innocent II had visited the abbey in 1132. In that passage the pope praised Bernard at length for his service to the church. This papal tribute, of course, concerned first of all the activities of the abbot in defense of the claims of Innocent II to the papal throne. But Geoffrey quoted this passage in a totally different context, to defend Bernard's controversial actions between 1141 and 1149 against Abelard and Gilbert de la Porrée.

Nevertheless, this statement in the *vita*, which was quoted verbatim from a letter from one of the predecessors of Alexander III, must have played an important role in the evaluation of Bernard's sainthood during the canonization process. The impression this statement made on the pope, who himself was confronted with a dragging schism, is apparent in the letters he circulated concerning Bernard's canonization. Innocent praised Bernard with these words:

> With what forceful and tenacious steadfastness your pious and discrete zeal has assumed the task to defend the cause of St. Peter and of your holy Mother, the Church of Rome, when the schism of Pierleone flared

23. *Apo*, c. XII, 28; SBO III, 104-106. For this attitude of Bernard, see also C. Rudolph (1990) and my review of this controversial study in CCM 37 (1994), 159-161. About the deliberate intention to make the new church in Cluny a place for pilgrims, see Werckmeister, "Cluny III."

up! And how much effort did you give, in positioning yourself as an impregnable wall before God's house, to lead the sentiments of kings and princes and other ecclesiastical and secular authorities back to the unity of the Catholic Church and to obedience to St. Peter and us, by continuously advancing sensible arguments! The enormous profit that ensued for the church of God and us is tangible.[24]

In his letter to the French bishops, Alexander III began by reminding his readers that he had laid aside the earlier canonization request. After this introduction, he explained which criteria he had decided to use with respect to Bernard's sainthood:

> . . . Upon a renewed request, we have again occupied ourselves with the memory of the holy and distinguished life of this blessed man; how, supported by the signs of a special grace, he not only excelled in personal holiness and piety, but also how through the light of his faith and teaching he radiated throughout the whole church. Even in the most remote parts of holy Christendom does everyone know about the fruits that he harvested in the house of the Lord through his word and example. He established the institutions of the holy religion in faraway regions and introduced these to "barbaric" nations. He saw to it that monasteries were established in more and more countries, and he was able to call an immeasurable number of sinners, who walked in the broad way of the world, back to the narrow path of spiritual life. In particular, he supported the most holy church of Rome, which we now lead with God's help, when it suffered a whirlwind of persecution. He did this not only through his virtuous life, but also through his divinely bestowed wisdom, in such a manner that we, together with all the sons of the church, should venerate him as behooves, and honor him with eternal devotion. . . .[25]

Pope Alexander added to this reason for Bernard's canonization yet another passage concerning his ascetic life, which had equaled the martyrium of earlier saints. But this latter argument applied to every saint who was officially recognized as such, and served only as a minor complement to

---

24. This privilege for Clairvaux dates from February 17/19, 1132. Text in P.L., CLXXIX, 126, and in J. Waquet (1950), 5-7. See for the passage quoted by Geoffrey of Auxerre: Vp III, c. V, 12; P.L., CLXXXV, 310. The notion of an impregnable wall, borrowed from Ezekiel 13:5, became a hagiographic *topos*, as a result of the exegesis by Gregory the Great in his *Regula Pastoralis* II, c. IV (P.L., LXX, 30). Cf. Van 't Spijker (1990), 78.

25. P.L., CLXXXV, 622.

the main arguments of Alexander III. The pope did not mention it in the letter he sent to the Cistercian abbots, but he did stress Bernard's significance for the church as a whole through his piety as well as through his defense of the faith.[26] The pope also underlined this significance in his letter to the monks of Clairvaux; while in his letter to the king of France, he asked that the king would show respect for this saint, promote his cult, and protect his monastery.[27]

꛷   ꛷

AT THE TIME of the canonization, the pope also determined which office was to be used in the liturgical commemoration of Bernard. His choice did, moreover, deviate from the line of reasoning he had followed in his explication of the canonization. For he chose an office for Bernard's feast that was rather general in character. Alexander III chose the varying eucharistic prayers, which were acceptable for those saints who had not been bishops. Canonized abbots, in particular, fell in this category; and this liturgy, commonly denoted as *os justi* (the mouth of the righteous), was part of the *commune abbatum* (what abbots as saints have in common). Its general character is already apparent in the Psalm verse at the beginning of the first prayer or *introitus,* which is applicable to practically all saints:

> The mouth of the righteous utters wisdom, and his tongue speaks justice. The law of his God is in his heart; his steps do not slip (Psalms 37:30, 31).

Alexander III used this office in the mass that he celebrated at the occasion of Bernard's canonization, and thus indicated that this liturgy was to be followed for his feast. However, it is clear that from the beginning this office failed to satisfy all Cistercians. Those who had requested Bernard's canonization in Rome were of the opinion that this liturgy failed to do sufficient justice to Bernard as a saint, that the special nature of his sainthood was not adequately expressed in this office. The final remarks in the account that Tromund, the main champion during this canonization process, sent after Bernard's canonization to Abbot Girald of Clairvaux, point in that direction:

26. Ibid., 624.
27. Ibid., 623.

> We advise you at this moment not to initiate any change in the office, which the pope sent for the solemn celebration of the mass of this saint.[28]

This passage indicates that Tromund and the other champions not only exerted influence on the pope's arguments for Bernard's canonization, but also voiced their preferences regarding the office that they felt would best suit his feast. For whatever reasons, Alexander III was unwilling to comply with these wishes.

The Cistercians seem to have complied with Tromund's counsel until the end of the twelfth century. But in 1201 they requested Pope Innocent III to change the office for Bernard, and the pope gave his approval in 1202. Innocent III may have wanted to make a gesture of good will toward the Cistercians at the moment when he wanted to assign the preaching against the Albigenses to them. They were to assume this task in the same area where Bernard had worked, when he had set out on a journey to Albi, in his attempt to counteract the influence of the heretical preacher Henry of Lausanne.[29] Whatever motives Innocent III may have had, he complied with the wishes of the Cistercian Order with regard to this request for a change in the liturgy for Bernard. The office that was chosen had until then rarely been used; the preamble of the *introitus*, in any case, agrees much better with the concept of Bernard's sainthood that had been defended by the leadership of the Cistercians as early as 1174. This *introitus* begins with a text from Jesus Sirach (15:5), which, translated from the Latin Vulgate text, reads:

> In the midst of the church the Lord has made him speak. He has filled him with the spirit of wisdom and insight and clothed him with the garment of glory.

This new office must have been more appealing to the Cistercians than the liturgy of 1174, since it implied a recognition of the view of Bernard's significance as saint that had been stressed in the canonization request. According to this view, which by now was more generally accepted, Bernard's significance was not limited to his own order, but extended to the church as a whole. Earlier the *prima vita* had expressed this view; it must gradually have won greater acceptance within the Cistercian Order, but

---

28. P.L., CLXXXV, 627.
29. *Christendom* (1994), 211-224.

was not honored with this office *in medio ecclesiae* until 1202. Innocent III's approval of this liturgy implied the recognition that Bernard deserved a place among the doctors of the church, even though it was not until the nineteenth century, in 1830, that he was officially proclaimed as such.[30]

4. THE DEFENSE OF BERNARD'S SAINTHOOD

AFTER BERNARD'S DEATH, many Cistercian monks who had known him as their spiritual leader and abbot were more interested in concrete, anecdotal memories than in what they mostly were offered in the *prima vita*. Often they were but little aware of his activities outside his monastery and his order. Expressions of their appreciation for Bernard were — as already mentioned — written down without much system between 1170 and 1180: in an as yet unpublished, anonymous *liber visionum et miraculorum*;[31] in two other documents already referred to — *De miraculis* by Herbert of Clairvaux and the *Exordium magnum* by Conrad of Eberbach; and also in the short, legendary *vita* written shortly after 1180 by John the Eremite, also presumably a monk from Clairvaux.[32] All these writings describe incidents that continued to be remembered by those who lived at Clairvaux.

But gradually this portrayal of Bernard's sainthood was to give way to that presented by the *vita prima*. For with the lapse of time, those who had personal recollections of Bernard eventually came to the end of their earthly existence. The *vita prima* was not only written in preparation for Bernard's canonization, but was also intended to emphasize, as extensively as possible, the significance of Bernard's sainthood in church and society. In retrospect, it seems likely that partly for this reason, after Rainald of Foigny had declined the authorship, Geoffrey chose the two subsequent authors to whom he entrusted the writing of this *vita*, from outside the Cistercian Order.

Because of their background, Geoffrey could expect that in their description of Bernard's sainthood they would pay due attention to his

---

30. A. van Velzen, "Het misformulier," COCR VI (1939), 110-112.

31. McGuire, "A lost Clairvaux *exemplum* found" (1983), 27-62. It probably concerns an incomplete collection, since we find in later medieval *exempla*-literature more stories ascribed to Bernard than to any other saint. Leclercq, "Le portrait de saint Bernard," COCR 50 (1988), 256-267.

32. P.L., CLXXXV, 531-550. Hüffer (1886), 153-157.

involvement with matters in the outside world. Choosing these outsiders as writers was not without risk, since it was precisely Bernard's activities outside the monastery that had been criticized by some contemporaries. But Geoffrey had apparently become convinced that reporting and answering this criticism would give a better understanding of Bernard's sainthood. That does not mean that the choice for this approach must have originated with Geoffrey. It may in fact stem from William of Saint-Thierry, the author Geoffrey subsequently asked to begin the writing of Bernard's *vita*.

On the other hand, in their portrayal of Bernard's sainthood, William of Saint-Thierry and Arnold of Bonneval also gave ample attention to the monastery Bernard had established and where he was supposed to live. William, in particular, paid attention to Clairvaux. But the impression he creates of monastic life in the early years of Clairvaux's existence tends to be a jubilant praise for the way the monks, through their mortifications and the simplicity of their buildings, came nearer to God, rather than a trustworthy account of the real way of life of this community.[33] And neither can the subsequent description of life at Clairvaux by Arnold of Bonneval — at the time when Innocent II visited this abbey around 1136, after a new monastery had been built — be considered a historically reliable account of how this community was run. His comments seem to be largely inspired by what Bernard himself wrote in his *Apology* about the lifestyle of the Cistercians.[34]

These stories about the early years of Clairvaux, when yields of the harvests were still insufficient, were probably more appealing to the Cistercians who had heard about these things than the other chapters of the *vita prima*, in which Bernard was defended against the criticism for his actions in the outside world. Because they preferred these stories about Clairvaux, the monks must have felt the urge to complement them with additional anecdotical details. But that this was contrary to the intent of the *vita* may be concluded from the way in which John the Eremite retold the *vita Bernardi*.[35]

This latter aspect also seems to clarify the distress of these older monks regarding the accounts in the *vita prima* about Bernard's activities outside his monastery, in particular about what William of Saint-Thierry

---

33. Vp I, c. VII, 35-37; P.L., CLXXXV, 247-249. Paul, "Les débuts de Clairvaux."
34. Vp II, c. I, 6; P.L., CLXXXV, 272. Rudolph (1990), 66, note 194.
35. Vp, II, c. 3; P.L., CLXXXV, 541-542.

reported with the intent of answering the charges. They probably found it difficult to understand this polemic, since their idea of Bernard's sainthood was one-dimensional; they were inclined to recognize only virtues in their saint. They must therefore have failed to notice that William did not ignore the objections of his critics and opponents, but confronted them in a provocative way, in order to prove that the aspects Bernard was blamed for constituted an essential part of his sainthood. For that reason this facet of the portrayal of Bernard's sainthood in the *vita prima* deserves some closer study.

We have already referred to this in the previous chapter, where we dealt with the manner in which the story of the dream of Bernard's mother prior to his birth had functioned. It was used as a response to those who ironically characterized Bernard's demeanor vis-à-vis Peter Abelard as the barking of a dog, and portrayed him as "the greatest master in opening his jaws." It seems likely that the allies of Abelard — after the intervention by Peter the Venerable, the abbot of Cluny, on behalf of their teacher — dared to qualify the deportment of Bernard as the barking of a dog. They must also have been acquainted with the exegesis of the texts in Isaiah (56:10) and the Psalms (67:24), and they may have been the ones who, in view of the ferocity of Bernard's interaction with Abelard, applied this by way of parody to Bernard.[36]

---

36. The use of parody based on a standard exegesis of certain texts of Scripture was not uncommon at the time. For instance, the constantly repeated explanation of the text from the book of Job (41:13; Vulgate) by Gregory the Great — "Scarcity precedes his coming" — as applying to the coming of the antichrist (*Moralia*, XXXIV, c. III, 7; P.L., LXVI, 721), was used around 1130 in an ironic parody by Matthew, the cardinal of Albano. With this parody he addressed the reform-minded abbots in the ecclesiastical province of Reims when they rejected the monastic customs of the Cluniacs. According to his ironic comments, they behaved in their reform-mindedness as the defenders of Christendom against the coming of the antichrist. *Christendom* (1994), 64-65 and 69-70; also *Cluny et Cîteaux* (1985), 132. Likewise, Berengarius Scholasticus, in his *Apology for Abelard*, used the weapon of irony and parody against Bernard, to whom this *Apology* was addressed. Berengarius described how during the Council of Sens, after they had enjoyed a heavy meal, the participating prelates time and again fell asleep, while Bernard fulminated with great eloquence against the teachings of Abelard. The abbot ended each section of his oration with: "Damnatis"? (Do you condemn?); the council fathers were no longer able to respond with: "Damnamus" (We condemn), but barely managed to say: "Namus" (We swim). Thomson, "The Satirical Works," M.S. 42 (1980), 114. The point of this short, satirical account of how this council condemned the "errors" of Abelard, was its parody of what Bernard himself had written fifteen years earlier about the drinking of wine and the subsequent choral prayers in Cluny (*Apo*, c. IX, 21; SBO III, 98-99; Rudolph [1990], 267-269).

Whatever may be the case, William elaborated upon the biblically inspired account of the dream that Geoffrey and Rainald of Foigny had presented as a proclamation of Bernard's sainthood in such a way that it could be explained as a divinely appointed manifestation of the sainthood of Bernard, who in his preaching barked against the enemies of the church. Thus understood, the story of the dream, employed by William of Saint-Thierry to introduce the concept of Bernard's absolute holiness, formed a first reaction to the various misgivings of his contemporaries regarding the activities of this abbot outside his monastery.

Regardless of the extent of this criticism, which was already heard when William wrote, the nature of his defense remained of great importance, since he rejected any criticism of Bernard by appealing to his sainthood. This line of defense must later, at the time of Bernard's canonization, have been quite effective, as subsequently the objections against his activities outside the monastery continued. For the irritation on the part of many members of the Curia that Bernard provoked by his strong influence on Eugenius III, especially in 1148 during the Council of Reims, where the trinitarian theology of Gilbert de la Porrée was at last condemned as a result of his insistence, was felt for a long time. This seems apparent from an apologetic dialogue written between 1192 and 1198 by Gilbert's pupil, Everard of Ieper, who had been a monk in Clairvaux since 1182.[37]

As indicated, William only alluded to these objections against Bernard in order to offer a more general defense. It provided him with an opportunity to present additional arguments for Bernard's sainthood and to place this in a broader context than would have been possible in the traditional, one-dimensional, hagiographic scheme. The author did subsequently adhere to this scheme in his writing. For it allowed for other matters, such as the proclamation of Bernard's sainthood prior to his birth; his consecration to God and his early education, both after the example of Samuel;[38] his virtuous endurance of sufferings and temptations, which ought to be related at some length;[39] the joyful suffering of hardships, with the inhospitable valley of Clairvaux being compared with the cave of Subiaco where St. Benedict stayed during the years of his

37. For the Council of Reims, see Chibnall, ed., *The Historia Pontificalis* (1956), c. 9; 19–21. For Everhard of Ieper, see Häring, "A Latin Dialogue," M.S. 15 (1953), 243-289. Von Moos, "Le dialogue latin au moyen âge," AnnESC 44 (1989), 939-1028. Also below, 101, with note 22.

38. Vp I, c. I, 2-3; P.L., CLXXXV, 228.

39. Vp I, c. III, 7-8; ibid., 230-231.

maturation;[40] the contemplative union with God: the fact that Bernard subsequently in his contact with his monks seemed like Moses, as the Jews once saw him descending Mount Sinai;[41] and finally, the gift of prophecy and the power to perform miracles that were entrusted to him by God. For all these reasons, he deserved to be venerated as *vir Dei,* a man of God.

Following this scheme was, however, inadequate for a full description of the various other activities of Bernard within and outside the Cistercian Order. In the *vita* this broad involvement, which, of course, was proof of the sainthood of Bernard in all its many facets, is simply designated as a divine endowment. Already in the interpretation of the dream before Bernard's birth, emphasis was placed on Bernard's calling as a preacher to protect God's church. This predestination was further evident in his physical weakness, a result of too much fasting, which made it impossible for Bernard to follow the daily rule of the monastic community. Thus, without any personal ambition in that direction, he was forced, because of his ill health, to be involved in worldly matters. William wrote as follows:

> For even at this time God's power shaped him for the great work of preaching, and as you remember, he had been marked out by a heavenly revelation while his mother was still carrying him in her womb. The whole development of his life trained him for this work, from the time he first went to Cîteaux and lived there under obedience as a simple monk, until the time when he was made the abbot of Clairvaux and ordained by William of Champeaux. And this training in the monastery, although he could not foresee where it would lead him, prepared him for work not only on behalf of his own order but also on behalf of the whole church.
>
> The first-fruits of his youth were dedicated to the work of restoring among his monks that fervor for the religious life which was found in the monks of Egypt long ago. He concentrated all his efforts by word

---

40. Vp I, c. V, 23; idem, 241; Burchard of Balerne made the comparison with St. Benedict in the postcript to this first book; ibid., 267-268. For a translation of the text, see below, 139-140.

41. Vp I, c. VI, 28; P.L., CLXXXV, 243. To arrive at this image, William distorted the conversation between Bernard and his brother Gerard about the material need of Clairvaux, as reported in the *"Fragmenta,"* into a somewhat brusque interchange between the two brothers, during which Gerard, who was the cellarer, accused his abbot of a lack of interest in that need. *Etudes,* 106-107.

and example on achieving this aim among the community in the monastery, but later, when his sickness forced him to adopt another way of life, as I have already told you, he could no longer play such an active part in the life of his monks. And this was how he was first forced into contact with men living in the world who flocked to him in large numbers so that he had to adapt his manner to their ways. . . .

. . . but wherever he went and whenever he spoke, he could not remain silent about the things of God, nor could he cease to carry out God's work. And so it was that his reputation spread among men so widely that the church could not afford not to use so valuable a member of Christ's body for its designs.[42]

In the context referred to above, in which the first book of the *vita prima* was written, this passage is to be interpreted as one of the attempts of William of Saint-Thierry to prevent the criticism Bernard had provoked from in any way disfiguring his portrayal of Bernard's absolute holiness. But this interpretation of the methodology of William is not to be seen as an accusation that he falsified history. We, who today differentiate between the cultic and the historical approach to Bernard, should also realize that such a distinction did not exist in the minds of the medieval hagiographers. To judge William of Saint-Thierry by the same criteria we would employ with regard to a modern biographer of Bernard would testify to a lack of historical insight.

Moreover, William's portrayal is in essence similar to the testimony about Bernard from another contemporary: Wibald, the abbot of Stavelot. In a letter written in 1149 to Manegold, a scholastic at Paderborn, he characterized the person and work of Bernard as he had viewed him in his preaching, writing, and activities. As far as we know, Wibald never had any direct contacts with the abbot of Clairvaux, nor did he ever perceive him as opposed to the convictions he held as a Benedictine abbot. For that reason his extensive testimony is important:

> From time to time situations in the church fully justify the exercise of eloquence, in particular by preachers. In such cases we may recognize a charisma. Of such Bernard, the abbot of Clairvaux, in my opinion, is a supreme example. I do not hesitate to state that he fully realized the traditional concepts of an orator: "a man who masters the art of the word, in defense of the good." His countenance, emaciated by the

42. Vp I, c. VIII, 42; P.L., CLXXXV, 251. Transl. Webb and Walker, 66.

austerity and the fasting in the desert, as well as his paleness, give him a spiritual appearance, so that just looking at this man will convince his hearers, before he has uttered even one word. God endowed him with a perfectly balanced character, a profound intellect, an immeasurable ability to express himself as the fruit of extended exercise, a precise diction and the proper accompanying gestures. No wonder that such a cumulation of all gifts, which characterize orators, awakens the sleepers, yes even, so to speak, the dead. With the help of God, who adds grace to his words, he changes the people; he alters the opponents in the chariots of Pharaoh into the humble prisoners under the divine yoke. You also will not hesitate to call him eloquent; he who does not destroy through his acts the building he has erected by his words, and who, outwardly a Cato, does not inwardly resemble a Nero. To see him is to receive wisdom; to hear him is to be edified; to follow him is to approach perfection.[43]

Concerning William's indirect defense of Bernard, we should also recognize that subsequently, once Bernard had been canonized, the historical memory of him was gradually more and more embellished by the cultic image that bit by bit developed in Cistercian liturgy.[44] This soon made it impossible for a reader of the *vita* to recognize anything of the apologetic character of the first book. Also, since this cultic image of Bernard was quite generally accepted as historical, for many centuries it remained unnoticed how ably William of Saint-Thierry had constructed his apology for Bernard's sainthood from a mixture of cult and history that was just as legitimate for him as it was in the testimony of Wibald of Stavelot. In view of the conviction of many that Bernard always behaved as a man of God, we can hardly accuse William of a conscious misrepresentation of history. At the time his approach was completely acceptable.

As indicated, the apologetic character of William's portrayal of Bernard's sainthood is not immediately recognizable as a rebuttal of the criticism regarding his conduct. Since William nowhere dealt with the actual activities of Bernard, his apologetic arguments are not immediately understood as an indirect defense of his sainthood. In particular, this is apparent in a passage following William's account of the official entry of Bernard and his companions into Cîteaux. The main argument hidden in

43. *Ep.* 147; P.L., CLXXXIX, 1255.
44. "San Bernardo: correlazione" (1975), 32-39.

this passage is the statement of the apostle Paul: "The spiritual man judges all things, but is himself to be judged by no one" (1 Corinthians 2:15). In defense of Bernard, William paraphrased this statement in these words:

> This was the holy beginning of the conversion of the man of God. I believe no one who himself does not live in the same Spirit from which this (man of God) lived, is able to relate his remarkable conversion, how he lived on this earth like an angel. Only he to whom this Spirit has been given and who has accepted Him may understand how from the beginning of his conversion the Lord "met" him with "goodly blessings" (Psalms 21:3); with what measure of grace He filled him, and how He made him "feast on the abundance of his house" (Psalms 36:8).[45]

Once again William describes Bernard's holiness as a special grace, which God gave him in an even greater measure after his entry in Cîteaux. In this connection William argues that unless a person himself lives in this "Spirit," he will never understand the special quality of this sainthood. And such a person would not be able to judge Bernard. This argument further implied that those who felt they could criticize Bernard's life and conduct evidently did not live in that "Spirit." Thus all critical assessments of any activity of this saint were inconsequential, since such evaluations remained inferior to the measure of Bernard's sainthood. Although the passage of St. Paul quoted above was not actually cited, his statement, which was known to most readers of the *vita*, was in fact used to silence any contemporary criticism. To substantiate this criticism with details was unnecessary and even undesirable when a rebuttal was attempted.

This interpretation of the statement referred to above is closely linked to what could be said about some other apologetic passages in the first book of the *vita prima*. These may be understood in the same sense. This is, for instance, true of the passage in which William of Saint-Thierry defended Bernard against the allegation that he sometimes went too far in his zeal for certain matters. In this defense William conveniently failed to mention that Bernard usually did not take the trouble to check the facts on which he based his opinions and, subsequently, his actions.[46] William provided, to some extent, a summary of these actions. He thereby emphasized in particular Bernard's accomplishments in his many interventions on behalf of the church.

---

45. Vp I, c. IV, 19; P.L., CLXXXV, 237-238.
46. Riché, "La connaissance concrète de la chrétienté," 383-399.

William here repeated the argument he had earlier used that Bernard had not initiated these activities himself; but that God in his providence had led him to these acts, making use of his physical weakness, which had caused him to regularly spend time outside the monastic life. No mention, however, is made of the fact that it was William himself who pushed Bernard to some of his actions outside his monastery and even outside the monastic realm — for example, in his intervention in an internal conflict in Cluny[47] and later in his opposition against Abelard, already referred to above. William began this apology with an outburst of praise:

> And while we certainly bemoan the distressing results of his illness, we are full of praise for the way in which his holy zeal strove after its object. His illness may well have been part of God's wise plan to abash the great and powerful things of this world, for never did he leave unfinished because of his infirmity any task which he could finish with the help of the grace that God gave him.
>
> Who in these days, be he ever so fit and strong, has ever done such wonderful deeds on behalf of the church and for the glory of God as Bernard did and still does in spite of his health bringing him to death's door? It would be hard to number the men whom, by his word and example, he attracted from the world and its ways, not only to a new life but even to perfection. The whole Christian world is dotted with houses — or should I say, cities? — of refuge to which men may flee and be saved after falling into deadly sins worthy of eternal damnation, and realizing their guilt and turning to the Lord. Think of how many churches he saved from falling into schism, how many heresies he exposed. Who can remember how often he calmed the troubles caused by nations and churches which threatened to break away from legitimate authority? But it is common knowledge that he did these things. How, then, could one list the great benefits and helps he bestowed on individual men for whatever cause, on behalf of whatever person, in whatever place, at whatever season?[48]

The things here enumerated by William as expressions of Bernard's sainthood repeatedly led to criticism of him, the more so since Bernard often got involved in controversies without adequate examination of the facts.[49]

---

47. *Christendom* (1994), 130-150.
48. Vp I, c. VIII; P.L., CLXXXV, 250-251. Transl. Webb and Walker, 64-65.
49. Above, note 46.

His contemporaries must have been aware of this; therefore, William could not, after such exuberant praise, simply ignore this criticism. Following this praise, he mentioned the criticisms, but in such a way that he implicitly answered them, or at least denied them:

> Even if one finds fault with Bernard for allowing his zeal to overstep his limits, one must remember that godly souls respect that excess of his, and, being themselves moved by the Spirit of God, they are very slow to blame him for it. The general run of men excuse this so-called fault easily, since there are few who are so bold as to condemn a man whom God vindicates by doing so many marvellous things in him and through him. That man is happy indeed who is judged guilty of fault by doing something that most people do for the sake of boasting and self-glory. . . . And in this respect, even if he did carry things a little too far, he left to devout souls not so much an example of excess, but rather an object-lesson in fervour and zeal. And yet why do we look for excuses for him about a thing of which he, even to this day, is not ashamed to excuse himself?[50]

This defense by William of Bernard's at times "somewhat overzealous actions" also applies to the experiences of others with this abbot and to their accusations that he meddled in things that were outside his domain and his competence. That they did not appreciate his involvements is also clear from a remark William made earlier in the first book. Some had accused Bernard of refusing to take full responsibility for matters in which he involved himself. This reproach concerns in particular Bernard's repeated refusal to accept the various episcopal sees that were offered to him after his interventions in these places.

This problem had, for instance, been quite acute in 1138, in the context of Bernard's actions in Langres — rather close to his home. The episcopal throne had been vacant; however, when someone had been elected, Bernard had succeeded in having the candidate removed after his consecration. The chapter then elected him as the new bishop. But he refused this post and saw to it that it was offered to Godefroy de la Roche Vanneau, the prior of his own monastery, whom he could ill afford to lose.[51] Without giving further attention to any such offers or even men-

50. Vp I, c. VIII, 41; P.L., CLXXXV, 251. Transl. Webb and Walker, 65.
51. Constable, "The Disputed Election," 119-152; reprinted in *Cluniac Studies* (1980).

tioning them individually, William answered this accusation by painting his constant refusal of such urgent demands as a special grace that God had given him. The (in retrospect rather obvious) argument that Bernard, in his work for the church, could not, considering his nature and the task he had taken upon himself, tie himself down to a local assignment, would not have fitted in the cultic explanation William used in his defense of Bernard:

> All his magnificent actions together manifest the purity of his motives in everything he did. For, since he did not arrogantly spurn the highest ecclesiastical offices and the favors of secular princes, which they continued to press upon him in their conviction that he was worthy of these, but declined them in piety and reasonableness, he manifested what he sought and strove for in all his works. But he knew, although he would have been worthy to have been persuaded [to accept the episcopal office] — through some divine decree unknown to me and through the respect for his extraordinary saintliness — how to arrange matters in such a way that he would never be forced to do what he did not want. But while thus escaping from the honor of the world, he did not refuse to submit to the authority of those honorable offices which he himself, who was feared and loved in the love and the fear of the Lord, would have been worthy to occupy.[52]

The *vita prima* deliberately pictured Bernard's sainthood in its relationship to the church and the world. During the canonization process, and later by the Cistercian Order in his official cult, this concept was consistently maintained. This outside involvement, however, forced William of Saint-Thierry in his hagiographic presentation constantly to defend Bernard against the criticism of contemporaries who had met him as their opponent outside his monastery. As a result, the first book of the *vita prima*, because of these arguments of William, may be regarded as an extremely valuable source of information about Bernard's life. For in his repeated defense, we find illuminating information about Bernard as the human being he remained, in spite of all the special grace God gave him. But this information is only accessible to those who know the art of *close reading* and are able to place the text in the context of the facts that other studies of Bernard's role in church and world have discovered and established.

William of Saint-Thierry's veiled presentation of Bernard's life merits

---

52. Vp I, c. XIV, 69; P.L., CLXXXV, 265. Transl. Webb and Walker.

admiration rather than disapproval. He had known Bernard for a long time, and while he knew about a number of negative aspects in the life of this man, he was convinced of his sainthood. His burden concerned this latter aspect. He wanted to testify to Bernard's holiness while the abbot was still alive, and while, as a result of the exercise of his authority and his actions, he was the object of criticism, jealousy, and hatred. His defense was therefore rather a matter of protecting Bernard against hostile sentiments, than a rebuttal of concrete charges related to his "predestined" sainthood.

William could therefore conclude his part in this *vita* with a word of praise: During his life Bernard never met jealousy or hatred, nor did he ever have any enemies. In his attempt to make this credible, William employed a rather far-fetched argument. A sixteenth-century Lutheran commentary remarks that this could not even be said of Christ or his disciples:[53]

> He [the Holy Spirit] kept people from envying him [because of his gifts], as he himself was above all envy; the evil of the human heart usually stops envying another person for what it itself cannot reach. At the same time, he was also able to kill all envy through the example of his humility, or to transform it into a more elevated sentiment through the challenge of his love, or — when this envy was too evil and too stubborn — to push it aside by the weight of his authority. For, where does one find such a person who, in such an efficient and loving manner, is able to stimulate any love that might be present, and to awaken it if it should still be absent? Who is so benevolent and charitable toward all? Who bestowes so many favors on friends and manifests so much patience toward his enemies? That is, if one can speak of enemies in the case of a person who does not want to have any conflict. For as friendship presupposes two people, and can only exists between friends, likewise there can only be enmity between two enemies. If someone refuses to love or even hates the person who loves him, he is unjust rather than hostile. However, a person who loves all men and who because of his virtue never had an enemy, may nevertheless suffer from enmity, when others for no reason, because of their unrighteousness which originates elsewhere, decide to be his enemies.[54]

53. This comment is found in Flacius Illyricus, *Historia ecclesiastica,* or "Maagdeburger Centurionen," vol. III, Basel, 1624, 814. "St. Bernard and the Historians" (1977), 35 with note 32.

54. Vp I, c. XIV, 69. P.L., CLXXXV, 266.

None of the other authors of the *vita prima* went as far as William of Saint-Thierry in his defense of Bernard.[55] The question remains whether such a portrayal of absolute sainthood was necessary — in the context of the world of those days — to shelter Bernard to such an extent against the objections and grievances of others, as was done in this first book. But when faced with the allegation implied in that question, we must remember that William of Saint-Thierry himself was somewhat entangled in the criticism Bernard had to face during his life. It was, as we already saw, precisely at the instigation of William that Bernard involved himself in two extremely controversial affairs in which he almost blindly followed William's suggestions. And it was in particular for those interventions that Bernard at the time was repeatedly criticized.

This fact must be considered in our evaluation of the apologetic character of the first book. But a critical analysis of the *vita prima* in its entirety must also pay due attention to the specific relationship that existed between each of the authors and Bernard. We have already referred to these relationships a few times, but in the next chapter we will deal with these more adequately and in a more systematic way.

55. A more erroneous view than William's apologetic portrayal of Bernard's spiritual personality is found in the twenty-fourth chapter of a subtle spiritual treatise that was written in English between 1350 and 1370, a well-known but anonymous document published under the title *The Cloud of Unknowing* (London: J. McCann, 1952). It incorporates the understanding of mysticism widespread in the later Middle Ages and regards it as impossible for a mystic to have an enemy.

IV

The Authors of the Vita Prima

ঽ৵   ঽ৵

OUR EXPLORATIONS concerning the *vita prima* in the previous chapter have clarified a number of aspects of this document. We found that it was prepared and written with the intent of securing Bernard's canonization. We also explained why in its portrayal of Bernard's sainthood it placed so much emphasis on his involvement with the church and society. In the remembrance of the saints, not only was the abbot to live on as a *vir iustus,* whose significance was mainly based on the saintliness he had manifested in his own surroundings, but, in their view, he was also entitled to be regarded as a saint *in medio ecclesiae.*

Each of the authors, inspired by his own personal relationship with Bernard, contributed to the broad hagiographic intent that characterizes the *vita prima.* Although we have already referred repeatedly to their role, the contribution of these hagiographers needs to be dealt with in a more coherent way. While this concerns the background of each of them, their direct ties with Bernard, and their involvement with his activities, we must also further clarify why the cooperation of the authors of the first and second book was solicited.

1. GEOFFREY OF AUXERRE

GEOFFREY OF AUXERRE may be viewed as the initiator of the writing of this *vita*. As Bernard's secretary, he began in 1145, from the moment Eugenius III had been elected pope, to make the first preparations and to collect materials for others. It seems that initially he had wanted to entrust Rainald, a fellow secretary, with the writing of this *vita;* therefore, Rainald also deserves to be mentioned.

In 1122 Rainald became abbot of Foigny. In 1132 he returned to Clairvaux, where he was engaged as Bernard's secretary. He succeeded William of Rievaulx, a monk who had originally come from England. This William had been at this post since 1120, but had been dispatched by Bernard in 1132 to become the abbot of Rievaulx, one of the earliest Cistercian foundations in England.[1]

As indicated earlier, Bernard was accompanied on a number of his journeys by Rainald, in particular between 1132 and 1138, when he worked for the recognition of Pope Innocent II. We know from the *Exordium magnum* that Rainald wrote an account of the journey to Milan that Bernard made in 1135 for that purpose.[2] This account has not been preserved, and we do not know whether he wrote any other travel reports. He also accompanied Bernard when he came to Paris in 1140 to preach to clerics who studied there. At that occasion Rainald even acted as Bernard's spokesman.[3] But even though Geoffrey in the first instance wrote his biographical *Fragmenta* to assist Rainald, their collaboration seems not to have been very fruitful.

Geoffrey may have viewed Rainald's assistance as important since Rainald had frequently accompanied Bernard and also because his office provided him with the opportunity to publish more freely. Furthermore, it seems likely that if there were other travel reports, they were used in the writing of the *vita*,[4] the more so since the biographical fragments that Geoffrey had collected were in part rewritten by Rainald. How much he actually rewrote is now difficult to ascertain since very little of his work had been preserved.[5] Rainald probably depended heavily on Bernard; the letters he wrote when he was still abbot of Foigny convey the impression that he hesitated to make independent decisions. That may have been the reason that Bernard made him return to Clairvaux.[6]

---

1. For the origins of the Cistercian Order in England, see Knowles, *The Monastic Order,* 1963, 208-266. Bethel, "The Foundation of Fountains Abbey," JEH 17 (1966), 11-27. Idem, 1968.
2. II, c. 16; ed. Griesser, 110.
3. II, c. 13; ed. Griesser, 107.
4. Vp II, c. II, 9; P.L., CLXXXV, 274. *Etudes* (1960), 113, with note 3.
5. Gastaldelli, "Le piu antiche testimonianze," 21-32.
6. *Epp.* 72, 73, 74, and 413; SBO VII, 175-181 and VIII, 396.

Later Geoffrey did not look for authors of the first and second book of the *vita* in Bernard's immediate circles. The persons he chose also possessed abbatial authority, but did not depend on Bernard. After Bernard's death, Geoffrey completed the *vita* by adding three more books. As we have seen, this work carried a special difficulty in that, as a monk, Geoffrey had to submit anything he wrote to an abbot or bishop, or even to the general chapter, for approval. For that reason he introduced his account of the last year and of the death of Bernard with a letter to Eskil, the archbishop of Lund.[7] Having completed the *vita*, he subsequently assisted a group of Cistercian abbots and bishops who had assembled in Clairvaux, probably at the request of the general chapter, to evaluate this work and who, in a collective prologue, presented themselves as the authors of these books. However, this text, which remained largely unknown, may well have been composed by Geoffrey himself:

> After the demise of our blessed father Bernard, abbot of Clairvaux, we as bishops and abbots, though unworthy to follow in his holy footsteps, have gathered as dedicated sons in order to more fully and more clearly proclaim what we know of this man of God, on the one hand through our long experience with him, and, on the other hand, as a result of the generosity he manifested toward us. We therefore considered it fitting that we preserve for posterity some things which have been recorded, and gather from this abundant meal, which to the glory of God has strengthened all of our generation, some fragments, so that they will not be lost. We were also of the opinion that we should not leave this work to others, as long as we are not lacking in the required skills and consecration for such a task. We trust that the godliness of our intentions will make up for our deficiency in eloquence. One usually reports more honestly and more correctly what one has seen than what one just happened to hear — just as water that is drawn near the source will taste better than when it is drawn further away from the river.
>
> But after careful examination we have preferred to accept rather than to rewrite and to approve rather than to change what we found to have been truthfully recorded about our father [Bernard] by the honorable abbots William of Saint-Thierry and Arnold of Bonneval. We gladly respect a style of writing when we agree with its testimony. The reader will therefore, after having read those books, find a third

7. For the text, see *Etudes*, 51-52.

book that consists of three parts. The first of these three deals mostly with the conduct, the lifestyle, and the teachings of this, our most blessed father; the second recounts his virtuous deeds; while the third, about the blessed end of his life, completes this work.

Where one of us was mentioned, we have preferred to refer to that person as to any other, to prevent a frequent alternation of persons which would result in confusion. If someone should not fully agree with this approach, the example of saints, who speak in their books about themselves as if they were others, should be sufficient — if such an example be even required.

It should also be noticed that in our account of events we have given more attention to coherence than sequence. We do not report signs or miracles in the order in which, as far as we can remember, they took place, but we have inserted some at a more advantageous point to underline more strongly what we wanted to convey. And we have inserted other matters at other points to tie things of a similar nature together. This approach is, in particular, visible in the first two books; in the third it follows mostly the actual sequence of events.[8]

The detailed account of how the subject matter was dealt with in these last three books clearly indicates Geoffrey's close involvement with the redaction of this prologue. Moreover, he maintained these details in the prologue that he subsequently composed to introduce these three books in redaction B of the *vita*. It is also remarkable that in the third book of the *vita*, which Geoffrey wrote himself, he never specifies his personal relationship with Bernard or mentions himself by name. He does refer to himself, however, in the letter to Archbishop Eskil that he used as the introduction to his account of Bernard's last year and death.

Of course, Geoffrey could not send an anonymous letter to Eskil, since he could not publish this report without Eskil's approval. But normally Geoffrey preferred anonymity. For in his report of Bernard's sermon in 1140 for an audience of Parisian students "About conversion" *(De conversione: ad clericos)*, he fails to mention his own presence, even though this encounter led to his own *conversio*. This visit to Paris preceded Bernard's more public protest against Abelard. Until that visit, Geoffrey had attended Abelard's lectures; but after this sermon, he turned away from Abelard and followed Bernard to Clairvaux. Likewise in his own prologue,

8. MGH SS XXVI, 110. *Etudes*, 40 and frontispiece (facsimile of ms Douai 372, vol. II, fol. 176b). For the role of these abbots and bishops, see above, 41-42.

added to the last three books in 1163, he remains reticent. He mentions his close relationship with Bernard during more than thirteen years and speaks with great respect about his abbot and about the loss his death had meant to him and continued to mean to him, but he retains his anonymity and does not describe this relationship in any detail.

His reticence in this *vita* to speak about his close ties with Bernard contrasts sharply with the uninhibited manner in which he referred to this relationship elsewhere. In his later sermons about Bernard, he often reminded his hearers of the close relationship between them, as he also did in the prologue of his substantial "Exposition of the Song of Songs."[9] Geoffrey also testifies of his close ties with Bernard in the *Fragmenta Gaufridi*, although therein he also refrains from referring to himself by name.[10] This testimony is important since it dates from the time when Geoffrey embarked upon what was to be his life's work. This text can therefore be viewed as a contemporary evaluation of what his encounter with Bernard, five years earlier, had meant to him as a young monk:

> Speaking about others (whom he healed), I must not omit to refer to myself, lest I be thought of as ungrateful. It once happened that the man of God departed on some business to Gallia *(sic)*. When on his way there and on his return he was to preach to the students in Paris about *conversion* — something he was accustomed to do — he became gloomy and sad as the evening fell. He said in his prayers to God: "I fear that You have completely forgotten me. For, contrary to normal experience, this journey has remained without any fruit, and I have accomplished nothing of what I set out to do. Neither was a door opened for me when I was with these members of the clergy." At the same moment God comforted him in such a way, that he clearly foreknew and prophesied: "I will not return from here empty-handed."
>
> This day on which the light began to dawn, for me who sat in darkness and in the shadow of death, be blessed by the Lord. Blessed be the day on which the sun of righteousness and compassion visited my poor soul from on high, to completely recreate a wayward and wrongly directed person instantaneously and in one single moment with only one word, by an unnoticeable movement of the hand of the Most High. As a result I began to be his creature. For all eternity I

9. Gastaldelli, ed., *Goffredo, Expositio in Cantica* I, 1974, 4-6.
10. About the authorship of Geoffrey, see Gastaldelli, "Le piu antiche testimonianze," 18-21.

will remember this compassion, which was given me in such full measure and changed me so suddenly, that I astounded the spirit of many people. Truly, during this catch many fishes became entangled in the nets of the Lord and during our journey many joined our company. After the probationary year had ended, twenty-one of us, who belonged to this group, became monks.[11]

As was stated earlier, some passages from sermons Geoffrey preached in later years agree with this testimony. For in these he very openly spoke of his close association with Bernard.[12] But as far as content is concerned, these sermons are also in full harmony with the praises of Bernard that Geoffrey repeatedly sang in the *vita prima*. This contribution has a strong panegyrical character. The first chapter of the third book, for instance, contains a tribute that could have been written for any saint, with the exception of the final passage in which he also praises the outward appearance of Bernard:

> Magnanimous in faith, patient in the hope, giving himself unconditionally in love, the highest in humility, the first in piety. Forward looking in giving counsel, efficient in taking care of business; . . . He cheerfully accepted criticism and was bashful when faced with servility. He was pleasant in his behavior, sanctified through virtues, and famous because of his miracles; finally, he was full of wisdom and virtue, and enjoyed the favor of God and his fellowmen.
>
> God had provided a helper for his holy soul which was on a par with it; He had prepared a body for the soul, ready to be of assistance because of a special blessing. His body exuded a certain charm, which was spiritual rather than physical. His face radiated with a bright splendor, which was not of earthly but of heavenly origin. His eyes radiated, so to speak, with the true purity of an angel and the simplicity of a dove. Such was his inner beauty that it manifested itself outwardly through undeniable indications; even his physical appearance overflowed with inner purity and an abundance of grace.
>
> His entire body was rather fragile and not plump, his skin was extremely soft, and his face carried a rosy complexion. And whatever natural warmth he possessed, he expended in his continuous thoughts and his zeal for penance. The hair on his head was fair; his beard somewhat reddish, but toward the end of his life it seems as if it was

11. *"Fragmenta,"* c. 49; ed. Lechat, 115-116.
12. P.L., CLXXXV, 573-588. Leclercq, *Etudes sur saint Bernard* (1953), 157-170.

covered with a thin layer of greyness. His physique was a good average, and made him in fact appear rather tall. . . .[13]

This text was certainly in the right place, at the beginning of the third book of the *vita prima*. Its first chapters present a rich palette of praises, sometimes undergirded by striking examples of Bernard's human virtues, and also of those virtues that were his through God's special grace. However, these chapters, together with the statement from the privilege given to Clairvaux by Innocent II in 1132,[14] serve as an introduction to a few rather delicate matters, which Geoffrey mentions next: Bernard's preaching of the Second Crusade, which proved to be a failure (1146-1147); his opposition against Abelard (1141) and Gilbert de la Porrée (1149); and his preaching in the south of France against the heretical Henry of Lausanne. In all these matters Geoffrey unremittingly praises Bernard's actions.

But even detached from this context, these songs of praise for Bernard constitute an important part of Geoffrey's contribution as one of the authors of the *vita prima*. The fourth book, with its emphasis on miracles and prophetic omens that occurred as a result of Bernard's intervention while he was still alive, was less suitable for explicit praise, but the fifth book once again gives ample opportunity for this. The account, for instance, of Bernard's appearance after his death to brother William of Montpellier — added by Geoffrey to this book only in redaction B when he himself was the abbot of Clairvaux — contains the following song of praise and petition:

> Well then, holy father, you, who while in this valley of tears already ascended in your heart, have now from Clairvaux [= the "clear valley"] joyfully ascended the Lebanon: the mountain of splendor, the fullness of light, the summit of clarity. With innocent hands and a pure heart you have climbed the mountain of the Lord, toward the riches of salvation; you have ascended toward the treasures of wisdom and knowledge, where you discern the pure truth in purity, where you and all saints have no other teacher but Christ, and where all are henceforth ready and prepared to be taught by God.
>
> Take us with you, we plead, and look in mercy from your high mountain upon your valley. Assist us in our labor, help those who are in danger, reach out to those who are ascending. This trust bestows

13. VP III, c. I, 1; P.L., CLXXXV, 303.
14. For this statement, see above, 73-74, with note 24.

your goodness, which we experienced in the past, upon us; a trust that has in no way been reduced, but rather has greatly increased. . . .[15]

Just as remarkable is the praise Geoffrey adds to his comment on the letter that Bernard supposedly wrote on his deathbed to Arnold of Bonneval, but which, in my opinion, was composed by Geoffrey after Bernard's death as part of the account of Bernard's final moments that he wrote for Eskil.[16] In his postscript to this letter, Geoffrey indicates how the attentive reader may learn about Bernard's emotions just before his death and may imagine the sorrow of those who lost this father. In this context he calls Bernard truly a father for the whole world. He adds some further remarks to this passage in the revised version of this report.[17] There he alternately addresses Bernard in the third and in the second person:

> Where he was present, the saints shouted with joy, the boasters kept quiet, and the recalcitrants changed their ways. Where he was present, a meeting came alive; if he was absent, the meeting seemed to have lost its purpose and became dull. . . . You were the example of perfection, the model of virtue, the mirror of sanctity. You were the pride of Israel, the joy of Jerusalem, the delight of your century, the only charm of your time, an olive tree full of fruit, a lush vine, a flowering palm tree, a many-branched cedar, and a high sycamore. . . . You were the strongest pillar of the holy church, a resounding trumpet of God, a lovely plaything of the Holy Spirit, which encourages pious people, activates those who shun work, and supports the lame. Your hand and tongue, both medicinal, fought illnesses; the former was focused on physical ailments, the latter on diseases of the soul. His stature was natural, as was his countenance; his face was friendly and his appearance was pleasant. His life, finally, was fruitful and his death precious. For also for you, to live was Christ, and to die was gain. . . .[18]

This and other texts express Geoffrey's adoration, dedication, and love for Bernard, as well as his gratitude that he had been privileged to know him intimately as his abbot, his monastic leader, and his spiritual father. But

15. Vp V, c. III, 22; P.L., CLXXXV, 364.

16. "Der Brief" (1988). See below, 104-107.

17. Geoffrey inserted this postscript, which is missing in the report sent to Eskil, when he wrote recension A of the fifth book, "Un brouillon" (1959), 54-55; see comment on line 342.

18. Vp V, c. II, 11; P.L., CLXXXV, 357-358. In redaction B this passage has been replaced by a much shorter text; cf. *Etudes*, 53-54.

Geoffrey also called him "a father for the whole world" and indicated that Bernard's significance reached far beyond the walls of his monastery and the monasteries that had been founded from Clairvaux. He probably realized this far-reaching significance already at an early date; for once he had listened to Bernard, he turned away from his teacher Abelard. This realization of Bernard's significance for the world at large greatly influenced Geoffrey's approach and intent with respect to the *vita prima*. This awareness of Bernard's importance outside his monastery and his order is in particular reflected in the emphasis on the sainthood as it has been portrayed in this *vita*.

THIS REALIZATION of Bernard's wider role in church and society is also clearly present in the contributions of William of Saint-Thierry and Arnold of Bonneval, no doubt an indication that this aspect was one of the reasons why Geoffrey selected these authors. The choice of William of Saint-Thierry was rather obvious, but that was much less so for Arnold of Bonneval. Geoffrey, however, tried to create a different impression by including in the fifth book a letter that Bernard was said to have written on his deathbed to Arnold. As I said earlier, I believe this to be a fictitious letter, written at some later date by Geoffrey himself. In this letter he gave an authentic account of Bernard's physical condition just before his death. This account could also, without further explanation, help readers to see Arnold's contribution to this *vita* as a logical choice.

Geoffrey's ideas about the structure of the *vita prima* were, of course, also influenced by the contributions of the two other authors, the more so since he, as the last writer, had to take into account what they had already written. Yet to a large extent this *vita* remains his work because in spite of the fact that he could not write without the approval of others, Geoffrey had the advantage that, as Bernard's secretary, he could freely examine his writings and correspondence and was even allowed to write and send letters in his name. Bernard complained that during his final years one of the other secretaries greatly abused this freedom.[19] This incident, which led to the dismissal of the secretary in question, may have prompted Geoffrey to write, after Bernard's death, the letter that sup-

---

19. *Ep.* 298; SBO VIII, 214. Cf. "Saint Bernard in his Relations" (1993). See below, 245.

posedly was addressed to Arnold of Bonneval and that — as already mentioned — served a dual purpose in the context of this *vita*.

The freedom Geoffrey could permit himself as author is also apparent in another passage in the fifth book, where he showed his support for Abbot Robert, who remained controversial as Bernard's successor. Geoffrey describes a revelation experienced by a monk at Clairvaux seven years before Bernard died and which this monk related to another monk. The vision concerned the moment Bernard was to die. The person who had received this revelation is said to have died even before Bernard passed away. Geoffrey continued the story as follows:

> We heard this fact through a remark of the other, who is still alive and who was extremely astonished about what he heard, when he saw it happen exactly as he had heard it in the past. He is the kind of person whose testimony we need not doubt and we believe that nobody who knows him will doubt it. But there was more. It seems no less wonderful that, according to him, he has known since that time, through what this same fellow-brother told him, the name and identity of that successor.[20]

Geoffrey clarified this text in his report to Eskil with these words: "That is to say: the one who is now our abbot." This indication sufficed for this archbishop, who was well acquainted with Clairvaux. Outsiders, however, needed more clarification. For that reason, Geoffrey provided further details when he used this report as the basis for the fifth book of the *vita prima*:

> For unequivocally this fellow-monk predicted at the same occasion: "Dom Robertus, who is presently the abbot of Ter Duinen, will succeed our blessed father as abbot of Clairvaux."[21]

We need hardly occupy ourselves with the question of the credibility of this anonymous revelation-story. It may be viewed as a prophecy after the fact. It is more important to ask for Geoffrey's intention. It is abundantly clear that the resistance that Abbot Robert continued to experience as Bernard's successor was the underlying reason. Geoffrey undoubtedly supported Robert unconditionally since he had been Bernard's own choice.

20. Vp V, c. III, 17; P.L., CLXXXV, 361.
21. "Un Brouillon" (1959), 43, lines 494-495, and 58. Retold in *Exordium magnum* II, c. XXI; ed. Griesser, 118.

He therefore invented this story and deemed it desirable, when he re-edited his account, to emphasize the point even more strongly. This story is also instructive with regard to Geoffrey's methodology. His information to the reader was in part determined by the underlying issues at stake. His most important objective with regard to this *vita* was, of course, Bernard's canonization. But he felt little inhibition in informing his reader in such in way that some secondary interests were also served.

This deliberately designed account reflects another aspect of Geoffrey's personality. He knew how to define long-term objectives.

This attribute is especially noticeable in his prolonged involvement with the *vita prima*. It was first visible when Geoffrey began with his preparations at the time when Eugenius III had become pope, and subsequently in his choice of authors for the first and the second books who did not belong to the "inner circle" of his own order. His dealings with the group of abbots and bishops who were to evaluate his contribution to the *vita* and the document as a whole also point to a calculated approach. The same is also evident in his revision of the complete *vita* after the first request for canonization had been put aside.

Later Geoffrey was unwilling to make any concessions with regard to the structure of the *vita* for which he had opted. He unyieldingly retained his design for this document — which, as we saw, to a large extent depended on his personal insight and understanding of Bernard's personality — against those in the Cistercian Order who resented his attitude in the conflict between Thomas Becket and King Henry II, and who attempted to utilize his ensuing removal as abbot of Clairvaux by the pope to replace the *prima vita* with a colorless excerpt.

Just as characteristic was the special way in which Geoffrey had learned to appreciate Bernard as abbot, to experience him as miracle worker, and, above all, to savor him as preacher and author. This, in particular, defined the relationship that had developed between the two over the thirteen years during which Geoffrey had known and experienced Bernard: a relationship between a monk and his abbot, on Geoffrey's side mainly characterized by feelings of dependency and unconditional acceptance of authority, as described in the eulogies that he continued to reformulate in the various editions of this *vita*.

The nature of this relationship between student and teacher not only comes to expression in the many praises, but also in the absence of any direct apologetic defense against the criticism of Bernard that was still heard at that time. Geoffrey's admiration for Bernard was such that he totally ignored any criticism of Bernard, even after his death. Years later he defended, in two smaller treatises, the controversial involvement of Bernard against Gilbert de la Porrée, whose condemnation Bernard had succeeded in obtaining. Forty years later, Geoffrey sent one of these documents as a letter to Albinus, who at the time was the cardinal-bishop of

Albano.[22] This shows that his approach as hagiographer with regard to this issue in the *vita* was not totally determined by the need to cling to this portrayal of absolute holiness, as was customary in every *vita*. He accepted this portrayal as self-evident.

Finally, we are left with the question of Geoffrey's significance as author. Usually he is not regarded as a very competent writer. In his works he shows a large measure of dependence on Bernard.[23] When compared with both other authors, Geoffrey is less competent, and his significance as author must therefore be found first of all in what he did to promote Bernard's cult, both during his life and after his death. The success in that task, in which he shared as author, is undeniable.

This success may explain why, at a later date, he was asked to write a *vita* of Peter, a Cistercian monk who became the bishop of Tarentaise (1175).[24] On the other hand, Geoffrey is partly responsible for the confusion in the transmission of the *vita prima*; something he probably did not lose any sleep over. For the rest, one might say that Geoffrey developed into an author after he had accepted the assignment to realize Bernard's canonization. His part in this process is well known; while the concept of Bernard's sainthood, which positioned him in "the midst of the church," was also strongly promoted by Geoffrey, even though he was not its originator.

In summary, Geoffrey's merits as an author mostly concern this *vita*, written in support of Bernard's cult. For that purpose he worked unremittingly, inspired by a strong attachment to his abbot, uncritically maintaining the admiration and veneration he had had for his master ever since he was a young monk. In whatever way we want to judge this *vita*, we cannot blame Geoffrey, in view of his contribution, for the fact that others have

22. *De condemnatione errorum Gilberti Poretani*, P.L., CLXXXV, 587-596. The other essay *(libellus)*, in which Geoffrey responds to four of Gilbert's propositions, most probably was an appendix to this letter; P.L., CLXXXV, 595-617. He wrote the letter a few years before Everard of Ieperen, then already a monk at Clairvaux, defended Gilbert in his *Dialogus Ratii*. Above, 80, with note 37.

23. At the beginning of his first book, Geoffrey describes Bernard as the first and greatest miracle he performed, just as Bernard had written about Malachias (Vp III, c. I, 1; P.L., CLXXXV, 303). De Ghellinck says about him as author (1955, 219): "Geoffrey of Auxerre, or of Clairvaux, has manifested in his writing about the saint, whom he served as a secretary, a constant warmth and a feeling of sincerity, with a use of language that is clear and natural; but he does not show a mastery of language, nor a richness in form."

24. *Acta Sanctorum*, Maii II, 323-345.

later interpreted his involvement as an attempt on his part to provide a historically reliable portrayal of this saint. Though it has later been suggested that his subsequent revisions of the text were inspired by his care for greater historical accuracy, we must conclude that Geoffrey, as the initiator, author, and revisor of the *vita prima,* had another goal in mind that fitted more naturally in the context of the time in which he lived.

2. ARNOLD OF BONNEVAL

THE AUTHOR OF THE second book of the *vita prima* is virtually unknown among historians. One looks in vain for his name in the *Lexikon des Mittelalters;* while in encyclopedias that do mention his name, one usually finds a short description based on what authors of repertories in the seventeenth and eighteenth centuries already copied from one another.[25] According to J. de Ghellinck's survey of twelfth-century Latin literature, early information about Arnold does not seem to have been fully consistent. Referring to the sermons of Arnold that have been preserved, he writes that this author is of less interest to historians of literature than, because of the fear and uncertainty that are evident in his scrupulous attitude to religion, to psychologists. But on the other hand, he recognizes in him "un veritable talent d'historien"; this, of course, is in view of his part in the *vita prima.*[26]

In any case, this Benedictine abbot is primarily known for his contribution to the *vita prima.* A recent attempt to highlight his achievements did provide some additional information about him, but failed to give a sharp picture of his personality.[27] Even his relationship to Bernard remains rather vague. Apart from the letter referred to above, which Bernard allegedly sent him from his deathbed and which speaks of a close friendship, no further details about this association have been discovered.

Nor did Arnold himself, in the second book of the *vita,* mention any personal ties between himself and Bernard. His contribution to the *vita* does indicate, however, that even while Bernard was still alive, Arnold was convinced of his sainthood. It also stands to reason that he must have known at least some of

25. Oury, "Recherches," RMab 49 (1977), 118, note 2.
26. *L'essor de la littérature* (1955), 220 and 395.
27. Oury, "Recherches," 97-127. Idem, "La Vie monastique," R.H.S. 51 (1975), 267-280.

Bernard's writings. In a short treatise of his own — a hymn of praise for Mary — he shows clear dependence on four famous sermons by Bernard about Mary's election as the Mother of God.[28] Furthermore, his description of the contemporary life of the monks in Clairvaux was largely inspired by what Bernard had written on that topic in his *Apology.*[29]

Likewise little is known about Arnold's background. It has generally been assumed that before his election as abbot in Bonneval, he was a monk in Marmoutiers, near Tours. But in the meantime, a document dating from 1127 has been discovered that mentions his name with the addition *monachus de Bonavalle.*[30] This suggests that he came from around Chartres, where this abbey had been founded in 841 by Charles the Bold. This monastery had, through the centuries, acquired large possessions and prestige. Considering that Arnold is first mentioned as abbot in 1129, his entry must have taken place sometime before 1127. He was abbot for thirty years. His relationship with a major part of the monastic community seems to have been characterized by some problems, in particular in the early phase of his abbacy. This was the reason that in 1134, or at the latest in 1135, he asked Innocent II, through the intervention of the papal legate, Cardinal Matthew of Albano, for permission to abdicate from his post. His plan was to retire to Cluny with a number of monks who had chosen his side in his conflict with the community. This we may conclude from a letter written by Peter the Venerable to Matthew of Albano in 1135 or 1136.

The abbot of Cluny, however, gave no details about the nature of this conflict, since, as he stated, this was known to the cardinal-legate.[31] Apparently Innocent II did not approve of this request by Abbot Arnold. There are also indications, however, that in later years the relationship between the abbot and the community was far from easy. Thus when Arnold, in 1159, requested Adrian IV to relieve him of his post as abbot, he cited as the reason that he felt no longer able to deal with this monastic community.[32]

After 1159 his name is not found in any other document. Supposing that he was probably about seventy years of age in that year, it is generally assumed that Arnold was not older than forty when he became abbot. But he may have received that appointment as early as in 1128. It is further believed that before his

28. Cf. *Libellus de laudibus beatae Mariae virginis,* P.L., CLXXXIX, 1725-1741, with *Sermones in laudibus virginis matris,* SBO IV, 14-58.

29. Above, 78, with note 34.

30. Oury, "Recherches," 119, note 3.

31. Ep. 2, *Letters* I, 5-6. In his annotations with this letter (II, 96ff.) Constable supposed that these remarks of Peter the Venerable to Matthew did not concern Arnold, but rather his predecessor, Abbot Bernier.

32. He made this request in the prologue of his *Liber de cardinalibus operibus Christi,* which he dedicated to the pope; P.L., CLXXXIX, 1610. Oury, "Recherches," 115 and 126, note 87.

entry into the monastery he studied at the cathedral school of Chartres. From the nature of his writings, it would appear that he did some studies, but concrete indications that he studied in Chartres are lacking.

A. Did Bernard Write to Arnold from His Deathbed?

It has generally been supposed that the reason for the choice of Arnold as the author of the second book of the *vita* was the letter, already referred to several times, that Bernard allegedly sent him shortly before he died.[33] This letter has always received considerable attention since it deals rather extensively with Bernard's physical and spiritual condition in those final moments, clearly giving it historical and cultic importance. Geoffrey of Auxerre later incorporated this letter in his report to Eskil and subsequently in the fifth book of the *vita*. In the report to Eskil, the letter carried this opening statement:

> *The letter to Arnold of Bonneval,* which in response to a gift sent [to Bernardus] informed him — via a courier — about his [Bernard's] health.

The text of the letter, as recorded in the report to Eskil, reads as follows:

> In love, but not with joy, I received the proof of your affection. What joy could there be, when bitterness claims everything. Only total fasting makes the situation somewhat bearable. Sleep has left me, so that pain fails to recede, even for a single moment, for the bliss of even a light slumber. My stomach illness is the cause of all my misery. Often, by day or by night, I need to get a little strength by taking something fluid, for my stomach resolutely refuses anything solid. And the little it allows to enter, it only accepts with great aversion, only because a state of complete emptiness would be even more fearsome. But it is far worse when it seems to have absorbed too much. My arms and legs are swollen as if I were a dropsical. Not wanting to hide from you, in your care for me, anything about the condition of your friend, I report (but I speak as an unwise person) that in spite of all this, my spirit, judged according to the inner man, is still strong in this weakened flesh. Pray the Redeemer, who does not want the death of the sinner, that He may not delay my timely departure, but guard it. Make sure to support with your prayers my journey that is without

33. *Ep.* 310; SBO VIII, 230.

any merits, so that the adversary may not find a place to put his teeth in and wound me.

I have written this by my own hand, in order that you may learn about my love for you through the handwriting that is known to you.[34]

This letter is found in a number of manuscripts containing the third version of the register of Bernard's letters, which had been produced in Clairvaux *(textus perfectus)*. In most of these manuscripts to this letter, a final remark is appended that has been included neither in the report to Eskil nor in the fifth book of the *vita prima*.[35] This final remark appears to have been added later. For it can be interpreted as a slight reproach to Arnold, and as such it seems to be contrary to the content of the letter:

> But I would have preferred to respond to a letter from you, rather than to write first myself.

In some manuscripts that contain Bernard's letter in accordance with that third register, however, this final sentence is missing, as it is in the *vita*. A few of these manuscripts date from the thirteenth century.[36] But one dates from as early as 1163-1166. This manuscript, which we have already mentioned several times, was at that time copied in the scriptorium of Anchin from manuscripts originating in Clairvaux. Since this codex comprises all of Bernard's writings, including his letters, and since it also contains the *vita prima*, this letter occurs in two places in this manuscript. In neither of these two locations, however, was this final remark appended to the letter. This is very remarkable since the scriptorium of Anchin obtained both manuscripts from Clairvaux, and it suggests that in Clairvaux also this final sentence was added only later to the third register.

But there may be some other aspects to the manuscript transmission of this letter. In this register the epistle has been added at the end, after the letters 407, 408, and 409. This is also the case in the letter register from the Ter Duinen monastery, though there the final sentence does occur (but this manuscript must be of later date than that from Anchin, since we find notations from copyists in the text of several letters in the Ter Duinen version). In other manuscripts of the *textus*

---

34. "Un brouillon" (1959), 39, lines 308-326. Vp, V, c. II, 10; P.L., CLXXXV, 356-357.
35. Leclercq, "Lettres de S. Bernard," *Recueil* IV (1987), 166-168.
36. Mss Arras 70, Dijon 191, Douai 374, and Pontarlier XIII. Cf. "Der Brief" (1988), 216-217.

perfectus, this letter, which Bernard allegedly wrote on his deathbed, is not in final position. For that reason these need at present not be considered.[37]

The fact that the text of this letter occurs in the Anchin manuscript is a problem in its own right. Since both texts of this letter in the manuscript of Anchin correspond verbatim, it is possible that the text, which is found at the end of the letter register, was copied to the text of the *vita prima* when Clairvaux made this available for copying. This, in turn, would mean that around 1163-1165 the letter register at Clairvaux — which had also been made available for copying — did not yet contain this letter to Arnold. This impression is further strengthened by the fact that this letter is also missing in some other manuscripts in which this register *(textus perfectus)* was copied. And this would be another indication that at some later date the letter must have been copied from the *vita prima* to the letter register.[38]

As indicated above, some of the manuscripts of the letter register that do contain this epistle do not have the final sentence. It may be that some later copyist wondered why Arnold, with whom Bernard according to this letter maintained a regular correspondence, had sent him a gift and no letter. Considering this letter as it appears in its original form in the *vita prima* incomplete, he possibly added this final statement. A second objection against the authenticity of this letter is related to this first observation. It has to do with the total absence, or the complete loss, of all other correspondence between Bernard and Arnold. Moreover, the *vita* does not even hint at other letters. Yet this letter implies that Arnold was supposed to be able to recognize Bernard's handwriting. If this was indeed true, there was no reason for Bernard to emphasize that he had written this letter with his own hand. Such information would have been totally unnecessary.

The statement that stresses this aspect calls for yet another, even more serious objection. Bernard was not in the habit of writing his letters himself, but usually dictated them or even had them dictated by others. In two other letters that he wrote during his last illness, he mentioned

---

37. Brughes, seminary library, mss 22-34. SBO VII, "Introduction," xiii. Mss BNL 2564 and 17462; Vatican, lat. 622.

38. Initially Leclercq agreed with this analysis. *Recueil* IV, 127: "Internal criticism of the text offers sufficient reasons that warrant questioning its authenticity: what person at the point of death is capable of this kind of writing, even to one he knows well? Everything suggests that this small literary work was intended to guarantee the authenticity of what the second biographer had written. External criticism, on the other hand, strengthens these doubts; the text occurs only in some of the manuscripts of the letter register; it has primarily been transmitted by the witnesses of the *Vita Prima*. And from there it seems to have found its way into some letter registers." For his later opinion, see below, note 40.

specifically that he had dictated them himself; in one of those cases he did so, he said, because no one was at hand to do this for him.[39] But apart from his habit of not writing his own letters, writing on parchment would, even under normal circumstances, require ample preparations. It therefore seems highly improbable that Bernard would still have been able to do so when he was so weak that he could no longer leave his bed, as we may conclude from the letter to Arnold.

But the decisive external argument against the authenticity of the letter is the fact that the final sentence is not found in the oldest manuscripts of the letter register, which had been composed or completed shortly after Bernard's death. This letter was apparently copied from the *vita* at some later date. Thus there are strong indications that Bernard neither wrote nor dictated this letter.

Geoffrey thus seems to have been guilty of "falsification," but, as we stated above, what he did was not so strange at that time. The opportunity was more or less an extension of his work — the secretaries sent many letters on Bernard's behalf, of which he knew very little or nothing at all. But since this letter provided a good, and even a penetrating account of Bernard's condition shortly before his death, we may in this case speak of an "authentic falsification." At the same time, Geoffrey tacitly solved another problem: Arnold is introduced to the reader as an intimate friend of Bernard, so that a further explanation of why this Benedictine abbot was one of the authors of the *vita* was not required. Here he used an approach that he may, to some extent, have copied from Bernard as letter writer. For some of Bernard's letters carried another meaning than they appeared to have at first sight.

These objections against the authenticity of the letter Bernard allegedly wrote on his deathbed were first raised some thirty years ago, but even today they are not accepted by all scholars. Some argue that it is unthinkable that this "beautiful" letter was not written by Bernard himself,[40] an argument that seems more cultic than historical. Twice there has even been an explicit

---

39. "Der Brief" (1988), 218-219, with notes 48 and 49, *Epp.* 304 and 307, c. 2; SBO VIII, 221-226.

40. Relatively recently this textual criticism has been rejected by Gastaldelli, *Opere* VI/2 (Lettere), Milan, 1987, 310-311, note 1. He states, "Una lettera scritta nel più pure stile di san Bernardo, che nemmeno vicino alla morte dimentica di scherzare con le paranomasie, i suoi giochi retorici preferiti" (p. 312). A similar emotional argument is advanced by Leclercq (1989), 90: "This document is so surprising that only one voice has been raised which maintains with insistence that it cannot be authentic. But other scholars, with good reason, maintain that it is."

response to the charge of inauthenticity.[41] In the first reply, the main argument is that this letter refers back to the Bible with such subtlety that no one but Bernard could have written it. But this substantial response fails to take into account that Geoffrey of Auxerre was also very familiar with the Bible and with the way in which Bernard in his writings used to refer to the Scriptures. Probably the letter even shows some excess in the use of Scripture. But the arguments of this response are particularly unconvincing because of the fact that they ignore the main objection: the haphazardness of the textual tradition and the absence of the letter in a number of manuscripts in which the letter register of Bernard in its most complete form has been preserved.

The second reaction extensively criticizes my opinion that we have no concrete evidence for the close friendship that according to this letter existed between Bernard and Arnold. This reply, however, ignores my argument that no further correspondence between the two abbots has been preserved, and that none of Bernard's writings were dedicated to Arnold, or vice versa. But the critic thinks he can prove that Arnold, because of his important connections with the Cistercian Order and through a common network of alliances, must also have had close contacts with Bernard himself.

To substantiate Arnold's ties with the Cistercians, the author points to a document that dates from 1129 concerning a business agreement with the abbey of Preuilly, which was founded from Cîteaux and was one the priories belonging to Bonneval. The agreement of which Arnold possibly approved was reconfirmed by the next abbot of Preuilly in 1158. He finds important support in the fact that, in 1158, one of Arnold's writings was found in Preuilly. These points, he feels, lead to the conclusion that there must have been a lasting friendship between Preuilly and Bonneval, in which Bernard himself must have been directly involved. His argument for this direct involvement is that in 1113 Artald, the first abbot of Preuilly, was a novice simultaneous with Bernard, and thus must have been a friend of his ever since. There is, however, reason to doubt this argument, considering the way in which Bernard impeded Abbot Artald in 1127, when the latter wanted to found a daughter-monastery in Spain, with the intent of reserving the establishment of the Cistercian Order in that country for Clairvaux. It seems

41. D. Farkasfalvy, "The Authenticity of Saint Bernard's Letter," AnCi 34 (1978), 263-268. R. U. Smith, "Arnold of Bonneval, Bernard of Clairvaux and Bernard's Epistle 310," AnCi 49 (1993), 273-318. Meanwhile Pietro Lerbi announced that he also wrote an article in defense of the authenticity of this letter, which will be published in the second volume of the *Miscellanea Prosdocimi*.

to me that this whole argument holds little water, since it fails to recognize the solid arguments that have in recent years been advanced against the traditional, and by the author still uncritically accepted, view regarding a *unanimité cistercienne* that supposedly existed at the time.[42]

With regard to the other argument about the close friendship that also supposedly began between Arnold and Bernard — that is, as the result of a broader friendship network that, the author believes, must have existed — it is important to discuss in more detail the difficulties Arnold experienced in the thirties with the majority of the monastic community of Bonneval. We do not give direct information regarding those difficulties. The author presupposes that this conflict between abbot and monks had its origin either in Arnold's support for Pope Innocent II (a choice that may be explained from his participation at the Council of Etampes in 1130), or from the difficult circumstances in which Bonneval found itself because of the lengthy struggle that erupted at that time between Louis IV of France and Theobald IV, the duke of Blois. The possessions of Bonneval must have suffered extensively as a result of these hostilities.[43]

This last supposition seems most probable, in view of the time when Arnold considered abdicating (1134 or 1135). Any controversy in Bonneval about this schism would have been dealt with from Cluny because of the close relationships that existed between Arnold and that monastery. But if the conflict was caused by material problems confronting Bonneval, we would be able to define more precisely the nature of the controversy between Arnold and his monks. For such a crisis inevitably had consequences regarding the observance of the Benedictine Rule — a matter which at an earlier date, in 1122, had led to intense disagreement within the Cistercian Order. In that year a similar divergence of opinion in Cluny, also related to an economic crisis, led to an irreconcilable friction between Pons of Melgueil, who at that time was the abbot of Cluny, and his conservative opponents.[44]

In Bonneval, contrary to what transpired in Cluny, Abbot Bernier and his successor Arnold had no plans to adapt the Cluniac lifestyle to the changed economic situation and social circumstances. This conclusion seems justified from the letter Peter the Venerable sent to Matthew of Albano in

---

42. See below, 258-259. The manuscripts of Arnold's writings, which in the twelfth century found their way into the libraries of Clairvaux, and from there into those of monasteries founded by Clairvaux, constitute an additional argument for his involvement with the Cistercian Order. But on the other hand, it must be noted that there is no proof whatsoever that these manuscripts were made or acquired in Clairvaux before the *prima vita* became well known.

43. Smith, "Arnold of Bonneval . . . ," 280-284.

44. Le rôle de l'agriculture dans la crise de Cluny en 1122" (1994).

reaction to the conflict between Arnold and his community. The latter, as was mentioned earlier, vehemently and successfully opposed the reform party in Cluny that was favored by an economic crisis, and also became the most significant opponent of Abbot Pons, who had supported this movement. Moreover, in 1132 Matthew had done everything in his power to prevent similar reforms, which the Benedictine abbots in the Reims diocese had wanted to introduce in their monasteries, from having any chance of success.[45]

We owe our information about the nature of this conflict between Arnold and his community precisely to the fact that because of this conflict, Arnold had contacted Matthew of Albano and, subsequently, also Peter the Venerable, to whom he had indicated his wish to retire to Cluny with a number of his loyal supporters. For that reason, this conflict provides an insight into Arnold's point of view concerning another aspect of the earlier internal controversy in Cluny — Bernard's role when he intervened as an outsider, which was greatly lamented by the conservative Cluniacs, who had triumphed in this conflict.

Therefore, one can hardly expect that during the conflict that erupted ten years later between him and his community, and that was comparable to the earlier internal problems in Cluny, Arnold would have been able to appreciate Bernard's unsolicited intervention in Cluny in the same measure as he subsequently did when Geoffrey of Auxerre asked him to write the second book of the *vita prima*. This discussion further suggests that during these thirty years, Abbot Arnold did not yet belong to the network of those with whom Bernard remained in regular contact. And it is impossible to deduce from Bernard's letters that he did, within the context of this network of friends, correspond with abbots who belonged to the Cluny milieu. Apart from his occasional letters to Suger of Saint-Denis and Peter the Venerable, he wrote to Cluniac abbots only when one of their monks intended to transfer to Clairvaux or one of its daughter-institutions or had already done so.

Precisely this personal stand of Arnold as the abbot of Bonneval in the controversy concerning the Benedictine Rule must have prevented a closer contact with Bernard. And Bernard himself had also become controversial as a result of the events of 1125/26.[46] As a result, Bernard subse-

---

45. Below, 230f.

46. It is clear from *Epp.* 17 and 18 — written by Bernard in 1126 to Cardinal-deacon Peter (SBO VII, 65-69), whom Pope Honorius II had dispatched to France to find out

quently avoided contact with the supporters of these different viewpoints in Benedictine circles — at least in France — and refrained from further involvement in the reform movement in that order. This does not exclude the possibility that Bernard and Arnold met at some occasion, or that Arnold had visited Clairvaux at some point in time. However, after his failed intervention in the Cluniac controversy, Bernard always carefully avoided once again becoming the subject of criticism with regard to this conflict.

Bernard had no other choice, in particular after Peter the Venerable had written a letter in 1127 or 1128 with a detailed report of the issues that caused problems in Cluny. This letter was addressed to all priors of Cluniac monasteries, but Peter the Venerable wrote it in such a way that this lengthy account would be perceived by outsiders as a direct response to Bernard's *Apology,* even though the letter also dealt with a number of items that the abbot of Clairvaux had not touched upon. Nonetheless, since the letter was addressed to Bernard, the impression was created that there had not been any internal controversy in Cluny over the practice of the Benedictine Rule; Bernard had simply written an aggressive tale about differences of opinion between Cistercians and Cluniacs.[47] This explains why Bernard subsequently was unwilling or unable to express himself about this conflict in Benedictine circles.

In addition, there was another problem: the papal schism of 1130, in which Bernard, when it finally came about, was to play an important role in defense of Innocent II. Faced with the increasing threat of this schism, two French cardinals (Cardinal-chancellor Haimeric and Matthew of Albano), who both had played a leading role in the condemnation of Pons of Melgueil, had, from 1128 onward, attempted to improve their relationship with Bernard. The latter was not totally unresponsive, probably in part because this helped to put an end to the discredit he had experienced as the result of his involvement in the internal conflict at Cluny.

But the condition was that Bernard would not meddle any further in this controversy. Haimeric would have preferred that Bernard would have been willing to refrain fully from *all* protests against abuses outside his own order, but a letter from Bernard to the cardinal, written around 1130, shows that he was not prepared to comply with such a request.[48] Nevertheless, from then on Bernard was willing to

---

what had happened in Cluny — that he had wanted to question him about his role in this matter, but that Bernard had succeeded in avoiding such questioning. *Cluny et Cîteaux,* 72, notes 147 and 313.

47. *Ep.* 28; *Letters* I, 52-101. *Cluny et Cîteaux,* 88, note 27.

48. *Ep.* 48; SBO VII, 137-140. Concerning this letter, see also Williams (1935), 196.

stay out of controversies about the Rule elsewhere in France. For that reason, in later years Peter the Venerable never found in him a willing ear for his repeated pleas for Cistercian support in getting his attempts at reform in Cluny off the ground.[49]

In view of Bernard's hesitance with regard to reform-minded Benedictines, we may safely conclude that, in spite of Arnold's admiration for him, Bernard felt little inclined to maintain a close relationship with him. On the other hand, this did not mean that Geoffrey of Auxerre, when looking for an author for the next part of the *vita prima* after the death of William of Saint-Thierry, could not get in touch with Arnold of Bonneval. Bernard, of course, was not involved in that choice; even if he knew about these plans — and that is not totally impossible — he must at least have pretended ignorance in this matter.

B. Arnold's Contribution to the *Vita Prima*

Geoffrey's choice for Arnold was determined not only by the abbot's later appreciation and worshipful admiration of Bernard, or by his notoriety as monastic author. Arnold was also able to provide additional information, especially with regard to the period of Bernard's life that he described in this *vita:* 1130-1145. This applies, in particular, to his involvement with the papal schism of 1130-1138. This schism receives ample attention in the second book, at least indirectly. Arnold derived much of his information about this schism from the bishop of Chartres, Geoffroy de Lèves, who was himself a major player in the dispute with anti-pope Anacletus and the ending of the schism. But even before this, the bishop and Bernard had known each other.

In 1129 Bernard wrote a letter to Pope Honorius II on behalf of Bishop Geoffroy; while his letter of around 1130 to Cardinal Haimeric seems also to have been written on behalf of Geoffroy.[50] After that, relations between them were very close, since Pope Innocent II, whom Bernard supported in 1130 on behalf of the whole French church, honored Geoffroy by making him a papal legate. In this position he replaced Gerard, the bishop of Angoulême, who had chosen the side of Anacletus II.

---

49. *Cluny et Cîteaux*, 240-244. Cf. "Saint Bernard in his Relations" (1993). See also below, 229-230.

50. *Ep.* 47; SBO VII, 136. For the letter (*Ep.* 48), which he wrote to Haimeric in 1130, supposedly also on behalf of Geoffroy, see above, note 48.

Geoffroy and Bernard must have cooperated closely in the struggle against Bishop Gerard and his ally, Duke William X of Aquitaine. In 1134 Duke William came to Aquitaine to deal with the supporters of Anacletus II and his legate Gerard, referred to above; while Bishop Geoffrey accompanied Bernard in 1135 on his journey to Pisa and Milan, where he worked on behalf of Innocent II. Although in both instances Arnold was not an eyewitness of Bernard's actions, the second book of the *vita* reports these extensively.[51] As indicated, Arnold received most of his information about these events and other activities of Bernard from Bishop Geoffroy. Gradually his ties with the bishop became closer; after 1140 he even accompanied him on some of his journeys.

Geoffrey of Auxerre, who accompanied Bernard on several journeys as his secretary, most likely met Bishop Geoffroy on more than one occasion, the more so since in 1140 the latter was involved in the conflict of William of Saint-Thierry and Bernard against Abelard.[52] It would therefore seem natural that when, after William's death (1147/48), he was looking for an author to continue the *vita,* Geoffrey consulted Bishop Geoffroy. The bishop may well have suggested the abbot of Bonneval and subsequently have brought the two together. Since Bishop Geoffroy died in 1149, this contact with Arnold cannot have been made later than 1148.

Probably shortly after this, Arnold accepted the assignment. In the final passage of the prologue to the second book of the *vita prima,* Arnold explicitly presents himself as the one who was to continue the work of William of Saint-Thierry:

> And now that lord William — blessed be his memory — who so faithfully and with full dedication has given an account of the illustrious early years of this holy man, has been taken away from us, I (in my lowly state) have been requested to continue this work; and love for the church has assigned me the task to prepare this meal for the sons of the prophets. If, through carelessness, I should mix some indigestible things (*lit.* wild gourds) with it, then, I trust, Elisha will scatter some flour on it, and my readiness to obey will serve as an excuse for my excessive folly.[53]

51. Vp II, VI, 32-34 and II, 9; P.L., CLXXXV, 286-287 and 273-274.

52. William of Saint-Thierry addressed a letter to both Bishop Geoffroy and Bernard to inform them about the teachings of Abelard. *Recueil* IV, 361-363.

53. P.L., CLXXXV, 268. For the "wild gourds" of Elisha, see 2 Kings 4:38-42 (Vulgate: 4 Kings 4:38-41).

Looking at this prologue in its entirety, we find that Arnold continuously apologized for his insufficient qualities to complete this work successfully. At the time, prologues were already often used by authors to make all sorts of apologies. The inclusion of such a *captatio benevolentiae*, or statement of humility,[54] was regarded as an acceptable literary convention. But the excessive apologies in this prologue do not necessarily preclude some sincerity. Could it possibly be that Arnold alluded through this emphasis on his own unworthiness to the fact that he felt poorly qualified for the assignment, since he knew Bernard only indirectly?

This suggestion seems to find support in the absence, in this prologue, of the usual assurance that the author is reporting events he himself has seen and experienced. Nonetheless, Arnold must earlier have heard about some of Bernard's activities: about the role Bernard was assigned in Etampes in 1130 to support — on behalf of the church and the king of France — Innocent II; about his subsequent actions in Aquitaine against the party of Anacletus; and about his efforts to mediate in the conflict between King Louis VII and Count Thibaut of Champagne. It could be that Arnold was more directly involved with this latter problem since he had accompanied Geoffroy de Lèves on his journey to Rome. Geoffroy made that trip to seek papal approval for the solution of the conflict that Bernard had been able to arrange.[55]

For the rest, in writing this second book, Arnold was fully dependent on the oral or written accounts of others for his information. We may safely assume that he used the report of Rainald of Foigny about Bernard's journey to Milan in 1136, which has already been referred to several times. He also utilized the remarks in the *Fragmenta Gaufridi* about Bernard's role in the last phase of the papal schism.[56] This is, for instance, the source for the details of his account of the conversation during which Bernard succeeded in convincing Peter, the cardinal-archbishop of Pisa, who was one of the foremost adherents of Anacletus, belatedly to choose the side of Innocent II.

54. Van 't Spijker (1990), 62-63, with note 2.

55. Oury, "Recherches," 106-107, with notes 61 and 62. Bernard is probably not to be credited for the fact that Louis VI at that time opted for the side of Innocent II. Their relationship made this improbable. Grabois, "Le schisme de 1130," 593-612. Gastaldelli, *Opere* VI/1, 569-570, note.

56. *Exordium magnum*, II, c. 16, ed. Griesser, 110. *"Fragmenta,"* c. 12-13, ed. Lechat, 96 (corresponds with VP II, c. II, 11); c. 35 (Lechat 107) is worked out in more detail in Vp II, c. 29-30; c. 43-44 (Lechat, 111-114) in Vp II, c. 43 and 45-47.

In this account Arnold deemed it unnecessary to mention that the see of Pisa, vacant as a result of Peter's abdication, which had been demanded by Innocent, had subsequently been given to Baldwin, a former monk from Clairvaux. This Baldwin had been made a cardinal as early as 1130, when it was in Innocent's interest to please Bernard. This aspect of Bernard's involvement in the matter was also not mentioned in the *Fragmenta Gaufridi*. A further reference to this first Cistercian cardinal may have seemed of little importance when Arnold was writing, since Baldwin had already died in 1145.

The facts that Arnold furnishes the reader about the further history of the schism suggest that he collected a fair amount of information about this. He must have received most of this, in any case, after the death of Bishop Geoffroy de Lèves, from Arnulf of Séez, Geoffroy's archdeacon. Around 1133/34 this Arnulf had already sent a highly biased pamphlet about the origin of this schism to Bishop Geoffroy.[57] In 1135 Arnulf participated in the Council of Pisa, and in 1141 he was, partly on Bernard's suggestion, elected bishop of Lisieux.[58] From his letters that have been preserved, we learn that Arnold later was in close contact with this bishop.[59] We may assume that his totally negative opinion of Pope Anacletus also, to a large extent, depended on information from that source.

Arnold must have received his information about what happened in Clairvaux while Bernard was absent in Italy, from some source in Clairvaux itself, although he also consulted Bernard's *Apology*. Possibly Geoffrey himself was the spokesman he relied upon. That Geoffrey also provided him with the guidelines for his contribution to this *vita* is evident, for instance, from the nature of the miracle stories incorporated in the second book. Apparently it was agreed that Arnold would emphasize those miracles of Bernard that concerned the exorcism of evil spirits, while Geoffrey would in the later books mainly deal with Bernard's miraculous healings.

In his contribution, Arnold also conformed to the manner in which Bernard had been portrayed in the first book. Likewise, he defended Bernard's rejection of some episcopal appointments;[60] and he refrained from listing in detail Bernard's church-political activities on behalf of Innocent II during Anacletus's schism. Although Arnold mentions Bernard's efforts in

---

57. This pamphlet was a barrage of abuse against Gerard, the bishop of Angoulême, who as papal legate had chosen the side of Anacletus. M.G.H., *Libelli de lite* 3, Hannover 1897, 81-108.

58. *Ep.* 348; SBO VIII, 291.

59. *Epp.* 15 and 48; P.L., CCI, 29 and 76. Barlow, ed., *The Letters of Arnulf of Lisieux*, 1939.

60. Vp II, c. IV, 26; P.L.., CLXXXV, 283.

that matter, he clothes many of his actual dealings in a narrative of miraculous deeds; for his task was to highlight Bernard's sainthood in all that he did in church and society. In his flattering characterization of Bernard's sainthood, he at times allowed himself to express, along with some truisms, his own thoughts, though with appropriate trepidation:

> These and many other things the man of God did when he was staying south of the Alps; he showed benevolence to the sick in many of the places through which he passed. He gave back the light to the blind, he helped the weak to rise, and healed those who suffered from fever, but, above all, he endeavored to cleanse those who were devil-possessed, and the souls which had been defiled by the evil spirit he dedicated as temples, pleasing to God.
>
> Many virtuous and praiseworthy characteristics were united in his person. Some admire his knowledge, others his behavior, and others again his miracles. I myself give him the honor that is due because of all of these characteristics. But as far as I can judge, this I consider the highest and this I proclaim as the most important thing: he never overstepped any boundaries and never dwelled on the miraculous events which transcended him, even though he was a vessel of pre-destination and unashamedly proclaimed the name of Christ to the people and the princes; even though the princes of this world obeyed him and the bishops of every country followed his suggestions; even though the Roman Church itself respected his counsels and acknowl-edged his privileged position and subjected, so the speak, nations and empires to him by granting him a general mandate; and even though his deeds and words — and this exceeds everything else in glory — were confirmed by miracles. But he always manifested humility and considered himself the serving executor rather than the designer of laudable works. And though in the opinion of all he was the highest, he considered himself the lowest. . . .[61]

When Arnold sent this second book to Geoffrey in 1149/50, he probably had already agreed to Geoffrey's revision of his text. We get that impression from the statement at the end of his prologue, alluded to above, about the flour the prophet Elisha was allowed to sprinkle over what, through his carelessness, had become indigestible, in order to make the meal he had prepared for the sons of the prophets edible. This allegorical reference to

---

61. Vp II, c. IV, 24 (end) and 25; P.L., CLXXXV, 282.

2 Kings 4:38-41 seems a request to Geoffrey to revise, where needed, his rather panegyrical text.

It is clear from the last chapter of the book written by Arnold that this indeed happened. With the exception of the conflict between Louis VII and Thibaud, the count of Champagne, the matters covered in that chapter fall completely outside the time frame (1130-1145) to which this second book of the *vita* limited itself. Arnold must have received the information about these events from Geoffrey. And it remains an open question whether Geoffrey might have been directly involved with the redaction of this chapter, either at the time when Arnold was still working on the second book, or later, when Geoffrey completed his own books. Since this last chapter of the second book in particular contains additional information that goes beyond the years assigned to Arnold, it is evident that Geoffrey of Auxerre at least exercised some editorial supervision over Arnold's contribution to the *vita prima*.

Nonetheless, the second book of this *vita* retained its special character. In it the person of Bernard is depicted with greater detachment, and this accords with Arnold's style. It enabled him to allow Bernard and other persons from time to time to tell their own story. This literary style was quite common at the time, and clearly improved the readability of the book. It helped Arnold to emphasize the prestige Bernard had acquired through his activities in church and society during the years 1130-1145, and how he developed into one of the most prominent figures of medieval Christendom.

But the historical information provided by this second book is disappointing. Bernard's significance for the Cistercian Order is not dealt with. Arnold fails to mention Bernard's efforts during all his journey to widen the network of his order. All he says on this topic is that for years a new building was under construction in Clairvaux, and that after the schism of Anacletus, Innocent II donated the Benedictine monastery Tre Fontane near Rome to the Cistercians. And in the last chapter he provides an incomplete, and subsequently by Geoffrey revised, list of the bishoprics that the pope had entrusted to Cistercian monks.[62]

Neither did Arnold deal at any length with the criticism Bernard evoked through his actions. To some extent this may have been unneces-

---

62. Vp II, c. V, 29-31, c. VII, 48, and c. VIII, 49; P.L., CLXXXV, 284-285 and 296-297. About the time when Arnold wrote and Geoffrey made later revisions, see above, 38, with note 38.

sary, since this criticism had been answered in the first book of the *vita*. Moreover, the criticism — at least in France — did not concern his dealings with the supporters of Anacletus. It is commonly assumed that Anacletus had little support in France, but considering the way in which Hildebert de Lavardin, the archbishop of Tours (1133) — in spite of Bernard's urgent plea — refused to take sides, it cannot be excluded that most of Anacletus's French sympathizers found it prudent to keep silent about their opinion regarding the schism.[63]

Whatever the case may be, like William of Saint-Thierry, Arnold avoided providing precise details about most of the facts that he mentioned and completely ignored the political aspects of Bernard's activities. Therefore, this second book of the *vita prima* can only be considered as of very limited importance for an understanding of Bernard as an historical person. For even when reading between the lines, this book provides but little information about the personality of the abbot.

3. WILLIAM OF SAINT-THIERRY

IN CHAPTER III we already dealt at length with the hagiographic contribution of William of Saint-Thierry to the *vita prima*. His part, the first book of this document, to a large extent defined its overall character. But more remains to be said about the person of William of Saint-Thierry, and about his relationship with Bernard. He began his career as a Benedictine monk, who around 1112 had entered the abbey of Saint-Nicaise near Reims. In 1119 he became the abbot of Saint-Thierry, also in the vicinity of Reims. From 1135 until his death in September 1147 or 1148, he belonged — at least officially — to the community of the Cistercian monastery of Signy, again situated close to Reims.

Many studies have already been devoted to the writings of William of Saint-Thierry. But the story of his life has usually received less attention. This is understandable, since his writings have had a major influence on medieval mystical theology, while we know but very little about the details of his life. Only a fragment of the *vita*, written after his death, has survived.[64]

---

63. Cf. below, 278, with note 165.

64. A good bibliography, covering the period 1900 until 1976, is found in *William, Abbot*, 261-273. Bell (1984), 260-273; and Piazzoni (1988), 205-215. For the *vita*, see A. Poncelet, ed., "Vie ancienne de Guillaume de Saint-Thierry" (1908), 85-96.

Nonetheless, we do have some information about his life. It is now generally believed that he was born in Liège, between 1075 and 1080. There he began his studies, which he later continued in Reims. He may have left Liège because of the fact that the local bishop had chosen the side of the emperor in the still ongoing investiture controversy. Some have suggested that William subsequently went from Reims to Laon, where he may have attended Anselm's lectures at the cathedral school. There he is believed to have met Abelard, who had already achieved notoriety through his criticism of Anselm's teachings. This, some scholars maintain, could explain William's later vehemence in his theological opposition against Abelard.[65] Concrete evidence is, however, lacking. But we do know that William, in spite of his studies — which, among other things, covered the *artes liberales* — did not opt for an academic career. In retrospect, he considered his study period an escape from the paradise where God had placed him since his youth.[66]

A. His First Contacts with Bernard

William's return to this monastic paradise took the form of his entry into the monastery of Saint-Nicaise, which — like Saint-Thierry — had some connection with Cluny. But there life was more strict, or at least more ascetic, than in that large abbey. At the end of the eleventh century both Saint-Nicaise and Saint-Thierry were directly influenced by the abbey of La Chaise-Dieu in Auvergne, the base from which several monasteries were reformed.[67] This stricter life apparently appealed to William. This is evident from his move to the Cistercian monastery of Signy, but also, prior to this (around 1130-1132), from his attempts to introduce a more ascetic lifestyle in the Benedictine monasteries of the ecclesiastical province of Reims. His new orientation toward the much younger Cistercian Order, instead of la Chaise Dieu, may be explained by the many contacts he had, in the meantime, developed with Bernard. These contacts began around 1119, about four years after Bernard had become abbot of Clairvaux.

These contacts evolved into a friendship, and it seems that as early as 1124 William wanted to transfer to the Cistercian Order. Bernard is said

---

65. Cf. Piazzoni (1988), 16.
66. *Meditativae orationes,* ed. Davy (1934), 202-207.
67. Gaussin, *L'abbaye de la Chaise-Dieu* (1962).

to have opposed this move, so that, for the time being, William stayed on as the abbot of Saint-Thierry. But in 1135, after his attempts to reform the lifestyle in the Benedictine monasteries of Reims had failed, he resigned from his post and withdrew to Signy. Although by that time he must have been around sixty, William's interest in meditative theology and his desire to write about this had not in the least abated. Most of his writings date from this later period, such as his treatises "The Mirror of Faith" and "The Riddle of Faith," his "Exposition against the Errors of Abelard," his treatments of "The Errors of Abelard" and "The Errors of William of Conches," and his "Golden Letter to the Carthusians of the Mountain of God." As earlier indicated, this letter was for a long time attributed to Bernard, and became well known as a result.[68]

In the capstone of his entire oeuvre — the first book of the *vita prima* — William explains in detail how the friendship between himself and Bernard developed. But we find only some indirect indication about the time when this friendship started. He does describe the peculiar environment in which Bernard found himself at that particular moment, but fails to mention the exact place or time. Various dates for the event have been suggested. William described the beginning of their friendship with these words:

> It was about that time that I myself began to be a frequent visitor to him and his monastery, and when I first went to see him with a certain other abbot, I found him in that little hut of his, which was just like the kind of shack built for lepers at cross-roads. I found him completely free from all the spiritual and temporal problems involved in the ruling of any monastery, and this, as I have already told you, was exactly what the bishop had commanded. As a result Bernard was able to open the innermost depths of his soul to the actions of God's loving grace, and to enjoy in his silence and solitude delights such as are the reward of the blessed in heaven.
>
> Going into the hovel which had become a palace by his presence in it, and thinking what a wonderful person dwelt in such a despicable place, I was filled with such awe of the hut itself as if I were approaching the very altar of God. And the sweetness of his character so attracted me to him and filled me with desire to share his life amid such poverty and simplicity that if the chance had then been given to me, I should

68. A. Wimart, "La série et la date des ouvrages de Guillaume de Saint-Thierry" (1924), 157-167. See above, 37, note 34.

have asked nothing more than to be allowed to remain with him always, looking after him and ministering to his needs.[69]

It is clear from this text that William was already abbot when this first encounter took place, for he writes about his visit to Bernard "together with another abbot." Since William was elected as abbot at the end of 1119, this statement implies that they first met after that date. An earlier date for this meeting is impossible, since it is unthinkable that these first contacts between them, as described by William of Saint-Thierry, could have occurred before William had become abbot. Differences in status, which were extremely important in medieval times, also weighed heavily in the ecclesiastical hierarchy; consequently, this close contact between Bernard and William could never have occurred if William had still been only a monk.

However, following Jean Mabillon (†1707), Vacandard has suggested that William had begun to visit Bernard at an earlier date: sometime during 1118 or 1119.[70] Later other scholars have suggested that these first meetings may have taken place as early as between the autumn of 1116 and 1117. In defense of this date, they suggest that William was abbot in another monastery before 1119, but this cannot be proven.[71] Still others think that this sentence refers to Bernard and another abbot, or that William, when he wrote these words, simply ignored the fact that he still was only a monk at the time.

The background for this alternative date was no doubt the opinion, generally accepted until 1963, that Bernard's open letter to his cousin Robert of Châtillon — after the latter had left Clairvaux for Cluny — had been written in 1119 or at the latest in 1120; while in reality he dictated it toward the end of 1124 or in the spring of 1125.[72] In this polemical letter Bernard presented a very negative opinion of monastic life at Cluny. As we have seen earlier, it has been thought that this judgment applied to the situation in this abbey under the abbatiate of

---

69. Vp I, c. VII, 33; P.L., CLXXXV, 246-247. Transl. Webb and Walker, 56.

70. *Vie de Saint Bernard,* 1895, vol. I, 76; later reprints, vol. I, 79. Van den Eynde, "Les premiers écrits," *Recueil* III, 357-359. His date of 1116-1117 for *Ep.* 441 (SBO VIII, 419), which Bernard sent from Clémentimpré to Gaucher, the prior of Clairvaux, also ignores the fact that William could not instruct Bernard before he himself had also become an abbot.

71. Milis, "William of Saint Thierry" (1987), 26.

72. *Ep.* I, SBO VII, 1-11. Cf. *Recueil* III, 395. The attempts of C. Holdsworth — "The Early Writings of Bernard of Clairvaux," *Cîteaux* 45 (1994), 21-60, to maintain the earlier dating have not been able to convince me. For he merely removes the consistent explanation, which could be reached through the dating that he rejects without good reasons, while he fails to provide another, solid explication.

Pons of Melgueil, who in 1122 had been forced to abdicate by Pope Calixtus; although it was also known that William, to whom Bernard had dedicated his *Apology*, had also been involved in his polemical initiatives in Cluny.[73]

The first book of the *vita prima* provides ample information about Bernard's situation when William of Saint-Thierry first visited him. It relates, for instance, how Bernard, when he established Clairvaux, encountered William of Champeaux. This William, a former teacher at the cathedral school in Paris and the founder (1108) of a school that was connected with the monastic community of the canons of St. Victor, had in 1113 been elected bishop of Châlons-sur-Marne. In 1115 it was his task to ordain Bernard as abbot of Clairvaux, since the bishop of Langres, who was responsible for the area where Clairvaux was situated, was unable to be present on that day. Soon an intimate relationship with frequent meetings developed between the bishop and Bernard.[74]

As a result of these contacts, the bishop began to worry greatly about Bernard's poor health, the more so since Bernard ignored the urgent advice to pay more attention to his physical well-being. When the physical condition of Bernard continued to deteriorate as a result of his rigorous lifestyle, William at last contacted the general chapter of the Cistercian Order and arranged that the young abbot be placed under his supervision for a year. Bernard spent all of that year outside Clairvaux, in Clémentinpré, a branch of the Saint-Bénigne abbey in Dijon.[75] He stayed there to recuperate, and for some time received dispensation from the strict rules of his own monastery with regard to eating and drinking.

What William has recorded about the exemptions allowed to Bernard because of his ill health may not be completely true. The food he received before must have been less poor than William suggests. But such a negative story fitted perfectly in this hagiographic account, since it showed how, as a young abbot, Bernard already pursued such virtues as patience, humility, and mortification. William failed to mention where Bernard stayed during this year. This silence must probably be explained by the fact that he was in Clémentinpré, which together with the Saint-Bénigne abbey, resorted under Cluny;[76] through the years William's relationship with Cluny was rather strained.

73. *Christendom* (1994), 140-143.
74. Vp 1, c. VII, 31; P.L., CLXXXV, 245.
75. Grill, *"Epistola de Charitate"* (1964), 45. See above, note 70.
76. Auberger (1986), 51.

The question of why, around 1120, William encountered Bernard cannot be answered by referring to the fame Bernard already enjoyed at that time.

In those years Bernard was still little known outside his immediate environment and his own order, even though since 1115 the influx of new monks in Clairvaux was such that in October 1118 a first daughter institution, the monastery of Trois-Fontaines, could be established. Most of these monks, however, had come from Châlons-sur-Marne, which is not strange, considering the involvement of Bishop William with the founding of that monastery. In view of his role in the actual preparations, we may assume that the bishop also played a role in the recruitment of new monks from his diocese.

Nor can the establishment of a second filiation — Fontenay, in 1119 — be taken as an indication that Bernard was already widely known at that time. The founding of this monastery was made possible by a number of his own relatives. Their involvement may in part be related to the fact that in those days many noble families considered monastic life as an alternative to be preferred to a place in the military, where they usually landed.[77] On the other hand, Bernard may also have been a source of attraction; this attraction, according to William in this *vita*, was so strong that mothers would hide their sons from him, and wives their husbands, while friends encouraged each other to stay away from him.[78]

The answer to the question of why William of Saint-Thierry came in contact with Bernard lies partly in determining in what year Bernard stayed at Clémentinpré. Apart from what we argued above — that William cannot have met Bernard before the end of 1119, after his consecration as abbot of Saint-Thierry — there can be no doubt that his stay at Clémentinpré cannot be dated between the founding of Trois-Fontaines and Fontenay respectively, that is, between October 1118 and October 1119. It is difficult to imagine that the founding of Fontenay was being prepared while Bernard was away from Clairvaux for an extended period and was not allowed to be involved with the affairs of his monastery.

For the same reason it must be excluded that Bernard stayed in Clémentinpré in the year prior to the founding of Trois-Fontaines, which officially took place in October 1118. He must have been personally involved in the preparations for the founding of the first daughter monastery. If we should insist on an earlier date for his year of absence, it must have

---

77. Murray (1978), 317-382. Duby, "Les 'jeunes' dans la société aristocratique," in Duby, *Hommes et structures* (1973), 213-225.
78. Vp I, c. III, 15; P.L., CLXXXV, 235. Dimier (1953).

been after the meeting of the general chapter of the Cistercian Order in September 1116, precisely in the period when many novices from Châlons-sur-Marne came to apply for entry in Clairvaux. But it is hardly imaginable that Bishop William would have encouraged them to apply in Clairvaux during Bernard's absence. This also leads us to conclude that the bishop's request to the general chapter to place Bernard in his care was not submitted until after the founding of Fontenay. And it cannot have been much later, since William of Champeaux died already in early 1121.

We know that during the meeting of the general chapter in September 1119 approval was given for a new version of the *carta caritatis et unanimitatis,* a written agreement between the Cistercian monasteries about their mutual relationships. This agreement — against which Bernard had some objections with regard to his own monastery — was ratified by Pope Calixtus II in September of the same year. Prior to this, the *carta* had been officially accepted by all of the twelve abbots that the order had at that time. Two of them could only indicate their agreement after the meeting of the general chapter had ended.[79] Bernard may have been one of the two, since at that time he was already too feeble to attend this chapter. The approval by the chapter of William's request to allow Bernard to stay outside his monastery for a year must also have been given during Bernard's absence. Bishop William could not have made this request and secured its approval if Bernard himself had been able to participate in the deliberations of the general chapter.

On the basis of this dating, we may conclude that William of Saint-Thierry was appointed as abbot shortly after Bernard, through the intervention of Bishop William, had been placed outside his monastic community. From the moment that William of Saint-Thierry had received this distinction, he could be in regular contact with the as yet little known, and temporarily inactive, abbot of Clairvaux. The main intermediary between the two must therefore have been Bishop William. For first he had seen to it that Bernard would stay at Clémentinpré for a full year. And it seems reasonable to assume that subsequently William of Champeaux made sure that Bernard would not be left in complete isolation, and that the bishop would have brought Bernard, as soon as he had somewhat recuperated, into contact with the newly elected abbot of Saint-Thierry, who already at that time enjoyed some fame as a mystical-theological writer.

79. J. Marilier (1961), 81-82. For the approval of this *carta* by ten of the twelve Cistercian abbots, see Auberger (1986), 33.

Bishop William's initiative in arranging this contact between the two abbots was no doubt related, on the one hand, to this reputation as a writer, but, on the other hand, also to the fact that Bernard had received only some preparatory education in the chapter school in Vorles. His later theological training, which initially he had hoped to take in Germany, had remained limited to a short period in Cîteaux. At this time, therefore, he did not have any real theological education. As a result, the religious receptivity of this highly talented young abbot could as yet not fully manifest itself. As a theologically trained man himself, Bishop William must have noticed this lack of training in Bernard; and he would naturally have looked for an opportunity to remedy this deficiency. This presented itself during this year of isolation that the bishop had arranged for Bernard, from the moment that the other William had been chosen as abbot of Saint-Thierry. For, as we said earlier, a person who was lower in the hierarchy could not serve as an authoritative teacher of someone higher in rank, even in a monastic setting.

To discover what William may have meant to Bernard as a teacher is much more difficult than to establish under what circumstances the abbot of Saint-Thierry first met Bernard. From a statement made by Bernard around 1125 in a letter to the Englishman Henry Murdach — about the joys of monastic life — we may conclude that as a rather young abbot, he showed but slight appreciation for knowledge gained through study and teaching. But possibly this remark by Bernard should rather be interpreted as an ironic figure of speech, since the addressee was addicted to his scholarship:

> Trust my experience: one learns more between the trees of the forest than in books. The trees and rocks will teach you a wisdom you will not hear from your teachers. Or do you expect to suck honey from a stone and oil from the hardest rock?[80]

This statement seems to correspond with the testimony of William of Saint-Thierry in the *vita* about his friend:

> Even to this day he will claim that it was by praying and meditating in the woods and fields that he discovered the deep meaning of Holy Writ. And he will jokingly say to his friends that it was only the oaks and beeches who were his masters in this subject.[81]

---

80. *Ep.* 106, c. 2; SBO VII, 266-267.
81. Vp. I, c. IV, 23; P.L., CLXXXV, 240. Transl. Webb and Walker, 42.

But to this William added his own comment:

> His aptitude in understanding Scripture is, however, evident to all who are privileged to hear him, or to read something of what he has written.[82]

This comment of William has remained virtually unknown, because Geoffrey of Auxerre eliminated it in his later revision of the text of the *vita prima*, and because it is not mentioned as a textual variant in any edition of this document. Geoffrey may have removed this statement because he was aware of Bernard's remark in his letter to Henry Murdach and considered the *topos* it included as important, without perceiving its ironic nature. William saw the statement that he quoted as a quip. As a matter of fact, it is also contrary to his further comments on Bernard's study of the Bible. He mentions how Bernard liked to read the canonical books of the Bible repeatedly and in their order, and how he best understood the meaning directly from the text itself. He believed that he had a better chance to taste its truth and divine virtue at the source than in the riverbed of the commentaries derived from it. But when reading the holy and orthodox exegetes, Bernard never considered his own insights as equivalent to theirs, but subjected himself to these in developing his own opinions.[83]

This remark points to the existence of a relationship between William and Bernard as between a teacher and a pupil. But Bernard, on his part, is also said to have been William's teacher when the latter stayed at Clairvaux during a period of illness. William reports that the two had discussions about the Song of Songs. According to Paul Verdeyen, this was the beginning of mysticism in the Latin-Christian world. William here suggests that at that time Bernard shared with him his insights and emotional experiences and instructed him about things that had hitherto been unknown to him, since this kind of knowledge could be acquired only through experience.[84] Undoubtedly this is an embellished account, presented by William in the context of his hagiographic assignment, which takes some liberty with respect to the real relationships between them.

The question remains whether Bernard acquainted his friend with the Latin translation of Origen's commentary on the Song of Songs, or

---

82. *Études* (1960), 31.

83. Vp I, c. IV, 24; P.L., CLXXXV, 241.

84. Vp I, c. XII, 59; P.L., CLXXXV, 259. So far Paul Verdeyen has made this suggestion only orally.

whether William brought this to Bernard's attention. For in the twelfth century this text was available in the library of Clairvaux as well as in the libraries of Saint-Thierry and of Signy, where William entered at a later date.[85] But although William may have recognized in Bernard a student of greater talent than he himself possessed, his account of the learning process they both experienced in their mutual friendship remains questionable. For when they first met — whether or not through the intervention of William of Champeaux — William of Saint-Thierry was the better educated and more experienced of the two with regard to mystical theology. This is evident, for instance, from the two treatises about the love to God written by him around 1120, which he undoubtedly discussed with Bernard during their meetings.[86]

B. The Continuing Relationship between William and Bernard

The friendship that thus developed between William and Bernard had consequences beyond this learning process. Bernard must have felt a special obligation toward William because of the assistance the latter had rendered him in his spiritual growth; for twice the abbot of Clairvaux, upon William's request, was willing to get involved in matters about which he had been insufficiently informed and which subsequently brought him serious criticisms. These matters, referred to earlier, concerned internal problems at Cluny in which Bernard got involved, around 1124, through two polemical writings; and later (around 1140), his vehement opposition to Abelard as a person and theologian. William and Bernard both regarded Abelard's ideas as substantial heresies, which were of direct importance to them since they saw the scholastic approach to theology as a threat to their monastic views and ideals.[87]

But the relationship between Bernard and William was not always characterized by close cooperation. After his intervention in Cluny had failed, Bernard (from about 1128) showed a more detached attitude toward those in the Benedictine Order who sought support for their interpretation of the Rule from the Cistercians. William of Saint-Thierry also experienced that detachment. Around 1130 Bernard declined a request from William

---

85. Deroy (1963), 11 and Bell (1984), 16-17.

86. *De contemplando Deo* and *De natura et dignitate amoris*, P.L., CLXXXIV, 365-408. For later editions and translations, see Bell (1984), 260.

87. Verger and Jolivet (1982).

to get directly involved in the attempts, initiated under William's leadership, to reform the lifestyle in the Benedictine monasteries in the ecclesiastical province of Reims in a more ascetic direction.[88] This refusal concerned an invitation for Bernard to participate in the provincial chapter of the abbots, held in Soissons either in 1130 or in 1132. He responded with a statement of strong sympathy, but also of regret that affairs elsewhere prevented him from being, at least physically, present. He wrote these abbots as follows:

> I cannot, I say, fail this assemply of holy men, nor can distance of place and absence of body sequester me from this council and congregation of the righteous, especially as it will not be a council at which the traditions of men are obstinately defended and blindly observed, but "where the good, pleasing, and perfect will of God is carefully and humbly sought" (Romans 12:2). Thither my whole heart carries me, there my devotion holds me, my love impels me; there do I cling with my approbation and remain by sharing in your zeal.

In this letter Bernard also wrote very negatively about those who wanted to thwart these plans for reform:

> Let them depart from me and from you who say, "We do not wish to be better than our fathers," proclaiming themselves sons of lax and tepid fathers whose memory is accursed because they have eaten bitter grapes and the teeth of their children have been set on edge. If they glory in the memory of good and holy fathers, then let them at least imitate their sanctity while maintaining as a law their dispensations and indulgences.[89]

But in spite of this manifestation of sympathy, we have reason to suppose that Bernard absented himself from this meeting because it was inopportune for him again to underline publicly his view regarding obedience to the Rule of Benedict, which he had once candidly expressed in his polemical writings. His willingness to stay away from this meeting has already been dealt with in our discussion of Bernard's relationship with Arnold of Bonneval. But the letter Bernard sent to the assembled Benedictine abbots did not mean that he had changed his opinion on any essential point.

---

88. Ceglar, "William of Saint-Thierry and His Leading Role," in *William, Abbot*, 34-49.

89. *Ep.* 91, c. 1 and 3. SBO VII, 239-240. Transl. James, 140.

And that was the reason he had been invited, either by William himself or at the latter's instigation, possibly with the expectation that he would, with his increased authority, reiterate his earlier views with regard to obedience to the Rule.

But Bernard indicated that he would be absent from this chapter because of church business elsewhere. He did not elaborate upon the nature of those duties. It may have been related to his intense involvement with the schism of Anacletus. In any case, he would have compromised his interests in that matter, if in Reims he would once again have expressed his criticism regarding the traditional interpretation of the Rule, which was still current in Cluny. For, as we already saw, the background of this schism in part also concerned the earlier conflict in Cluny in which Bernard had intervened. He had been heavily criticized after his efforts had failed.

Not long after this, upon the invitation of Cardinal Matthew of Albano and Cardinal Haimeric, he had agreed to assume, at some future time, the role of referee in the question of the legitimacy of the papal candidate desired by the two cardinals as the successor of Honorius II — an offer that rehabilitated him after the previous failure. In view of the background of this schism, Bernard, when accepting this offer, must have agreed to the implicit condition that he would refrain from meddling once more in the Benedictine controversies about obedience to the Rule. Later it would become clear that this had placed him in a dilemma. For it prevented him from publicly expressing himself, during the meeting of provincial abbots chaired by William, in favor of this reform movement; while Cardinal Matthew of Albano, who had been responsible for placing Bernard in that position, could do so. In his speech he brusquely attacked Bernard's *Apology* and criticized the Cistercian lifestyle with these words:

> Since in our times and in many places the clearing of land and manual labor are inappropriate and unprofitable, our holy fathers, under divine inspiration, have entrusted the monks with the immeasurably great and most elevated task of chanting psalms and observing other sacred customs, which many regard as a more worthy occupation than the uprooting of trees and the digging out of stones.[90]

90. *"Acta primi capituli provincialis ordinis s. Benedicti, Remis A.D. 1131 habiti":* Epistola Matthaei, lines 239-243, *Saint Thierry, une abbaye,* 330. For this pamphlet, see *Cluny et Cîteaux* (1985), 127-131, and also "Le rôle de l'agriculture" (1994), 117-118.

Like Haimeric, the papal chancellor, this cardinal-legate had, from 1128 onward, shown some courtesies and favors toward Bernard;[91] in so doing they must have succeeded in gaining his support for their strategy in the college of cardinals.

Both cardinals wanted to prevent at any price having Pope Honorius II after his death succeeded by Cardinal Peter Leonis. This Peter came from a powerful family of bankers that was of Jewish origin but had converted to Christianity already three generations earlier. Before he had become a cardinal, he had himself been a monk in Cluny under Abbot Pons. In 1126, when in Rome the struggle of the conservative opponents of this abbot went through its final phase, Peter Leonis undoubtedly belonged to the opposition against Matthew, together with Gilles of Paris, the cardinal-bishop of Tusculum, who was also from Cluny. Gilles had been very devoted to Abbot Pons and later to Anacletus.[92] Matthew's appointment as cardinal, after the condemnation of Pons, must have heightened the existing tensions in the college of cardinals.

In 1130, after the death of Pope Honorius II, the discord among the cardinals indeed led to a dual choice. The majority rejected the minority choice of Innocent II — partly because it immediately followed a hastily arranged, secret funeral of Honorius — and elected Pietro Leone as pope. He called himself Anacletus II.[93] When Innocent was unable to maintain his position in Rome, he fled to France, where he could count on considerable support. For at that moment, Cardinal Haimeric and Cardinal Matthew had already succeeded in winning Bernard fully to their side. Thus, without too much risk, they could entrust him with the honor of determining, at least on behalf of the church in France, which of the two candidates ought to be recognized. They were certain that in the meeting in Etampes, where this official recognition was to take place, Bernard would unconditionally support the claims of Innocent II. To further increase that certainty, just prior to that meeting Innocent had elevated the Cistercian monk Baldwin, one of Bernard's secretaries, to the rank of cardinal.

91. "Saint Bernard in His Relations" (1992), 321, with notes 19 and 20.

92. Gilles went to Rome in 1120, together with Pope Calixtus II. There he wrote, upon Pons's request, a *vita* of his predecessor, Abbot Hugh. During the schism, Hugh had chosen the side of Anacletus; he remained loyal to him, in spite of the effort of Peter the Venerable to make him join the party of Innocent II. F. Barlow, "The Canonization and Early Lives of Hugh I, Abbot of Cluny," 308. *Letters*, vol. I, 195-197 and vol. II, 141; *Ep.* 66.

93. "De paus uit het Ghetto" (1962). M. Stroll (1987) and the bibliography there cited. Gasteldelli, *Opere* VI/1, 568-572. The great-grandfather of Pope Anacletus II, Baruch Judaeus, was baptized about 988 and then named Benedict Christian.

As we discussed earlier, Matthew of Albano had been the most tenacious opponent of Abbot Pons, during Pons's condemnation in 1126. His opposition against Abbot Pons concerned especially the latter's departure from the traditional way of life in Cluny, and subsequently he continued to oppose forcefully all who tried to tamper with this tradition. As its defender he wrote, around 1131, an extremely disagreeable pamphlet against the efforts at reform of William of Saint-Thierry in the Benedictine monasteries of the church province of Reims. Although the cardinal-legate did not directly mention the *Apology,* in which six to eight years earlier Bernard had criticized this Cluniac conservatism, some of his arguments were clearly directed against this treatise.[94]

If in this new controversy Bernard would have openly sided with William of Saint-Thierry, he would have affronted inplicitly the party he was so strongly supporting during the schism. But other interests had already obliged Bernard to relinquish the freedom to choose William's side. William of Saint-Thierry, of course, experienced the greatest difficulty because of this quandary in which Bernard found himself. In view of the statements in Matthew's letter, quoted above, in which William sought to convince the abbots of the chapter that Bernard's absence should in fact be seen as a presence, it seems likely that he would have been more successful in his reform efforts if he had had Bernard's verbal backing for his reponse to this pamphlet. Had that been the case, the abbot of Saint-Thierry would probably not have lost.[95]

Since he could not afford, even at a later date, to give any publicity to this turn-around of Bernard, William was, of course, unable to deal in the first book of the *vita prima* with the earlier conflict in Cluny, although at the time he had utilized Bernard's writing talent. As a result of this situation, William was ever after completely ignored by Peter the Venerable. An additional constraint for his saying anything about the Cluny issue was Bernard's systematic avoidance of any further involvement with the Cluniac reform problems, in spite of Peter's frequent urgings to the contrary. A few years after William's death, this attempt to persuade Bernard even led to a split between the two abbots.[96]

94. *Cluny et Cîteaux* (1985), 130-131.

95. Idem, 135. For a discussion of the polemics of Matthew, see "Le rôle de l'agriculture" (1993). Also above, note 90.

96. Concerning the relationship between William and Peter the Venerable, see *Cluny et Cîteaux,* 119, with note 26. For the split between Bernard and Peter, see "Saint Bernard in His Relations" (1992) and below, 227-248.

The only thing William felt he could do was to retell the legendary story — earlier reduced to writing by Geoffrey in his *Fragmenta*[97] — about the origin of the letter from Bernard to Robert of Châtillon that marked the beginning of Bernard's meddling in the internal controversy in Cluny, at William's instigation:

> Brother Robert, one of Bernard's monks and also a relative of his, was misled and cajoled in his early youth into changing his allegiance from Clairvaux to Cluny. Bernard did nothing about it for a while, but later he decided to try and bring the brother back where he belonged by writing him a letter. He dictated it to William, afterwards the first abbot of Rievaulx, who took it down on a parchment. Both of them were sitting in the open since they had secretly gone outside the monastery enclosure so that Bernard could dictate the letter without being overheard. Suddenly an unexpected shower of rain began to fall, and William, as he himself told me afterwards, wanted to put the sheet of parchment under cover. But Bernard said to him, "The rain is sent by God, so carry on with the writing and have no fears." He did as he was told and took down the letter while it rained without a single drop of water falling on the sheet, for although it was raining heavily all around him, the love which inspired the letter sheltered the parchment and kept the writing and the sheet quite unspoilt.[98]

William relates this incident as part of a series of stories about miracles and wonders allegedly performed by Bernard when he was still alive. Several of these stories were intended to neutralize criticism of his various activities.

---

97. *"Fragmenta,"* c. 26; ed. Lechat, 103.

98. Vp I, c. IX, 50; P.L., CLXXXV, 255-256. Transl. Webb and Walker, 70. Relating this miracle story, William may have had another intention. For it shows some relationship to what happened earlier to Saint Odo, the first abbot of Cluny. His *vita* informs us that a manuscript, which contained the life of Saint Martin of Sulpicius Severus and in which he had corrected some writing errors, had through negligence been left behind in the scriptorium. During the following night, as a result of heavy rains, this room had been totally flooded and the manuscript had been submerged in the water. But the text of this *vita* had not been damaged and the ink of the letters had not been affected. Possibly William of Saint-Thierry thus wanted to draw a parallel between the holiness of Bernard and this abbot of Cluny. Cf. *Vita sancti Odonis,* scripta a Joanne monacho, ejus discipulo, liber II, c. 22; P.L. CXXXIII. S. *Odonis vita altera,* auctore Nalgodo, cluniacensis monacho saeculi XII, c. 45; ibid., 102.

William subsequently attempted, for instance, to recast the criticism that had resulted from Bernard's opposition against Abelard in 1141, as a quality given to him through God's grace. To that end, as we saw above, he used the story about the vision of the barking dog. He succeeded at least to some extent in that tactic, for John of Salisbury and Otto of Freising, together with others who later blamed Bernard for his attitude toward Gilbert de la Porrée, later phrased their objections in a different way. They argued that Bernard involved himself with matters he had insufficiently understood.[99] Both John and Otto had studied under Abelard in Paris when he taught there in the 1130s. John later testified of his appreciation for this period of study, while Otto candidly referred to Bernard's dealings with Abelard as an indication of his lack of insight with regard to secular philosophy.[100]

Returning to the story about the letter that was dictated in the rain, we may compare it in some ways with the story of the barking dog. Since many Benedictines continued to be uneasy about Bernard's polemical writings concerning Cluny, William — unable to find any excuse on the basis of the actual facts — tried, by mentioning the incident, to underscore that in any case Bernard's involvement with this matter was divinely ordained. In so doing, he attempted by means of this miracle story to prevent further criticism from contemporaries of this notorious piece of polemical writing by Bernard, and to present his interference in the Cluniac controversy, which some Benedictines had openly condemned,[101] as a sign of his sainthood.

C. William of Saint-Thierry's Contribution Reevaluated

William mainly differed from the two other authors of the *vita prima* in his constant references to Bernard's sainthood in rebuttal of the critics of Bernard's actions. The previous chapter dealt at length with this aspect of

99. Chibnall, ed., *Historia Pontificalis*, c. 9; 19–21. *Ottonis et Rahewenini Gesta Friderici imperatoris*, vol. I, c. 48–51; ed. Waitz and Simson (SRG B. 46), 67-74 and 80-88.

100. For the opinion of John of Salisbury, see *Christendom*, 237-238, with note 22. For Otto of Freising, who after his stay in Paris and prior to his election as bishop had been a monk and an abbot in Morimond, see *Ottonis . . . Gesta Friderici*, vol. I, c. 49; 68. In his evaluation of Bernard's dealings with Abelard, Otto called him a fanatic *(zelotipus)* in his zeal for the Christian faith. He further remarks that Bernard was usually quite gullible, and that because of his strong loathing for the *magistri*, who in their secular wisdom placed far too much weight on rational arguments, he often listened to simple rumors about their supposed deviations from the Christian faith. Also Diers (1991), 259-269.

101. *Cluny et Cîteaux* (1985), 70-71, note 134.

his work. Nevertheless, it deserves some further attention. William's approach differs clearly from that of Geoffrey of Auxerre, as can be easily demonstrated by comparing a few of Geoffrey's hagiographic fragments with William's later usages of these in the first book of the *vita*. He was able to reshape this information to support his unequivocal portrayal of Bernard's sainthood.

We find a clear example of this dissimilarity in Geoffrey's account of a discussion between Bernard and his brother Gerard (who, as the cellarer at the time, was in charge of the material cares of Clairvaux), by putting this alongside its revision by William of Saint-Thierry. In his *Fragmenta*, Geoffrey described this discussion and what followed in these words:

> It happened in that same year, that at the beginning of the winter the highly revered Gerard, the cellarer of the monastery, had to make major purchases to satisfy the needs of the brethren, while there was absolutely no money. For that reason, when he complained about this situation to the abbot, the latter told him to examine even more precisely whether there would be any way to obtain this money from what was available in the monastery. When Gerard had assured the abbot there was nothing in the monastery that could provide him with the money, the man of God wanted to know how much money would be enough to see him through for the moment. Gerard answered that he needed eleven pounds. Then the abbot dismissed him, admonishing him to trust in God's mercies, since, he said, it is his responsibility to provide for us. Shortly after Gerard had disappeared from his view, he returned with the message, "There is a woman from Châtillon at the gate, who wants to see you." He [Bernard] then approached her and recognized her as the wife of Martin, a very rich man. The woman knelt before him and said, "Since last night my husband is seriously ill and close to death. He has sent me to you and asks you to pray for him. He also begs your holiness to accept the gift which he requested me to hand to you." The gift was a purse with twelve pounds. Sending the woman away, he said, "Go in peace, for you will find your husband in good health." Arriving at home, she found her husband as he had predicted.[102]

William condensed this account, but then commented at length on the nature of the relationship between Bernard, who was always focused on God, and his more secularly inclined fellow-brethren.

---

102. *Fragmenta*, c. 20; ed. Lechat, 100.

Not long before the winter was due to fall, Bernard's brother Gerard, who held the office of the cellarer in the monastery, complained to him explicitly that there was a great shortage of the various things necessary for the support of the community and the upkeep of the house. There was no money to buy what was needed, he said, and mere words were no use in trying to rid him of his worries since they had no possessions to barter for what was required. When Bernard asked him how much money would cover their wants, Gerard told him that eleven pounds would be just enough. And so Bernard sent him away, and began to call urgently on God for help. In a little while Gerard came back to tell him that a certain woman from Châtillon was outside and wished to speak to him. When she saw the young abbot, the good woman threw herself at his feet and asked him to accept a gift of twelve pounds, begging the brethren to help her with their prayers on behalf of her husband who was dangerously ill. Bernard stayed and talked with her for a while, and eventually left her with the words: "Go home now and you will find your husband restored to health." And when she arrived home, she found that what Bernard had told her had come true. And in this way he made Gerard even more undaunting in relying upon God's help in their every need after he had reassured his anxiety and trustlessness.

It is well known that this is not the only occasion of its kind, for often when they were in dire need the Lord sent help from an unexpected source. And this made those who were wise in the ways of God and who knew that the hand of the Lord was with him, wary of burdening his mind with the cares of everyday life. They knew that all his thoughts dwelt on the delights of heaven, and so they would try to cope with their worries among themselves as best as they could, and would ask for his advice only on matters which concerned their souls or consciences.

For them the situation was very similar to what happened to the people of Israel when, after he had spent a long time speaking to the Lord on Mount Sinai, Moses came out of the shadows of the cloud and went down to the people waiting below. After his long conversation with God his face seemed to send forth beams of radiance, which filled the people with such fear and trembling that they fled from him whenever he came near.[103]

103. Vp I, c. VI, 27-28; P.l.., CLXXXV, 242-243. Transl. Webb and Walker, 46, 47.

William had more than one purpose in telling this story. It not only gave him the opportunity to report the immediate answer Bernard received to his prayer, but also to compare him with Moses in his encounter with God. Moreover, William creates the impression that Bernard was not really interested in the material affairs of his monastery, and that his fellow-brethren preferred not to involve him in these matters.

As a result of the last-mentioned aspect, William considered himself free from any obligation to furnish more details about Bernard's actual part in the growth of his order and the establishment of so many daughter institutions. Others, however, were at times irritated by his activities in that area, for instance, with regard to the acquisition of the abbey of le Bueil (or Buillon) in 1148. This monastery fell under the jurisdiction of the abbey of Dalon, which remained outside the Cistercian Order until 1162. Referring to the affiliation of Buillon with Clairvaux, Abbot Robert in a letter allegedly compared Bernard with a man who, while in possession of ninety-nine sheep, secretly stole the sheep of the poor man and then received this poor man as a long-lost friend.[104]

But, on the other hand, William made it appear as if the growth of the order was largely due to the aura of Bernard. In this context, he advanced the story that Cîteaux had been saved from extinction by Bernard's presence, and that subsequently the order could expand in all directions as a result of Bernard's spiritual impulse. Apart from the fact that Bernard brought thirty companions with him, any precise information about this aspect is lacking. William found it unnecessary, and probably also undesirable, to elaborate further upon the many direct involvements of Bernard with the establishment and acquisition of monasteries — which, as we saw, evoked anger and criticism from some of his contemporaries. For centuries this presentation by William of Bernard's disinterest in material problems was considered so credible that no research was done about the actual facts surrounding the development of the order. Moreover, his views led Vacandard to date the year of Bernard's birth as early as 1190.[105]

This remarkable, but biased, presentation of the information William of Saint-Thierry offers his readers can be viewed as an important characteristic of his intentions and design for the first book of the *vita prima*. It stands also in these respects in sharp contrast with the contributions of the two other authors. Of course we should not put Geoffrey's share in this document on a par with the notes he collected in his *Fragmenta*. For in that work he made no effort whatsoever to present these

104. See *Gallia Christiana*, II, Paris, 1873, col. 632. *Recueil* IV, 126, note 3.
105. "Saint Bernard, est-il né en 1090?" (1994). Below, 202-204.

individual stories in a common framework. But when later he did attempt to do so, he also failed to portray Bernard's sainthood in such a way that it would really transcend a series of stories about his sainthood. In compensation, Geoffrey almost invariably resorted to panegyric passages. Arnold's contribution to this *vita* shows a similar deficiency. His book likewise does not present a portrait of Bernard as saint that convincingly transcends the sum of its individual chapters.

This contrast between the work of William of Saint-Thierry and that of the two other authors is partly also the result of the fact that their role as authors was limited to a largely factual expansion of William's work, as William had explicitly commanded them in his prologue. There William explained his decision to write the first part of this *vita*, and concluded by stating that it was not his intention to relate all the external facts in detail to prove Bernard's internal sainthood, but he trusted that others would do so after Bernard's death. Apparently William knew, at least in outline, that his work would be continued and by whom.

Prior to this remark in his prologue, William clearly described his overall design and aim in the writing of this first book:

> However, when I tried to take the measure of myself and thus compared myself with myself, I did not take the task upon me to cover the life of the man of God in its entirety, but only in part, that is: some experiences which show how Christ lived and spoke through him, some of his accomplishments as he lived with the people; I refer to what those, to whom that was granted, did see, and what we also in part have seen and heard, and what our hands have been allowed to touch. But since in essence we must say about him what was also stated of the one who said, "It is no longer I who live, but Christ who lives in me" (Galatians 2:20), and who elsewhere asks: "Or do you desire proof that Christ is speaking in me?" (2 Corinthians 13:3), I have decided not to give an account of the invisible life of the Christ who lived and spoke in him, but to limit myself to some external testimonies of his life. They concern the purity of his inner sainthood and of his invisible conscience, expressed through external deeds, which radiate to the external senses of the people, and which can just as easily be described by anyone, as they are known to all.[106]

106. Vp I, prologue; P.L., CLXXXV, 226.

This characterization by William of his contribution to the *vita prima* (though left out by Geoffrey from his redaction B), which he succeeded in anchoring in a largely apologetic description of the external actions of Bernard, determines the difference between the first book and the other books of this *vita*. But this difference is also related to the dissimilarity in the ways in which the authors each knew and experienced Bernard. William not only venerated Bernard as a saint, but also knew, understood, and at times criticized him as a human being. Nonetheless, he continued to defend his sainthood. Arnold in essence offers the reader an account of the life, or in any case of the actions, of a saint, whom he knew and admired from some distance. With Geoffrey, finally, we encounter an almost uncritical admiration and devotion for this saintly abbot, who had saved him from this world.

This difference also has to do with the fact that William already knew Bernard from his youth. Consequently, he also reflects some of his own ambitions in connection with Bernard's intentions in and through Clairvaux, which were not always realized in the way he had initially expected.[107]

Some Cistercians who had also known Bernard personally later objected to the manner in which William of Saint-Thierry characterized Bernard's sainthood. This was in part because of the veiled reference to the criticism Bernard had evoked in some circles through his church-political actions. We have already dealt with this matter at length in the third chapter.

But from the beginning, others in the order did appreciate this document. This was stated by Burchard, at the time still the abbot of Balerne, after William's death, and probably also after Bernard had died. He supplied an epilogue to the first book, which is found in virtually all manuscripts of the *vita prima*.[108] Geoffrey most likely had good reasons for accepting this epilogue to the first book. For this postscript, written no later than 1157, offers an explicit, positive evaluation, which somewhat counterbalanced the criticism of the *vita prima* from other members of the order.[109]

---

107. Lobrichon, "Répresentations de Clairvaux" (1991), 250-251.

108. The epilogue is only missing in ms Douai 372, a copy of a lost codex that was submitted to Alexander III at the occasion of the first request for Bernard's canonization and was subsequently used as a working copy when the text of this Vp was revised, resulting in redaction B.

109. Until 1157 Burchard was abbot of Balerne, an Eremite monastery that had sought affiliation with Clairvaux in 1136. He became the abbot of Bellevaux in 1157, which in 1119 had been established as the first daughter institution of Morimond. Cf. B. Chauvin, "Un disciple méconnu de saint Bernard," *Cîteaux* 40 (1989), 5-66.

This epilogue may also be regarded as a formal conclusion to what we have said about William of Saint-Thierry as Bernard's hagiographer. Therefore it also serves as the epilogue to this chapter:

> It is well known that this treatise about the life of the most holy man Bernard, the abbot of Clairvaux, which had been produced by the honorable William — at one time the abbot of Saint-Thierry, but later a monk of the Signy monastery, where he had gone in a desire for solitude and peace — covers the period until the time of the schism, initiated by Petrus Leonis against Pope Innocent. This faithful man, referred to above, had a special reason for writing: the friendship and intimate tie which had bound him for such a long time to the man of God. He had found so much favor with him that there was in fact nobody else who was closer to him in the exchange of their mutual love and was more suited to discuss with him the mysteries of the spiritual life. The privilege of this intimacy was in particular manifested by the several letters which this saint wrote to him; the reader of these letters immediately senses what Bernard felt for him. Bernard also sent him an apology and a book about grace and the free will.[110]
>
> However, William also had a more general reason to write this book, which was of more importance than his personal motive: the benefit for the church as a whole. He wanted to prevent that, when a vessel is filled with a highly desirable treasure, the treasure itself remains hidden. Those who ask that the treasure be shown, do not complain unjustly: "What use has an invisible treasure and a hidden wisdom?" (Jesus Sirach 20:32). He laid bare the riches of salvation, a most desirable treasure, a pearl of great value, which, since it is not a ball of earth, should not be hidden with the earth. But things did not go for him as he wanted. For, as — according to his prologue — he feared, he was overcome by death and had not finished to entrust to his pen what his spirit had prepared.
>
> Thus, those who begin to read this work will rather easily understand with what perfection the pious and god-fearing boy Bernard, as a second Benedict, began his conversion; and they will also see how he accepted his sainthood already in his mother's womb. This is the basis for the predictions of the future saintliness of his life and teachings. [Just as it is said about him that he was never nursed at the breast

---

110. *De gratia et libero arbitrio*, SBO III, 165-203. Bernard completed this work shortly before he wrote letter 52, addressed to Cardinal Haimeric. The letter dates from 1128.

of a wetnurse, but only at the breast of his mother, so that he would not with the milk suck up any error, but only the godliness of his mother. There are children who, dangling at their mothers' breasts, with their impetuous look and hostile eyes prefigure what they will later become. And there are other children who, while sucking, beat the breasts of the ones who feed them with their fists and heads.

But as a child Bernard always gave evidence of his gentle nature. When he came from his mother's womb he was accompanied by indications of his gentle disposition: a pleasant appearance, a calm face, and innocent eyes. What in his case was a sign of goodness as a natural gift was, as a result of the grace bestowed upon him, transformed in virtue. Though still unable to speak, as a baby he already seemed able to speak by means of the grace he had received. When he was no longer nursed, but had grown into a boy, he already manifested the maturity that enabled him to transcend childish manners.] What he did as a youth has been described in this treatise. He is therein portrayed until he reached the maturity of a man, that is, as was mentioned earlier, to the extent this excellent painter, who died such an untimely death, has been granted to do.[111]

111. P.L., CLXXXV, 266-268. The section between square brackets is missing in redaction B and has not been included by Horstius, Mabillon, and Migne in their editions of the Vp. For the Latin text of this passage, see *Etudes* (1960), 35, line 5.

140

V

Saint Bernard and the Historians

❧   ❧

THROUGH THE CENTURIES many historians have paid attention to St. Bernard, all with their own motives and from their own perspectives. As a result, this medieval abbot inevitably was characterized incidentally and evaluated by some in an almost inimitable way. More than once we find an emotional appreciation or disapproval of his actions. Thus developed — even outside of the hagiographic tradition — a number of historically questionable portraits of his person, which persisted for a shorter or longer period. Alexander Lenoire in 1814 provided a remarkable example of this phenomenon. This lodge member argued that Bernard's unblemished life and compassion resulted from his intimate knowledge of the deepest secrets of freemasonry, which enabled him to draft the Rule of the Templars.[1]

Obviously not all more or less cursory portraits of Bernard were as flattering as that of Lenoire. At times we find extremely negative judgments, based on just a few isolated passages from Bernard's writings or from the *vita prima*. To these a commentary or interpretation would be added, with no attention to the context within which these passages were written or, rather, dictated.

It has been established that the frequent presupposition that Bernard was anti-intellectual is based on a remark with an ironic undertone made by Bernard around 1125 in a letter to Henry Murdach about Henry's

---

1. "Saint Bernard and the Historians" (1977), 44, note 55.

armchair learning. The fact that the addressee was completely addicted to his learning, and that this remark of Bernard's was clearly relativized by William of Saint-Thierry in the A-redaction of the *vita prima*, is totally ignored. In redaction B this relativizing remark was eliminated. This suggests that this hagiographer intended to confirm this anti-intellectual image of Bernard; the more so, since none of the versions of this *vita*, which incorporated some passages from redaction A, pay any attention to William's comments. They seem to be utterly unaware of its existence.[2]

A passage at the beginning of his treatise *De consideratione*, where Bernard deals with the meaning and the usefulness of "considering," shows how ill-conceived it is to accuse him of anti-intellectualism. This is what he has to say:

> First of all, "considering" purifies the source from which it springs, i.e., the spirit. It also regulates our emotions, gives direction to our actions, corrects deviations, builds our character, bestows honor and order to our lives; to put it in one word: it provides knowledge of divine and human things. It clarifies what is confused, unifies what is disjointed, collects what is dispersed, grasps what is hidden, searches for truth, and discovers what is treacherous and disguised. It foresees and organizes what must be done, checks what has been done, so that nothing remains in the spirit that has not been improved or needs no further improvement. In times of prosperity it foresees misfortune, and it hardly feels the latter when it has arrived. This last ability is called strength, the first one prudence.[3]

The characterization of Bernard by the French medievalist Jacques Le Goff, in his study of medieval civilization, offers another ill-conceived interpretation of an isolated remark by this abbot.[4] This interpretation was based on the last part of a letter, written by Bernard, sometime between 1124 and 1135, in which he provided an ironic answer to a question from the abbot of the Premonstratensian monastery of Cuissy. The passage in question reads as follows:

> There is yet another matter on which I will give you my opinion with my usual lack of inhibition. I refer to that particular mill, where the

2. See above, 125-126, with notes 80-82. Diers (1991), 198-208. Häring, "Saint Bernard and the litterati."
3. II, c. VII, 8; SBO III, 404, lines 1-9.
4. *La civilisation de l'occident médiéval,* 266.

lay brethren who are charged with its supervision, may allow frequent visits by women. If you ask me, it must be one of three things: either the women must definitely be prevented from entering, or the supervision of the mill must be left to outsiders and not to these lay brethren, or the mill must be completely abandoned.[5]

This text deserves some clarification. In their supervision of the mill, the lay brethren of Cuissy were confronted by women who came to this place to engage in prostitution. That was not uncommon at such a meeting place as this mill provided. Apart from those who came to the mill to have their wheat ground, there were prostitutes who also came, looking for their share. Since this caused embarrassment to the lay brethren, the abbot of Cuissy had asked Bernard for advice about how to proceed in the matter. In response he received a threefold, somewhat ironic suggestion, which may have prompted him to choose Bernard's second option as the most practical solution.

In view of the importance these water mills had for the Cistercian monasteries in Bernard's day — the abbey of Pontigny built no less than three of these mills — and considering that this problem nowhere else figures in the writings of Bernard, we may conclude that Bernard dealt with this problem only because he had received a question about it. He certainly did not have to worry about the problem of how prostitution could be prevented at mills belonging to Cistercian monasteries.

Nevertheless, le Goff felt he could justifiably come to a different conclusion on the basis of this passage. He remarks that when the Cistercians constructed mills, Bernard threatened to destroy them, since they proved to be places where people met, arranged contacts or meetings, or — worse — engaged in prostitution. Le Goff finds support for his conclusion in a passage from chapter LXVI of the Rule of St. Benedict, which, among other things, stipulates that provisions such as water, a mill, a garden, and maintenance sheds were to be situated within the confines of the monastery, "so that monks do not have to roam around outside their monasteries, as this is detrimental to their souls."

I regard the conclusion Le Goff draws from this isolated passage as doubtful, since there are no further indications that Bernard intended to fight against the construction of mills, and since his letter was not addressed to a Cistercian abbot. Perhaps it ought therefore to be viewed as a challenge, intended — as is often Le Goff's strategy — to provoke a rebuttal that will enhance our understanding. In this case, the reply would be that here two totally unconnected elements are linked

---

5. *Ep.* 79, c. 3; SBO VII, 212. Transl. James, 119-120. The letter from the abbot of Cuissy is not extant.

together. Apparently the abbey of Cuissy had to admit outside customers to its mill. We are here dealing with a mill with seigneurial rights. In the Cistercian monasteries such a situation never occurred; for when acquiring estates, they systematically precluded any future rights of others.[6]

Nonetheless, in the meantime this conclusion of Le Goff has begun to lead its own life, not only because the book in which the author first proposed it has been translated into several languages, but also because it has been repeated, even more blatantly, in a popular book about the "industrial revolution of the Middle Ages." There this conclusion is presented in such a way that Bernard would have seriously delayed the economic development of Europe, if he had been able to put his "plea" for measures against prostitution into practice.[7] This suggests that Bernard also turned against the economic progress of his times, in spite of the fact that the Cistercians — of whom, according to this author, Bernard was the leader — in fact did much to promote it.

There are other dubious portrayals of Bernard by historians, based on biased or incorrect interpretations of particular passages from his writings. Two of these have become rather widespread. The first of these, to which we already referred in the Introduction, concerns Bernard's observations in his *Apology* with regard to the luxuriance of the abbey church that was being constructed in Cluny.

There will never be unanimity regarding the exact intentions of Bernard in writing the two short chapters of this treatise. In this particular document Bernard had more than one purpose, and as a result it is open to more than one interpretation. But in spite of this, it has often simply been assumed that Bernard had no eye for beauty and ought therefore to be classified among the iconoclasts, since he demanded that the monks manifest austerity in the building and furnishing of their own churches. Moreover, he allegedly wrote these chapters because the passion of Cluny "à faire de luxe pour Dieu" was an eyesore to him.[8]

In the next chapter we will deal at greater length with this assault of Bernard on the extravagance of the building program in Cluny. But there

---

6. Berman, "Les cisterciens et le tournant économique," 155-177.

7. Gimpel (1977), 3: "Saint Bernard, the leader of the Cistercian Order in the twelfth century, was scandalized to hear of the prostitutes' activities and wanted to have the mills closed. If such a thing had occurred . . . the European economy would have grown at a far slower rate."

8. Van der Meer (1950), 103-114. Evans (1950). Mortet, "Hughe de Fouilloi . . . ," 105-137. Rudolph (1990).

is another, even more common, misleading portrayal of Bernard that ought to receive our explicit attention in this context. It concerns the views Bernard supposedly had on the relationship between church and state, and the support he therefore gave to the papal demands for more power over the church, at the expense of the authority of the bishops. This misleading characterization presents Bernard and Gregory VII (1073-1085) as kindred spirits, and holds him partly responsible for the theoretical foundation of this papal theocracy, which to a large extent determined the political strategies of the popes in the thirteenth and fourteenth century in church and society. The section that follows deals with this complicated issue and may also help us in determining what actual value may be attributed to the political statements in Bernard's writings.

I. BERNARD AS THE IDEOLOGIST OF PAPAL THEOCRACY

IN HIS WRITINGS Bernard speaks several times about the relationship between the spiritual and the secular powers, using the common image of the spiritual and the worldly sword.[9] He mentions this metaphor three times. One of these instances is in "Praise to the new militia," which he wrote between 1128 and 1138 for the knights of the recently established Order of the Templars. The passage is usually, and justifiably, ignored in this connection, since in this treatise the metaphor was not applied to the pope.[10] The two other passages where Bernard uses the same metaphor are found in a letter and a treatise, in both cases addressed to Pope Eugenius III. Those who tried to stress the large degree in which Bernard was co-responsible for this theocratic ideology attach great importance to them.

But at the same time these historians, who were more interested in the history of the papal claims concerning power over church and society, often ignored the fact that Bernard's relationship to this pope cannot be understood when their earlier relationship of abbot and novice is ignored.

---

9. For this image, see Jacqueline (1975), 119-124. Hoffmann, "Die beiden Schwerter . . . ," 78-114. Turrini, "San Bernardo e l'allegoria delle due spade," 5-41.

10. *Liber ad milites Templi de laude novae militiae*, c. III, 5; SBO III, 217-218: "May both swords of the believers fall on the enemies, to cut down every height that rebels against the knowledge of God, that is: against the Christian faith."

This would perhaps bring some elucidation, or at least clarify that some of Bernard's political thoughts in his *De consideratione* may have had less ideological significance than has repeatedly been assumed.[11]

As mentioned earlier, seven years before being elected pope Eugenius III had entered Clairvaux as monk. At the time, his name was still Bernard Paganelli. He had been a canon in Pisa, where he was authorized to represent the cardinal-bishop in temporal matters as "vidame." He met Bernard in 1135, when Bernard attended a council in Pisa chaired by Innocent II. The meetings must have impressed Paganelli deeply, for in 1138 Paganelli entered Clairvaux as novice. At that time the schism of Anacletus was about to end, and Cardinal-archbishop Hubert of Lefranc had died, to be succeeded by Baldwin, a Cistercian monk who had been made a cardinal as early as 1130.

Paganelli returned to Italy in 1139 and subsequently became the abbot of Tre Fontane in Rome. This abbey had remained loyal to Anacletus, and shortly afterward the end of the schism was offered by Innocent to Bernard. Early in 1145 the cardinals elected Abbot Paganelli as the successor of Lucius II, a choice that caused Bernard, in a letter to the cardinals of the Curia, to react with anxiety rather than with approval. With obvious exaggeration he remarked that through this choice the cardinals had called back into the midst of men, someone who was dead and buried, and had shattered the decision of a poor, needy, and sorrowful man to lead a silent life. Bernard further spoke of his fear that Paganelli, with his delicate physique and sensitive reluctance, would not be able to fulfill the papal duties with the required authority.[12]

This anxiety of Bernard was perhaps partly caused by the circumstances in Rome that had led to the death of Pope Lucius II, the immediate predecessor of Eugenius III. Lucius fell victim to a popular uprising in Rome in 1144. This uprising came as the climax of the popular resistance that the rule of Innocent II eventually evoked after the schism of Anacletus had been ended. The resistance was at first supported by the Roman aristocracy, which had taken the capitol and then attacked the senate. For that reason the capitol was besieged by a papal army, albeit in vain. The resistance by the senate was led by Giordano Pierleone, a brother of Anacletus II. But the opposition of the people was headed by Arnold of Brescia, who continued to claim the power over Rome for himself and his

---

11. Kennan, "The *De consideratione* of Saint Bernard . . . and the Papacy in the Mid-Twelfth Century," 107: "It seems more fruitful, therefore, to evaluate what Bernard said by the relation it bore to the events and the literature of his own time. . . . Perhaps the most obvious fact about the period in which Bernard lived as an adult was the absence of any major struggle between Church and State."

12. *Ep.* 237. SBO VIII, 113-115. For the exaggeration by Bernard, see Diers (1991), 208-210.

followers even when, toward the end of 1145, the senate party concluded an agreement with the recently elected pope, Eugenius III. Papal authority was only reestablished in Rome in 1146 by Emperor Conrad, who for that purpose came with an army to Rome.

There must have been some direct link between the election of Eugenius III as pope and the subsequent intervention by Emperor Conrad III. And no doubt Bernard played some role in the affair. The violent death of Lucius II must have convinced the cardinals that only an intervention by the emperor would restore papal authority in Rome; just as in 1133, during the schism of Anacletus, the assistance of Emperor Lotharius II to Pope Innocent II had temporarily provided the latter with access to Rome. At that occasion the emperor had decided to intervene upon Bernard's instigation.

Thus, in considering a possible successor for Lucius II, the cardinals must have realized that once again imperial intervention would be necessary to restore order in Rome. On the other hand, they also undoubtedly realized that this time, too, such intervention from the emperor would depend on Bernard's cooperation, in view of the latter's influence on the emperor. This explains why the cardinals could do little else but elect the abbot of the Cistercian monastery Tre Fontane near Rome as pope, although he was no member of the college of cardinals.

To repeat: they could do little else. For in electing Eugenius III, they must have been aware that this choice would cause Bernard to get involved with papal policies, as indeed happened. After the intervention of Emperor Conrad II, for which he was rewarded by the pope through the canonization of his predecessor, Emperor Henry II, who had died in 1024, Eugenius III traveled to France. He stayed there until the spring of 1148. During this time this pope twice visited Clairvaux, while Bernard, who already in 1146 had been charged by him to preach a new crusade, often accompanied Eugenius III during his travels throughout France.

This made Bernard better acquainted with the papal administration; and as a result, he increasingly became the most important adviser of Eugenius III. This was clearly evident during the Council of Reims in 1148, which was still chaired by this pope. There, against the opinion of the participating cardinals, Bernard succeeded in forcing the condemnation of Gilbert of Porrée's views about the Trinity. This resulted in a certain tension between him and some members of the Curia, which is somewhat reflected in Bernard's criticism of this ecclesiastical administrative body in the fourth book of the *De consideratione*. Bernard began to write this treatise, in which he continued to advise Eugenius III, shortly after this pope had returned to Rome.

Already in the first book of this treatise, Bernard posed the question of how the pope ought to view his task. He suggested that Eugenius consider what did and did not belong to his papal duties, and also ponder what place he should give in his life to contemplation if he were to function as pope as he should.[13] A second book followed in 1149. Bernard began this part of his work by looking back on the failure of the Second Crusade, which he had preached as commanded by the pope. Next he asked Eugenius to consider four things: himself, the church he was to lead, the Roman Curia around him, and, finally, the things above: heaven and the angels. Bernard dealt with these four points in the second book and in the other three books, which he wrote between 1149 and 1152/53 to complete his treatise on "considering."

Since Bernard completed this work only toward the end of his life, we may view it as his spiritual testament. Many continued to be attracted or impressed by it because of its sharp criticism of the conduct of those who were supposed to assist the pope: the Roman Curia. Many also detected that Bernard did not always speak in favorable terms about the immediate predecessors of Eugenius III.[14] One of these was Innocent II, who in 1139 had not involved Bernard in the Second Lateran Council, in spite of the fact that for eight years Bernard had with great zeal devoted himself to the recognition of Innocent as the legitimate pope. During the council, Innocent had demoted Peter of Pisa, a former supporter of Anacletus, who at Bernard's instigation in 1137 had belatedly chosen Innocent's side, in such a way that the abbot of Clairvaux felt he had to protest sharply and firmly.[15]

These critical comments of Bernard explain why through the centuries some individuals have used this treatise as a basis for their complaints about the way in which the Roman Curia operated in their day. In view of their own negative experiences, they could easily agree when this saint criticized the highest ecclesiastical center of authority. A clear example of this in the later Middle Ages is the attitude of the followers of John Wycliffe (1384). They appealed to the *De consideratione* in their protest against the papal claims to increased power over the

---

13. It has been suggested — without any proof, however — that originally Bernard intended only to write the first book. G. R. Evans, "The *De Consideratione* of Bernard . . . A Preliminary Letter," 129-134. This theory seems to be contradicted by the first sentence of book II; SBO III, 410.

14. Book I, c. IX, 12; SBO III, 407. Bernard advised Eugenius to concentrate on the examples of his good predecessors, and not only on that of recent popes.

15. *Ep.* 213. SBO VIII, 73-74. For the deportment of Innocent II, see Vacandard, *Vie de Bernard,* II, 56-59. For other reasons why Bernard was critical of this papal reign, see Stroll (1987), 121-135; (1991), 100.

churches under Rome's jurisdiction. Luther also repeatedly appealed to this treatise.[16] A much later example is the commotion in 1870, particularly in Germany,
when the dogma of papal infallibility was proclaimed during the First Vatican
Council. Some German theologians separated from Rome and founded the Old
Catholic Church. At the same time one of them published a new German
translation of this treatise with a commentary.[17]

Since in this treatise Bernard deals with many aspects of the papal office,
it is no wonder that he also discusses the relationship between the pope
and the secular authorities and the church as a whole. In this connection,
Bernard also touches upon the doctrine of the two swords, a common
metaphor to describe the claims of the pope to both spiritual and secular
power. And in this treatise Bernard also feels free to make some remarks
about the papal claim to total authority within the church, the *plenitudo
potestatis* — a matter which he also discusses elsewhere.

Already in 1149 Bernard had presented Eugenius III with his first
exposition of the doctrine of the two swords. This was when the Second
Crusade had proven a failure and a new expedition was being planned. In
a letter he urged the pope to launch an appeal to come to the rescue of
the church in the East:

> In this second passion of Christ we must draw those two swords that
> were drawn during the first passion. And who is there to draw them
> but you? Both of Peter's swords must be drawn whenever necessary:
> the one by his command, the other by his hand. It seems that Peter
> was not to use one of these swords, for he was told "put up thy sword
> into thy scabbard." Although they both belonged to him, they were
> not both to be drawn by his hand. I believe that the time has come
> for both swords to be drawn in defense of the Eastern Church. You
> hold the position of Peter, and you ought also to have his zeal. What
> should we think of one who holds the primacy but neglects its re-
> sponsibility?[18]

The plan to organize a new crusader army after the failure of the Second
Crusade was advanced in 1149 after the fall of Antioch, in particular by

16. De Vooght, "De *De consideratione* de saint Bernard . . . ," 114-132. T. Bell
(1993), 138-150.
17. *Papst und Papsttum nach der Zeichnung des h. Bernhard von Clairvaux.* Ueber-
setzung und Erläuterung von Jos Reinkens. Münster, 1870.
18. *Ep.* 256, c. 1-2. SBO VIII, 163-164. Transl. James, 471.

persons in the entourage of Louis VII, and later by the king himself. With this army the king supposedly wanted to attack not only the Muslims, but also the Byzantine emperor, Manuel Comnenus, whom Louis had accused of treachery. When the king was in the process of repatriating his army, the emperor had attacked the French fleet. At that occasion even the king himself and his wife had, for a short while, been in danger. The plan of a new crusade was also promoted by Abbot Suger of Saint-Denis, Peter the Venerable, and the bishop of Langres, Godefroy de la Roche Vanneau, who himself had participated in the failed expedition.[19] Bernard also favored a new attempt. The reasons he listed in his letter to Eugenius III indicate that he was motivated by religious pathos rather than by a sense of political reality.[20] This is also apparent in the fact that he did not immediately refuse the offer to be in charge, however difficult he found this.

> I expect you must have heard by now how the assembly at Chartres, by a most surprising decision, chose me as the leader and commander of the expedition. You may be quite sure that this never was and is not now by my advice or wish, and that it is altogether beyond my powers, as I gauge them, to do such a thing. Who am I to arrange armies in battle order, to lead forth armed men? I could think of nothing more remote from my calling, even supposing I had the necessary strength and skill. But you know all this, it is not for me to teach you.[21]

As we have already seen, in the letter Bernard used the doctrine of the two swords as a convenient argument in favor of a new crusade. Against that background it is difficult to characterize Bernard, on the basis of this argumentation, as an articulate supporter of a papal theocracy. Moreover, Bernard remains silent about the plan for a new crusade at the beginning of the second book of the *De consideratione*, where he defends himself regarding the failure of the earlier crusade that he had promoted. Neither does he deal with the question of the spiritual and secular power of the pope.[22] And when Bernard — in the fourth book, written in 1152 — does discuss the papal claim to the dual power and refer again to the metaphor

19. Runciman, II (1952), 286-287. Vacandard, II, 439-446.
20. Gastaldelli, *Opere* VI/1 (lettere), 184, note.
21. *Ep.* 256, c. 4; SBO VIII, 164-165. Transl. James, 472.
22. Book II, c. I, 1-4; SBO III, 410-413.

of the two swords, the earlier argument in defense of a new crusade is not mentioned. Here he ties this metaphor to a totally different political problem: the pope's attitude toward the rebelling citizens of Rome. In this context, however, Bernard does refer to his earlier statement about the distinction the pope is to make in the exercise of both powers that have been entrusted to him:

> You instruct me to feed dragons and scorpions, not sheep, you reply. Therefore, I say, attack them all the more, but with the word, not the sword. Why should you try to usurp the sword anew which you were once commanded to sheath? Nevertheless, the person who denies that the sword is yours seems to me not to listen to the Lord when he says, "Sheathe your sword" (John 8:11). Therefore this sword also is yours and is to be drawn from its sheath at your command, although not by your hand. Otherwise, if that sword in no way belonged to you, the Lord would not have answered, "That is enough" (Luke 22:38), but, "That is too much," when the Apostles said, "Behold, here we have two swords." Both swords, that is, the spiritual and the material, belong to the Church; however, the latter is to be drawn for the Church and the former by the Church. The spiritual sword should be drawn by the hand of the priest; the material sword by the hand of the knight, but clearly at the bidding of the priest and at the command of the emperor. But more of this elsewhere. Now, take the sword which has been entrusted to you to strike with, and for their salvation wound, if not everyone, if not even many, at least whomever you can.[23]

There is a distinct difference between the two explanations of Bernard regarding the papal claims to secular power to be exercised by the princes on his behalf. In a letter in which he asked Pope Eugenius to launch a new crusade, he called the pope's task of seeing to it that others would draw the secular sword in his name inescapable — that is to say, if Eugenius wanted to honor the office of Saint Peter as he ought. But in *De considera-tione* Bernard chose a different point of departure. He advised the pope only to handle the spiritual sword and to leave the secular sword to the soldier, who had to wait not only for a signal from the priest before he would initiate any action, but also for the command of the emperor. The specific task of the emperor in this interaction between the two powers receives considerably more attention in this treatise than in the letter about

---

23. Book IV, c. III, 7; SBO III, 454.

the plans for a new crusade. In any case, it seems that these plans were soon discarded, since the Cistercians did not want to hear about them.[24] With their rejection of this project, they delivered Bernard from the quandary in which he had landed as a result of the decision of the Council of Chartres.

But apart from this latter aspect, a comparison of the two texts, each within its own context, shows how in both cases Bernard based his arguments about the temporal and spiritual power of the pope on concrete situations as they occurred. His main concern in his letter about plans for a new crusade was to win the pope for such a proposition; while the *De consideratione* dealt with problems of a different sort, relating to the position of the pope in his own city. In that case, Bernard counseled the pope to be reluctant to commit troops on his own authority to end the communal reign that Arnold of Brescia had been able to reestablish in Rome.

As mentioned above, already during the papal reign of Pope Lucius II, Arnold of Brescia had established a rival government in Rome. After his election as pope, Eugenius II had been confronted with this problem. Subsequently Emperor Conrad III, at the request of Bernard, had eliminated this popular rule by coming to Rome with his army. Eugenius later pardoned this tribune of the people. But as a result of the pope's extended stay in France, Arnold had been able to reestablish his communal reign. Once again imperial intervention seemed necessary, but according to Bernard's remarks to Eugenius in book IV of the *De consideratione*, this time he deemed it inadvisable for the pope to initiate military action. He would do better to wait for an imperial initiative.

The flattering letter in which Bernard had earlier, in 1146, urged Conrad III to intervene in the city of Rome, gives a clear indication of Bernard's understanding of the appropriate relationship between spiritual and temporal power:

> The crown and the church could not be more sweetly, more cordially, or more closely united and grafted together than in the person of the Lord, since he came to us according to the flesh from the royal and priestly tribes, as both our King and our High Priest. And not only this, but he has also so mingled and combined both these characters in his body, which is the Christian people with himself as their

24. *Chronicon Sigeberti*, cont. premonstratensis, 455: "sed per monacos cistercienses totum cassatur."

head. . . . Therefore what God has joined together let no man put asunder. Let us rather try to concur with the divine plan by uniting ourselves in spirit with those to whom we are united by constitution. Let us cherish each other, defend each other, and carry each other's burdens.

This letter also clarifies that the harmonious relationship between pope and emperor, as suggested by Bernard, did not imply that the emperor could only wait until the pope would give him his orders. In this interaction between the two powers, according to Bernard's thinking at that particular time, the emperor was entrusted with a second, equally important task. The protection of his own crown was a prerequisite for the protection of the church:

> Wherefore I say unto you, gird your sword upon your thigh, most powerful one, and let Caesar restore to himself what is Caesar's and to God what is God's. It is clearly the concern of Caesar both to protect his own crown and to defend the church. The one befits the king; the other the defender of the church.[25]

Considering this difference in tone, which, depending on the circumstances, we detect in Bernard's statements regarding the relationship between temporal and spiritual power, there seems to be insufficient evidence to conclude that Bernard was an unqualified defender of the papal theocracy, as formulated by Gregory VII in his *Dictatus papae*.[26] Thus this portrayal of Bernard remains controversial. The question that remains, however, concerns the correctness of what has been said about Bernard's opinions with regard to the papal claims to authority within the church. How did Bernard use the term *plenitudo potestatis* in that context?

We find this term, with some variations, at least six times in his writings. He did not coin the term, and through the centuries it did not always have the same meaning.[27] During the twelfth century, the concept of *plenitudo potestatis* was often contrasted with that of *pars sollicitudinis* in ecclesiastical circles. This latter term comprised the authority and power of a bishop, who could only claim part of the care: the ecclesiastical

---

25. *Ep.* 244, c. 1; SBO VIII, 135. Transl. James, 394. The letter dates from 1146. Gastaldelli, *Opere* VI/2, 126-129, note 1.

26. Text in Tierney (1964), 49-50. Pacaut (1989), 66.

27. Jacqueline (1975), 205-207.

jurisdiction in a certain region, but always subjected to papal authority. With regard to both terms, Bernard remarks in his *De consideratione* that he used them *iuxta canones tuos;* that is, according to ecclesiastical law.[28]

There is only one passage in Bernard's writings where his description and interpretation of the *plenitudo potestatis,* the fullness of papal power, closely corresponds to the guidelines of the *Dictatus papae,* even though Gregory VII himself did not use the term. Bernard offered that explanation in a letter written to the citizens of Milan in the summer of 1135, after they at last had turned their backs on Anacletus II and had declared their willingness to accept Innocent II as the legitimate pope:

> . . . for the Apostolic See, by a unique privilege, is endowed with a full authority over all the Churches of the world. Anyone who withstands this authority sets his face against the decrees of God. She can, if she judge it expedient, set up new bishops, where, hitherto, there have been none. Of those which already exist she can put down some and raise up others as she thinks best; so that, if she deem it necessary, she can raise bishops to be archbishops or the reverse. She can summon churchmen, no matter how high and mighty they may be, from the ends of the earth and bring them to her presence, not just once or twice, but as often as she sees fit.

But the threat that we notice in Bernard's explication of the full extent of papal power must not be viewed as a solid testimony on his part of his willingness to execute unconditionally all of Gregory's demands. The implicit reference to Gregory's *Dictatus papae* was rather determined by the circumstances under which he wrote this letter: the earlier attitude of the citizens of Milan during the schism of Anacletus. The remaining portion of the letter emphasizes Rome's supremacy over the church in Milan in such a threatening way in an effort to prevent the Milanese from once again becoming disloyal to Innocent II:

> Furthermore she is quick to punish disobedience if anyone should try to oppose her wishes. This you have discovered at your cost. . . . Who was able to stand up for you against the most just severity of the Apostolic See when, provoked by your excess, it determined to deprive you of your ancient privileges and cut off your members? . . . But now, were you to provoke her again, none could save you from far greater

28. Book II, c. VIII; SBO, 424.

penalties. So be careful that you do not suffer a relapse, because, unless I am very mistaken, you would not find a remedy for the consequences so easily. If anyone should advise you to obey in some things but not in others, you should know, since you have experienced once the severity of the Apostolic See, that he is either deceived or a deceiver.[29]

In this explanation of the manner in which the pope could manifest the fullness of his power, Bernard clearly referred to the earlier rebellious attitude of those to whom his remarks were addressed. That he could interpret the *plenitudo potestatis* in a different way is clear from what he states elsewhere in the *De consideratione* about the complaints of the local churches concerning the full scope of papal power, which caused the hierarchical structure of the church to be ignored or even to be trampled upon:

> Do you wonder where this is leading? Are you still unaware of what I wish to say? I will not keep you in suspense any longer; I speak of murmuring complaints of the churches. They cry out that they are being mutilated and dismembered. There are none, or only a few, who do not suffer the pain of this affliction, or live in fear of it. Do you ask what affliction this is? Abbots are released from the jurisdiction of bishops, bishops from that of archbishops, archbishops from that of patriarchs and primates. Does this seem good? I wonder whether this practice can even be excused. In doing this you demonstrate that you have the fullness of power, but perhaps not of justice. You do this because you have the power; but the question is whether you ought to do it. You have been appointed, not to deny, but to preserve the degrees of honor and of dignities and the ranks proper to each, as one of yours says, "Render honor to whom honor is due" (Romans 13:7).[30]

At times Bernard had a personal interest in the circumstances that caused him to appeal to the pope to use this power. In three letters he asked Innocent II, Lucius II, and Innocent III, respectively, to intervene in a conflict on the basis of the fullness of power that was rightfully theirs. He requested, for instance, Innocent II in 1141 to use his special authority to protect the abbot of the Cistercian monastery of Cherlieu against Pierre de Traves, the deacon of Besançon.[31] The two other letters, written during

29. *Ep.* 131, c. 2; SBO VII, 327-328. Transl. James, 208-209.
30. Book III, c. IV, 14; SBO III, 442.
31. *Ep.* 198, c. 2; SBO, 55.

the last quarter of 1143 and in March 1145, belong to the so-called York file. This collection comprises no fewer than twenty-two letters, dictated by Bernard between early 1142 and no later than May 1147. They deal with the appointment of William FitzHerbert as archbishop of York and his consecration on September 26, 1143, three years after the death of Thurstan, the previous archbishop.[32]

Bernard found William FitzHerbert's appointment unacceptable. He argued that it had not been a free choice since William allegedly had acquired his position by money. In reality, Bernard saw this appointment as contrary to the interests of the Cistercians in this archbishopric. For that reason Bernard continued to be opposed to this choice and to object and agitate even after William's consecration, until at last Eugenius III, during his stay in France in May 1147, was prepared belatedly to remove this archbishop.

Bernard had addressed seven letters about this appointment to four consecutive popes: four letters had been sent to Innocent II, Celestine II, and Lucius II respectively;[33] and the three remaining ones to Eugenius III.[34] As indicated, in two of these letters Bernard explicitly referred to the *plenitudo potestatis*. He wrote his letter to Eugenius III in May 1145, repeating his request of two years previously to Lucius II to use his legitimate authority in immediately deposing this unsuitable archbishop.

Bernard's insistence in urging the removal of this archbishop was also related to the appointment of Richard, the abbot of Fountains, as archbishop, and after Richard's death in 1147, of Henry Murdach as his successor. This tenacity suggests that in his opposition to archbishop William, Bernard may also at other occasions have called Pope Eugenius's attention to his papal authority in an attempt to have his way in this matter. In this, however, he succeeded only after he had been in close contact with this pope for over a year and had become intimately involved in papal politics.

This approach of Bernard may have given the impression to his contemporaries that in fact Eugenius allowed him to share in the exercise of the

---

32. *Epp.* 520 and 239; SBO VIII, 480-482 and 120-122. For the York file, see Gastaldelli, *Opere* VI/2, 79, note.

33. *Epp.* 346 and 347 (early 1142); *Ep.* 235 (later in 1142); *Ep.* 520 (early 1145). SBO VIII, 286-289; 108-110; 480-482.

34. *Epp.* 239 and 240 (March 1145); 252 (Feb. 1146–May 1147). SBO VIII, 120-124. In this last letter Bernard maintained that Eugenius would damage his reputation if he refused to depose the archbishop. After the death of his successor, Henry Murdach (October 14, 1153), FitzHerbert was reappointed by Pope Anastasius IV. Baker, "San Bernardo," 134.

fullness of his power. This may explain why Arnold of Bonneval, in the second book of the *vita prima,* which he wrote in 1148, used this expression in his description of the role Bernard played in convening the Council of Pisa in 1135:

> During all this time the holy abbot attended the meetings, the discussions and decisions. All expressed their respect and besieged his door. The commotation, rather than any ceremonial, prevented people from reaching him. As soon as some departed, others entered; it seemed as if the humble man, who did not attribute any of that honor to himself, did not share in the *sollicitudo,* but rather in the *plenitudo potestatis.*[35]

On the other hand, Bernard disapproved of others who in Rome attempted to influence the pope for their own ends. This is apparent in some passages in the third book of the *De consideratione.* In one of the passages, cited above, he explicitly used the term *plenitudo potestatis.* But another passage, in which he did not explicitly employ the term, contains an even stronger indication that Bernard was aware of the disadvantages of the exercise of this power by the Curia for local churches:

> Can you be of the opinion that it is lawful for you to cut off the churches from their members, to confuse the order of things, to disturb the boundaries which your predecessors have set? If the role of justice is to preserve for each what is his, how can it befit a just man to take from each what belongs to him? You are wrong if you think your apostolic power, which is supreme, is the only power instituted by God. If you think this, you disagree with him who says, "There is no power except from God." Equally, what follows, "Who resists the power, resists the ordinance of God." Even though this is principally on your behalf, it is not solely on your behalf. The same one also says, "Let every soul be subjected to higher powers" (Romans 13:1-2). He does not say "to a higher power" as if in one person, but "to higher powers" as if in many. Therefore, yours is not the only power from God; there are intermediary and lesser ones. And just as those whom God has joined together must not be separated, so those whom God has made subordinate must not be made equal.
>
> You create a monster if you remove a finger from a hand and make it hang from a head, above the hand and on a level with the

---

35. Vp II, c. I, 8; P.L., CLXXXV, 273C.

arm. So it is in the body of Christ if you put members in places other than where he arranged them. Unless you think it was another who placed "some in the church as apostles, some as prophets, others as evangelists, others as teachers and pastors, for the perfection of the saints, for the work in the ministry to build up the body of Christ" (Ephesians 4:16). . . . You should not think this form is to be despised because it is on earth; it has an example in heaven. For the Son cannot do anything unless he sees the Father doing it; especially since it was said to him under the name of Moses, "See that you make everything according to the pattern which was shown to you on the mountain" (Hebrews 8:5).[36]

Among other things, Bernard pleaded in this text that the unique responsibility of the bishop in the church be respected. He attributed great importance to the episcopal duties, and in his letters to Eugenius III he repeatedly supported the interests and rights of individual bishops. His letter to Hughes, the cardinal-bishop of Ostia and former abbot of Trois-Fontaines, is also remarkable. Therein he complains about the conduct of the cardinal-legate Jordanus, who unashamedly abused his position to enrich himself at the expense of local churches.[37] Considering further the ample attention Bernard gives in the fourth book of the *De consideratione* to the misconduct of members of the Curia against bishops,[38] it becomes clear that we can inaccurately picture Bernhard as an unconditional supporter of the Gregorian ideology of a papal theocracy by simply pointing at his statements of approval regarding the *plenitudo potestatis*. He agreed with its philosophy, and at times it suited him, but we must also underline that he repeatedly criticized it because of the abuses that resulted from it.

Therefore, with respect to the ecclesio-political statements of Bernard — regardless of his stubbornness — we must always look at the moment when, and the place from which, he made these statements. Moreover, when Bernard was still alive, the Cistercian Order did not yet show any interest in exemption privileges that would remove its monasteries from episcopal jurisdiction and place them directly under the authority of the pope[39] — a strategy that always found approval with Ber-

---

36. Book III, c. IV, 15. SBO III, 444-445.
37. *Ep.* 290; SBO VIII, 207. Gastaldelli, *Opere* VI/2, 266-268, note 1.
38. Book IV, c. IV,9–V,16; SBO III, 455-481.
39. *Cluny et Cîteaux* (1985), 38-39 and 61-62, notes 72, 73.

nard. But in spite of all this evidence, many are still inclined to accept this portrayal of Bernard as the ideologist of papal theocracy. This may be the result of the fact that, since the days of the Enlightenment, many prefer to characterize Bernard as a narrow-minded fanatic — a view that, at the time, was defended by men like Pierre Bayle and Friedrich Schiller. Their caricature of Bernard fits the image of an intransigent, overzealous propagandist of the medieval theology of a papal theocracy.

As far as I know, this portrait of Bernard has nowhere been presented in a more exaggerated manner than in a study by two well-known medievalists at the former Karl Marx University in Leipzig. They maintain that in the 1140s Bernard served as the leader of an ecclesio-political group, of which the Cistercians constituted the hard core. According to these historians, their program comprised the following repressive points:

1. Superiority of the church over the state, according to the doctrine of the two swords.
2. Maintaining the educational monopoly of the church by rejecting the rational theology and lay schools in the cities.
3. Reconquering the Holy Land with the assistance of the orders of knights.
4. Resisting the communal movements in the cities and stabilizing the episcopal rule in urban centers.
5. Eliminating all heretics.
6. Subjecting the Greek church to the primacy of Rome with the intention of conquering Constantinople.[40]

I want to make just two remarks regarding this ambitious program that Bernard and his order supposedly supported and promoted: First, this program with all its ramifications was not yet relevant during Bernard's life, certainly not in France. Secondly, Bernard's involvement with ecclesio-political matters was far less consistent than would have been necessary for the execution of such an ideological program. For that reason, the motivation for Bernard's ecclesio-political activities must be sought elsewhere. This topic is reserved for the final section of the next chapter.

40. Werner and Erbstösser (1986), 222-223.

2. THE HAGIOGRAPHIC TRADITION AND THE "ENLIGHTENED" RESISTANCE AGAINST IT

AFTER HIS CANONIZATION, when his liturgical cult gradually found acceptance beyond Cistercian circles, the story of Bernard as a human being became increasingly concealed behind his carefully constructed saintly image.[41] Due to popular preaching, Bernard's sainthood soon gained in popularity, in particular with illiterate laypeople. This is clear from *exempla*-collections of that time. These story collections for use by preachers to edify their audiences gave much more exposure to Bernard — that is, to his statements and to the miracles attributed to him — than to any other saint.[42] Of no other medieval saint were more miracle stories in circulation than of Bernard.[43]

These stories also gained in popularity through the *legendaria,* which listed the *lives* of saints in a more concise manner, following the church calendar. These were an important part of the literature for preachers, a fact that has often been overlooked in studies of medieval *exempla*. Anecdotal accounts included in these *legendaria* have often, as a result of popular preaching, increased the popularity of many saints. In particular, this is clear from the *Legenda aurea* by James de Voragine, completed about 1260. Thus in the late Middle Ages, Bernard also developed into a popular saint,[44] even though very few people had the opportunity to visit his tomb.

Not everybody at the time, however, was happy with Bernard's popularity. This we learn, for example, from the satire an Englishman, Walter Map, wrote toward the end of the twelfth century in his *De nugis curialium: Courties' Trifles* — about miracles Bernard had intended to perform when he was still alive, but that had been failures.[45] However, Map's parody of the miracle stories that were in circulation remains an exception. We find, for instance, even in the writings of Giraldus Cambrensis (1146-1223), a prolific writer who was a close friend of Walter Map and shared Map's disgust for the Cistercians, a few stories in *exempla* form about

---

41. "San Bernardo: Correlazione" (1975), 23-48.
42. Leclercq, "The Image of Saint Bernard . . ." (1979), 291-302.
43. Sigal (1985), 18-20.
44. McGuire, "A Saint's Afterlife. Bernard in the Golden Legende" (1994), 197-211.
45. Walter Map, *De nugis Curialium: Courties' Trifles,* dist. 1, c. 24, ed. by M. R. James, revised by C. N. L. Brooke and R. A. B. Meyers (Oxford, 1983), 73-80. For the probable reason for Map's negative opinion of Bernard, see Türk (1977), 158-160.

Bernard's miraculous powers. Moreover, he was also willing to praise other aspects of the activities of this abbot.[46]

But most of all, Bernard was renowned for his writings. The history of their textual transmission indicates a growing interest in his works during the late Middle Ages.[47] A totally different kind of indication of the appreciation for Bernard as a mystical writer is the thirty-first song of Dante's *Paradiso*. In this song the poet is first accompanied in the hereafter of the blessed by Beatrice; but because of God's nearness, he is further escorted by Bernard.[48] This growing appreciation is also seen in the increasing number of translations that were beginning to circulate. The title *doctor mellifluus* — 'honey-sweet teacher' — which he acquired at an early stage, also reflects his reputation as spiritual author.[49]

The edifying merit attributed to his writings is also quite apparent from a remark in the chronicle of Saint Albans: In 1423 John Whetamstede, the abbot of that monastery, known for his interest in humanist studies, became seriously ill during a journey to Rome. The chronicler tells us that the abbot did not recover until Bernard had appeared to him in a dream, and had made him promise to read and distribute no other writings than his.[50] Yet the interest for these writings in medieval times was not limited to those who were literate. Often stories about Bernard were visualized. This was the case, for instance, with the popular story of Bernard's objec-

---

46. For his agreement with Walter Map's opinions, see Giraldus Cambrensis, *Speculum Ecclesiae*, lib. I, c. III, 14; *Opera Omnia* (ed. J.-S. Webster), R.S. 21/4 (1873), 219-225. For the *exempla*, idem, *De Rebus a se Gestis*, lib. II, c. XVIII; R.S. 21/1 (1861), 76; idem, *Gemma Ecclesiastica*, lib. I, c. LI and LIII; lib. II, c. XI; R.S. 21/2 (1862), 152, 160, and 222. Cf. de Ghellinck (1955), 135-145; Türk (1977), 207, and Bartlett (1982).

47. Constable, "The Popularity of Twelfth-Century Spiritual Writers," 5-28. Idem, "Twelfth-Century Spirituality," 27-60.

48. Botterill (1994); Masseron (1953).

49. This name is inspired by Joel 3:18: "And in that day the mountains shall drip with sweet wine, and the hills shall flow with milk, and all the stream beds of Judah shall flow with water." Peter the Venerable cited this text in a letter to Bernard, in reference to the way in which Bernard had replied to an earlier letter from him; *Ep.* 149; *Letters* I, 364-365. Hugh Metellus paraphrased this compliment in a letter to Bernard; *Ep.* 479; *Inter epp. S. Bernardi;* P.L., CLXXXII, 687, 688. Bernard cited this text twice in full: in *Ep.* 106 (SBO VII, 267, lines 2-3) and in *Sermo* I, I, *Super missus est* (SBO IV, 14, lines 8-9). There he also used (line 15) the word *mellifluus* in connection with the eloquence of the evangelist Luke. This is a sermon that is often read. "Bernard and the Historians" (1977), 29, note 9.

50. *John Amandesham, Annales monasterii S. Albani,* ed. by H. Riley, R.S., 28/1 (1870), 151. Constable, "The Popularity . . . ," 17-18.

tion against the feast of Mary's Immaculate Conception in a letter to the canons of Lyon. The story relates how for that reason he had appeared once in a vision with a dark stain on his white hood.[51]

A. The Reception of the *Vita Prima*

Our discussion has shown that during the first centuries after Bernard's death there was hardly any demand for a historically correct portrayal of Bernard that would do justice to circumstances of time and place. The historical information in the *vita prima* remained adequate as long as no essential distinction was made between his cultic and his historical image. The text of this extensive *vita* must frequently have been copied in the late Middle Ages, considering the rather substantial number of copies that have been preserved, in spite of the many manuscripts that must have been lost through fire, or during the looting and destruction of monasteries in the period of the wars of religion, or as a result of their continuous moving about in the days of the commendatory abbots, and, finally, because of the confiscations of monasteries during the French Revolution. In any case, this is true of the Latin text. Translations of this *vita* were considerably less widespread; and, remarkably enough, they were absent in convents of nuns, where usually little or no Latin was read.[52]

The late-medieval copyists who duplicated the text must have been totally unaware of the existence of two editions or redactions of this *vita*. This is probably true of most of those who copied the text of the *Life* at the end of the twelfth century and in the early part of the thirteenth

---

51. "Bernard and the Historians" (1977), 30, with note 13. R. M. Dessi and M. Lamy, "Saint Bernard et les controverses Mariales au moyen âge," I and II, *Cîteaux* 42 (1991). The concept of Mary's Immaculate Conception was quite generally taught in the late Middle Ages. It was accepted as a dogma during the Council of Basel. The decisions of this council were, however, not accepted by Rome; and the official promulgation of this dogma did not take place until 1854.

52. A monk from Clairvaux translated the Vp into French in 1396; at least two copies of this translation are extant: BNF, no. 917 and "Nouvelle acquisition," 1079. The remaining mss that have been preserved in Clairvaux offer an abbreviated translation: NBF, nos. 13496, 22962, and 25665. BNF, 2465 is a revised version of the Vp, produced in the 17th century for a young nun. In this ms the chastity temptations are missing, but some stories about Bernard's obedience as a novice to his superiors are added. This seems to indicate that the integral text of the Vp was not deemed suitable for monials. For printed 16th-century translations, see Janauscheck (1891), nos. 428, 429, and 636. For abbreviated translations, based on the Vp: nos. 222, 332, and 391.

century. Only a few manuscripts have a kind of intermediate redaction, which, however, is not based on the manuscript from Anchin.[53]

It is therefore hardly amazing that we find, almost without exception, the same version of the text in the approximately fifty editions of the Latin text of the *vita prima* that were printed before 1641. In all but two of these, we also find the writings of Bernard himself; the text of the *vita prima* was simply added to these. Since these editions are related — before 1550 they appeared only in France — we may expect that the text of the *vita* that most publishers copied from colleagues follows the same redaction. It is hardly unexpected that they follow redaction B, since this is also the version we find in most of the manuscripts originating from France.

The oldest printed edition of the *vita* dates from about 1480. It appeared in Italy and was produced by the Milanese humanist Boninus Mombritius. He included this *vita* in a book of all *lives* of saints according to the church calendar — a *legendarium* that published the original *vitae* of the respective saints in full. Mombitrius himself called his work a *sanctuarium*.[54] It is improbable that he would have investigated whether there existed any other versions of the *vitae* that were included in his work, and he was most likely unaware of the fact that the text of the *vita prima* that he published followed redaction B. Also in Italy this was the most current version.

The only other printed edition of this *vita* before 1641, which follows redaction A, is part of another hagiographic collection: the four-volume series of *lives* of saints, published in Cologne by the Carthusian Laurentius Surius between 1570 and 1575, entitled *De probatis sanctorum historiis*, and subsequently reprinted at least twice.[55]

It is not strange that this publication followed redaction A since this redaction of the *vita prima* was most widely distributed in Germany and Austria. In these countries the Morimond monastery in particular contributed to the growth of the Cistercian Order.[56] Surius's choice of redaction A may lead us to conclude

---

53. *Etudes* (1960), 19.

54. *Sanctuarium seu vitae sanctorum*, 2 vols. (Milan, ca. 1480). Vp in vol. I, fol. 96 recto to 140 verso (in reprint, Paris, 1910).

55. In the third ed. of 1618 the title was: *De probatis sanctorum vitis*. Vp in III, 197-243.

56. For the selective distribution of the Vp mss in the "Morimond region," see *Etudes* (1960), 63-68.

further that the printed editions of Bernard's works, to which almost invariably the text of the *vita prima* was added, were not yet distributed very widely. For if Surius had availed himself of one of those printed editions for his publication, he would also have followed redaction B. That Bernard's writings were only available in a limited region is also apparent from the names of the cities where his writings, and thus also the *vita prima,* had already appeared in print. The first edition of the *Opera sancti Bernardi* (or: *divi Bernardi*) was published in Paris in 1508 and was reprinted there four times: in 1513, 1517, 1520, and 1527. In 1515 this publication also appeared in Lyon, with reprints in 1520, 1538, and 1546. The earliest editions were printed only in these two cities. They did not appear elsewhere before around 1550: from that year onward Bernard's works were printed in Venice, from 1552 in Basel, from 1576 in Antwerp, and only from 1620 in Cologne.

As mentioned above, almost all the editions of the writings of Bernard prior to 1641 also included the *vita prima*. At first this text was found in the same place as it had been given in some of the manuscripts: at the end, after the *vita* of Archbishop Malachias. The text of the *vita prima* is absent only in the two oldest editions from Paris.

The role of the Cistercians in these publications was at first rather limited. They were mostly the initiative of humanists and theologians, the so-called *theodidacti*. The edition of 1508 was prepared by magister Andreas Bocardus, who is presented on the title page as an extremely learned individual. It was printed by Jehan Petit (Johannes parvus), who as "bibliopola" assumed the responsibility for the costs. The title page further informs the reader that this edition of the angelic writings *(seraphica scripta)* of Bernard was based on the manuscripts from Clairvaux. These allegedly had been improved by some monks of this monastery to help the reader more easily distinguish between Bernard's writings and those that were incorrectly attributed to him.

This acclaim for the *"editio seraphica"* is rather dubious. Andreas Bocardus probably did little else than copying or making arrangements for the copying of manuscripts, which, at his request, had been made available to him in Clairvaux. That this was initially done without much care or expertise is apparent from the fact that the *vita prima* is missing, while the *vita secunda* has been included. In the reprints published in Lyon, this was immediately exchanged for the *vita prima*, but the *vita secunda* was still maintained in the first Parisian reprint, in 1513. In all other editions of the *Opera Bernardi*, the text of the *vita prima* was, however, included.

The Clairvaux community was not really satisfied with the so-called *editio seraphica,* in spite of the replacement of the *vita secunda* with the *vita prima.* Thus in 1520 a new edition appeared in Lyon, prepared by two monks from this abbey. This was already reprinted, also in Lyon, in 1530. In both of these editions the *vita secunda* was incorporated. The *editio seraphica* also lost its popularity in Paris; the new text edition of the two monks from Clairvaux, in the meantime revised by Franciscus Comestor, was reprinted there between 1536 and 1545 no less than four times. But in these cases the *vita secunda* was omitted. After that there appeared to be little interest in that document. Not until 1667, when the first edition of Jean Mabillon appeared, was this *vita* again added to the *opera Bernardi.*

New publications of the edition of Comestor, most of which appeared in Paris, were usually prepared by university theologians. They added a few more texts, found in an unidentified manuscript that was in the possession of the Sorbonne. Nonetheless, the name of Comestor remained on the title page as the official publisher. Only from 1572 onward did reprints of this edition carry the name of Johannes Gillotius, since he had added new commentaries. This version also contained improvements and additions based on the newly printed edition of Johannes Hervagius, published in Basel in 1552.

We do not know, even approximately, how many of these *vita*-manuscripts were sacrificed in the preparation of these early editions. But there is no doubt that a number of these manuscripts were lost in the process. The humanists of those days felt there was no need to preserve the manuscripts they had utilized for their text editions. For many of them, their only further use was to utilize the parchment for repairing book covers, and to heat it so that it would yield glue, which could then be used for gluing folios together.

When we survey all the editions of Bernard's works that appeared before 1600 and that also include the *vita prima,* we must conclude that these (at least) thirty-six editions offer at the most six to eight different versions. Moreover, most of them are based on manuscripts originating in Clairvaux. From the seventeenth century onward, other manuscripts were preferred as the basis for new text editions. Also from that time onward, more manuscripts were consulted and manuscripts were more carefully compared when text editions were prepared.

The first person to use this method was the Cistercian Edmundus Lancelot Tiraqueus. He also based his edition of 1601 on manuscripts from Cîteaux, where he himself had entered as monk. His work became somewhat of a standard text, since the other printings of the writings of Bernard that appeared between 1600 and 1643 were all based on it. The differences between these various editions are mainly limited to the annotations and commentaries that were subsequently added by Johannes Picardus. For that reason his name was mentioned after 1609 on the title page.[57]

A second difference between these editions and those from the sixteenth century concerned the increased amount of space that was later devoted to the hagiographic texts about Bernard. In addition to the *vita prima,* some other texts were incorporated under the caption of *miracula.* The new title of the collected writings became: "Books about miraculous matters, performed by Bernard before and after his death,"[58] and included miracle stories written down before the end of the twelfth century. These *miracula* were in part derived from Conrad of Eberbach's *Exordium magnum.* In part they also comprised the miracles Bernard allegedly performed when he promoted the crusade in Germany, which from the twelfth century onward were added to some *vita*-manuscripts as a *liber sextus,* a sixth book.

This addition of *miracula* received even more attention in the new edition of Bernard's works published in 1641 in Cologne by Jacob Merlo Horstius. Until recently all subsequent editions of Bernard's writings were based on his work, and this continues to be the case for the *vita prima.* Horstius, a scholar from the northern part of Dutch Limburg, worked in Cologne as priest. This fact may possibly explain why in his edition he gave a different place than had been customary to the hagiographic writings about Bernard. He did not view these as an appendix to Bernard's writings, but rather as an introduction, which could be of importance for the readers of these writings. He therefore placed the *vita prima* at the beginning of his edition.

Horstius added the other miracle stories about Bernard to the *vita prima* as a sixth and a seventh book. For the sixth book, he used — as mentioned earlier — the *vita*-manuscripts in which the account of Bernard's journey to Rhineland had already been incorporated as *liber sextus.* But he also included in this sixth book an account of Bernard's journey to the south of France in 1145, to counter the influence of Henry of Lausanne, the popular preacher who had been condemned as a heretic.[59]

---

57. The last edition of Picardus appeared in 1642. For the authors of the various editions, see Clémencet, *Histoire littéraire* (1773), 390-395. Janauschek (1891), xvi-xix and 496.

58. *Mirabilium rerum a sancto Bernardo ante et post mortem gestarum.* The pagination in these editions is usually 2275-2306.

59. Above, 25, with note 5. "Studien" (1958), 331-343. "Henri de Lausanne" (1983), 108-123.

Horstius himself introduced the title "seventh book" for the remaining *miracula.* Later Jean Mabillon, in his editions of the *opera Bernardi,* also presented the text of the *vita prima* in seven books, with the same title as in Horstius's edition: *Sancti Bernardi abbatis vita et res gesta, libris septem comprehens.*[60]

Horstius based his text edition of the *vita prima* on more than one manuscript. The reason for this may have been that he knew the text of the *vita* from the edition by Surius as well as from one of the editions of the *opera divi Bernardi,* probably the one that appeared in Cologne in 1620. In comparing these editions, he must have noticed a number of textual differences, without, however, tracing their sources. But he deemed the differences too important simply to ignore them in his own text edition, the more so when he found the same textual variations that he had detected in Surius's edition in at least one and possibly more manuscripts originating from his own region. From the manuscripts and editions he consulted, he could only conclude that both redactions had existed from early times. He therefore felt he could not just follow the text of one of the two redactions as had been done in earlier editions.

Horstius solved this textual problem by using the shorter version, redaction B, as his basis, with additions from the longer version. He placed these additions between square brackets. Since this method did not make clear what were the essential differences between the two redactions, this did not really help the reader very much. Moreover, this indication of textual variations was not consistent. Horstius did not add all passages that he had found in Surius's edition, nor did he mention which version he followed in his own edition where the redactions differed. Thus the relationship between the two versions and their relative age remained unclear.

After 1641 Horstius had intended to work on another improved edition, but his death in 1644 prevented this. Thus we still have to depend on his arbitrary edition of this *vita,* which saw a rapid distribution. A first reprint of Horstius's work appeared as early as 1642, and in France at least five reprints followed. The first of these reprints, which appeared in Paris in 1667, coincided with the publication of the first Bernard edition by Jean Mabillon.

Mabillon's new text edition formed part of the ambitious project undertaken by the congregation of Saint-Maur to promote the writings of Christian authors from

---

60. "The life and works of the holy father Bernard of Clairvaux, collected in seven books."

the early centuries and the Middle Ages. This French Benedictine congregation, established shortly before 1620, counted six research monasteries, of which Saint Germain-des-Prés in Paris became the best known. At least forty scholars of Saint-Maur were entrusted with the task of preparing reliable editions of these writings. For that purpose they collected manuscripts from the monasteries of their congregation in order to compare the different copies of texts of a particular author.[61]

Naturally, the Maurists were also interested in the writings of Bernard. When Horstius's edition appeared, one of them, Dom Claude Chantelou, compared it with manuscripts he had at his disposal. In doing so, he detected so many textual variations that he felt it would be necessary to prepare a new, corrected edition of Bernard's writings. After Chantelou's death in 1664, his coworker, Dom Jean Mabillon, completed his work, which — as indicated above — appeared in Paris in 1667.[62] On the title page Mabillon referred to Horstius's edition, which he had improved and to which he had added certain passages after comparing this edition with other manuscripts.

Thus, Mabillon's edition also included the *vita prima* — not, however, as an introduction to the writings of Bernard, but rather as an addendum at the end. At the beginning of his text — that is, of his edition of 1667 — Mabillon placed the text of the *vita* written by Alanus of Auxerre, known as the *vita secunda,* a text also found in three sixteenth-century editions.

Mabillon spent only little effort in comparing textual variants of the *vita prima,* in any case with regard to Horstius's edition. Mabillon incorporated Horstius's text with all its additions, mentioning in the margin some notes about variants he had encountered in manuscripts he had at his disposal in Saint German-des-Prés; manuscripts from French monasteries that all followed redaction B.

Even in his definitive edition of the *opera Bernardi,* first published by Mabillon in 1690, he similarly based his *vita prima* on Horstius's work. With regard to the hagiographic *finale* of his work, there is some difference between the two editions of Mabillon. In the 1690 edition the *vita secunda* followed the *vita prima* (which still consisted of seven books). After these he included a *vita tertia* and a *vita quarta.*[63]

This revised edition of Mabillon saw many reprints. His hagiographic capstone was accepted by the Bollandists for their *Acta Sanctorum* without further changes. This publication paid no attention to new textual variants and added

61. Knowles, *Great Historical Enterprises,* 33-62.
62. Clémencet (1773), 396-397.
63. For these *vitae,* see above, 25, note 4.

only some explanatory comments to the text. In the last edition of the *opera Bernardi*, prepared by Jean Leclercq and Henri Rochais, and in its later reprints, the hagiographic texts about Bernard were no longer included. Consequently, as far as the *vita prima* is concerned, we must still make do with the text prepared by Horstius and Mabillon, which is most readily accessible in its presentation of 1860 in J. P. Migne's *Patrologia Latina*. Migne's edition, in fact, added even further to the confusion concerning the text of the *vita prima*. The marginal notes in which Mabillon listed the textual variants he had found in his comparison of manuscripts were now inserted in the text itself and also placed between square brackets.

After Horstius and Mabillon, no one had the courage and persistence to prepare a new edition of the text of the *vita prima*. But the attempts that were made did help to give a glimpse of the complexity of both textual redactions. Ludwig Bethmann, one of the early editors of the prestigious series of sources — *Monumenta Germaniae Historica* — made a start after beginning his employment in 1837. He began his search in several libraries, where he discovered a dozen manuscripts, which he described. After his early death, his work was continued by George Waitz, one of the major figures in this *Forschungsgesellschaft*. This resulted in a fragmented edition of the *vita*[64] — a method of publishing the *Monumenta* often followed at the time.

Waitz had also encountered both redactions in other manuscripts, which enabled him more clearly to distinguish between redaction A and B. This further enabled him to adduce reasons why redaction B must have been of later date, without, however, discovering when and why this later redaction was produced. He did conclude that an earlier version had preceded the fifth book of redaction A, written by one of Bernard's friends as an account of the last year of his life. Waitz especially emphasized the "sixth book" of the *vita*, the text of which he published almost in full. However, he did not in this edition clarify the relationship between this sixth book and the other books. Waitz also failed to notice that there existed an older version of some of the passages of this sixth book, even though he did have access to the manuscript of this older version.[65]

With regard to the text of the actual *vita*, Waitz may have limited himself to a number of shorter fragments, since work was in progress elsewhere

64. MGH, SS XXVI, 91-142.
65. Ms Douai, 372, vol. II, from Anchin. "Studien" (1958).

on an integral edition of the *life* of Bernard. George Hüffer, a private teacher in Münster, was engaged in this project. In 1884 and 1885 he published three articles in which he reported on his research, which concerned a search not only for extant manuscripts of the different Bernard *vitae,* but also for manuscripts of letters from Bernard, which until then had not been found. When Hüffer published the results of his study in 1886 in a book, it became clear that he had not undertaken his journeys in preparation of a new edition of the text of these *vitae,* but rather as a preliminary study for a new biography of Bernard, which, however, remained unfinished, or, in any case, unpublished.[66]

Nevertheless, Hüffer's preliminary study proved to be very useful, even though it did not provide full insight into the complexity of the history of the origin of the *vita prima,* and in spite of the fact that the information he provided was inadequate to serve as the basis for a new text edition. But Hüffer did point out that Geoffrey of Auxerre at the time revised the full text. He believed that Geoffrey undertook this revision in order to give a more complete portrayal of Bernard, and to make some stylistic and material improvements. But since Hüffer did not fully report on the results of his comparisons of different texts, he could not be specific enough in his account of his findings. He also ignored the relationship that existed between Geoffrey's textual revision and Bernard's eventual canonization. We should remember, however, that in those days any comparison of widely dispersed manuscripts was extremely difficult, and that almost nothing was known about the canonization procedures that had developed in the twelfth century. Hüffer also gave but scant attention to the other hagiographic texts.

Hüffer's work was appreciated by many, in particular by Vacandard, who had already published a few monographs in preparation for his biography of Bernard. Vacandard devoted a subsequent detailed study to a survey of the main results of Hüffer's research.[67] Among other things, Vacandard remarked that someone who wanted to prepare a full and impeccable edition of the different *vitae* had only to retrace Hüffer's steps.

This conclusion has been proven to be quite wrong. In fact, the question arises whether Vacandard did not too easily accept that Hüffer had given definitive answers to questions that he himself — as Bernard's biographer — should have

---

66. Hüffer (1886). Idem, "Handschriftliche Studien," H.J. 5 (1884), 576-624; 6 (1885), 31-91 and 232-270.
67. "L'histoire de saint Bernard. Critique des Sources," 337-389.

posed, and that he therefore did not need to examine the sources any further. His judgment is too uncritically positive to be accepted as totally unbiased.

In this article, Vacandard focused in particular on the *vita prima,* and pointed to the *Fragmenta Gaufridi* as the "source" for the *vita.* He also gave considerable attention to the date of the second redaction, which, following Hüffer, he established as between 1162 and 1165. Furthermore, he dealt with the nature of Geoffrey's corrections, which he believed mostly related to supernatural events related in the *vita,* in particular to predictions. These textual corrections caused him to conclude that Geoffrey had attempted to lend extra weight to this document as a testimony about Bernard. By eliminating a few remarks, Geoffrey supposedly tried to emphasize more strongly the authenticity of what was said about supernatural matters. This conclusion of Vacandard presupposes that some contemporary readers of the *vita* would already have had the ambition to compare both redactions — an untenable idea.

Like Hüffer, Vacandard fully accepted the credibility of the miracles reported in the *vita prima.* This was, in particular, true of the miracles described in the sixth book, even though only a minor portion was repeated in the actual *vita.* But the discussions about such questions, which at the time were very controversial, led them astray as far as textual criticism was concerned. The main weakness of both authors was that they were unable to do very much with the data they had been able to collect from the manuscripts. For Vacandard also failed to discover that this *vita* was written for the purpose of obtaining the canonization of Bernard, and that the sixth book had been composed precisely in the preparation of the *vita* that was to serve that specific purpose. This failure of Vacandard is the more significant when we notice how in the review of Hüffer's book he evaluates the difference between the historical-biographical value of this *vita* and of the other hagiographic writings about Bernard:

> There is no doubt that his biographers regarded Bernard as a saint. Moreover, his supernatural works must be viewed as signs of his sainthood. It should therefore not amaze us, that they wanted to bestow on their hero not only all the prestige that went with the pursuit of virtue, but also the prestige that went with the status of a miracle worker. We should not suggest that this was a vicious circle, which originated in the minds of over-enthusiastic persons, who conspired to mislead themselves and others. If I may say it in this way: Bernard's disciples just focused on what would ensure the canonization of their master. It was much later that (other) disciples conceived of the idea

to make a written collection of the miraculous events they had witnessed, primarily to edify later generations, rather than their contemporaries.[68]

This quotation does not indicate that Vacandard saw any direct relationship between Bernard's official canonization, which demanded considerable preparation, and his hagiography; as a matter of fact, he believed that the *vita prima* had nothing to do with that canonization. He therefore viewed this *life* as a reliable source, certainly in its second version. However, he presented a slightly different opinion in his *Critique des documents,* which in 1895 introduced his *Vie de saint Bernard.* He then saw a connection between the canonization of Bernard and the *vita secunda,* which he correctly regarded as a censored, abbreviated revision of the *vita prima.* He commented:

> No doubt a legitimate purpose, but less favorable for the impartiality of the historian, whose only aim must be to proclaim the whole truth. The author of the *vita secunda* has concealed the deficiencies, or things that should be viewed as such, in his hero. Some years later there would be other authors who would be prepared to attribute powers to their hero which in fact he did not possess or, at least, to attribute works to him which he did not perform. Bernard supposedly had at that time already been canonized, but this well deserved honor also brought him praise which he did not deserve. His life story, intended for use in the liturgy of the church, was to be falsified and deformed, due to the perspective of some admirers; and before the end of the twelfth century this life story would end up in the domain of legends.[69]

Vacandard believed that when the *vita prima* was written there was not yet any legendarizing approach to Bernard's life — in any case, not on the part of the authors of this *vita.* They had written Bernard's life story, as could be expected of historians, and only for that reason had one of them subsequently rewritten its text. But would Vacandard, if he had known that this first revision had been undertaken when the pope had rejected the first request for Bernard's canonization, have been just as negative about the *vita prima* as he was about the *vita secunda?*

---

68. Ibid., 364-365.
69. *Vie de S. Bernard,* I, p. XLIII.

This is difficult to imagine, since Vacandard also belonged to those who unconditionally accepted Bernard's sainthood. Had he been aware of this, he would
probably have concluded only that this initial rejection must have been due to a
too human, historical portrayal of Bernard in this *vita;* this can be said with some
justification when it is compared with the *vita secunda.* But in that case, it would
have remained difficult for Vacandard subsequently to characterize the textual
revision that resulted in redaction B as a mere touching up, which Geoffrey at
some later stage in his life had done, since in the meantime he had developed a
more critical disposition and more respect for historical accuracy.

The positive opinion of Vacandard regarding the nature of the text revision
by Geoffrey of Auxerre and his reasons for undertaking it remained widely
accepted for a long time, since no one felt the need to verify it. It was
repeated as recently as in 1953, the year in which the eighth centennial of
Bernard's death was commemorated.[70] Due to the authority that continued to be attributed to Vacandard's statements about Bernard, cult and
history appeared difficult to separate even in the twentieth century, although Vacandard himself made a modest attempt to do so.

B. Reformation, Enlightenment, Romanticism, and Restauration

One of the consequences of the fragmentation of Latin Christianity in the
sixteenth century was that the evaluation by historians of the previous period,
when Rome's authority extended over all of Europe, would henceforth to a
large extent be determined by their attitude toward the religious controversies
that then developed, and which in turn would largely depend on the camp to
which they belonged. This leads us to ask what repercussions this new
situation had for the way in which Bernard was viewed in Reformation circles.

We notice, first of all, that the early Reformation in its protest and
resistance against Rome sometimes appealed to Bernard. This was, in particular, true of Luther. Already as monk in the monastery of the Augustinian
Observantists in Erfurt, he had been acquainted with the writings and
thinking of Bernard. Luther saw his theology and spirituality confirmed in
several aspects by Bernard. He found this same confirmation from Bernard

---

70. Aigran (1953), 311: ". . . l'âge venant, son sens critique s'affinait, et dans la
recension qu'il a donnée de l'oeuvre commune il retouche ses fragments en vue d'une
exactitude de plus en plus scrupuleuse, exemple assez rare au moyen âge et d'autant plus
digne d'être salué."

in his abhorrence for the scholastic method and in his devotion to the suffering Christ. He had inherited both of these inclinations from the *devotio moderna* of the fifteenth century. Likewise, Luther appealed to Bernard with regard to his opinion on repentance and in his rejection of free will. But in this respect, he became more careful when his opponents also claimed to find support for their views in Bernard's writings.[71]

Luther felt some kinship with Bernard in yet another area. In an open letter that he sent, in 1520, to Leo X, together with his treatise "About the freedom of a Christian," he twice advised the pope to read Bernard's *De consideratione.* He said that Bernard's example also gave him the boldness to write in this brotherly fashion to the pope. Although Luther rejected monastic vows, since the making of these vows was based on the idea that man must earn his salvation by works, he was willing to make an exception for Bernard, since he had lived according to the gospel. Moreover, in his preaching, Bernard to a major extent had tried also to address the world at large, outside the monastery.

After he had left the Roman Church, Luther gradually distanced himself more from Bernard, but he continued to read his writings and referred to him in his own works more than five hundred times. He counted Bernard among those who shared his belief that the Scriptures are the only source of revelation. In this connection Luther quoted what William of Saint-Thierry had said in the *vita prima* about the meticulous way in which Bernard studied the Scriptures. Luther emphasized that Bernard knew the Bible especially through meditation. But Luther condemned Bernard's allegorical method of interpretation, as well as his devotion to Mary and his excessive asceticism, which undermined his health.

This frequent criticism of Luther must, however, be viewed in the context in which he stated it; that is, against the background of the concrete problem about which his opinion was asked. In this respect we could even speak of a remarkable resemblance between Luther and Bernard.

Luther is no exception among the early pioneers of the Reformation in his mostly positive attitude toward Bernard. Calvin also knew Bernard's writings and quoted from them, though with reservations.[72] Remarkably enough, the first Lutheran historian, Flacius Illyricus (1575), explicitly listed Bernard among the witnesses of the truth, and categorized him with the approximately four hundred precursors of the Reformation that he

---

71. T. Bell, "Pater Bernardus. Bernard de Clairvaux par Martin Luther," *Cîteaux* 41 (1991), 233-255. Idem (1993).

72. Lane, Hilary Hill (1982, B.D. thesis, Oxford).

counted in past centuries. His later church history — often referred to as the *Maagdenburger Centurionen* — in which he offered a sharp polemic against the Church of Rome, was, as far as Bernard was concerned, mainly based on the *vita prima*.[73]

But there he also found his reasons for criticizing Bernard. He accused him of a negative attitude toward marriage, since he recruited even married men for monastic life, and also of neglect for his physical well-being. He also stated that Bernard had been guilty of idolatry, since he attributed to the host — detached from the celebration of the Lord's Supper — a power of healing and conversion, and thus of performing ridiculous and blasphemous miracles. Furthermore, in his defense of the pope, in particular with respect to his authority toward the emperor, Bernard had acted as a fierce supporter of the antichrist, because he regarded the papacy as a divinely ordained institution.

On the other hand, he praised Bernard for the virtues and skills that were mentioned in this *vita:* his knowledge of Scripture and of the church fathers; his self-accusations of ignorance, error, and sacrilege. Finally, Flacius showed much appreciation for Bernard's sharp criticism of the pope, the cardinals, the bishops, and other clergy, who had behaved in such an ungodly manner that they were to be regarded as servants of the antichrist.

Later, during the "Second Reformation," when many Protestants focused on medieval-Christian spirituality, this appreciation for Bernard even increased. Through the influence of his writings, Bernard acquired the status of a precursor of the Reformation, rather than that of one who had been co-responsible for the deterioration of the Church of Rome. In the course of the seventeenth century, this positive appraisal diminished somewhat. One of the reasons probably was the expanding cult of Bernard in the Roman Church. The decrease in esteem for Bernard was also visible in the polemics between Protestant and Catholic Christians concerning Bernard's place in Christendom. The Protestants in particular blamed him for his preaching tour against the heretics in the South of France, and for his agitation against the activities of Arnold of Brescia in Rome; while he was also criticized for his share in the condemnation of Peter Abelard and Gilbert de la Porrée. Nonetheless, Protestants continued to appreciate what he had done for the Christian faith and for Christian spirituality.[74]

---

73. *Catalogus testium veritatis* (Strasbourg, 1562), 643-644. *Historia ecclesiastica* III (ed. Basel, 1624), 804-821.

74. "St. Bernard and the Historians" (1977), 34.

Another reason for the diminished respect for Bernard in Protestant circles was the growing menace of Rome's endeavors to regain lost terrain in Europe. The Protestants were in particular afraid that the Catholic princes might be prepared to support this objective with secular means. This also created negative attention for Bernard's memory. This was the case, for instance, when Louis XIV proclaimed Bernard, at the occasion of the solemn commemoration of the fifth centennial of his death, the protector of the throne. The immediate political background of this decision probably was the attitude of the French Jansenists, especially of the group around Blaise Pascal in the Port Royal monastery. They appealed to Bernard in their resistance to the church from within and to the absolutism of Louis XIV. The king's answer was the incorporation of Bernard into the French monarchy. By so doing, Louis wanted to defuse their appeal to this saint.[75]

But this explanation is incomplete in the sense that in the panegyric for Bernard held in Metz by Jacques-Bénigne Bossuet, the minister at this occasion (August 20, 1653), in the presence of the king, we also find allusions to the victory gained one year previously in the Battle of Blénau. There an army that sided with the king had defeated the forces of the Huguenot Condé, which signaled the end of the Fronde uprising and of the further resistance of the nobility against the authority of the king.[76] This made the title "protector of the throne" a barrier for the esteem for Bernard in Protestant circles. Already at the time of his coronation, Louis XIV had shown himself as quite intolerant toward the Huguenots. He then promised under oath to eradicate the heretics from his country. Subsequently he commanded every citizen to confess the Catholic faith, which led, in 1679, to a repeal of the Edict of Nantes — a decision taking away religious liberty from the Huguenots.

❦ ❦

THE EXTREMELY NEGATIVE evaluation of Pierre Bayle in his *Dictionaire historique et critique,* which first appeared in 1697, must be viewed against this background. Therein he remarked sneeringly that Bernard of Clair-

---

75. Flasche, "Bernhard von Clairvaux als Geistesahne von Pascal" (1953), 333-337. Mesnard, "Pascal et Bernard de Clairvaux" (1994), 375-387.

76. Mellinghoff-Bourgerie, "Bernhard von Clairvaux in der französischen Frömmigkeitsliteratur" (1994), 389.

vaux had enjoyed such respect that all kinds of ecclesiastical matters were submitted for his counsel, while kings and princes sought his service as a peacemaker in their quarrels with each other. Bernard, Bayle writes, possessed valuable qualities and an enormous zeal. But according to many, his zeal made him too jealous of those who had gained a reputation as scholars in the humanities. In his gullibility, Bernard had listened too much to slander about those scholars, and had, in particular, become altogether prejudiced with regard to Abelard. Driven by human passion, he had been indefatigable in his efforts to have all those whom he suspected of heresy condemned. Often he had reacted against imaginary opponents and against heresies that were either nonexistent or unimportant.

But, so the author continues, whether Bernard was right or wrong, he had always sounded his alarms in a masterful way, and made the thunder of his victories reverberate. He felt more at ease in the elimination of heretics than in the destruction of unbelievers. Nonetheless, he had also attacked the unbelievers with the customary weapon of eloquence and the special weapon of prophecy. But when all the beautiful promises that had enabled Bernard to assemble a huge army of crusaders had proven to be in vain, and people wanted to complain that he had led this army to slaughter without himself ever leaving the country, he had dismissed the whole matter with the excuse that the conduct of the crusaders had nullified the fulfillment of his prophecies.[77]

The background sketched above, against which this sharp criticism must be viewed, does not explain everything. We should also consider the volatile character of the author himself. Pierre Bayle (1647-1706), the son of a Calvinist pastor, was converted in 1669 during his studies in philosophy with the Jesuits in Toulouse to the Catholic Church, but joined the Huguenots a year and a half later. He then moved to Geneva, where he came in contact with Descartes' rationalism and underwent the influence of scepticism. For a while he earned his living as a private teacher. In 1675 he was appointed professor at the University of the Huguenots at Sédan. After this institution was closed by order of Louis XIV, he received an appointment as philosopher at the Illustrious School of Rotterdam, where he was dismissed in 1693, due to his agnostic, rationalistic criticism of the Christian revelation, and the aggressive radicalism he employed in his statements.

In writing the entry about Bernard in his encyclopedia, Bayle undoubtedly utilized a biography of Bernard that first appeared in 1647 and saw four

77. Vol. I, 559-561. In the fifth edition (Amsterdam, 1734), I, 778-780.

reprints within four decades. This *Vie de Saint Bernard* consisted of a translation of the first three books of the *vita prima*, to which the author had added another three books. In these additional sections, he dealt with some aspects of Bernard's life that had been largely or completely ignored by his contemporary hagiographers. The author presented himself as "le sieur Lamy," a veiled reference to his real name: Antoine le Maistre (†1658).[78] Le Maistre was a well-known lawyer at the tribunal of Paris, but entered Port Royal, and — with his brother Isaac (1684) and Blaise Pascal (†1662) — became an important Jansenist leader. His biography left Bernard's sainthood untouched, but emphasized in particular Bernard's attitude of independence in his dealings with ecclesiastical and worldly rulers.

The traditional, hagiographic portrayal of Bernard as presented in this study by Antoine le Maistre was elaborated upon in the early years of the eighteenth century in a more erudite way by Joseph François Bourguoin de Villefore (1652-1737), a man with Jansenist sympathies who belonged to the circle of the Oratorianists of Saint Sulpicius in Paris. Villefore, who owed his fame as author to a number of hagiographic studies, published a translation of letters and sermons of several saints, Bernard being one of them. He also wrote an extensive hagiography about Bernard.[79] We do not know how these studies about Bernard by Le Maistre and Villefore were received, unless we assume that there are some references to Villefore's work in the Bernard biography by Rattisbone.

Significantly enough, however, French church historians, who already at the beginning of the eighteenth century were open to "enlightened" ideas, for the time being preferred the more traditional hagiographic portrayal of Bernard to the more shocking view of Pierre Bayle, who became more influential only in the second half of that century. The historians of that era found it fashionable to criticize rather than to praise Bernard for his worldly activities. This happened even more strongly by German than by French authors.[80] Apparently Bernard's contribution to France's fame mitigated the disapproval of him that the French, as enlightened spirits, would have been expected to express.

The most negative appraisal of Bernard dates from 1802. It came

---

78. *La Vie de saint Bernard de Clairvaux, divisée en six livres dont les trois premiers sont traduits du latin,* par le sieur Lamy (Paris, 1647). The fifth printing was published in 1684.

79. *La vie de saint Bernard, premier abbé de Clairvaux, père et docteur de l'Eglise* (Paris, 1723). Cf. Janauschek (1891), 1394 and 1474.

80. "St. Bernard and the Historians" (1977), 38-40, in particular note 51.

from the poet Friedrich Schiller, who as professor in *Universalgeschichte* in Jena devoted some time to the study of Bernard. His assessment, stated in a letter to Goethe, has often been cited. It resembles a torrent of abuse. It shows that Schiller found it unnecessary to pay any attention to Bernard's own writings:

> Recently I occupied myself with Saint Bernard and this encounter gave me much pleasure. It might be difficult to find another figure in history who was so wise in worldly ways and yet, at the same time, such a spiritual crook, who through his elevated position, however, could play his role with such dignity. He was the oracle of his days, and dominated these, in spite of the fact — or rather: because of the fact — that he remained a private person and let other persons be in positions of leadership. Popes were his students and kings his creatures. He hated and suppressed all progress as much as he could and favored the greatest stupidity of monks. He himself had only the intellect of a monk and had no other qualities than shrewdness and hypocrisy.[81]

We hardly need to say that this judgment totally ignored all the positive values Bernard also represented. It is the typical testimony of an eighteenth-century rationalist, who was incapable of any historical relativizing. Yet, this conviction of Schiller, as that of Bayle, must be viewed as highlighting the inconsistencies that the historian tends to discover in Bernard. Bayle and Schiller could arrive at such conclusions because of the fact that rationalism has no eye for those values in Christianity of which the social importance is not immediately evident. The supporters of the Enlightenment of that period had no appreciation for the non-rational religious values of the twelfth century. That made their evaluation of Bernard's ideas one-sided and negative. They could see in Bernard only a direct contradiction between the monk who wanted to escape from the world and the politician who wanted to influence all areas of contemporary society.

The traditional historical-hagiographic approach had accepted a priori Bernard's canonized sainthood, and for that reason had been able to ignore this disparity. Since the eighteenth century, however, historians could no longer so do, unless they were willing to reject completely what that century brought to the West.

---

81. For the German text, see *Bernard im Widerstreit* (1966), 26.

ॐ   ॐ

ROMANTICISM LED NOT ONLY to an idolizing of the Middle Ages, but also
to a closer study of that period. It did not simply return to the earlier
historiographic traditions. Instead of the marginal commentaries about
Bernard to which the proponents of the Enlightenment had limited themselves and which receive a faint echo in the work of Jacob Burckhardt,[82]
some extended biographies about him were now published, based on new
research. Even in Protestant circles interest in this medieval saint was
rekindled, partly because of some current developments. Protestants were
opposed to the revived attempts within the Church of Rome to declare
Mary's Immaculate Conception an official dogma — a teaching against
which Bernard had strongly protested in his letter to the canons of Lyon.[83]

The first Protestant theologian who dared to write a biography of
Bernard was the church historian August Neander, a "convert" from
Judaism. His study *Der heilige Bernhard und sein Zeitalter* was published
in 1813. Later, Bernard continued to intrigue him: in 1848 a second, revised
edition appeared, which saw several reprints.[84] Neander recognized the
contradiction between Bernard's external and internal life, but did not
make any explicit statements about this aspect, although it was implicitly
dealt with in his biography. He also acknowledged that Bernard's sainthood
was accompanied by some human shortcomings. He had no difficulty in
accepting this, since he understood sanctity in the biblical sense.[85]

Neander's work soon inspired others, both in England and in France. In 1863
James C. Morisson, an Anglican, published *The Time and Life of Saint Bernard*.
This work was clearly dependent on that of Neander, but was inferior in quality.
Nonetheless, it was reprinted four times. The most significant difference between
the two authors was that Morisson was less critical in his admiration of Bernard,
knew less about his spirituality, and showed a lesser understanding of the medieval
world in which the abbot lived. Some Catholics, in particular Vacandard, also

82. *Weltgeschichtliche Betrachtungen* (1947), 354.
83. Ep. 174; SBO VII, 388-392. See above, 162, with note 51.
84. Prior to his baptism in 1806, Neander's (1789-1850) name was David Mendel.
From 1813 he taught in Berlin. The revised edition was reprinted five times. The original
edition of 1842 was also translated in French and English; the revised edition appeared in
a Dutch translation in 1858.
85. "St. Bernard and the Historians" (1977), 42, with note 57.

accused Morisson and his Protestant kinsmen of daring to rank Bernard with Luther; while others objected that he showed too little empathy in his account of the miracles that Bernard — according to his contemporaries — performed.[86]

But Morisson was not the only Englishman with a special interest in Bernard. Mention must also be made of Richard S. Stores, an Anglican theologian who in the 1890s published a series of lectures about Bernard, which he had held at Princeton. His admiration for this abbot and his appreciation for his significance for later centuries are remarkable. Although Stores admitted that Bernard had not been sinless, he nevertheless extensively defended his at times controversial actions, among others his actions with regard to Abelard. And based on a comprehensive knowledge of Bernard's writings, he underlined his universal significance for Christians of all ages.[87]

Among the nineteenth-century biographies of Bernard, the French contribution is certainly the largest. This is due to the Catholic Restauration in France, which was one of the phenomena accompanying Romanticism. Within a period of fifty-five years, three two-volume biographies of Bernard appeared, which were repeatedly reprinted. Each of these was written by a Catholic clergyman. The first in this series was by Théodore Ratisbonne (1802-1884). He was followed by Gustave Chevallier, and, finally, by Abbé Elphège Vacandard (1849-1927), who at the time really broke new ground and became the best known.

In France the climate was rather favorable for these biographies since, under the influence of Romanticism, Bernard was not so negatively evaluated by those outside the church. Even Jules Michelet (1798-1874), France's preeminently national historian, and his vulgarizer Henri Martin (1810-1883), who clearly lacked sympathy for the Church of Rome, had some appreciation for Bernard. From what they said about him, however, it is evident that they knew and understood but little of him and, in any case, had not read any of his writings.[88] The reason that they did mention him in their work in all probability lies in the fact that — as indicated earlier — a man as politically important as Bernard must receive a place in the history of France.

Other historians also gave attention to Bernard for the same reason. Thus the author of a survey of contemporary French historiography published in 1867 felt he had to mention Ratisbonne's biography of Bernard of 1840. By including him, he indicated that Bernard deserved the attention of French historians. The

---

86. "The Conflicting Interpretations" (1980), 60.

87. *Bernard of Clairvaux: The Times, the Man and his Work* (London, 1892).

88. Pacaut, "Saint Bernard dans l'historiographie française du dix-neuvième siècle" (1994), 421-430.

author showed his chauvinistic appreciation for this biography, since Ratisbonne through his work had attempted to compensate for the regrettable negligence of French authors. This negligence allowed the German church historian Neander to appropriate a subject that above all deserved a place in French historiography.[89]

The authors of those three biographies of Bernard differ in their points of departure, and their products display a divergence in motivation and quality, even though each of them was part of the Catholic Restauration — a reaction of the church against the Enlightenment and the French Revolution. Each author in his own way shared in the cultural, social, and theological reflection to which the French episcopacy had inspired its clergy in the course of the century. The history of France received special attention in this intellectual advance, in particular as a result of the efforts of Mgr. Felix Dupanloup, the bishop of Orléans. This led to an extensive interest in historiography on the part of many clergymen.[90] In addition, hagiography was a large and extremely vital part in the Catholic historiography of that period. Edification was the main object, but gradually these historians were expected to show greater erudition, which enabled them to situate their *lives* of saints in a historical context, so that these cultic writings could also claim some scholarly respect.[91]

In the first instance, the difference between Ratisbonne, Chevallier, and Vacandard has to do with their backgrounds and the various times when they wrote. Ratisbonne was of Jewish descent and had first studied law. In 1830, three years after he had been baptized, he was ordained as priest. From that moment on, he served the religious interests of the French church in numerous ways with great energy and dedication. Among other things, he founded a congregation of sisters that was dedicated to converting Jews. The writing of an easily readable biography of Bernard fitted well within the framework of his activities. Within seventy years this biography was translated into another language and reprinted ten times. However, his book contained no new insights, and what was presented as new research pertained only to minor matters. Ratisbonne defended Bernard unconditionally against the criticism that had earlier been voiced by "enlightened" spirits about certain aspects of his activities.[92]

---

89. Carbonelli (1976), 517: ". . . ce saint du Moyen Age nous appartient doublement par la naissance et par le bon sens mêlé a l'exaltation religieuse."

90. Den Boer (1995), Chapter I, 1, "The First Estate."

91. Carbonelli (1976), 95-108.

92. *Histoire de saint Bernard et son siècle* (Paris, 1840). One of the reprints served as the introduction to *Oeuvres de saint Bernard,* transl. by A. Ravelet (Paris, 1870), 5 volumes. This edition had to compete against that of Abbé Charpentier and P. Dijon, which had been on the market since 1865 in 8 volumes and was reprinted thrice.

Gustave Chevallier, the second Bernard biographer, whose lengthy *Histoire de saint Bernard* appeared in 1888, was, from a scholarly point of view, rather unique.

The work certainly did not meet the norms that, since the founding in 1866 of the journal *Revue des questions historiques* and of *Polybiblion*, a journal with reviews, which appeared from 1868 onward, had gradually been required from the Catholic historiography of France.[93] These requirements included adequate documentation and careful dating on the basis of authentic sources, allowing a factual and coherent account of events. In formulating these requirements, the historiography by the Catholic clergy to a large degree followed the program that the *Revue historique*, which had been founded in 1876, intended to realize — a program, however, that gave priority to political history.[94]

Abbé Chevallier primarily intended his book to be the final volume of the *opus magnum* that Charles, count of Montalembert (1810-1870) had earlier written about the history of monasticism from Benedictine of Nursia until Bernard's time.[95] The last two volumes of this work, which had met with a favorable reception, did not appear until seven years after Montalembert's death. But it still lacked the life story of the one who had inspired the author to undertake this project: Bernard himself. For that reason, Chevallier decided to write a book that would offer the reader this culmination that was still missing. He therefore also paid much more attention to Bernard as monk than to his involvements with the world at large.

At the same time, the author tried to imitate the style of Montalembert; thus some of the events were related in such a way that the reader could imagine himself to be an eyewitness of Bernard's activities. Nevertheless, this biography, introduced by Chevallier as a sequel to Montalembert's work, did not attain the same literary level. Yet within a short time this sequel saw three reprints. For this the recommendation from the bishop, and eventually even from the pope, for this biography must have been at least partly responsible. On the other hand, Chevallier's work no doubt offered what a Catholic audience would expect of

93. Carbonelli (1976), 325-365.
94. Pacaut, "Saint Bernard dans l'historiographie . . ." (1994), 421-422.
95. *Les moines d'Occident depuis saint Benoît jusqu'à saint Bernard* (Paris, 1860-1867), 5 vols. (Lyon, 1875-1877), 7 vols. For the initial involvement of Mgr. Dupanloup with this work, see "The Conflicting Interpretations" (1980), 68, note 44.

such a hagio-biography. But the author had to go to great lengths to prevent a negative review of his book in *Polybiblion*.[96]

Finally, the biography by Vacandard — *Vie de saint Bernard* — was such a high point in the nineteenth-century Catholic hagiography about Bernard that even now, after more than a century, we must still depend heavily on it although the latest reprint dates from 1927. Soon after its publication in 1895, this biography received an award from the Académie Française; while in 1897 the author was congratulated for his work by Pope Leo XIII in the form of his apostolic blessing. The book was favorably received in the French as well as the foreign press. Critical remarks mostly concerned minor details about which opinions could differ. Protestants regretted that Vacandard had failed to put Bernard, in his (verbal) evaluation of Rome, on a par with Luther; while Cistercian circles complained that he had not written with the intent to edify his readers.[97]

The review in the *Revue historique* likewise was extremely positive; it recommended the book to all friends of the Middle Ages.[98] The review almost creates the impression that the historiography, as it was pursued by those who were involved with this "journal of professors," differed but little from the aims of the *Revue des questions historiques,* in which since 1885 Vacandard had published some of his earlier studies about Bernard. But nothing of this euphoric sentiment was present in the article "Saint Bernard" by Achille Luchaire, published in the *Revue historique* in 1900. Vacandard's book is not mentioned, except in the only footnote Luchaire added to his article. In this footnote, Luchaire remarks that in spite of its merits, Vacandard's book can only be viewed as a well-documented survey.[99]

Most likely Luchaire was subsequently reprimanded for this footnote, which also implied a totally negative opinion of the editorial management of the *Revue des questions historiques.* In any case, he omitted this footnote when he incorporated

96. *Histoire de saint Bernard* (Lille, 1888). For the recommendations and the review in *Polybiblion,* see "The Conflicting Interpretations" (1980), 69, with note 45.

97. Vacandard, "La vie de saint Bernard et ses critiques," R.Q.H. 62 (1897), 198-211. For the Cistercian reactions, see "St. Bernard and the Historians" (1977), 43, note 63.

98. Vol. 58 (1895), 111-113 (Bulletin historique). A. Molinier was the reviewer.

99. Vol. 71, 225-242. Luchaire says (225, note 1), "La plus recente biographie de saint Bernard, celle de Vacandard, malgré ses mérites, n'a que la valuer d'une esquisse bien documentée." This footnote is missing in *Les premiers capétiens* (987-1137) (Paris, 1911, repr. 1980), 279-295.

this erudite article about Bernard in his book about the early Capetingians in 1910. In his evaluation of Vacandard's book in this footnote, we detect an anti-clerical sentiment that was quite common with many of the historians around the *Revue historique,* as well as a touch of the rivalry that existed between the two journals. Vacandard's reaction to some of the reviews of his work possibly must also be seen against that background. He simply dismissed these as "critiques de sentiment"[100] stemming from prejudice.

Vacandard's book also displayed a bias, inasmuch as it accepted Bernard's sainthood a priori as a historical reality. This presupposition ran contrary to the principles of the positivistic historiography espoused by historians such as Luchaire. The Catholic church historians, who wanted to safeguard their position beside the rapidly advancing "universitaires" of the *Revue historique,* also claimed to accept these principles, but were unable to do so with all their implications.

The opening paragraph of Luchaire's article about Bernard remained — as we saw earlier — a well-known quip.[101] In these first lines the author called this abbot of Clairvaux the synthesis of his times. By his eloquence and holiness, Bernard ruled Western Christendom and personified the entire political and religious system of a period of the Middle Ages that was dominated by the moral power of the church. Following this introduction, Luchaire lists all the requirements of a Bernard biography, while adding that the author of such a book should also seek to understand and describe Bernard's human nature. In this context Luchaire included his footnote about Vacandard's work, which, in his opinion, was fully inadequate in this respect.

Luchaire must have had great difficulty in understanding and accepting Vacandard's portrayal of Bernard, in spite of the ample documentation he provided. Vacandard, however, was convinced that the book conformed to the scholarly norms of his days. For in a few places he had actually dared to criticize Bernard's actions, in spite of his generally acknowledged sainthood. This must not have come easy to him, since he had to give up the hagiographic image of Bernard. However, since giving this up completely was beyond his capability, he combined the occasional moral criticism of Bernard's dealings with the presupposition that the grace bestowed on Bernard from his birth must have left him temporarily at such critical moments.[102]

In response to the disapproval that came from Cistercian circles, Vacandard stated that his task as a historian did not include the writing

100. Above, note 97.
101. See above, 9, with note 18.
102. "The Conflicting Interpretations" (1980), 72-74.

of a panegyric; his duty rather was to judge Bernard's actual deeds. This, however, the book only in part delivers. For Vacandard retained the concept of a sainthood bestowed on him from before his birth, as related by contemporary hagiographers of Bernard and regarded as an objective fact by the hagiographic tradition.

Thus, for someone like Luchaire, who as a historian belonged to the tradition of the Enlightenment, Vacandard was, in spite of his incidental departure from the current portrayal of Bernard's sainthood, a representative of the hagiographic naïveté that was characteristic of the hagiobiographers of this saint even in the nineteenth century. A century later it still seems difficult to turn away from this tradition,[103] and innovative Bernard biographies have not been forthcoming. Considering this, it is remarkable that already in his day Vacandard dared to distance himself from that tradition, for instance in his treatment of Bernard's attitude toward Abelard. For that reason his work remains important as a first attempt to make a transition between a cultic and an historical understanding of Bernard, his sainthood included.

3. THE CHIMERA OF THE TWENTIETH CENTURY

IN 1949 AN AUSTRIAN, Friedrich Heer, published a study about the rise of Europe in the twelfth century that caused considerable excitement. The subtitle indicated that the central theme of this work concerned the transition from feudal-political religiosity, which the author labeled as Roman, to a new approach to religion, which supposedly was characteristic for the Gothic period. A separate chapter of the book was dedicated to Bernard's role in this development.[104] But however important Bernard's share therein may have been, it was, says Heer, paradoxical. He maintained that in Bernard, Romanesque and Gothic aspects competed, as was continually apparent in the tensions displayed by the abbot of Clairvaux, his extreme mobility, and his constant impetuosity.

Bernard was tied to the old feudal-political religiosity, according to Heer, in particular in his political activities. Among other things, this led him to remind temporal kings of their subjection to the King of

---

103. *Christendom and Christianity* (1994), 181-197. See below, 191-193.
104. *Aufgangs Europas* (1949), 182-235. The professional quality of this book was justly criticized by F. L. Ganshof in M.I.ö.G., vol. 61 (1953), 434-440.

kings, and even to pressure them to participate in the crusade, which he preached in the name of the Lord of hosts. On the other hand — inspired by his spirituality and his mystical piety as author and preacher — he sharply criticized the old feudal way of life, especially of ecclesiastical authorities, who had no qualms in combining spiritual and temporal interests. But he also criticized the new lifestyle these prelates assumed, which was based on a confluence of scholasticism with canon law and Roman law, and on the fact that the papal court developed a system of governance adapted to the monetary economy. Likewise, in the ecclesiastical legal system, the papal court acquired a central place through the right of appeal and the privilege of bestowing exemptions, while the development of this new power of the Curia was consolidated through a network of papal legates.

Heer felt that in yet another respect Bernard represented both the new world that was then being born, and the old way of life. Bernard is said to have shown the progressive side of his personality in his polemic with Cluny about the lifestyle of the monks; while in the struggle against Abelard and against the heretics, he supposedly displayed the "old-conservative, sacramental-symbolical, and politico-religious part of his character." In protesting against the opulence of Cluny, he defended the poor in Christ (*pauperes Christi*), who were viewed with compassion only by the populist preachers.[105] On the other hand, Bernard is reported to have turned against them when, as inhabitants of the city of Rome, they supported the rebel Arnold of Brescia, one of Abelard's students.

The further suggestion is that Bernard was the victim of an intense and prolonged inner conflict, mainly due to his close identification with the feudal-political religiosity and, at the same time, his association with the new piety that focused on the imitation of the incarnate God in Christ. Internally, he was faced with the contrasting concepts of God as the King of terrifying majesty whom no man can see and live, and of the God-man in the manger, the compassionate leader of mankind, who after his suffering and death had ascended into heaven; the bridegroom of the human soul, who had transformed the old, submissive relationship between God and man of "give, that I may give in return" into an experience of love. The course of this inner struggle of Bernard supposedly can be detected in the concept of God that he developed in the more than eighty sermons on the Song of Songs that he wrote through the years. The fact that Bernard

105. Van Moolenbroek, *Vital l'ermite, prédicateur itinérant* (1990).

continued to carefully amend the texts of these sermons afterward was still mostly unknown in 1949.

Although at first this presumptuous view of Bernard provoked but little debate, it did receive attention, the more so since the chapter in question with the subtitle *Die Schimäre des Jahrhunderts* (the Chimera of the Century) referred to the final passage in a letter written by Bernard to his namesake Bernard of Varey, the prior of the Carthusian monastery of Portes, shortly after the disaster of the Second Crusade. This passage contained a candid statement about his life at that particular time:

> It is time for me to remember myself. May my monstrous life, my bitter conscience, move you to pity. I am the chimera of my age, neither cleric nor layman. I have kept the habit of a monk, but I have long ago abandoned the life. I do not wish to tell you what I dare say you have heard from others: what I am doing, what are my purposes, through what dangers I pass in the world, or rather down what precipices I am hurled. If you have not heard, enquire and then, according to what you hear, give your advice and the support of your prayers.[106]

Friedrich Heer's views to some extent correspond with what others had earlier remarked about the inconsistencies that strike us in Bernard's personality and activities. For this reason Heer at times found it difficult to recognize him as a saint.[107] But not all concluded, on the basis of this confidential confession, that Bernard must have been an internally torn chimera. Achille Luchaire, for instance, had already characterized him as someone with a totally inconsistent temperament. As a monk, Bernard had been contemplative, mystical, ascetic; as a preacher, counsellor of princes and popes, and *de facto* leader of the church of the West, he was a busy and over-excited politician. This inconsistency even touched his physical nature. Bernard combined mildness with agitation, and genuine humility with haughtiness and loathing.

But contrary to the opinions of later authors, who in their appraisal of Bernard referred back to this statement and attempted to interpret it psychologically as in indication of an inner dichotomy in his being, Luchaire felt that these inconsistencies did not bring him into conflict with

---

106. *Ep.* 250, c.4; SBO VIII, 147. This is the only instance in Bernard's works where the word *chimera* occurs. About the content of this letter, see Gastaldelli, *Opere* VI, 148, note 1. James (402) translates "Cimaera mei saeculi" as "a sort of modern chimera."

107. "St. Bernard and the Historians" (1977), 44-48. Diers (1991), 1-6 and 105-106.

himself. For even though Bernard was perhaps unable to reconcile fully these inner contradictions, he did, through a peculiar logic, show their coherence. This harmony, Luchaire stated, was rooted in his absolute faith that totally rejected human reasoning, as well as in the conviction that the church represented a higher interest than the world. Bernard subjected all his acts to this faith and this conviction. He sacrificed without hesitation his own affection, however dear this sometimes was to him, his own interests, and those of his friends and colleagues. Thus people who were close to him could, in their turn, become his victims. This sums up the earlier, somewhat superficial view of Luchaire.[108]

A serious objection against Friedrich Heer's suggestion regarding Bernard's inner conflict is that the author too strongly projects the cultural transition that occurred in the twelfth century and formed the primary subject of his book onto the person of this abbot. Subsequently, he concludes that Bernard was internally torn in two. For two reasons this suggestion is unacceptable: first, because the passage cited above must be read in its immediate context; and secondly, because the testimony of Bernard's contemporaries about his ambivalence leads to a different conclusion. To me this chimera image, therefore, seems primarily a historiographical problem. In particular, it illustrates the difficulties of historians of the twentieth century, who want to understand this saint as an historical figure without really distancing themselves from the cultic tradition that pays attention only to the saintly life story of Bernard.

THE LETTER IN WHICH Bernard called himself "the chimera of the century" was sent in 1150 to Bernard of Varey, in response to the charge that had reached him from the monastery of Varey. Bernard was accused of the fact that as a result of his intervention, one of the monks from this Carthusian monastery, who had been proposed for the episcopal see of Grenoble, had been turned down by Eugenius III, after he had received objections against this candidature from the Grande Chartreuse. Bernard of Clairvaux, however, insisted that he was not involved in this rejection.

Bernard claimed that he was totally ignorant about the pope's intentions in this matter. He did not go into any detail, but only stated that, in retrospect, he could

108. Luchaire (above, 184, note 99), 226 (or 280-281).

agree with the pope's decision. He had learned that the monk himself, or the community of Portes, had felt spurned by this rejection; while in fact, the candidate concerned, as a Carthusian, had opted for a life as recluse.

So much is clear, that a conflict about the occupancy of this see had arisen between the monastery of Portes, in the diocese of Belley, and the Grande Chartreuse, situated in the bishopric of Grenoble. Hugh II, Grenoble's bishop and a former Carthusian from Portes, had been appointed in 1148 as archbishop of Vienne. When that happened, the prior of Portes had proposed one of his monks as a candidate for the see of Grenoble. The Grande Chartreuse objected in Rome against the appointment of this monk because of his youth; but in reality, this abbey wanted the appointment to go to one of its own monks.[109] Bernard may in principle have agreed with the claims of the Grande Chartreuse, considering his own meddling in episcopal appointments elsewhere when Cistercian monasteries were involved. But we do not know whether he did communicate his opinion to Eugenius III, as was stated by the prior of Portes.

Bernard's critical comment about the improper ambition of the Portes community to have one of its monks elected as bishop was misplaced, considering his own activities, which corresponded just as little to the lifestyle he had chosen as a monk, certainly at the time when this problem occurred. Just prior to this, during a council in Chartres, Bernard had been chosen to lead a new crusade, which was to compensate for the failure of that of 1147 — a task he did not feel he could simply reject, even though it brought him into an impossible position.[110] This predicament possibly explains why Bernard, at the end of his letter, refers in such a dramatic way to the extremely contradictory situation in which he, as a monk, found himself at that particular moment.

None of the other texts of self-pity that are found in Bernard's writings corresponds with this statement of the inner conflict he suffered,[111] not even the assertion in one of his sermons on the Song of Songs that his sins were camouflaged by his habit. This sermon, dating from 1145/1148, was written prior to the letter he addressed to the prior of Portes. He made this confession in a comment on a text from Zephaniah: "At that time I will search Jerusalem with lamps" (1:12):

---

109. Bligny, "Les chartreux," 153.

110. Above, 149-152, with notes 18-24.

111. About statements of self-pity in Bernard's writings, as a result of too heavy burdens laid upon him, or about his inability to satisfy all expectations and obligations, see Diers (1991), 150-176.

What is safe in Babylon if Jerusalem is about to be examined? For I think that the prophet here employs the term Jerusalem to indicate those who live a religious life in this world, who through a respectable and orderly conduct try to imitate the life of the heavenly Jerusalem as well as they can, and do not — as the inhabitants of Babylon — through shameless passions and disorderly behavior destroy their life. In any case, their sins are clear and precede them to the judgment (1 Timothy 5:24). They do not need further scrutiny, but deserve judgment. But the sins of me, who is supposed to be a monk and a citizen of the heavenly Jerusalem *(Jerosolymita)*, are securely hidden, overshadowed by the name and the habit of a monk. Therefore, it will be necessary to bring these to light in a minute examination, to bring them out of the darkness into the light, by illuminating them, as it were, with a torch.[112]

This statement of Bernard about his monastic state and his wearing of a habit, which enabled him to hide his sinfulness, is so different from the complaint in his letter to the prior of Portes that we should attach only incidental, circumstantial meaning to this passage about the duality of his life. For that reason we cannot draw any conclusions from it regarding any inner conflict that Bernard experienced because of his continuous involvement with the world. Two statements from contemporaries point in that same direction: because of his ability to lead a contemplative life and simultaneously to act when necessary, they compared him with Jacob the patriarch, who begot his descendants through Leah, but also spent joyful nights with Rachel.[113]

Both of these testimonies express a genuine admiration for Bernard's ability to combine so easily a contemplative and an active life. That to me would seem another reason that this portrayal of Bernard as a chimera primarily represents an approach to his person that could only

---

112. *Sermo in Canticum* 55, c. 2; SBO II, 112. This sermon is part of the fourth group of sermons on the Song of Songs, which Bernard began to write before 1145 and the last of which was written shortly after the end of the Council of Reims, held in March 1148. See *Recueil*, I, 232.

113. See, in particular, Peter of Celles and Hilderbert of Lavardin. "St. Bernard and the Historians" (1977), 41, note 53. Diers (1991), 148, note 189. For this comparison by Peter of Celles, see his *Sermones* 76 and 77, P.L., CCII, 873-878. Hildebert used it in a letter that he sent to Bernard between 1125 and 1130; *Ep.* 122; SBO VII, 302-303. Below, 222-229. For the complete correspondence between Hilderbert and Bernard, see Gastaldelli, *Opere* VI/1, 78-79.

have been invented in the twentieth century.[114] In fact, the appeal to this characteristic of Bernard typifies the ineptitude of those who still want to maintain their a priori concept of Bernard's sainthood, but also insist on giving him the place he occupied as a human being living in the twelfth century. An historian who does not distance himself from the portrayal of Bernard in the prevailing hagiographic-cultic tradition cannot avoid creating his own inner conflict.

The inner struggle that is thus believed to have plagued this abbot has less to do with Bernard himself than with the effort needed to distance oneself from the traditional portrayal of his sainthood when trying to arrive at an historical understanding of his person. For a picture totally different from that of the current hagiographic image of his absolute sainthood emerges as soon as we are also willing to consider, in our evaluation of his person, the opportunism that is time and time again expressed in Bernard's writings, and his often offensive attitude toward those who disagreed or even opposed him, as well as the very controversial manner in which Bernard repeatedly, at his own initiative, meddled in all kinds of ecclesiastical and temporal matters.

The extremely sensitive nature of this matter is in particular apparent in the monastic comments on an historical judgment of those moments in Bernard's public life when he failed to exhibit his sainthood. These regard the events that seem to contradict the common portrayal of his sainthood as of secondary importance for those who recognize him as a saint. Thomas Merton is one of the spokesmen for this view.[115] We meet this approach also with Jean Leclercq, even in his *Nouveau visage de Saint Bernard* (1976), in which he dealt once again with this problem. In this book he, in fact, reiterated the apologetic evaluation that he had already in 1948 presented in his *Saint Bernard mystique*:

> With regard to Saint Bernard, the historian is confronted with the problem of the relationship which God maintains between sainthood and human temperament. Bernard is a human being: we can study his acts. But the scholars, whose duty it is to give an account of these acts in their annals and chronicles, sometimes claim the right to sit in judgment over them. They often forget this other principle of history,

---

114. For the present status of this chimera theory, see Diers (1991), 1-6. About Bernard's own thinking with regard to the contrast and cohesion between action and contemplation, see Diers (1991), 105-149.

115. (1954), 27-28; "Saint Bernard, moine et apôtre," BdC, VIII-X.

that is just as undeniable: "Bernard is a man of God." He says things which only the Spirit of God can put in a human heart. His writings likewise are essential for an understanding of his actions. We cannot hope to comprehend Bernard's role in the politics of his time or in the controversies in which he got involved, if we are unwilling to give attention to his sermons on the Song of Songs and all of his writings which he has left us. In his pamphlets, as in his preaching and his letters, we perceive how his entire soul was in the grip of grace. Everything in him was supernatural and yet human. He knew of no vulgarity and no bigotry, but only of loftiness and magnanimity.[116]

A knowledge of Bernard's writings is indispensable for all who want to understand his role in the politics of his time. But that knowledge should preferably be based on the manner in which Michaela Diers recently reexamined them. Her comments about Bernard's role in church and society, however, do not sketch the full picture. Bernard was often careless and opportunistic in formulating his own standpoint, while he repeatedly abused others who disagreed with him. And there remains Bernard's personal testimony that the title and habit of a monk could easily overshadow his sins, and that therefore even Jerusalem — that is, his own monastic life — ought to be "searched in the light of lamps." We continue to derive most of our knowledge about this from the writings of Bernard's hagiographers. For that reason it may be useful also to give attention to this Jerusalem of Bernard; that is, to this abbot in his own monastic *Umwelt*. Such a study might lead to a better or, in any case, a different perception of Bernard's role in temporal matters and, as a result, also of his sainthood.

---

116. (1948), 236. For an evaluation of Leclercq's *Nouveau visage,* see *Christendom* (1994), 181-197, and CCM 22 (1979), 44-48.

VI

"Jerusalem Searched in the Light of Lamps": Bernard in His Monastic Umwelt

❧   ❧

BERNARD FASCINATED many readers and listeners by his ability to give a vivid account of his religious experiences. To some extent this depended on how familiar the other was with the Bible texts that Bernard either quoted or paraphrased. As he had himself remarked, they could taste such a text again and again, like the innocent livestock that chews the cud.[1] For instance, he succeeds in hitting his readers verbally with an image of the place occupied by the church on earth through the ages. Referring to a text in the letter to the Hebrews: "Are they not all ministering spirits sent forth to serve, for the sake of those who are to obtain salvation" (1:14), and to the Psalmist (whom he calls "the prophet"), where he says: "The angel of the Lord encamps around those who fear Him" (34:8), Bernard continues as follows:

> If this is indeed true, it must mean that two things offer comfort to the church in this time and in the place of its diaspora: with regard to the past, this undoubtedly is the memory of Christ's suffering; but for the future she thinks and trusts to share eventually in the destiny of the saints. She keeps her sight, with eyes before and behind her, trained on these two in an insatiable desire. Both ways of seeing make

1. *In festivitate omnium sanctorum*, sermo I, c. 5; SBO V, 330, line 23: "vos estote animalia munda et ruminantia." *Super Canticum*, sermo 53, c. 9; SBO II, 101, line 26: "Ruminemus ergo, tamquam munda animalia."

her grateful, and both are a place of refuge against the sadness of evil and against sorrow.[2]

With this image of the church, Bernard distances himself from current threats that confronted this institution of salvation in the world of that era. This view, so characteristic of his approach to history in general,[3] fitted perfectly with the monastic way of life, in which the spirituality of the monk received form and content through his withdrawal from the profane world. He lives with the meditative memory of the suffering of the Lord; while looking into the future, he views his monastery as the Jerusalem in which heaven descends on earth. Those who are familiar with the time-lessness of monastic life and with the monastic expectation of salvation will always recognize Bernard in his writings as a monk.

And he must have been recognizable as such in his own times, even when his work took him outside his monastery. This is apparent, for instance, in the testimony about him from Anselm, the bishop of Havel-berg (1158). This former Premonstratensian knew Bernard only casually, since he worked mainly east of the Elbe. Nevertheless, he wrote about him, around 1149, as follows:

> At one time, when I visited the Church in Rome, I saw and heard the abbot of Clairvaux. In his coarse habit, and emaciated by mortification, he was in all respects a virtuous man of God; not a pretender, but a genuine disciple of the blessed Benedict. At the command of Pope Innocent II, a great and incomparable man, he was, in the midst of the clerics who were seated around him, interpreting and clarifying the words of the Holy Scriptures. Yet, he acted more from his obedience to the pope, than from a priestly duty.[4]

Bernard's continuous willingness to involve himself with matters outside his monastery completely contradicts his repeatedly expressed desire not to leave his monastery again. For, in spite of his assertions that he was a loyal observant of the monastic life, he was always prepared to react positively to a request from ecclesiastical authorities to assume tasks in the world.[5] Yet he

---

2. *Super Canticum,* sermo 62, c. 1; SBO II, 154. Following Jewish custom, Bernard in his writings often used the word *propheta* instead of *psalmista.*

3. For Bernard's view of history, see Diers (1991), 311-348.

4. *Epistola apologetica;* P.L., CLXXXVIII, 1128B.

5. Diers, 163-170. Bernard's willingness in this regard is recognized by Geoffrey of Auxerre, but he attempts to play it down. Vp III, c. III, 8; P.L., CLXXXV, 308.

usually acted only at his own initiative, if a monastic interest was threatened by developments or events outside his monastic world. However, he must have repeatedly concluded that such was the case, in particular with regard to episcopal appointments, which he opposed whenever he felt that these jeopardized or harmed the interests of his order.[6] He must also have viewed the approach to theology by Abelard and Gilbert de la Porrée as a menace to monastic life. He saw it as an attack on the monastic practice of theology, since in the scholastic method that was taught in classrooms, the personal dialogue between leader and pupil was eliminated. In monastic theology this dialogue was regarded as essential for spiritual formation.[7]

When Bernard launched out into the world at his own initiative, he assured himself beforehand of episcopal support. He could then refer to this backing, if he subsequently wanted to inform Rome about complaints and objections to things he disapproved. This was not a matter of pure calculation, but rather of his consciousness that his zeal for temporal causes was limited, on the one hand, because of his monastic status, but on the other hand it offered him more scope. His repeated refusal to accept an episcopal appointment clearly shows his unwillingness to relinquish his status as monk and as abbot, but he usually made few objections if capable members of his order accepted the sees that were offered to them. His own refusal was undoubtedly also inspired by the realization that as bishop he would have fewer possibilities to involve himself in ecclesiastical matters; while from his nonofficial position in the church, he was able to signal a prophetic protest. When others accepted an office, however, his possibilities to intervene increased.

But his repeated refusal of the episcopal office was also influenced by the consideration that as a bishop he would be alienated from monastic life.[8] From the very beginning, he had unconditionally opted for this life; he did not see this as important only for himself, but for all who wanted to reach eternal salvation. For that reason he never tired of urging others to accept the same state of life. The frequently quoted remark of William of Saint-Thierry that mothers kept their sons, wives their husbands, and men their friends, hidden from Bernard in order to save them for this world, may well be primarily applicable to the period prior to his entry in Cîteaux; but the accompanying character-

6. Pacaut (1957), 103-104. *Cluny et Cîteaux* (1985), 137, note 19.
7. Cf. S. Teubner-Schoebel (1993).
8. Diers (1991), 219-227.

ization of Bernard as "a fisherman in God's service" remained valid during his whole life.[9]

The regular appeal to Bernard to get involved in matters outside his monastery is an indication that he performed those tasks for which he had been asked and which he had accepted most loyally, and that these involvements did not detract from the spiritual/monastic self-interest that he thereby simultaneously pursued. For that reason we must see Bernard's involvements in the world — however far he sometimes went — in the context of the monastic state of life he had chosen; that is, with the meaning and the worth he ascribed to it for himself and for others. He could legitimize his worldly exploits insofar as these presented him with opportunities to lead others also to this redemptive state of life.

BERNARD WAS REMARKABLY successful in recruiting others for the monastery. On the one hand, we can detect this success in the number of Cistercian abbots and monks whose names occur in Bernard's letters or are mentioned in charters and other documents. On the other hand, this success is apparent in the rapid expansion of the Cistercian Order during Bernard's life, even though he only partly deserves the credit for its organizational development. This phenomenon therefore demands our attention, even though it does not explain everything.

When, in 1113, Bernard entered the monastery Cîteaux, this fifteen-year-old abbey had only one daughter institution: Ferté-sur-Grosne, which had recently been established. Forty years later, at the time of Bernard's death, the order counted 345 monasteries for men, spread out all over Europe. Bernard's own abbey — Clairvaux — together with its own affiliate institutions was responsible for about half of this growth.

To what extent does this indisputable increase reflect Bernard's own recruiting power? We cannot explain this growth by simply looking at statistics. Moreover, the endearing, pious accounts about the origin and early development of these monasteries more often than not offer a misleading distortion of the way in which Cîteaux in a short period could develop into an order with a vast geographical distribution. Often the establishment of such a new monastery was not the direct result of an influx of new monks that forced the existing community to establish a daughter institution. Also, the preference for an area of uncultivated

9. Vp I, c. XIII, 61 and 62; P.L., CLXXXV, 260, 261. Dimier (1953).

wilderness, which often features in these stories, did not always determine the choice of location.

Many Cistercian abbeys had their own past history, which ended at the moment when the previously existing community was incorporated in the order and was subsequently, so it seems, intentionally ignored. Such an incorporation was not always voluntary. Sometimes hermitages or monasteries of regular canons or abbeys of Benedictine monks without direct ties with Cluny, and at times even larger monastic conglomerates, were the object of negotiations that could lead to concessions in the rules governing the life of the monks. Besides religiously inspired recruitment, there were also instances where economic interests and political manipulations played a role. A critical analysis of the sources during many years has enabled us to have a clearer picture of these aspects of the early developments of the Cistercian Order.[10]

On the basis of the research that enables us to reconstruct the early history of the Cistercians, and the role of Clairvaux in particular, it may now be profitable to search the "heavenly Jerusalem" of that time "in the light of the lamps"; that is, to give more attention to the primarily material problems and resources that were of significance in this expansion. This may also enable us to say more about Bernard's personal involvement in this development. Until recently this latter aspect received only scant attention, for Bernard's role was effortlessly deduced from the cultic-charismatic image his hagiographers presented. Objective data for a more balanced treatment are virtually nonexistent and are not found in their writings, even though the expansion of the order does not remain unnoticed.

William of Saint-Thierry's account of Bernard's involvement in material matters even creates the impression that his dealings with temporal things were almost negligible. For William suggested that the Clairvaux brethren continuously tried not to burden their abbot with external matters, so that he would be free for his mystical contemplation of the blessings of Paradise that the saints may taste in their ascent to God.[11] Geoffrey of Auxerre — though indirectly — paints a somewhat different picture of Bernard's involvement with his monasteries. As Bernard's

---

10. Locatelli, "L'implantation cistercienne dans le comté de Bourgogne," 167-225; idem, "L'extension de l'ordre cistercien au temps de saint Bernard," 103-140. Berman, "Origins of the Filiation of Morimond in Southern France," *Cîteaux* 41 (1990), 258-262 (further references to relevant literature in note 1).

11. Vp I, c. VI, 28; P.L., CLXXXV, 243. Cf. above, 137.

secretary, he naturally possessed more information about his concern for material matters related to the growth of the order.

But Geoffrey broaches the subject only once. He relates how Bernard missed a considerable sum of money that had been made available by the abbot of Farfa for the purpose of founding a monastery in Italy from Clairvaux. The abbot had deposited this money in Rome, and had then sent the receipt, a chirograph, to Clairvaux. When Clairvaux wanted to draw the money, it had already been spent. Geoffrey then relates how mildly Bernard reacted to this blow, and to other occasions when the material preparations for the founding of new monasteries did not transpire as foreseen:

> Yet, upon receiving the news, the man of God only said, "Blessed be the Lord, who saved us from this burden. And it would be better to simply forgive the thieves, for they are Romans: the amount of money seemed enormous and the temptation was too big." He also used to congratulate himself that he could point at about ten monasteries or at least locations that would be suitable for new monasteries, which had been seized from him through deceit or violence. He did not even want to argue about these things, but regarded it as more joy to be the victim than to triumph over others.[12]

In this hagiographic comment, Geoffrey implicitly acknowledged that already existing monasteries did not always become affiliated with Clairvaux, in spite of an agreement to that effect. This acknowledgment confirms what has now been established by research concerning the way in which a significant part of the expansion of the Cistercian Order in Bernard's time took place — an expansion that also helped to curtail the unbridled proliferation of monasteries that earlier had been founded with great idealism.

꙰   ꙰

THE EXTENT AND INTENSITY of Bernard's possible involvement with the expansion of the order, in particular with the many filiations of Clairvaux,

---

12. Vp III, c. VII, 24; P.L., CLXXXV, 517. A chirograph was a private document, of which each of the parties concerned received a part. The cut between the parts often was intentionally crenated, with the word *chirographicum,* written in large letters, cut in two. LdM III, 1844-1845.

is only one of the subjects that need to be discussed. That topic will be dealt with in the third section of this chapter. It will not only consider Bernard's role in the expansion of his own abbey, but will also pay attention to two images Bernard used with regard to Clairvaux: "the home of the poor in Christ" and "the heavenly Jerusalem." Prior to this, we will discuss in the first section how Bernard acquired his unique position in the Cistercian Order: how he entered Cîteaux, and what kind of relationships developed during the life and abbacy of Stephen Harding — that is, until about 1134 — between this monastery and Clairvaux, which was founded by Bernard in 1115.

A second section deals with Bernard's association with the Cluniac Order, which during his lifetime was surpassed by the Cistercians. This expansion to a large extent influenced the relationship between the two organizations, which also in part was determined by Bernard's own activities. For that reason in this second section we will discuss the background and motivation of Bernard's polemical writings against Cluny, and also his later contacts with Peter the Venerable, which have often been described in glowing terms as a friendship between two saints. In this connection we must also mention the unusual role of Nicholas of Montiéramy in the relationship between the two abbots. This Benedictine monk, who liked to mingle with the great men of church and society, gave some secretarial assistance to Bernard in 1141. He entered Clairvaux in 1145/46, and became Bernard's chief secretary. But in 1152 he was rather brusquely dismissed, which must have led to a rupture in the relationship between the two abbots.

The third section, which has already been mentioned above, will deal with the two most contrasting aspects of Bernard as a person: his actual involvement with the expansion of his own Clairvaux (which according to his hagiographers was almost negligible), and the manner in which he developed the spirituality of this monastery, of the many affiliate institutions that sprang from it, and of the Cistercian Order in general. For this we must turn, in particular, to his writings. The question is, How can these contrasting aspects in Bernard be reconciled? And how do they relate to his frequent political and diplomatic missions in the world outside his monastery?

The chapter — and the book — are concluded with a short epilogue about the way in which these two, or possibly three, aspects of Bernard can be brought together. Such an epilogue can hardly be more than very preliminary. But it must be expected in a study undertaken to illuminate Bernard as an historical person, detached from the usual cultic portrayal. In our evaluation of Bernard's constant efforts to assure an important status for Clairvaux as the "Jerusalem of the monks," we can hardly limit ourselves to a description of his secular involvement with the required material and social provisions. While engaged in his never-ending activities, Bernard continued his dialogue with God and experienced God's love for him. His writings so clearly manifest his religious motivation that they cannot be ignored in a study of these aspects.

I. BERNARD AND CÎTEAUX (1113-1133/34)

A. Cîteaux until 1115

The *vita prima*, and subsequently also the *vita secunda*, relate how in 1113, at the age of about twenty-two, Bernard entered Cîteaux, together with more than thirty others. This "new monastery" (*novum monasterium* — as it was called until about 1119 because of its program) had been founded some fifteen years earlier by reform-minded monks from Molesme.[13] William of Saint-Thierry remains silent about the problems the arrival of this group created for this monastic community. They must, however, have been considerable; for this new influx meant at least a doubling of the community. According to William, this community was, humanly speaking, at that particular moment doomed to disappear:

> The new, and insignificant, Cistercian community lived in those days under the leadership of its abbot, the revered Stephen. It gave great grief to him that there were so few monks and he lost all hope for a posterity to which this inheritance of sacred poverty could be transferred.[14]

William no doubt derived this information from the *Fragmenta Gaufridi*. The author of that work, in turn, depended on a remark in the *Exordium*

---

13. Vp I, c. IV, 19; P.L., CLXXXV, 237. Vs, c. IV, 15; 478. For the term *novum monasterium* until 1119, see Marilier (1961), 24-26. That this term was subsequently no longer used for Cîteaux may be due partly to the fact that in the meantime it had become more suitable to describe the place and importance that Clairvaux had since acquired in this monastic renewal, which had been initiated earlier from Cîteaux.

14. Vp I, c. III, 18; P.L., CLXXXV, 236-237.

cisterciense. This document, written in Clairvaux around 1124, mentions such an influx of monks under Stephen Harding's abbacy that Cîteaux at a given moment had to make provisions for thirty newly entered novices.[15] However, this remark receives a different connotation when cited by Geoffrey and William. Their account indicates that all of these novices entered together with Bernard; and this led to a sudden and complete change in the affairs of this monastery. William's account of how Bernard won his brothers and some relatives and friends for his monastic ideal, and how they subsequently followed him in his decision to enter Cîteaux, makes it clear that he did not arrive alone. Nonetheless, William's suggestion that there had been no earlier growth was not true; and the suggestion of a sudden turnaround of events in Cîteaux was equally incorrect.

There are clear indications that the expansion of this "new monastery" must have begun at an earlier date. This is apparent, for instance, from the founding of the first affiliate institution, the abbey La Ferté-sur-Grosne, on May 18, 1113. This had been possible as a result of the cooperation of the bishop of Chalon-sur-Sâone and some counts in that region. The abbot of Cluny must also have given his prior approval, since this new monastery was situated near Cluny. An extant excerpt of the founding charter gives as the reason for this new monastery the fact that the number of brothers in Cîteaux had increased to the point that they could no longer provide for all, and that the space where they had to live and work had become insufficient.

That the preparations for this first affiliate monastery had been started a considerable time before may be inferred from a deed of gift for this monastery dating from 1112.[16] This resembles the care exercised by abbot Stephen in the founding of subsequent monasteries. Thus it appears that William intentionally ignored the expansion of Cîteaux prior to Bernard's arrival during the abbacy of Stephen, and possibly already during that of his predecessor Alberic. The nature of the *vita* required the author to give a biased account of the development of the order. His task was not to write a history of Cîteaux, but to present a story that would promote Bernard's canonization.

---

15. Bouton and Van Damme (1974), 113. See below, 212, with note 36.

16. For a summary of this founding charter, see J. Marilier (1961), 66, no. 42. For the donation of 1112, see Hümpfner, "Archivum et bibliotheca . . . ," 132. Winandy, "Les origines de Cîteaux," 62, no. 1.

The chronological problems resulting from this biased reporting led in a number of manuscripts in Clairvaux — probably already at the end of the twelfth century — to a correction of the year of Bernard's entry into Cîteaux. The year 1113 was erased from the parchment, and 1112 was substituted. Elsewhere the year 1111 was given instead of the original date. Both changes in dating are also found in some later manuscripts. When Abbé Chomton discovered this antedating at the end of the nineteenth century, he concluded that Bernard must have entered the monastery in 1112, and that therefore he was born in 1090 and not in 1091, as had until then generally — and correctly — been assumed.[17]

An additional argument for Abbé Chomton was the fact that at the time of his death, Bernard was already 63 years old; while this researcher had inferred from other data in the first book of the *vita prima* that his arrival in Cîteaux could not have taken place in 1113. For from William of Saint-Thierry's account, it could be deduced that Bernard must have entered shortly before Easter. In 1113 Easter was as early as March 28, and according to Chompton this same report from William shows that Bernard could not have entered Cîteaux in 1113 before the month of May. For on a Sunday about six months before his arrival in Cîteaux, Bernard had, when he had attended a church service together with his earliest fellow-brethren, heard a text from the Epistles, which in the liturgy of those times was read on the twenty-third Sunday after Pentecost. In 1112 this particular Sunday fell on November 17; that is, on a date less than five months before March 28, 1113. This difficulty, caused by a literal interpretation of William's account, disappears if one assumes that Bernard became a monk in 1112.[18]

These conclusions of Chomton, together with his arguments, were accepted by Vacandard, who incorrectly added his assumption that the Easter style had been followed in those manuscripts that mentioned 1111 as the year of Bernard's entry into the monastery, so that, according to our chronology, these manuscripts in actual fact also supported the 1112 date.[19] The authority that continues to be attributed to Vacandard's *Vie de saint Bernard* has resulted in the fact that it is still quite generally assumed that Bernard must have been born in 1190, since he entered Clairvaux in 1112; although it has been known for some time that in actual fact the expansion of the Cistercian Order had already begun prior to Bernard's entry. Since scholars have begun to compare the manuscripts of the *vita prima,* the misunderstanding resulting from this dating can be traced more precisely. Moreover, through the progress in hagiographic research, it is now possible to

---

17. "Saint Bernard est-il né en 1090?" (1994), 233-245.

18. Chomton, *Saint Bernard et le chateau de Fontaines-lès-Dijon,* II, 25. He also saw the founding of La Ferté as the result of the large number of men who entered together with Bernard.

19. *Vie de saint Bernard* (first ed.), I, 1, note 1.

imagine that details in a story of William, such as the attendance of a church service where Bernard made his decision to become a monk,[20] do not necessarily have to be taken as factual.

There is yet another factor that speaks against William of Saint-Thierry's account of the situation in Cîteaux. During the abbacy of Stephen Harding (1108/9-1133/4), in the years prior to the arrival of Bernard and his associates, the scriptorium of Cîteaux had already experienced a tremendous development. Moreover, this scriptorium would also have remained renowned for the earlier manuscripts it produced and illuminated, even if Cîteaux would have had to do without him and his followers. In that case, this particular style of illuminating manuscripts would have continued even after 1134. But due to Bernard's intervention, manuscripts with this type of illumination were no longer produced.

We find clear support for this presupposition in a short chapter of Bernard's *Apology*, where he speaks about sculptures that apparently were placed in the cloister of Cluny. It has gradually been realized that in this passage Bernard mainly criticized the illustrations in extant manuscripts from Cîteaux, which had been produced previously, during the abbacy of Stephen Harding. Their style of illumination did not conform to the norms Bernard required for the monastic lifestyle. Taken from its Cluniac context, the passage seems to convey a veiled, satirical criticism:

> But apart from this, in the cloisters, before the eyes of the brothers while they read — what is that ridiculous monstrosity doing, an amazing kind of deformed beauty and yet a beautiful deformity? What are the filthy apes doing there? The fierce lions? The monstrous centaurs? The creatures, part man and part beast? The striped tigers? The fighting soldiers? The hunters blowing horns? You may see many bodies under one head, and conversely many heads on one body. On the one side the tail of a serpent is seen on a quadruped, on the other side the head of a quadruped on the body of a fish. Over there an animal has a horse for the front half and a goat for the back; here a creature which is horned in front of an equine behind. In short, everywhere so plentiful and astonishing a variety of contradictory forms is seen that one would rather read in the marble than in books, and spend the whole day wondering at every single one of them than in meditating on the law of God.

20. Phil. 1:6. Vp I, c. III, 13; P.L., CLXXXV, 234.

After this excursus about the illuminations in the manuscripts of Cîteaux, Bernard resumed his description of Cluny, with its enormous financial problems. He adds ironically:

> Good God! if one is not ashamed of this aburdity, why is one not at least troubled at the expense?[21]

Archaeological research in Cluny has in the meantime shown that there were no such sculptures right there as described by Bernard in this passage, while his characterizations correspond remarkably to the pictorial embellishments in manuscripts produced around that time in Cîteaux. Around 1134, however, the production of such representations and the adding of such polychromous ornamentation ended in Cîteaux; that is, since the moment that Rainald de Bar, originally from Clairvaux, became its abbot. But we do find this polychromous technique and the representations Bernard criticized, as they originally appeared in the manuscript of Gregory the Great's *Moralia in Job*, which was produced in Cîteaux, and in a copy made in 1134 in the scriptorium of La Ferté.[22]

As mentioned earlier, the oldest manuscripts from Cîteaux date from before 1113. Among other items, a four-volume Bible, which contains the text of the Vulgate as revised by Stephen Harding and for which he had consulted some rabbinical scholars, has been preserved. According to a *monitum* in this work written by Stephen himself, the first volume of this manuscript was produced in 1109, while in 1111 the work of copying and illuminating the *Moralia,* the commentary of Gregory the Great on the Book of Job, was begun.[23] The quality of the illuminations and their own peculiar style seem to indicate that the expertise in the production of these costly manuscripts was developed at some earlier stage, and that Cîteaux could already afford such expensive monastic trade. The implication is that the monastery must have been prosperous at that time, since it did not lack for workers. This is confirmed by the use of *lapis lazuli* in the illumination of these manuscripts.[24] Apparently Cîteaux could afford to buy this expensive material already at such an early date, as was later also the case for La Ferté.

21. *Apo,* 29; SBO III, 106. Transl. Rudolph (1990), 11-12.

22. Stratford, "A Romanesque Marble Altar-Frontal in Beaume and some Cîteaux Manuscripts," 223-239. Rudolph (1991), 125-157. Zaluska (1989), 113-117. For the manuscript from the scriptorium of La Ferté sur Grosne (Chalon-sur-Sâone, Mun. Library, mss 7, 8, 9), idem, 260.

23. Dijon, Mun. Library, mss 15 and 168. Zaluska (1989), 75-79.

24. Idem, 74, note 25. Also Zaluska, "L'enluminure cistercienne," 271-285.

ည်း   ည်း

WILLIAM OF SAINT-THIERRY'S account that prior to Bernard's arrival, Cîteaux was threatened with extinction because the severity of its rules kept novices from entering it, can, on the basis of what was said above, only be viewed as a hagiographic commonplace. It would rather seem that the influx of new monks to Cîteaux had begun somewhat earlier, and that Bernard and his companions were only part of a larger group of thirty men who entered Cîteaux between 1108 and 1115.

This finds further confirmation in the fact that the founding of Pontigny, a second affiliate institution, in 1114, took place one year after La Ferté had been established; however, preparations for this new monastery must have started already earlier. We know that the first abbot of this abbey, Hughes of Vitry from Mâcon, was among those who entered together with Bernard; but there is no evidence that the other eleven or twelve members of this community all belonged to this group of Bernard's companions. That Hughes was elected as abbot of Pontigny may be explained by the fact that he was older and had been ordained as priest prior to his entry.[25]

Furthermore, at least one monk who entered Cîteaux around 1113 most probably did not belong to the followers of Bernard. This monk, named Arnold, studied before his entry at the cathedral school in Cologne.

A passage from the *Fragmenta Gaufridi* has led some to suppose that Bernard first encountered Arnold in Germany, when his brothers urged him to continue his studies there. At that time Arnold supposedly joined Bernard. But there exists no solid proof, and there are no convincing arguments to assert that Bernard did indeed go to Germany, nor that they knew each other before they entered Cîteaux. For the *Fragmenta Gaufridi* tells us that Bernard refused to make this journey. Neither is there proof for the suggestion that Arnold was a brother of Frederick, who was the archbishop of Cologne between 1099 and 1131. Although Arnold died already in 1125, and thus probably was Bernard's senior, the age difference between him and bishop Frederick was such as to make a family relationship between the two highly unlikely.[26]

25. "Erat autem clericus et iam maturioris etatis," *Fragmenta,* 11; 94.
26. *"Fragmenta,"* 10; 94. Further: Grill, "Morimond, soeur jumelle de Clairvaux," BdC, 118-125. In his argumentation the author follows the cultic tradition. Another monk who entered Cîteaux around 1113 and who did not belong to Bernard's followers was Artald, who became abbot of Preuilly in 1119. See below, 259, note 124.

We also know that Stephen Harding sent Arnold, in 1115, to become the abbot of a small, already existing Eremite monastery in the eastern part of the bishopric of Langres, close to the borders of the bishoprics of Toul and Besançon, just inside the borders of the German Empire of that time. From 1102 onward, the monks of Moiremont had been assisted regularly by Vilain d'Aigremont, an uncle of Bernard, who was a canon with the cathedral chapter of Langres. His involvement facilitated the entry of this community in 1115 into Cîteaux, or in any case into the Cistercian Order. By then there was a spiritual-juridical statute, which had earlier (in 1113/14) been developed by Stephen Harding, prior to the founding of Pontigny. The charter of this abbey mentioned a *carta caritatis et unanimitas,* an agreement that governed the relationship between the monasteries affiliated with Cîteaux.[27]

Stephen Harding paid ample attention to the transfer of the Moiremont hermitage — which now received the name Morimond (i.e., the place where one dies to the world) — just as he previously had to the founding of La Ferté and Pontigny. This is clear from the charter that was drawn up. Before Morimond was actually founded, Stephen visited the place where the monastery was to be established and contacted the local bishop and those who were to donate the required land. We are also explicitly informed that the abbot of the "new monastery" charged Monk Arnold, who was appointed by Stephen as abbot of Morimond, to instruct the monks how to faithfully observe the Rule of Benedict.[28]

But Stephen Harding seems to have been far less directly involved with the founding of Clairvaux. Apparently he did not take part in the decision about where precisely this abbey was to be located. Its location differed significantly from that of the other filiations of Cîteaux, in the founding of which he did play a direct role, even after 1115. Initially Clairvaux seems to have been built on a rather unfavorable spot, halfway down the slope of a narrow valley in a hilly area; whereas other monasteries founded through Cîteaux were all situated in a low, flat area, near water and surrounded by forest — which ensured a large measure of isolation.[29]

27. Marilier (1961), 66, no. 43. The text of this *carta* has not been preserved. Several points must have differed from the *carta caritatis prior,* which in 1119 had been accepted by the chapter general and was subsequently ratified by Calixtus II. For this *carta* itself, see Auberger (1986), 25-28; also below, 212, note 36.

28. Ibid., 67, no. 45.

29. Auberger (1986), 94-96. Kinder, "Les églises médiévales de Clairvaux," 207. Lobrichon, "Représentations de Clairvaux dans la *Vita Prima sancti Bernardi,*" 245-258.

It remains difficult to say why Bernard, at least initially, preferred a less ideal spot for his own monastery and its earliest filiations. It must not be excluded, however, that Bernard initially opted for a less favorable place for his monasteries in order to aggravate the living circumstances.

With regard to the founding of Clairvaux, we do not know whether Stephen personally consulted the bishop of Langres and the regional lords who were to provide the land. Most of these lords belonged to Bernard's family; this would indicate a closer involvement of him with the preparations. Moreover, these arrangements required less time than had been the case with the founding of Morimond and the two earlier affiliated monasteries.[30] Bernard apparently made haste, in order to prevent the official founding of Clairvaux from following that of Morimond. There may well be a dual reason for this: Bernard probably acted from religious motives, but his haste may also be interpreted as the corollary of his dynamism and assertiveness.

Even in choosing the date for the official founding — that is, the date when the new abbot would receive his confirmation from the church — Bernard showed no concern for the schedule of the bishop of Langres, who normally would have performed that task. Most likely the bishop had previously accepted the invitation to be that day in Morimond, where he was to confirm the new abbot for this monastery. This obvious haste in the founding of Clairvaux may also explain why Bernard was confirmed as abbot by William of Champeaux, the bishop of Châlons-sur Marne.

One of the remaining questions in the story of William of Saint-Thierry about the entry of Bernard and his companions into Cîteaux concerns what Bernard did before he entered. For about six months he lived in his parental home, together with those he had found prepared to become monks. There they already formed a religious community. When exactly did they decide to enter Cîteaux? Had they intended to do so from the very beginning, or was it their initial plan to form their own eremitical group, as so many did or would do in those times? In the latter case, the decision in favor of Cîteaux must in fact be viewed as a second choice, at least initially. It was made because Bernard's original intention to found his own "new monastery" was as yet beyond their reach. William of Saint-Thierry's story remains unclear on this point, and thus we have no certainty about the decision process.

30. Auberger (1986), 91-101.

❧   ❧

NEVERTHELESS, WE MUST confront another question: should the entry of Bernard and his companions not also be viewed as a detour on the road toward the establishment of his own community, which he eventually realized when he founded Clairvaux in 1115 in his native country? A desire to have his own "new monastery," where he himself could be the abbot, would certainly have corresponded to his nature. Moreover, as has already been indicated, the manner in which Clairvaux was founded differed in a number of respects from the way in which other affiliated monasteries were founded from Cîteaux between 1112 and 1115. Moreover, we cannot fail to notice that most of those who followed Bernard from Cîteaux to Clairvaux had been among his earliest companions.[31] This may be an indication that they remained a separate group even in Cîteaux.

But these factors, including the fact that the founding of Clairvaux occurred on the same day when that of Morimond had been planned, do not imply that Bernard acted against the express wishes of Stephen Harding. Even though Stephen at times must have found it difficult to deal with this promising but strong-willed monk, he undoubtedly was able to shape him into a Cistercian monk, though of a special kind. And Stephen must have surmised that if given enough opportunity, Bernard could be of great use for the realization of the ideals Cîteaux pursued as a monastic community. He therefore provided Bernard with that opportunity within the confines of the young Cistercian Order. But the rules he instituted to give stability to the Cistercian Order also encapsulated — at least in principle — Bernard's zeal for expansion in such a way that disunity and division could be prevented. And the benefits of Bernard's charismatic contribution to this order were thus partly due to Stephen Harding's ability of adaptation.

Stephen Harding's significance for the order usually remains underexposed, or rather overshadowed, since attention tends to go to Bernard.

---

31. Vp I, c. V, 25; P.L., CLXXXV, 241: ". . . misit in cor abbatis Stephani ad aedificandum domum Clarae-Vallis mittere fratres ejus." Redaction A reads: ". . . fratres ejus et cum eis viros alios religiosos." *Etudes* (1960), 31. It remains unclear whether William of Saint-Thierry is responsible for the exact wording of this first version. It is possible that the words "et cum eius viros alios religiosos," which are missing in redaction B, were added only in 1155/56 by the abbots and bishops who gathered to examine the text of the Vp. Lobrichon, "Représentations de Clairvaux" (1991), 250, with note 25.

Moreover, we have but little direct information about this third abbot of Cîteaux. Born around 1060 in England, Harding had been entrusted by his parents, who belonged to the Anglo-Saxon nobility, as an oblate to the abbey of Sherborne in Dorsetshire. When the Norman conquest of England in 1066 ruined his family, Stephen fled to Scotland and from there to France, where he concluded his education in Paris. Around 1085 he made a pilgrimage to Rome, where he decided to become a monk. And so, on his return journey, he turned to the Molesme monastery in the Langres diocese.[32]

This abbey, founded in 1075, was populated by reform-minded monks led by Abbot Robert. Previously this Robert had been in charge of a Cluniac abbey. In 1072 he had resigned as abbot there to become a monk elsewhere, since he could not agree with the traditional lifestyle of this order. Two years later he joined a group of Eremites. When this group became too large, he founded, in 1075, a new monastery for the group in Molesme, where his family owned land. His stricter view of monastic life, according to the Benedictine Rule, appealed to many. Bruno of Cologne was one of those who stayed for some time in Molesme before he founded the Grande Chartreuse near Grenoble in 1084.

When Stephen Harding entered Molesme in 1086, this monastery already had a number of daughter institutions, mostly based on pre-existing eremitical communities; and their number continued to grow. In addition, Molesme received a wealth of donations. But these possessions and the close contact with the donors, who belonged to the nobility and who frequently gathered in this monastery, forced the community once again to conform to a more traditional life pattern. This created internal tension in the community that Robert was unable to handle. Shortly after 1090, therefore, he left for a community of Eremites, where for a number of years, unburdened by further responsibilities, he was able to experience his monastic spirituality according to his own ideals.

But Robert had left Molesme without officially abdicating and without arranging for a successor. This led to a crisis in this monastery, which eventually was solved by Urban II, who — at the request of the community of Molesme — made Robert return as abbot. The tensions in the community regarding obedience to the Rule of Saint Benedict were, however, not dissolved by Robert's return. Insistence upon a stricter discipline, as some monks urged, would inevitably have caused the community to fall apart. For that reason Robert decided to leave once again, this time accompanied by as many as twenty-one monks from this community. Among them was Stephen Harding, who had already served as Robert's secretary while he was at Molesme.[33]

32. Lekai, *The Cistercians: Ideals and Reality* (1977), 17-18.
33. Lackner (1972), 217-274.

The founding of Cîteaux was the direct result of an exodus of monks from Molesme, which was unique because of the numbers involved. Because of its far-reaching consequences, this event always receives ample attention in the sources that describe the beginnings of the Cistercian Order. Those reports are not always identical, and certainly not with regard to the precise problems and considerations that played a role. We find the oldest account of these events in the *exordium parvum* (chapters I-XII and XVI). Using information from five letters and decrees, this documents deals with the origin of this order.

Most likely this *exordium* was written during the abbacy of Alberic — that is, before 1108 — by a monk who had received his information from Stephen.[34] He mentions, among other things, that at the time, Abbot Robert had left Molesme for a desolate area (a *heremum*) in the bishopric Chalon-sur-Saône, at the advice of Archbishop Hugh of Lyon, the papal legate. This had been put at his disposal by the Duke of Burgundy, at the request of the archbishop of Lyon. Upon arrival, all renewed their vow according to the Rule of Saint Benedict, as they had earlier done at the time of their profession.

It would prove to be important for this "new monastery" that Robert, who, after a complaint from Molesme, had once more been ordered by Urban II to return, allowed those of his followers who had found it difficult to abide by this stricter obedience to the Rule to return with him. This probably saved the recently founded Cîteaux from the tensions and conflicts that caused so much turmoil in the Order of Molesme and in many other eremitical foundations.[35] Likewise it is of importance that Stephen Harding, as Robert's secretary, was intimately familiar with the earlier problems at Molesme, and that subsequently, as the right hand of Alberic, Robert's successor in Cîteaux, he was able to follow closely the later developments.

Stephen Harding, who had personally experienced the circumstances that led to the founding of this "new monastery" and its actual beginnings earlier at Molesme, had therefore had a close view of the confusions that governed the relationship between this monastery and its many filiations. When in Cîteaux he once again experienced how the type of obedience to the Rule that Robert proposed appealed to many, he decided not to commit the same mistakes as had been made in Molesme,

34. Auberger (1986), 43-52.
35. Leyer (1984), 102.

and so arranged the mutual relationships between the filiations that all abbots had equal authority in the administration of the order.

For that reason, when Cîteaux acquired filiations and thus developed into an order, he formulated a spiritual-juridical statute: the *carta caritatis et unanimitatis* to which we already referred. This charter dealt with the relationships between the Cistercian monasteries. One of its precepts was the instituting of a general chapter, in which the abbots would assemble annually at Cîteaux to make collective policy decisions. The oldest extant version of this statute dates from 1119, the year when it was confirmed by Pope Calixtus II. But as was mentioned earlier, it was first drafted in 1113/1114, when La Ferté and Pontigny were founded. In 1114 this version was confirmed by the bishop of Auxerre, who played a role in the founding of Pontigny.[36]

Undoubtedly this statute was once again confirmed when Morimond and Clairvaux were founded in 1115, this time by the bishops of Langres and Châlons-sur-Marne. The statute also provided the abbots of Cistercian monasteries, though under the supervision of the general chapter, with the possibility of establishing and administering their own filiations; and the abbots of Clairvaux and Morimond made ample use of this provision. On the other hand, the statute prohibited the abbots of abbeys with filiations to form their own general chapter with the abbots of these daughter monasteries.

B. Clairvaux besides Cîteaux

When Stephen abdicated as abbot of Cîteaux in 1133, the order already had more than forty filiations.[37] Since the founding of Pontigny in 1114, the number of abbots assembling in September in Cîteaux for the general chapter had increased each year. We may assume that Bernard was always an important voice in the chapter, even when he was absent due to illness

---

36. Marilier (1961), 66, no. 43: "Cartam vero caritatis et unanimitatis inter Novum Monasterium at abbatias ab eo (scl. Stephani) propagatas compositam et corroboratam idem pontifex et canonicorum conventus ratam per omnia habuerunt." For the confirmation of this statute by Calixtus II, see ibid., 81. See also above, 124, with note 79. For the text of the *carta caritatis*, see Bouton and van Damme (1974), 89-102. Auberger (1986), 328-339.

37. Stephen himself mentioned this number in the only letter from him that has been preserved. It was written around 1131 to the monks of Sherborne, the first monastery where he entered. See Bouton, "Bernard et l'abbé de Cîteaux," 175.

or important duties elsewhere. We know but little about his relationship with Stephen Harding, or about his association with Rainald de Bar, Stephen's successor (1133/34-1150). The latter had previously been a monk in Clairvaux and may well have been one of the first companions of Bernard. There is good reason to suppose that Rainald, as the abbot of Cîteaux, stayed in close touch with Bernard, and that he owed his appointment as abbot to Bernard's support.[38]

With regard to the relationship between Bernard and Stephen, they must regularly have met during meetings of the general chapter, and must have had other contacts as well. So much at least is clear from two letters that Bernard sent on his behalf to Louis VI and Pope Honorius II respectively, as well as from some deeds of donations witnessed by both. We further know that Bernard and Stephen at times assigned themselves the task of mediating in conflicts between two monasteries; while in a letter written in 1124, Bernard remarked to the abbot of Morimond that shortly before that, Stephen Harding had visited him when *en route* to Flanders.[39]

While this information should not be taken as evidence of a close cooperation between the two, neither is there proof to the contrary. Bernard does, however, explicitly and formally express his own ties with Cîteaux in a letter to Adam, a monk from Morimond, who together with his abbot had left this monastery in 1124, and had thus broken his promise of "stability" *(stabilitas loci)*:

> But perhaps you will ask how I reconcile the stability I confirmed at Cîteaux with living elsewhere. I answer that, while it is true that I was professed a monk of Cîteaux in that place and was sent by the abbot to live where I do, yet I was sent in peace, without any scandal or discord, according to the customs and common observance of our Order. Therefore, so long as I persevere in the same peace and concord wherein I was sent, so long as I stand fast in unity, I am not preferring my private judgment to the common observance. I am remaining quietly and obediently where I was put. I say my conscience is at peace

38. Initially Stephen was succeeded by Guy, until then abbot of Trois-Fontaines, and also from the school of Bernard. For unknown reasons (see below, 253-255) his abbacy lasted only a few months. He was succeeded by Rainald de Bar, a son of Milon, the count of Bar-sur-Aube, who had supported Bernard in material ways. In a letter to Eugenius III, Bernard described the death of Rainald as a great loss for the order. *Ep.* 270, c. 3; SBO VII, 180.

39. *Epp.* 45 and 49; SBO VII, 133 and 140. Bouton, "Bernard et l'abbé de Cîteaux," 174-175. *Ep.* 4, 1; SBO VII, 24.

because I have not broken the bond of unity, because I have not left the firm ground of peace. And if under obedience I am absent in body from Cîteaux, yet by a fellow devotion, by a life in all things the same, I am always there in spirit. But the day on which I begin to live by other rules (which may God forbid!) and other habits, to keep other observances, to introduce new things and follow different customs, on that day I shall no longer believe I keep my promise of stability.[40]

Nonetheless the question arises whether during Stephen Harding's abbacy Bernard fully complied with the guidelines he mentioned. He did not completely agree with the lifestyle current in the Cistercian monasteries during Stephen's abbacy. He himself lived quite ascetically and desired that the lifestyle of the Cistercians would in all respects be characterized by asceticism. For that reason, in his *Apology* he indirectly protested against the attention given in Cîteaux to the costly illumination of manuscripts.

But there must have been other differences of opinion between the two abbots, among other things about accepting a female branch of the order. Bernard usually provided a home for his female relatives, whom he had led to choose the veil, in the Benedictine monastery of Jully, which had been founded from Molesme at some earlier date. Among these was his sister Humbelinde, who, according to the *vita prima,* at first led a worldly life, but repented through his influence. In doing so, Bernard distanced himself from an initiative of Stephen Harding. Partly at the instigation of Stephen Harding, a group of monials had left Jully in 1125 and founded the monastery of Tart. Unlike in Jully, in Tart the monials were offered a kind of spirituality that included more than the normal weeping over past sins that these women were supposed to have committed, in particular in their married state.[41]

It seems that Bernard did not consult Stephen Harding with regard to all initiatives that were developed from Clairvaux, for instance, concerning the filiations that soon were founded from there. The choice of location for these abbeys often deviated from the kind of place that was usually chosen by Cîteaux. But even if the example of Clairvaux was initially followed, often that monastery was subsequently relocated.[42]

40. *Ep.* 7, c. 16; SBO VII, 43. Transl. James, 35-36.
41. Bouton, "Saint Bernard et les moniales," *Mélanges saint Bernard,* 225-247. Thompson, "The Problem of the Cistercian Nuns in the Twelfth and Early Thirteenth Centuries," in Baker (1978), 227-252.
42. Auberger (1986), 103-107.

However, there is another significant indication that Bernard initially wanted to go his own way within the Order of Cîteaux. This is found in the divergent versions of both the *exordium parvum* and the *carta caritatis et unanimitatis*, often referred to as the *exordium cisterciense*, and the *summa cartae caritatis*. The latter two texts appear to have originated in Clairvaux.

The interrelationship of these four texts has long remained unclear. Since several manuscripts were discovered that transmitted these oldest texts from Clairvaux, widely divergent theories were developed and vehement polemics were carried on.[43] One of the difficulties was to ascertain whether the legal status of the *carta caritatis prior* and of the *summa cartae caritatis* were comparable.

In 1986 Jean-Baptiste Auberger was able to solve this mystery. He showed convincingly that the *summa cartae caritatis* offered a new redaction rather than a summary of the *carta caritatis prior*. There is evidence that it came from Clairvaux.[44] The *summa cartae caritatis* served as a model for the statute that Norbert proclaimed for the monasteries of the Premonstratensian Order. We learn from a letter from Bernard that Prémonstré was founded in 1120 with assistance from Clairvaux. The similarity between the statutes of this order and the *summa cartae caritatis* thus reflects their origin in Clairvaux.[45]

Another indication is the fact that this revision lacks the stipulation that the abbot of a mother abbey may not hold a general chapter with the abbots of its own filiations. The manner in which Clairvaux as the mother abbey in the days of Bernard exerted its authority over its filiations, indicates that this rule was there experienced as a nuisance, in particular during the period of Stephen Harding, when Bernard's influence on the policies of Cîteaux was still limited.[46] This explains why this prescript does not occur in the *summa cartae caritatis*, which must have been drafted long before 1133.

The text of the *exordium cisterciense* precedes the *summa cartae caritatis* in three of its oldest manuscripts. Moreover, this text contains several expressions that have been directly borrowed from Bernard's linguistic usage. Since the content of this *exordium* leads us to date it around 1124, this Bernardine use of language can be explained only if we assume that the text originated in circles close to this

43. Knowles, "The Primitive Documents of the Cistercian Order," in *Great Historical Enterprises* (1963), 197-222. De Place, "Bibliographie raisonnée (1098-1220)," *Cîteaux* 35 (1984), 7-54.

44. Auberger (1986), 34-41 and 52-57.

45. *Ep.* 253, 1; SBO VIII, 150, lines 5-8. Bouton, "Bernard et les Chanoines reguliers," in BdC, 294-296. Van Damme, "La *summa cartae caritatis*, source de constitutions canonicales," *Cîteaux* 23 (1972), 5-54.

46. Pacaut, "La filiation claravalienne" (1991), 135-147. Cf. below, 250-256.

abbot, that is, in Clairvaux. In addition, since the later *carta caritatis posterior,* which dates from 1165 and was regarded as the official constitution of the order, agrees only with the *carta caritatis prior,* this indicates that subsequently the two texts from Clairvaux, which were already in use in Clairvaux when Stephen Harding was the abbot of Cîteaux, did not acquire any official status in the order.

In any case, the special character of the *summa cartae caritatis* and of the *exordium cisterciense* exhibits a unique tradition and the specific ideas that developed in Clairvaux just at that time when Bernard still had to consider the differences of opinion between him and Stephen Harding. It is there-fore possible that from 1133/34 onward, Bernard was less inclined to em-phasize a special tradition for Clairvaux with regard to the Cistercian Order, since he was now able to influence Cîteaux through Abbot Rainald de Bar, who, of course, was not appointed without his approval. We will return later to Rainald's appointment as abbot of Cîteaux.

That before 1133/34 Bernard at times dealt with certain matters in the order on his own authority, thus bypassing Stephen Harding, is also clear from the manner in which he interfered in the crisis at Morimond. This was, among other things, the result of a failed harvest after an extremely severe winter.

But there was also rivalry between Morimond and Clairvaux. In 1118 Clairvaux, which by then had two daughter monasteries, acquired the same rights as La Ferté-sur-Grosne and Pontigny. The abbots of these monasteries had the right of visitation in Cîteaux and its filiations. Morimond had not as yet acquired the same right, even though this abbey had been founded on the very same day as Clairvaux. Arnold was no doubt displeased with this discrimination, which may explain his efforts to ensure that Morimond would not remain behind in its expansion.

When Clairvaux founded Foigny in 1121 as its third filiation, Morimond had already caught up; and in 1123, with the founding of Camps, it even took the lead. Moreover, Morimond had by then been able to increase its social standing, since in 1120, in spite of heavy opposition from his family, a son of the duke of Bavaria had entered as a novice. But Abbot Arnold had been forced to invest so heavily in these filiations that the essential expansion of the estates of his own monastery had been neglected. This proved disastrous after the severe winter of 1123/24 — even more so, since he rejected assistance from Clairvaux to alleviate the food shortage in his community during the famine that occurred.[47]

47. *Etudes* (1960), 65, with note 2. Grill, "Der heilige Bernhard von Clairvaux und Morimond," in *Festschrift,* 31-118.

For that reason, in 1124 Arnold decided to travel to Jerusalem together with some fellow-brethren. This was an emergency measure, which at the time was regarded as befitting the hopelessness of the situation. But his decision was at variance with the obligation of *stabilitas loci* prescribed by the Rule, and it led to the excommunication of Arnold and his companions by the general chapter. The pilgrims did not get any further than Cologne, where early in 1125 their leader died. Prior to the ruling of the general chapter, Bernard had sent Arnold a letter on behalf of Stephen Harding (whom, he said, he had not yet informed about Arnold's departure), ordering him to return to Morimond. He also wrote about the same matter to Bruno, the provost of Sankt Gereon in Cologne, to Pope Calixtus II, and twice to Adam, a monk who had followed his abbot to Cologne.[48]

Due to Bernard's intervention, this crisis was indeed resolved. The estates of Morimond were enlarged; and Gaucher, until then the prior of Clairvaux, became its new abbot. After his death in 1138, the abbey received complete independence. Otto of Freising, who had already before 1124 become a member of this community, was then chosen as Gaucher's successor. The monks of this abbey did not afterward foster any hard feelings against Bernard because of his interference.

But Morimond did continue to protest against its subordination to Clairvaux, which lasted until after Bernard's death. Only in 1157 did the abbot of Morimond also acquire the right of visitation in Cîteaux and its filiations. As far as Bernard's writings and the oldest *vita* are concerned, these found wide distribution in the monasteries within Morimond's sphere of influence. But, as was said earlier, these monasteries preferred the earlier version, which they apparently regarded as more authoritative, to the official redaction, which, due to the influence of Clairvaux, gradually became the norm in the Cistercian Order after the canonization of Bernard.

The most likely explanation of why, after this crisis of 1124, Bernard continued to be held in high regard in Morimond, in spite of its rivalry with Clairvaux, is found in another conflict that occurred at roughly the same time, in which the abbot of Clairvaux also played a major role. For the Cistercians this conflict implicitly meant less attention for internal controversies, as far as these existed, and, in particular, a closing of the ranks. In 1125 Bernard wrote his notorious *Apology*, which would unintentionally create lasting discord between Cluniacs and Cistercians.

---

48. *Epp.* 4, 6, 359, 5, and 7; SBO VII, 24-27, 29-30; VIII, 304-305; VII, 28-29 and 31-46. The excommunication is mentioned in *Ep.* 7, 19; *Receuil* III, 392, with note 5.

2. BERNARD AND CLUNY

A. Bernard's Interference in the Crisis in Cluny (1122-1126)

The chartulary of Clairvaux contains a charter in which Peter the Venerable confirms an exemption from the payment of tithes granted by his predecessor, Pons of Melgueil, to Bernard and his fellow brethren, as well as their successors.[49] This exemption, granted between 1115 and 1122, points to an initially positive relationship between the two monasteries. It also refutes the idea that a longstanding rivalry between Cluniacs and Cistercians prompted Bernard, at some time between 1119 and 1125, to attack Cluny in two polemical writings by fiercely castigating its prevailing lifestyle, with the intent of creating or increasing friction between the two orders.

For a long time, Bernard's criticism in these writings was regarded as directed against the policies of Abbot Pons, who allegedly was responsible for the disorderly behavior that was said to have been rampant in Cluny. For that reason, after complaints had reached the ears of Pope Paschal II, Pons had been forced to abdicate in 1122. The pope was also motivated by protests from bishops who felt thwarted in the execution of their office by the many exemption privileges the Cluniac abbeys had received from Rome. Another reason mentioned for Pons's abdication was a change in papal policy with regard to these exemptions for monasteries, which supposedly had already been agreed upon before the First Lateran Council of 1123.

This view concurred with the presupposition that Robert of Châtillon's move from Clairvaux to Cîteaux must have occurred while Pons of Melgueil was still the abbot, and that the first reaction of Bernard on this luring away of his young nephew, which is known as "the Letter in the Rain," was written as early as 1119, that is, during Pons's abbacy. This idea received further support from the fact that the letter register that Geoffrey of Auxerre arranged in consultation with Bernard begins with this letter, which was therefore considered as one of his earliest epistles. But the suggestion that Bernard's polemics were directed against the Cluny of Abbot Pons has become extremely dubious, since external evidence has shown that this letter was not written before 1124. Even so, many find it difficult to abandon the traditional view.[50]

---

49. Waquet (1950), 7, no. V.
50. Holdsworth, "The Early Writings of Bernard of Clairvaux" (1994), 20-56, esp. 48. Cf. above, 129, with note 90.

In all their speculations about what happened in Cluny in 1122, these historians failed to consider to what extent Bernard's criticism of the monastic lifestyle in Cluny could have been prompted by the restorative changes effected in the period after the involuntary abdication of Abbot Pons. Yet it made sense to examine this relationship, for it would be unthinkable that a matter that proved to be a major concern for Benedictine monks everywhere else would have left the Cluniac communities completely untouched. In addition, from the beginning of the twelfth century onward, Cluny had to search for an answer to the question about the degree to which the monastic observances that had been prevailing since the ninth century, with their liturgical emphasis, could be relevant in a world that was undergoing enormous change — a world where the use of the plow was becoming of equal importance with the wielding of the sword. For that reason society was justified in expecting a different kind of social interaction than one that consisted solely of full-time choral prayer in support of a continuously warring knighthood.

Taking these social changes into consideration, the decadence of Pons's rule consisted mainly of the fact that he was open to a renewal of contemporary monastic life — a renewal that actually proposed a return to the lifestyle of the earliest monks. This attempt not only led to the founding of new hermitages, but also found response in already existing monasteries, including those of the Cluniacs. There this response repeatedly led to tensions and conflicts between supporters and opponents. These were more intense in Cluny, since the movement for renewal wanted more emphasis on manual labor, which was prescribed by the Rule but had been sadly neglected in Cluny.

Compliance with this desire meant, however, that there would be less time for liturgical matters than the Cluniacs were accustomed to. And this, in particular, was viewed by many as proof of spiritual decline, as was made abundantly clear by Cardinal Matthew of Albano, the chief opponent in Cluny. As late as 1131/32, when Peter the Venerable was already contemplating reforms, he vehemently resisted the plans of some abbots of Benedictine monasteries in the diocese of Reims, which were affiliated with Cluny, to reform the lifestyle of their monks. In his rebuttal he expressly rejected manual labor as inferior.

On the other hand, such a modification of the lifestyle also offered an economic perspective. Abbot Pons must have realized the importance of such changes in view of the major expenses Cluny was facing. (Among other things it had to care for the building of a new, monumental abbey church. The costs were to be recovered from the pilgrims who traveled via Cluny to Compostella, but there was an acute cash-flow problem.) Also the extensive income that this abbey used to receive in cash from Spain and elsewhere had decreased and was less regular than before. This drop in income could be compensated for only if new donors were found or if the agricultural profits from its own estates, which had been neglected and had therefore declined, could once again be boosted.[51]

Pons's choice for this solution, inspired by the economic depression in Cluny, implied a violation of the constitution in which the Cluniac lifestyle was formulated. Thus there ensued an irreconcilable difference of opinion about this change and modification of the customs, which for many had become more sacrosanct than the Rule itself. This subsequently led to a complaint against Pons in Rome, resulting in his involuntary abdication. But that did not end the conflict in Cluny.

The reformers, who wanted stricter observance of the Rule, as was the case elsewhere — for instance, in the Cistercian Order — began to stir once more when Pons returned from his Jerusalem pilgrimage, undertaken after his abdication. He had found shelter in a small hermitage in Northern Italy, which was a filiation of Cluny. His stay there prompted Calixtus II and Honorius II in 1124 and 1125, at the request of Peter the Venerable, to forbid the monks of Cluny to visit Pons without prior approval of their abbot.[52]

At the instigation of William of Saint-Thierry, who himself was an outspoken supporter of this desire for reform in the existing Benedictine monasteries, Bernard interfered in this new commotion. William knew what was happening in Cluny and wanted to intervene, but he needed Bernard's pen in doing so. The latter was willing to get involved in the conflict, in the first instance with the open letter he wrote in 1124, or more probably at the beginning of 1125, to his nephew Robert, who had been in Cluny for some years.[53]

In this letter, which, as mentioned above, has remained known as "The Letter in the Rain," Bernard sharply protests against the injustice the grand prior of Cluny had inflicted upon him as the abbot of Clairvaux by

51. "Le rôle de l'agriculture" (1994). Also *Christendom and Christianity* (1994), 130-150. For the construction of Cluny III as a church for pilgrims, see Werckmeister, "Cluny III and the Pilgrimage to Santiago de Compostella," *Gesta* 27 (1988), 103-111.

52. *Cluny et Cîteaux* (1985), 122 and 138, note 39.

53. Above, 122, with note 72. *Recueil* III, 395-396.

luring away this young and inexperienced monk on the pretext that, when he was a child, his parents had promised him to Cluny. In this letter Bernard also criticized Cluny because its lifestyle had been relaxed by modifications in the liturgical *consuetudines*. He contrasted these with the observance of the Cistercians, to which the supporters of Pons were more inclined. William, however, was not satisfied with this letter, since it did not deal openly enough with the internal controversies in Cluny. He therefore requested Bernard to redo his homework; Bernard then wrote his *Apology*.

William's request to Bernard to take up his pen once again has not been preserved, but we do have Bernard's assent. Since Mabillon, this letter had been regarded as an introduction to the *Apology*. But Jean Leclercq has shown that William had already received the letter before Bernard had written the earliest version of the *Apology*:

> I am happy to accept your assignment to devote myself to a work which is intended to take away the vexation from the kingdom of God, but it is still unclear to me how you want me to go about this task. For in the gratifying reading and even more gratifying re-reading of your most enjoyable letter, which gave me more pleasure each time I read it again, I understood that you wish me to vindicate myself against those who complain that we deprecate the Order of Cluny. It must show that the evil, which they attribute to us or make others attribute to us, is untrue. But if, after such a vindication, I *once more* deal, in the way you suggest, with the luxuriance of the Cluniacs in food and clothing, and with other things also mentioned by you, I cannot but create the impression that I contradict myself. And this inevitably will cause new irritation, unless I combine praise for this Order and reproach for those who castigate it with criticism of this opulence. Indicate more clearly whether I should proceed in such a way, or whether you prefer another approach, and pray earnestly to God, that I may be able to do what you desire, in the way you desire. Nonetheless, you must know, that this kind of writing disturbs me considerably, as it greatly impedes my religious exercises and interferes with my devotion to prayer, the more so, since I am not used to writing and do not have the time for it.[54]

This letter indicates that the twofold task expected of Bernard was to praise the Cluniac Order and protect it against criticism from others, but, at the

---

54. *Ep.* 84 bis; SBO VII, 219.

same time, to show disapproval for the abuses that were current in Cluny. Bernard did not identify himself with this scornful reproach, which, as he admitted in his *Apology*, was also resorted to by Cistercians who prided themselves for their asceticism. As proof of his loyalty to the Cluniacs, he emphasized how he had sent back a monk from one of their abbeys who had sought entry into Clairvaux.[55]

In a following section of this tract, Bernard stated that he felt compelled to defend the Cluniac Order against its critics because of his respect and appreciation for it. But this also forced him to criticize some abuses that had gained entrance, including the generally accepted opulent lifestyle. This more specifically had to do with the attention given to food, drink, clothing, comfort, adornments, housing, and other practices that were contrary to the letter or the spirit of the Rule. He also censured the luxuriousness in the building and furnishing of their churches, which was unbefitting, in particular for monks.

That Bernard was more circumspect than he usually was is apparent from the fact that he wrote three different versions, of which two have been preserved. He did not immediately submit the oldest version of this treatise, which is not extant, to William of Saint-Thierry, but asked for the opinion of someone who was not directly involved with this internal conflict in Cluny: Oger, a regular canon from the Mont-Saint Eloy monastery near Atrecht.

This does not imply that Bernard at the time found it difficult to rely on William's judgment. From a letter sent by Bernard to Oger during the Lent period of 1125, we learn that the latter had already received the text of some other recent writings of Bernard.[56] From a second letter, addressed to him in the summer of 1125, we further learn that at that time Oger had also received the initial version of the *Apology*. This letter was Bernard's answer to a message from Oger that has not been preserved. He had therein notified Bernard that in the meantime he had copied the text of the *Apology*, in order to submit this copy to William of Saint-Thierry. The second letter to Oger also contained an instruction how he was supposed to appraise the first version:

> Do not hesitate, I beg you, to find an opportunity of going to see him, and do not on any account allow anyone to see or copy the aforesaid

55. *Apo* II, 4; SBO III, 84, line 11.
56. *Ep.* 89, 3. *Recueil* III, 394-395.

booklet until you have been through it with him, discussed it with him, and have both made such corrections as may be necessary, so that every word of it may be supported by two witnesses (Deuteronomy 19:15; Matthew 18:16). I leave to the judgment of you both whether it shall be published, or shown only to a few, or to none at all. I also leave to you both to decide whether the preface you have put together out of my other letters will stand or whether it would not be better to compose another.[57]

Bernard further mentioned in this letter that at the time of his visit to Clairvaux, Oger could take another tract for his evaluation. A passage in the *Apology*, occurring in both extant versions, in which Bernard directly addresses Oger, indicates that this visit did indeed take place. Oger therefore came to Clairvaux before even one of the versions that have been preserved was written. This implies that Oger also was allowed to judge the oldest extant version of this treatise.[58]

Besides three major variants, there are a few smaller differences between the two extant versions. In the final version, two passages were added to the text, while one remark that Bernard had initially included was eliminated. This remark concerned an incident that Bernard would have doubted if his own eyes had not been able to confirm what someone had reported to him.[59] The additions deal with subjects that Bernard had not referred to earlier, and were made at the request of William. This suggests that at some earlier moment, William may well have made a proposal to Bernard about the things he felt ought to be dealt with in the *Apology*. And that, in turn, would tend to confirm the supposition that in this tract Bernard touched upon an internal conflict in the Benedictine monasteries. Initially this was relevant to the Cistercians only inasmuch as they served as a role model for the reform party in Cluny.

From Bernard's consultations with Canon Oger, it is clear that he ran the risk that his *Apology* would be misunderstood, and that he sought to safeguard himself against that. This explains why it took him a year to write the *Apology*, and why it was distributed only from 1125 onward. Bernard apparently took his time. But in another respect, he was somewhat less conscientious in preparing this tract. The examples that were to illustrate his criticism of the opulence that had entered Cluny were not all

57. *Ep.* 88, 3; SBO VII, 234. Transl. James, 136-137.
58. *Apo* XII, 30; SBO III, 106, line 26 to 107, line 3. *Recueil* III, 401-402.
59. SBO III, 68.

from Cluny itself. This surfaced in a rather interesting way, as we have already seen, in his criticism of the sculptures that were supposedly used to embellish the capitals in the cloisters, but in reality referred to illuminations that had been produced in Cîteaux in its own manuscripts. And there were other examples of Cluniac wealth, which in actual fact he had seen or encountered elsewhere. It has been reported that he must have seen some of the liturgical objects that he disapproved of in Saint-Denis rather than in Cluny;[60] while the abbot of Cluny, who traveled with many horses, accompanied by a large party, with much pomp and splendor, may have been modeled after Abbot Suger of Saint-Denis. In any case, this characterization cannot have been true of Abbot Pons.[61]

Bernard had a good reason for this seeming carelessness in the choice of his examples. The two paragraphs in question toward the end of his *Apology*, where he scolded the extravagance in the manner in which the abbey church of Cluny was built and furnished, followed his criticism of the Cluniac lifestyle. He made a clear transition between the preceding comments and his final chapter, which dealt with the extravagance in the abbey churches. He begins his chapter with these words:

> But these are small things; I am coming to things of greater importance, but which seem smaller, because they are more common.

In this chapter Bernard broaches some inappropriate things that not only occurred in Cluny, but were also quite noticeable in abbey churches elsewhere. These things would have been permissible in parochial churches, but not in churches of monasteries:

> I will overlook the immense heights of the places of prayer, their immoderate lengths, their superfluous widths, the costly refinements, and the painstaking representations which deflect the attention while they are in them of those who pray and thus hinder their devotion. To me they somehow represent the ancient rite of the Jews. But so be it, let these things be made for the honor of God.
>
> However, as a monk, I put to monks the same question that a pagan used to criticize other pagans. "Tell me, priest," he said, "what

---

60. Rudolph (1990), 57-69.

61. The relationship was first referred to in the *Chronica Sancti Bertini* of around 1388, on the basis of Bernard's portrayal in his Apology of the abbot of Cluny, who traveled with great pomp. *Cluny et Cîteaux* (1985), 322.

is gold doing in the holy place?" I, however, say, "Tell me, poor man, if indeed you are poor men, what is gold doing in the holy place?"[62]

In this final chapter, Bernard *en passant* addressed a much wider monastic public, confronting them with abuses that also prevailed outside Cluny, even in Cîteaux.

From a passage quoted earlier in this book,[63] we discover how Bernard was aggravated by the fact that precisely in Clairvaux manuscripts were illuminated in a similar way. However, since in his *Apology* he officially addressed only matters related to Cluny, he had to mention his criticism of this kind of illumination more indirectly. He therefore pretended to speak about sculptures that could be admired in the cloister of Cluny. Such veiled reference seemed acceptable, since elsewhere cloisters were embellished with somewhat similar images. This excursus, in which Bernard moved away from his topic, shows that, if necessary, he had no qualms in introducing a different matter in a text about a more or less well-defined subject — naturally for those who had ears to hear.

As was mentioned above, in 1125/26, after the *Apology* had been distributed, some rather drastic events happened in Cluny, which neither William nor Oger, and certainly not Bernard, had foreseen. While Peter the Venerable sojourned in Spain, among other things in order to find new supplies of money, Pons returned in 1125 to Cluny. Whether he was led to this decision by what Bernard had written is unknown. But upon his arrival, his earlier adherents once again rallied to his support and drove the followers of Peter the Venerable away. In the following year Peter's party had to use force to reconquer the abbey and to spend scarce money for a small army of mercenaries.[64] Subsequently this scandal led to a process in Rome, where Pons died a little later as a prisoner.

These events damaged Bernard's reputation to such a degree that henceforth, in any case in France, he stayed away from the internal controversies that for a long time would keep the older Benedictine monasteries and congregations divided. This attitude was further reinforced, at least initially, by the letter Peter the Venerable sent to him in which he accused the Cistercians of pharisaical self-complacency, and which was

---

62. *Apo* XII, 28; SBO III, 104. Transl. Rudolph (1990), 10. Bernard quotes Qersius, *Satires* II, 69.

63. Above, 204-205, with note 21.

64. Cowdrey, "Abbot Pontius of Cluny," 234-243.

simultaneously addressed to the priors of Cluny's filiations. This extensive document also contained Peter's argumentation for insisting upon the continued observance of the customs of his order.[65]

In so doing, Peter created the impression for the outside world that Bernard had not written his *Apology* to interfere in an internal conflict in Cluny, but had intended only to confront the lifestyle of the Cluniacs with that of the Cistercians, while there were no problems in Cluny itself. This approach served to hide the scandals of the present for future generations, as was considered wise in those days. And he definitely saw the events that had transpired during the early years of his abbacy in Cluny as a scandal. Also, in his later account of these events in the *vita* of Matthew of Albano written after Matthew's death, Peter the Venerable — improperly — suggests that at the time almost all had turned against Pons, and that the violence used to chase him from Cluny should in fact have been employed by Pons in his attempt to reestablish himself in this abbey.[66] The *vita*, of course, did not allude to any internal conflict in Cluny, nor to what Bernard had written about it.

As a result of this strategy of disguise, Bernard's polemical writings, in which he supported the reform-minded Cluniacs, were usually regarded as an attack on Cluny from the outside. He thus failed in what he had set out to do. Subsequently Bernard remained silent; and he later ensured that other Cistercians did the same, or at least did not write about it while he was still alive,[67] since Matthew of Albano and Chancellor Haimeric had succeeded in enlisting his support in the papal schism after the death of Honorius II, which they regarded as inevitable.[68] Thus the portrayal by Peter the Venerable of Bernard's intentions with his satire about the monastic life of Cluny contributed to the fact that ever after, the differences

65. *Ep.* 28. *Letters* I, 52-101. For the date of this letter see II, 270-274. For the distribution of this letter to the Cluniac priors, II, 206, notes with *Ep.* 161.

That Bernard's reputation was somewhat damaged as a result of his interference in this Cluniac controversy can be deduced from letters 17 and 18 (SBO VII, 65-69). Bernard wrote these in answer to questions from the Cardinal-dean Peter, who was sent from Rome as a temporary legate to investigate this scandal. Cf. *Cluny and Cîteaux* (1985), 72-73 and 313-315. Knowles, "Cistercians and Cluniacs" (1964), 59.

66. *Petri Cluniacensis abbatis. De miraculis,* liber II, c. XII; ed. Bouthillier, CC, cont. med. 83 (1988), 117-120. In *Ep.* 192, written by Peter to Bernard in May 1152, he admitted that many had left during the schism of Pons: "cum innumeri declinaverint"; *Letters* I, 446.

67. The first Cistercian polemic against Cluny — the *Dialogus duorum monachorum* — was not written until after Bernard's death. *Cluny et Cîteaux* (1985), 249.

68. Cf. above, 130. Also "Saint Bernard in His Relations" (1992), note 19.

between Cluny and Cîteaux were interpreted as a contrast that already had the seeds of hostility within it.

Of course, that alleged hostility of Cistercians against Cluniacs then began to lead a life of its own. The resulting enmity between the two orders also influenced negatively the relationship between Bernard and Peter the Venerable. In spite of all the cultic praise that until the present has been showered on their relationship and the jubilation about their bond as one of a friendship between two saints, their association was, in fact, strained, or even very strained. The dissimilarity in their characters may also have played a role in this respect.

B. The Relationship between Bernard and Peter the Venerable

In 1773 the Maurist Dom Charles Clémencet published a synopsis of the life stories and the writings of Bernard of Clairvaux and Peter the Venerable. In this work — a kind of descriptive summary — the author gives only cursory attention to the relationship between the two abbots, even when dealing with the letters they wrote to each other. However, he does state in his introduction that the gifts of head and heart of both saints, as well as the nobility of their sentiments, together with their consensus with regard to virtue, constituted a mutual bond that manifested a renewal of Christian friendship such as at one time, in the fourth century, had existed between Saint Basil and Saint Gregory of Nazianzus.[69]

Several nineteenth-century authors have tried to describe this friendship in more detail. They based their opinions on the letters in which both abbots, back and forth, testified in lofty terms of their friendship for the other. But such statements were inevitable commonplaces in medieval correspondence, and no solid conclusions regarding friendships should be drawn from them. This applies *a fortiori* for the correspondence between monks, who more or less repeated the expressions of praise that they chanted in their prayers.

This style of correspondence had to do with the fact that medieval letters were far from private. They therefore seldom contained concrete

---

69. *Histoire littéraire*, p. V. This statement is quoted in "Saint Bernard in His Relations" (1992), note 1. This paragraph is heavily dependent on this article. The article "The Controversy between Peter the Venerable and Saint Bernard of Clairvaux" (1956), 53-71, is now completely outdated.

information, which was usually conveyed orally by the person who delivered the letter. Letters between monks and religious were usually comprised mostly of pious statements and abounded in expressions derived from oft-cited texts of Scripture that had become current in monastic parlance.[70]

On the other hand, there is no doubt that external circumstances complicated the relationship between the two abbots. To a large extent it was determined by the context of their formal and informal roles and by the vested interests related to those roles. In some ways these interests differed, and in some ways they coincided. Moreover, their relationship cannot be detached from their respective ties to others, such as between Peter the Venerable and Matthew, cardinal of Albano and papal legate in France, and between Bernard and William of Saint-Thierry, the abbot of a monastery affiliated with Cluny, who continued to be blamed by Peter the Venerable for his share in Bernard's *Apology*.[71]

At a later time they were diametrically opposed to each other regarding Peter Abelard, who was chased by one and protected by the other. They also differed with regard to Nicholas of Clairvaux. (We will return to this in more detail in the next section of this chapter.) In addition, Peter the Venerable had stronger anti-Jewish feelings than Bernard, who in turn was less interested in Islam than his colleague from Cluny. We should acknowledge, however, the attempts of both abbots to pursue the virtue of Christian love, which prompted them in their letters to give a literary testimony of their lofty feelings for each other.

With the passing of years their actual relationship must have changed by virtue of the fact that the social importance attached by others to their person and function must also have changed. When Peter the Venerable was elected as abbot of Cluny in 1122, his social status at first greatly surpassed that of Bernard; but later Bernard's social importance exceeded that of Peter the Venerable when he became known for his preaching and miracles, his many activities outside his monastery, and the rapid growth of the Cistercian Order, of which — certainly after 1134 — he became the most significant exponent.

Nonetheless, the nature of their relationship was largely determined

70. For this idealizing description and the criticisms it evoked, see "Saint Bernard in His Relations" (1992), 315-316, notes 2 and 3. Also Constable (1976), 52-55. Idem (ed.), *Letters* II, 23-28.

71. When William's successor in Saint-Thierry (1136) entered into a communion of prayer with Cluny, he had to insist that his predecessor would not be excluded from this communion. *Cluny et Cîteaux* (1985), 138, note 26.

by their earliest contacts. The manner in which they reacted to each other, and then experienced and judged the attitude of the other, were decisive. Not having known each other before, they nevertheless succeeded in maneuvering each other into a difficult position; while Bernard became the subject of criticism. This peculiar start of their relationship resulted in the fact that both, each in his own way, again and again had to focus on the permanent results of their first encounter, in any case in situations where their interests diverged. Moreover, such situations, at times for the one and then again for the other, were rather more the rule than the exception.

However, the manner in which in 1127/28 Peter the Venerable, in a letter to Bernard, defended his order's observance of its own *consuetudines*, was no longer realistic. Five years later he was already forced to plead for a modification of some of these immutable customs, which eventually, in 1146, led to a series of statutes of reform.[72] Possibly Peter the Venerable only began to change his mind regarding these matters after his visit to the abbey of Peterborough in England in 1130. This community resisted the Cluniac abbot who had been forced upon them. The sources do not inform us about the nature of the conflict; but the disagreements, which simultaneously caused a crisis in Saint Mary near York and led to the founding of the Cistercian monastery of Fountains, lead us to conclude that this same desire for a reformation of lifestyle, which had earlier led to schism in Cluny, later also caused division in some English Benedictine monasteries.[73]

Peter's experiences in Peterborough, in any case, influenced his decision in 1132 to assemble the priors of all filiations in Cluny, including those from England and Italy. The guidelines for reform of the Cluniac customs that were subsequently issued, however, provoked so much resistance that through the years Peter had to do everything possible finally to realize some changes. Eventually he found he could not succeed without support from the Cistercians, in particular from Bernard himself. This policy change, which began around 1130, led him in 1144, some eighteen years after he had written the letter that had brought public embarrassment to Bernard, to propose a measure of cooperation between Cluniacs and Cistercians. Such collaboration would earlier have been unthinkable, and was still unacceptable for Bernard at that late moment.

72. Constable (ed.), "Statuta Petri Venerabilis," CC Mon. VI, 19-106.
73. Knowles, *The Monastic Order*, 102-104 and 231-235.

An excuse for his initial attitude toward Peter the Venerable might have been that Bernard's early position must in part have been determined by the views of Cardinal-legate Matthew of Albano. The latter may well have advised Peter how he could restore things to normal in Cluny, and how he could reduce Bernard's involvement with the internal difficulties in Cluny to differences between Cluniacs and Cistercians.

As mentioned earlier, Matthew of Albano, previously the prior of Saint-Martin-des-Champs, was the most indomitable defender of the Cluniac traditions. Undoubtedly he exerted a heavy influence on Peter the Venerable, who began his abbacy in Cluny under Matthew's supervision as grand prior. Matthew was also the one who removed Robert of Châtillon from Clairvaux, since this Robert had earlier been promised by his parents to Cluny. His status within the order was further enhanced by his role in the process against Pons, the more so since he was then elected as the cardinal-bishop of Albano and also designated as the papal legate in France.

Considering the close relationship between Peter the Venerable and Matthew, we may assume that Bernard must initially have had little confidence in what Peter, around 1132, had in mind with his intentions of reforming the Cluniac Order. For while the abbot of Cluny called a large number of delegates from the numerous Cluniac monasteries to a meeting in an attempt to introduce some cautious modifications of the *consuetudines,* we find Matthew of Albano resisting — with all his power and with a degree of success — the efforts of some Benedictine abbots, in the diocese of Reims under the direction of William of Saint-Thierry, to initiate some substantial reforms in their monasteries.

Bernard must have felt frustrated by the counteroffensive of the cardinal-legate, the more so since Matthew had succeeded in preventing the abbot of Clairvaux from participating in the reform-minded chapter of the Benedictine abbots in the archdiocese of Reims. But this offside position, into which he had maneuvered Bernard, did not apply to England. At about the same time Bernard there interfered in a controversy regarding the observance of the Rule of Saint Benedict, which had led to a split in the abbey of Saint Mary, near York, and a little later, in part through his involvement, resulted in the establishment of the Cistercian monastery of Fountains.[74]

When he first heard rumors about these attempts at reform by Peter the Venerable — which probably had somehow received publicity — Bernard must, because of Matthew's resistance, have paid little attention to this report, the more so since Peter the Venerable had not clearly distanced himself from Matthew's defense of the Cluniac traditions, through which he had torpedoed the chapter of the abbots at Reims, in spite of their difference of opinion on this matter.

Peter the Venerable also continued to cherish the memory of Matthew after

74. Ibid., 236-239.

the cardinal's death in 1136. He wrote a *vita,* probably in preparation for his canonization.[75] But, as already indicated, Bernard must have regarded Peter's account therein of the chaos Abbot Pons allegedly caused in Cluny, and of what Matthew of Albano then did to limit and to repair the damage, as biased — if indeed he ever set eyes on this document.

We do not know how and when the two abbots first met. It may have been already at the assembly at Etampes, where the majority of the French church acknowledged Innocent II as the lawfully elected pope. But they became closer during the Council of Pisa in 1135. There they worked closely together to end the papal schism. This presented no problem, since there were no conflicting monastic interests. Peter the Venerable in particular was very impressed by this encounter. Two years later he reminded Bernard in a letter how they had opened up to each other; he expressed his appreciation and joy for the spiritual experience this encounter had brought:

> Only He, who I worship and embrace in you, knows how much respect and how much love my innermost soul retains for you. This I also did, when your absence kept your physical countenance hidden from me, since the countenance of your blessed soul — which, we know, can move faster than your body — remained vividly before me.[76]

Some reservations regarding this and other expressions of friendship that we find in this letter seem to be justified, since it fails to mention why Peter sent this complimentary letter to Bernard, except perhaps to encourage him in his attempts to end the papal schism in Italy.

Early in 1138 Peter the Venerable wrote another short letter to Bernard in which he reminded the latter of this first epistle, to which he had not responded. This letter was delivered to Bernard by the Archdeacon Gebuinus, who would further inform him orally. This may also have been the case when Bernard received the first letter, since that epistle also contained no material information. Peter sent yet a third letter to Bernard, which has not been preserved, but which was answered by Bernard in 1138. Once again, it contained no factual information.

---

75. "La canonisation de Saint Hugues" (1990), 166-167. See also above, 35, with note 31.

76. *Ep. 65. Letters* I, 194. For the date of this letter, see II, 140-141. Cf. "Saint Bernard in His Relations" (1992), 324.77.

Bernard merely responded to the compliments of Peter and expressed his satisfaction that the schism had been ended after the death of Anacletus. He further told Peter that he longed for a good opportunity to meet him.[77]

We can only guess about the nature of the oral messages that may have been delivered by the carriers of these letters. For around the same time a conflict arose between the Cluniacs and the Cistercians that kept them divided. Since Bernard was in Italy, he most likely was not directly involved in the controversy; but through the carrier of his lofty letter, Peter may have wanted to inform Bernard, naturally with the request to mediate in this conflict. The problem concerned the exemption of the payment of tithes that the pope, already in 1132, had granted the Cistercians for all their estates. Peter the Venerable had earlier protested against this privilege in two letters, which he addressed to Innocent II and Haimeric, the cardinal-chancellor, between 1135 and 1137.[78] This protest was prompted by a conflict of interest that had arisen between the Cluniac priory of Gigny and the abbey of le Miroir, near Gigny.

This Cluniac priory was entitled to the tithes of the profits from estates that subsequently had been donated by a third party to le Miroir. As a result of this papal privilege, the abbot of le Miroir now refused to pay these tithes to the community of Gigny. Peter the Venerable protested twice against this situation to the general chapter of the Cistercians. In his first letter he described this papal privilege as a bone of contention between the two orders. Since this letter remained unanswered, he sent another in the following year, in which he argued that the indignation that so he had heard, his first letter had caused, was fully unjustified.[79]

This expectation of Peter the Venerable that Bernard, with whom he had had such a good relationship in Pisa, would solve this problem between the two orders — conceivably why he may have written this letter — was in vain. For years this controversy between the two monasteries over these tithes continued. It was further intensified in 1151, when both parties even resorted to violence. These rather significant incidents obliged Bernard to repeatedly contact Peter the Venerable, but without any results, since the pope sided with the Cistercians. In 1152 Eugenius III went so far as to force the monks of Gigny, at the risk of

---

77. *Ep.* 73. *Letters* I, 206. About Gebuinus, see *Letters* II, 144-145; *Ep.* 147; SBO VII, 350-351 (= *Ep.* 74, *Letters* I, 207-208).

78. *Epp.* 33 and 34; *Letters* I, 107-113. Probably written between 1135 and 1137; cf. II, 123.

79. *Epp.* 35 and 36; *Letters* I, 113-117.

an interdict and excommunication, to reimburse the damage le Miroir had suffered.[80]

Only shortly after Bernard's death was this conflict permanently resolved by Pope Anastasius IV, the immediate successor of Eugenius III. He decided in favor of the Cluniacs, who before had been on the losing end. He ordered the Cistercians to pay the amounts they owed and to repay the fines that more than once the Cluniacs had been required to pay because of their acts of violence.[81]

In view of the fact that Peter and Bernard were constantly involved in this unsavory conflict of interests between the two monasteries, we must probably see these friendly letters that they exchanged, and that failed to resolve the ongoing controversy between the two orders, as an interchange of diplomatic compliments rather than as expressions of genuine, personal friendship that bound them together.

This conclusion is confirmed by the course of another conflict, which was shorter in duration but no less intense. It began in 1138 and concerned the election of a bishop in the diocese of Langres. This bishopric, in which not only three major, older Benedictine abbeys, but also the monasteries of Molesme, Clairvaux, and Morimond were situated, had been governed since 1125 by Vilain d'Aigremont, a relative of Bernard. After his death in 1136, the episcopal see remained vacant for about two years because the chapter of Langres could not agree on a successor of Vilain. A number of canons, led by the deacon of the chapter, proposed a Cluniac monk as their candidate. Others rejected this candidate categorically, perhaps because they considered Cluny, with its exemption privilege, a threat for the episcopal authority and thus for the influence of the chapter. This animosity against Cluny was shared by some of the canons from Lyon, where the current archbishop himself was originally from Cluny.

This archbishop found the Cluniac candidate for Langres fully acceptable. He was supported in this by the bishops of Autun and Mâcon; while Peter the Venerable gave him permission to accept the post. As a result, he was appointed to this office by Innocent II in 1138, to be followed by his consecration when Louis VI had granted him the investiture over the bishopric. This matter was very much alive when Bernard returned

---

80. Constable, "Cluniac Tithes and the Controversy between Gigny and Le Miroir," 591-624. For this decision of Eugenius III, ibid., 620. For a report of the negotiations that Bernard sent to this pope, *Ep.* 283; SBO VIII, 197-198.

81. *Bullarium cluniacensis*, 63.

from Italy. Since he had not been able to get involved in the case while in Italy, he belatedly protested against both the election and the consecration of this Cluniac. He objected, on the one hand, against the person of the candidate, who he felt was leading an unworthy life and did not have a virtuous reputation; and, on the other hand, against the procedure that had been followed. This supposedly had not been correct, and therefore he considered the consecration of the candidate as illegal.[82]

Another argument that Bernard used in his report to Innocent II about the whole process was that he had not been consulted, contrary to the promise of the archbishop and the deacon of the chapter of Langres. Both had travelled to Rome in connection with this succession and had been told by Innocent II to consult other "religious persons" in the election of a bishop; that is, to contact the abbots of the monasteries in the diocese. Since they had not consulted him, Bernard later felt that they had failed in their task.[83]

Other letters from Bernard not only show that he continued to firmly resist this choice and consecration until the pope ruled both to have been invalid, but also that he saw no need to get in touch with Peter the Venerable about this matter, even though this abbot and his friends at Cluny were held responsible by Bernard for this unacceptable affair.[84] Naturally, Peter the Venerable could not just let this pass, and therefore he sent the abbot of Clairvaux a letter in which he presented his side of the story with regard to the choice and consecration. He defended the person in question against all charges and accused Bernard of having been gullible in believing the lies and slander of the enemies of Cluny. He also blamed Bernard for not having sought further information about this candidate from him, who, he believed, had as much appreciation for the Cistercians as for the members of his own order.[85] As far as we know, Bernard never answered this letter.

This is not so strange, since Bernard had other problems to deal with after he had been successful in this affair. First, there was his own candidature as bishop of Langres, which had been decided by its chapter. He, of course, rejected this

---

82. *Ep.* 501; SBO VIII, 458-459.

83. *Ep.* 164; SBO VII, 372-375.

84. *Epp.* 165-169; SBO VII, 375-382. Constable, "The Disputed Election at Langres in 1138," 119-152. Also Cantarella, "Cluny, Lione, Roma" (1119-1140), 63-87, and Gastaldelli, *Opere* VI/1, 696-699, note.

85. *Ep.* 29; *Letters* I, 101-104.

offer, but did advise the canons to offer the position to his prior, Godefroy de la Roche Vanneau. When they did elect Godefroy, Bernard was faced, early in 1139, with the task of convincing Louis VII to accept this choice, since the king opposed this candidate. After his intervention in Langres, he was also obliged to contact Innocent II with the request not to listen to what the enemies of Godefroy were telling about him. Finally, when a vacancy occurred in the archbishopric of Lyon in that same year, Bernard had to seek the support of Innocent II for the candidature of the deacon of this archiepiscopal chapter.[86] For Bernard had been able to get his way in Langres partly because of the support of this deacon.

Although Bernard apparently did not see any need to respond to Peter the Venerable's letter about his role in the episcopal election, he could not restrain himself in that same year from correcting the abbot of Cluny in a short epistle with regard to Saint Bertins, or urging him, in any case, to tone down his claims to authority over this monastery. The monastic community there had at that time not been consulted about the incorporation of this monastery into the order of Cluny, and therefore persisted in its attempts to annul this incorporation.[87] To some extent, this letter gives the impression that Bernard wanted to recover himself for the critical message he had earlier received from Peter the Venerable. For two years after this the two had no further contacts.

This changed in 1141 when, during the Council of Sens, Bernard succeeded in having the writings of Peter Abelard condemned as heretical. Since Abelard had appealed to Rome, the council could not proceed to condemn Abelard personally as a heretic. To achieve this, they had to submit a request to the pope. In the meantime Abelard had departed for Rome, but had gotten stranded in Cluny, where he asked permission to stay because he felt sick. Peter the Venerable took him in and, in general, felt sympathy for him. At some earlier time he had invited Abelard to enter Cluny, and at last this took place. Abelard in fact had little choice, for after his condemnation in Sens, Peter the Venerable was the only person with enough authority to urge Bernard's moderation.

A letter sent by Peter the Venerable to Rome on behalf of Abelard further indicates that in the meantime Bernard and Abelard had met, partly due to the mediation of Rainald de Bar, the abbot of Cîteaux. At this occasion they made peace, after which Abelard could no longer be con-

---

86. *Epp.* 170, 502, 503, 171, 172; SBO VII, 383-385; VIII, 459-460; VII, 385-386.
87. *Ep.* 149; SBO VII, 353; *Cluny et Cîteaux* (1985), 105-106.

sidered a heretic. Maintaining the accusation would have been possible only if he had persisted in the views that had been condemned. But in that case there could not have been a reconciliation between Bernard and Abelard.[88]

We do not know how this all happened and how Peter the Venerable succeeded in bringing Bernard to this magnanimity, which was not without limit, however. Bernard deemed it advisable also to include a letter from Innocent II about this subject in his letter register, which in principle contained only his own letters. In this letter, which was addressed to the archbishops of Reims and of Sens and their suffragan bishops, the pope confirmed the condemnation of Abelard's views, as pronounced by the Council of Sens. In the letter Abelard was also personally condemned; furthermore, he was to be silenced forever, and possible followers were threatened with the ecclesiastical ban.[89]

But this agreement with Bernard may have led Peter the Venerable to hope that he would also be able to involve him in his attempts to reform the lifestyle of the Cluniacs, or at least to create the kind of cordial relationship between the two orders that such a reform required. In any case, during 1143 the two abbots once again began to write to each other, and this time the initiative might have come from Bernard. This, however, is not absolutely certain, since some letters have been lost. The earliest letter from Bernard that we possess begins with these words:

> So you are pleased to jest? Courteously and kindly I would admit, if I could be sure you were not ridiculing me. Do not be surprised at my saying this, for your sudden and unexpected urbanity makes me a little uneasy. It is not so long ago that I greeted you in a letter with all the respect that is your due, yet you never answered one word. And it is not long since I wrote you again from Rome, but even then I did not get a reply. Are you therefore surprised that I did not presume to trouble you with trifles when you got back from Spain?

The last sentence indicates that Bernard here reacts to a letter Peter had at last sent him, though he no longer expected it. He had been encouraged by this answer:

---

88. *Ep.* 98; *Letters*, I, 258-259. *Christendom* (1994), 242-245.
89. *Ep.* 194, SBO VIII, 46-48. About the inclusion of this letter and two other letters addressed to Bernard, see below, 243 n. 102, 247 with n. 109, and 276.

I welcomed your letter with open hands. I have read it and re-read it greedily and gladly, and the more often I read it the better pleased I am. I must say I enjoy your fun. It is both pleasantly gay and seriously grave. I do not know how it is you are able to be both gay and grave, so that your fun has nothing about it of frivolity, and your dignity loses nothing by your gaiety. You are able to keep your dignity so well in the midst of your fun that those words of the holy man [Job] might be applied to you: "I smiled on them though they were never so ill at ease, and the encouragement of my glance never failed them."[90]

The ensuing letter from Peter the Venerable, or rather the tract with which early in 1144 he tried to prolong their correspondence after the flattering message from Bernard, makes it clear that with his humorous letter to which Bernard reacted so playfully, the abbot of Cluny had intended to initiate a serious discussion about the hostility that had developed between the Cistercians and Cluniacs, which caused him so much anxiety. In this tract, characterized by "wishful thinking," he referred to Bernard's jest as an expression of the love that existed between them and would continue to exist, and would undoubtedly also begin to flourish between the monks of the two orders, considering the tenacity Bernard manifested in fostering it. For, so he remarked subtly, the love between them had even survived the torrent of Langres.

Peter then candidly dealt with the misunderstandings and hard feelings that existed between the members of the two orders. The letter further shows Peter attempting to relativize the differences in lifestyle and clothing that had developed into an emotional abyss between the orders:

Why, O white monk, do you so abhor the blackness of your brother, that is: not of his soul, but of his garment? And you, black brother, why are you so amazed about the whiteness of your brother, that is: not of his soul, but of his habit? Do not both of you belong to the flock of the Lord, who says: "My sheep hear my voice, and I know them, and they follow me; and I give them eternal life, and they shall never perish, and no one shall snatch them out of my hand" (John 10:27-28)? And what human shepherd, let alone God, has ever objected to the color of the hide of his sheep? Who has ever made trouble about such a thing? Who has ever believed that the white ones belonged more to the flock than the black ones, or the black ones more than

90. Job 29:24; *Ep.* 228, 1-2; SBO VIII, 98-99. Transl. James, 375.

the white ones? What shepherd ever paid attention to whether they were white or black, rather than to the question whether these particular white sheep and these particular black sheep were part of his flock? How evil is man, and how innocent are the animals. . . .

Who then will be so childish or so stupid as to think that, if one is a new creation in Christ, a different color or a different custom will make any difference with regard to our salvation? And if this makes no difference when it comes to salvation, why should monks be separated from each other by the fact that their clothing differs in color?[91]

A comparison of this tract, which was written in the form of a letter, with the treatise Peter the Venerable addressed to Bernard in 1127, shows how he modified his views about the Cluniac monastic life in the course of almost twenty years. The main thing these two letters have in common is that they were probably both intended for a much larger audience, in particular for the Cluniacs themselves. Peter may further have expected that this second tract/letter of his would also be distributed in Cistercian circles. But this depended to a significant degree on Bernard's cooperation, which he solicited in particular in the second half of the 1140s.

Precisely in those years Peter the Venerable tried extremely hard to make the Cluniac lifestyle conform to the much stricter ways in which the Rule of Saint Benedict was observed elsewhere. We detect this, for instance, in a circular letter that he addressed to all Cluniac priors soon after he had sent his tract/letter to Bernard. In this letter he criticized the abuses in their monasteries just as strongly as Bernard had done in his *Apology*. The efforts of Peter the Venerable in this direction are also apparent from the statutes he issued in 1146 and, finally, from the economic reforms he ordered at that time.[92]

Bernard, however, showed no sympathy for the anxieties of Peter the Venerable. He did not answer the tract he received in 1144; furthermore, the few short, polite letters that he addressed to Peter in the second part of the forties were intended only to prevent possible incidents and misunderstandings between the two orders.[93] We should, of course, take into

91. *Ep.* 111; *Letters* I, 286-287.

92. *Ep.* 161; *Letters* I, 388-394. For the statutes issued by Peter the Venerable, see above, 229, note 72. For his economic reforms, see Duby, "Le budget de l'abbaye de Cluny," *Hommes et Structures*, 61-62.

93. One letter deals with the entry of a Cluniac monk in Clairvaux (*Ep.* 267; SBO VIII, 176). The other letter about the choice of Henry of France, a brother of Louis VII

consideration that Bernard had little time to get involved in the affairs of the Cluniac Order, since he had in the meantime been entrusted with the preaching of a new crusade. On the other hand, there are some indications that he refused to be drawn into these problems.

C. Nicholas of Montiéramy as Intermediary

These indications that Bernard did not want to get involved in Cluniac affairs are found mainly in what we have managed to discover about Bernard's objections to the relationship from 1149 onward between his secretary Nicholas and Peter the Venerable. Bernard apparently considered this relationship inappropriate. This Nicholas was not just another monk of Clairvaux. Initially he had been a Benedictine monk in Montiéramy, and subsequently he had become a *cappelanus* (secretary) in the service of Hatto, the bishop of Troyes. In this role he had the opportunity to cultivate contacts and friendships with numerous influential persons.

In this way Nicholas also came in contact with Peter the Venerable. Their relationship had continued until the end of 1141. Around that time Nicholas had become acquainted with Bernard, probably during the Council of Sens, which Hatto attended. Following this, Bernard found Nicholas prepared to help him with the backlog in his correspondence with Innocent II, and to deliver to the addressees in Rome the letters in which he had stated his charges against Abelard to the pope and the Curia.[94]

When Hatto resigned from his episcopal office in 1145 and withdrew to Cluny, Nicholas at first returned to Montiéramy. Rather soon after this, however, he departed for Clairvaux, where he became a kind of chancellor for Bernard, and thus his most important secretary. The reason that Bernard brought Nicholas to Clairvaux was in part his involvement with the preaching of the crusade. This work was not limited to oral recruitment. Bernard also used written appeals and sent crusade-encyclicals throughout Europe. He also dispatched diplomatic correspondence to prelates and

---

who was a monk at Clairvaux, as the bishop of Beauvais, has been lost. The letters of Peter the Venerable about this subject, however, have been preserved: *Epp.* 145 and 146; *Letters* I, 360-362.

94. *Ep.* 436; SBO VIII, 415. Gastaldelli, *Opere* VI, 2, 594, note 1. For the delivery of the letters in Rome, see *Letters* II, 316-320. J. Benton, *Dictionnaire de Spiritualité*, II, 255-259.

princes. Nicholas was charged in particular with the preparation of these letters. He possessed considerable literary skills and had experience in directing a chancellory. Nicholas — as mentioned earlier — had previously assisted Bernard on a temporary basis when the latter combated and hounded Abelard with his letters.

Nicholas found this post very appealing, since it offered him new opportunities to be in contact with many important persons and even to correspond with some of these himself; therefore, he had few objections to Bernard's proposal to exchange his black habit for a white one. The social relations he would be able to cultivate in this role tickled his vanity, which expressed itself in particular in his imitation of Bernard's style in his own letters and sermons. As his first secretary for a considerable time, Nicholas enjoyed Bernard's confidence and was afforded great freedom in handling Bernard's correspondence, the more so since the abbot himself was too busy to give ample attention to the final version of his letters — a freedom in which his other secretaries shared.

But this method was not without risks, as became apparent in the summer of 1149 from a letter Bernard was obliged to send to Peter the Venerable about the unkind words that had found their way into one of the letters addressed to this abbot. Bernard, as well as Nicholas, had failed to check the final version of this letter. This disturbing omission was detected when Peter informed Nicholas about it. The two men had met once again in 1149 during a visit of Peter to Clairvaux and had resumed their correspondence. Because Peter the Venerable so far had not had any response to his requests to Bernard for assistance in his reform efforts in his own order — by improving the relationship between the Cistercians and the Cluniacs — he hoped it would possible to get this support through the intervention of Nicholas.

The letters between Bernard and Peter the Venerable that followed the incident in their correspondence referred to above are rather amusing. Bernard opened his letter with an extremely flattering introductory statement:

> To his most reverend father and dear friend Peter, by the grace of God Abbot of Cluny, health and greetings in the source of all true health, from Brother Bernard, styled Abbot of Clairvaux.
>
> Would that I were able to express in this letter all that I feel towards you! Then you would certainly see clearly the love for you which God has inscribed upon my heart and engraved upon my very

bones. But what need is there for me to commend myself to you in this way? For a long time now we have been united in the closest friendship, and an equal affection has rendered us equals. What could a person of my lowly attainments have in common with a man like you, if you were not so tolerant of my limitations?

Thus it has come about that both my lowliness and your magnanimity have been so blended that I could not be lowly without you nor you magnanimous without me.[95]

Then Bernard stated that sometimes he had no time to check the words of his secretaries in the letters that he had dictated. "Their mutual son" Nicholas, who would deliver this letter to Peter, would further explain this.

Nicholas brought a response with him on his return. This letter was at least five times longer than the one from Bernard. Of course he also complimented Bernard with similar flatteries. He concluded that part of his letter by stating that he was satisfied — yes, more than satisfied — if in his relationship with the other he were allowed to claim the terms of brother, friend, dear friend, or dearest friend. He did not attach too much attention to the incident that had occasioned this exchange of letters. His secretaries at times made similar mistakes. Much more important than all this was what Bernard had written about their friendship, and he added that he would remind him of his words:

Can one read such words thoughtlessly? Does reading them not fascinate the eyes, delight the heart and unite our souls? You, my dear friend, who wrote them, are the one to indicate what they mean. I can only accept them in their literal meaning *(sic!)*, and declare that I will hold to what has been said by one so great, true and holy. And as you have said yourself, I will also refrain from recommending myself to you once again. Our love in Christ dates from when we were still young; how could we, in our old age, begin to doubt such a holy and enduring love? Never! To cite your own words once more: Trust the one you love. The thought has never even occurred to me, nor have I ever said a word, that I ever doubted anything you said in earnest. I therefore accept, retain and cherish what you have written about this in this letter.[96]

95. *Ep.* 387; SBO VIII, 355-356. Transl. James, 378.
96. *Ep.* 149; *Letters* I, 365.

Bernard could hardly leave this letter unanswered. He wrote that together with only Nicholas, "who is so dear to you," for a short moment he had been able to taste its charm. But, unfortunately, he was not able to respond in a similar way. Most likely Bernard also used this moment together with Nicholas to discuss what the latter was to write in answer to the practical points Peter had raised in his letter. Nicholas's personal involvement with this response to Peter is clear from its concluding sentence:

> And I Nicholas add my undying affection for you and for all your household.[97]

A month and a half later, in mid-October 1149, Peter the Venerable once again referred to the constant animosity between Cluniacs and Cistercians. In order to prevent Bernard from once more failing to pay any attention to this subject, Peter sent with his letter an accompanying short note to Nicholas, requesting him to urge Bernard to take proper notice of this letter:

> I am writing a letter to the abbot of Clairvaux, which I want you to deliver to him. Read it to him carefully and attentively, and exhort him as much as you can, so that what I have written, with a view to love, will be brought to a good effect.[98]

We do not know whether the assistance Peter the Venerable sought from Nicholas had any result. If there was a response from Bernard, it has not been preserved, nor is there any indirect indication in the form of a subsequent reaction from Peter the Venerable. In any case, there does not seem to have been any direct result, since in a letter about other matters, Nicholas informed Peter about his plans to pay a visit to Cluny in order to give him an oral and reliable report. The letter indicates that he planned this visit for early 1150.[99] We learn from two other letters, written in the autumn of 1150 and addressed to Bernard and Nicholas respectively, that Peter expected to see Nicholas in Cluny for some longer time. The extremely congenial tone of Peter's letter to Bernard and the praise Peter therein expressed for him lead us to believe that at that particular moment the abbot of Cluny must have been keenly interested in a visit of Nicolas

---

97. *Ep.* 389; SBO VIII, 356-357. Transl. James, 380.
98. *Ep.* 150; *Letters* I, 367-371; *Ep.* 151; *Letters* I, 371-372.
99. *Ep.* 152; *Letters* I, 373; cf. II, 202.

to his monastery. The letter begins with a resounding *captatio benevolentiae:* "To the strong and splendid pillar of the monastic orders, yes, of the entire Church of God, to Bernard, abbot of Clairvaux, the humble abbot of Cluny: the light which God promised to those who love Him."

> Since it happens only rarely (that I receive messengers from you), I desire that your holiness will send me someone, who loves you, as soon as possible, but no later than the octave of Easter; the person I would prefer is Nicholas, who, I believe, represents your spirit in a large measure and mine fully. In him, holy brother, I shall see you, and listening to him, I shall hear you, and through him I shall let you know some things that I privately want to submit to your wisdom.[100]

Peter apparently expected that through his contact with Nicholas he might be able to improve his relationship with Bernard, which he greatly valued, if only for pragmatic reasons. But this proposal must not have appealed to Bernard. His reply to Peter contains only one indirect remark about this request and left no doubt that he did not regard it as having any importance:

> And so I will now answer the trifling request with which you concluded your letter. He for whom you have asked is not with me now, but with the Bishop of Auxerre. I am told he is so ill that he cannot come either to me or to you without grave inconvenience.[101]

Because of this absence and illness of Nicholas, Bernard did not need to say openly that he did not at all appreciate this close relationship between Peter and Nicholas. But a letter from Nicholas to the abbot of Cluny, written in the spring of 1151, once again shows Bernard's dislike for granting Peter's request. In an attempt finally to convince Bernard to approve a visit around Easter, Nicholas advised Peter to ask Bernard that he be given permission to deliver the manuscripts that he had in the meantime acquired for Cluny.[102] Since both the prior and the cellarer of Clairvaux were also involved in this transfer of manuscripts, Nicholas suggested to Peter that he inform these two

---

100. Letter to Bernard: *Ep.* 175; *Letters* I, 416-417. Letter to Nicholas: *Ep.* 176; *Letters* I, 417. *Ep.* 175 is one of the three letters addressed to Bernard that were included in the register of his letters; *Ep.* 264; SBO VIII, 173-174.

101. *Ep.* 265; SBO VII, 175. Transl. James, 378.

102. *Ep.* 179; *Letters* I, 420-422. At some earlier date (in 1149 and 1150) Nicholas had also assisted in the exchange of manuscripts between the two monasteries; *Epp.* 153 and 176; *Letters* I, 373 and 417.

men in separate letters about his request. Peter then sent a short and hasty note to Nicholas, to confirm that he would follow his suggestions and would soon write him a more substantial letter.[103]

When Peter referred to this matter in a letter to Bernard, he reminded him of Bernard's earlier questions about why he wanted to see Nicholas in Cluny. This time his answer was rather direct:

> You want to know my reason? Is it not reason enough to see a person whom one loves? He is yours indeed, but he is very dear to me, and you are not pleased with me liking what belongs to you? Does it not please you that one, whom I believe more dear to you than many who belong to you, should be still more dear to me? And what greater proof of true friendship is there than to love what my friend loves?

Peter also mentions in this letter that he and Bernard had recently met in Cluny because the conflict between Gigny and le Miroir had flared up. This provided Bernard once again with an opportunity to ask Peter why he was so keen on a visit of Nicholas to Cluny. He had been wrong, Peter says in this letter, in stating that this was a matter of minor importance. He had given this answer since Bernard had been unwilling to listen to the response he had given already two or three times to this question that he had been asked. And Bernard should have been able to guess the real reason for his request, for he ought to know that Peter was not trying to get something from his storehouse or cellar, or to make him give gold or silver from his treasury (supposing that indeed he possessed these):

> What then am I asking? That you should send me Nicholas — and not only now, but whenever I send for him. For I shall, as far as possible, not ask anything that can be reasonably denied or which may in any way annoy you, not to say myself.[104]

No response from Bernard to this letter has been preserved. He may not have responded at all. Neither do we know whether Nicholas finally received permission to travel to Cluny. It has been suggested that he might have gone there around Easter 1151, but it is just as possible that this visit did not take place until early 1152, shortly after Peter had returned from a

---

103. *Ep.* 180; *Letters* I, 422-423.
104. *Ep.* 181; *Letters* I, 423-425. Transl. in "Saint Bernard in His Relations" (1992), 339.

five-month journey through Italy.[105] If Nicholas did go in 1152, his visit must have coincided with the discovery, made during his absence from Clairvaux, of his fraudulent activities. Books, money, a lot of gold, and three seals were found: one of Nicholas himself, another of the prior of Clairvaux, and the third a new seal of Bernard himself. We have no precise details about this deception by Nicholas, nor do we know whether these items were found in his cell or at his place in the scriptorium.

The only available information about this scandal is found in a letter that Bernard sent to Eugenius III after May 1152.[106] This letter also tells us that as a result of this deceit, Nicholas was no longer tolerated in Clairvaux and had left. The charge against him, however, was rather vague. It probably concerned mainly his traffic in manuscripts, his private correspondence, and his sermons and tracts in which he plagiarized the writings of Bernard — at the time not considered a crime. His use of several seals that were found in his possession cannot have been too serious since secretaries in those days often worked rather independently. Insiders must therefore have considered Bernard's charge against Nicholas as rather exaggerated. The church did not begin any legal proceedings against him, and he kept his contacts with important people.

૨૯   ૨૯

THUS THERE REMAINS the question of what results this incident had for the relationship between Bernard and Peter. It is clear, of course, that Nicholas could no longer fulfill any role as intermediary. But that does not answer the question about the consequences of this incident. However, it is important to note that from approximately the moment when Bernard informed the pope about Nicholas's deception, we have no data about any further contacts between the two abbots. Peter the Venerable's letter register, arranged by his secretary Hugh of Poitiers, ends with a letter to Bernard and one to Nicholas of Clairvaux, both written in May 1152. There are no later letters from Bernard to Peter.

But the letter Bernard wrote between the end of 1151 and early 1152 to Eugenius III about Peter the Venerable has been preserved. The reason for his letter was the rumor that Peter was planning, during his Italian journey, to ask the pope, whom

105. *Letters* II, 325 and 327.
106. *Ep.* 298; SBO VIII, 214.

he met in February 1152 in Segni, for permission to resign from his post. In this letter, in which he lavishly praised Peter, Bernard asked the pope as a special favor that he would under no circumstance accept such a request.

Bernard's letter of November 1151 to Peter, at the time when the latter was making preparations for his journey to Rome, is not extant. We know from a letter Peter sent to Bernard in May 1152, after his return from Italy, that it was written.[107] It leads us to conclude that Bernard's letter of November 1152 to Peter was mainly intended to urge him not to resign. Peter's letter further indicates that Bernard's message to Eugenius III in favor of Peter had not gone without effect. Peter the Venerable reports with joy and great satisfaction that the pope and Hugh, the cardinal-archbishop of Ostia — who until shortly before had been the abbot of the Cistercian abbey of Trois-Fontaines — had been very accessible to him.

Peter also reported to Bernard how during his meeting with the Curia the problems of authority, which the abbot of Cluny encountered in his order and for which he needed papal support, had been discussed. These problems may have resulted from his attempts at reform. Peter tells Bernard in this letter how he always had exercised his authority in his order with great openness and without force or violence. As an example, he referred to his strategy during the schism of Abbot Pons. The countless persons who had failed him at that time, and those members of the order who had committed criminal or unacceptable deeds, had never experienced his sword, dagger, or spear. At the most, they had heard him speak some angry words.

In this same letter Peter also announced his plans to visit Bernard in Clairvaux or Dijon. During that visit they were to discuss once again the conflict between Gigny and le Miroir, which had been re-ignited the previous winter. This meeting was supposed to take place on June 9, but in the end it did not occur. From a letter that Peter sent at this same time to Nicholas, we know that he had counted on Nicholas's presence at that meeting.[108] This particular letter was also a reply to several letters from Nicholas that had reached him in Italy. But for an account of his journey, Peter referred to a letter he had written on that subject to Bernard.

As we saw above, Nicholas's relationship with Bernard, as well as his stay at Clairvaux, ended around 1152 because of the fraud he was accused of by the abbot. Considering the nature of the charges against Nicholas, which Bernard expressed in a letter to Eugenius III, we may assume that these charges were rather a pretext than the real reason for Bernard's insistence on Nicholas's departure. The real reason is mainly to be sought in the relationship that had developed between this secretary of Bernard and Peter the

---

107. *Ep.* 277; SBO VIII, 189-190.
108. *Ep.* 192 and 193; *Letters* I, 443-450.

Venerable. Peter tried to exploit this association by attempting to use Nicholas as his intermediary with Bernard in order to get his cooperation in improving the relationship between the Cluniacs and the Cistercians.

Peter deemed such an improvement necessary if he was to realize reforms in his own order. But all his attempts of many years to win Bernard's support for this venture had remained without success. When he became reacquainted with Nicholas in 1149, the latter wore the Cistercian habit. His motive for exchanging his black habit for a white one made him in Peter's eyes a suitable go-between. Considering his many contacts, Nicholas must have been a skillful diplomat, another reason Peter would have tried to use him in his continuing efforts to get Bernard's support for his plans. But Bernard refused to become involved and found a regular personal contact between Nicholas and Peter the Venerable unacceptable.

However, having received the letter in which Peter the Venerable reprimanded Bernard about this and reminded him how amenable he had always been toward Cluniacs who wanted to become Cistercians, it became almost impossible to continue to refuse Nicholas permission to go to Cluny from time to time. The only remaining way for Bernard to put an end to this undesirable contact between these two men was to force Nicholas to leave. This could be accomplished by accusing him of fraud and on that basis forbidding a further stay in Clairvaux. This strategy was certainly beyond all proportions, but it did result in the fact that Bernard would no longer be faced with requests to get involved with the internal problems of the Cluniac Order.

We already posed the question of how this eviction of Nicholas influenced the relationship between Bernard and Peter the Venerable. The answer can be short: it ended. The two abbots did not resume their correspondence, even during Bernard's final illness. If at that time Peter the Venerable had written him another letter, he might have received a friendly reply, considering the courteous way in which the two abbots addressed each other, in spite of all difficulties. Others who inquired after his condition received the same kind of polite response. Such an answer would then have been included as the last entry in the register of Bernard's letters.[109]

---

109. That such a letter is missing may have been the reason why the extremely flattering letter, which Bernard received in late 1150 from Peter the Venerable, was posthumously added to his letter register (*Ep.* 264; SBO VIII, 174-175) in an attempt to obscure the break in the relationship between the two abbots that occurred in 1152.

The analysis presented above of the relationship between the two abbots finds strong confirmation in the total absence of the name of Peter the Venerable in the *vita prima,* while — humanly speaking — his association with the first abbot of Clairvaux could hardly have been omitted in this document. That there must have been such a rupture may also explain why it was not until 1321 that Bernard received his commemoration as a saint in the Cluniac liturgy.

3. CLAIRVAUX: ITS EXPANSION AND SPIRITUAL SIGNIFICANCE

IN THE first book of the *vita prima,* William of Saint-Thierry tells us that as soon as Clairvaux had been founded, Bernard was less concerned about the hardships he and his community were suffering than about the future blessings this abbey would bring to the souls of mankind:

> His greatest desire was for the salvation of all mankind, and this has been the great passion of his heart from the first day of his life as a monk even to the day on which I am writing this, so that his longing to draw all men to God is like a mother's devoted care for her children. All the time there is the conflict in his heart between his great desire for souls and the desire to remain hidden from the attention of the world, for sometimes in his humility and low esteem of himself he confesses that he is not worthy to produce any fruitful increase for the Church, whilst at other times his desire knows no bounds and burns so strongly within him that it seems that nothing can satisfy it, but the salvation of all mankind. And so it was that his love for God and his creatures gave rise to an unfaltering trust and faith in God, although this too was held in check by his humility.
>
> It was about this time that the brethren were called slightly earlier for Matins on one occasion, so that when the office was finished there was a rather long delay before Lauds could begin. During the interval Bernard went outside to walk in the grounds of the monastery, and as he walked he prayed that God might find acceptable the obedient service which he and his brethren offered. Longing for his work to bear rich fruit filled his heart, and as he stood still and closed his eyes for a moment in prayer, he saw coming down from the mountains round about him and down into the valley below such a great company

of men of every type and standing that the valley could not hold them all. Today everyone realizes what that vision meant. . . .[110]

The last sentence in particular suggests that William later invented this vision. The story seems to agree with what had actually happened, and it is therefore clear what William wanted to convey. For in and through Clairvaux, Bernard's spiritual fruits grew to maturity. The crowd referred to in this vision, which was larger than the valley could hold, indicates that William counted the many monasteries that had been founded and were directed from there as part of Clairvaux. But William did not explain how this functioned in actual practice. This held no importance for him as a hagiographer. He wanted the readers of the story to understand that the expansion and splendor of Clairvaux was God's will, and that Bernard served as God's visible instrument in all this.

But by following this approach, William brushed aside the kind of questions that must be asked if we want to differentiate between cult and history: How can this growth and development, to the extent that they can still be traced, be explained? And what role did Bernard have or assume in the many foundations and incorporations that were effected from Clairvaux during his abbacy? These questions refer to three distinct aspects: the expansion of Clairvaux and its resulting status within the order; the indirect, diplomatic involvement of Bernard with the founding of new monasteries by Clairvaux; and finally, the attraction of the monastic life-style of Clairvaux. This third aspect can be discovered only in the picture Bernard sketched by means of the metaphors in his preaching and writings for the benefit of others. We cannot leave these three aspects untouched.

A. The Expansion of Clairvaux

In descriptions of the exceptional status of Clairvaux in the Cistercian Order during the abbacy of Bernard, reference is usually made to the many monasteries that were affiliated with Clairvaux in this particular period. The significance of this number becomes apparent when a comparison is made with the number of filiations of Cîteaux and three other daughter institutions: La Ferté, Pontigny, and Morimond, which, like Clairvaux, occupied a special place in the order. Their special status allowed these abbeys to build their own family of filiations.

110. Vp I, c. V, 26; P.L. CLXXXV, 242; Transl. Webb and Walker, 45, 46.

Father Anselme Didier has calculated that in 1153, the year of Bernard's death, the Cistercian Order may already have had as many as 345 monasteries. Cîteaux could boast 57 filiations; La Ferté, only 8; Pontigny, 26; and Morimond, 87. Clairvaux by itself had 167 filiations — almost equal to the number of the other four combined.[111]

But we learn more about Clairvaux's expansion if we also include in this comparison the genealogy of the monasteries that were part of its network and then use this to determine the status of the abbey in the order. For this we need to compare once again the size of the five networks of monasteries; but this time we must, in particular, look at the monasteries that were *directly* related to Cîteaux and the four oldest daughter institutions. And to avoid confusion, we should exclude the abbey of Savigny in Normandy, which in 1147, together with over thirty filiations — mostly in England and the western part of France — were incorporated into the Cistercian Order as filiations of Clairvaux.

According to this way of counting, in 1153 Cîteaux had a total of 16 daughter monasteries in the direct line, while La Ferté had only 3, and Pontigny and Morimond had 13 and 22 direct daughters respectively. Against these four networks with a total of 67 monasteries that were directly dependent, Clairvaux could boast of 66 or possibly 67 daughter institutions that were fully dependent. Another, related point of comparison is the information regarding the number of filiations each of these daughter institutions in its turn founded. We are able to determine that in the period until 1153, only 3 of the 16 filiations of Cîteaux did not found any daughter institutions themselves. For La Ferté we are able to discover that each of its 3 filiations founded at least one daughter monastery, while 6 of the 13 Pontigny-filiations did not found any institutions of their own. And only 6 of the 22 filiations of Morimond did not realize new foundations, while this is the case for no fewer than 44 of the 66 or 67 filiations of Clairvaux.

Finally, when we add as a third point of comparison the total numbers of daughter monasteries founded by the direct filiations of Clairvaux and Morimond, we find a very remarkable difference between the

---

111. "Le monde claravallien à la mort de saint Bernard," 249; in *Mélanges Anselme Dimier,* I, 2:595. For the genealogy of the Cistercian monasteries, see Janauschek, *Originum Cisterciensium,* and van der Meer, *Atlas* (1965), 22-28. For the shortcomings of the *arbre généalogique de l'ordre cistercienne,* included in van der Meer's work, see Cocheril, "L'Atlas de l'ordre cistercian," 119-144.

ways in which these two abbeys, which experienced the greatest expansion, realized their expansion. Clairvaux reached 68 granddaughters and great-granddaughters from 22 filiations, while Morimond reached a total of 78 from 16 filiations. Considering also that 44 daughter monasteries of Clairvaux did not have filiations of their own, we may conclude that this abbey, to a far lesser degree than one of the other mother institutions, left the founding or acquisition of new monasteries to its own daughters, but rather kept the ongoing expansion in its own hands.

And then we should not forget that 40 of these 67 granddaughters of Clairvaux, that is, more than half of the total number, owed their origin to only 5 of its daughters: Trois-Fontaines, founded in 1118 and situated in the bishopric of Châlons-sur-Marne, founded 6 filiations; Rievaulx in York, founded in 1132, acquired 11 daughters, as did the monastery of Fountains, established in 1135 in the same bishopric. In addition, Mellifont, founded in 1142 in Ireland, in the archbishopric of Armagh, had 7 daughter institutions; while Grandselve, incorporated by Clairvaux in 1145/46, had 5 filiations. This abbey was situated in the bishopric of Toulouse, which at the time did not belong to France.

These data indicate that during Bernard's life, Clairvaux clearly differed from the other four mother abbeys in the way it built a network of filiations. This difference must also have influenced the way in which this abbey directed its filiations. The uneven way in which these 67 new filiations, founded by no more than 22 daughter monasteries of Clairvaux, were spread over these monasteries is rather striking. For as was mentioned above, 40 of these granddaughters belonged to the 5 daughter institutions already referred to: Trois-Fontaines (6), Rievaulx (11), Fountains (11), Grandselve (5) and Mellifont (7).

The explanation for the development of these five abbeys is roughly the same, except for Trois-Fontaines. For this abbey was situated in the bishopric of Châlons-sur-Marne; while its six daughters were in the bishoprics of Verdun, Trier, and Châlons-sur-Marne. Like Trois-Fointaines, they could easily be reached, by contemporary standards, from Clairvaux. Rievaulx, Fountains, and Mellifont were much more difficult to reach. These abbeys were so far from Clairvaux that the network of Cistercian monasteries that developed around them could hardly be governed from Clairvaux. For as we saw, Rievaulx and Fountains were both in the bishopric of York in England; while Mellifont was even further away, in the archbishopric Armagh in Ireland.

A similar explanation also applies, in fact, to the abbey of Grandselve, which at an earlier date (between 1114 and 1118) had been founded by Gerard of Sales. Grandselve was transferred to Clairvaux in 1145 when Bernard visited Toulouse for a preaching tour against Henry of Lausanne in this region. Previously, Henry's successful attacks on the church in Languedoc had contributed to the fact that the Cistercians had been unable to settle in this region, the more so since the French king could not give any support in that region. At the time of its transfer, Grandselve took a daughter monastery with it: Fontfroide, situated in the diocese of Narbonne. The daughter monasteries that Grandselve later acquired were also situated in the region of the Pyrenees and the North of Spain.[112]

With regard to Trois-Fontaines, when we compare this oldest daughter monastery of Clairvaux (1118) with other daughter monasteries founded at an early date (Fontenay, 1119; Foigny, 1121; Igny, 1126; Reigny, 1128; Ourscamp, 1129; and Cherlieu, 1131), we find that, remarkably enough, only Reigny had no filiations. In 1153 Cherlieu had four daughter monasteries; Fontenay and Ourscamp had three each; while Foigny, like Igny, founded only one daughter, even though this daughter acquired a granddaughter in 1153/54.

On the other hand, the Trois-Fontaines abbey, with its six filiations, as well as Rievaulx (11), Fointaines (11), Mellifont (7) and Grandselve (5), can be included in the "extended family" of Clairvaux. But since Trois-Fontaines and its daughter monasteries were within easy reach from Clairvaux, we must find another explanation for its larger number of filiations. We have already seen that practically all the daughter monasteries that were founded in the early years of Clairvaux acquired filiations of their own. This may indicate that initially the filiation process was less centrally directed from Clairvaux. But this is no more than a hunch, for it may also have been — especially when Bernard had not yet acquired his fame — that at that time Clairvaux found it inopportune to initiate the founding or acquisition of additional monasteries.

We also find, however, that Trois-Fontaines retained its traditional prerogative of founding or acquiring daughter monasteries even until the year 1153. In later years Trois-Fontaines may have regarded this privilege to place daughter institutions under its own authority as a kind of "right

112. Calers, 1147, in the bishopric Toulouse; Candeil, 1150(?), in Albi; Valldaura (later called Santa Creuz), 1151/52, in Barcelona; and Poblet (a filiation of Fontfroide), 1151, in Tarragona. See Passerat, "La venue de saint Bernard à Toulouse et les débuts de l'abbaye de Grandselve" (1992), 34.

of the first-born," somewhat comparable to the position in the order of
the four oldest daughters of Cîteaux. Since Abbot Guy of Trois-Fontaines,
who had succeeded Abbot Roger in 1127, and the abbot who in turn
succeeded Guy in 1133 were able to found, during their abbacies, two and
three monasteries respectively, it cannot be excluded that in other respects
they also preferred to keep a measure of independence vis-à-vis Clairvaux.

It appears that Clairvaux put no obstacles in the way of Trois-Fontaines with
regard to the founding or acquisition of its own daughter monasteries. It has been
suggested that Abbot Guy, with Bernard's support, made an unsuccessful attempt
to found a third daughter. The acquisition by Trois-Fontaines in 1138 of the
Cheminon monastery, which belonged to the congregation of canons of Arrouaise,
must have been the result of negotiations. Most likely Bernard himself was
involved with these.[113] But, as has been mentioned, in another respect Abbot
Guy and his successor also maintained a more independent stance vis-à-vis Clairvaux than the other daughter monasteries usually did. Bernard may not have been
pleased with this and possibly tried, after the death of the third abbot of Trois-
Fontaines in 1147, to end this situation by appointing one of his own monks,
Hugh of Châlons, as the next abbot. But if this was his strategy, it was thwarted
as early as 1149 by Eugenius III, who appointed Hugh as the cardinal-bishop of
Ostia — an appointment that certainly met with Bernard's approval.

It then proved difficult to find a suitable successor for Abbot Hugh in
Clairvaux. Not until 1152 did Trois-Fontaines get a new abbot: Thorald, who had
been the abbot of Fountains from 1147 to 1149. He had resigned from that post
after two years, with Bernard's consent, after difficulties between him and Henry
Murdach, who had been made archbishop of York with the support of Bernard.
Since 1149 Thorald had lived in Clairvaux until, in 1152, he was enlisted to solve
the impasse of leadership in Trois-Fontaines. However, he did not fully succeed
in ending the urge for more independence on the part of this community; for in
1153 it acquired the Châtillon abbey in the diocese of Verdun, and another, sixth,
daughter monastery.[114]

This possible deviation by Trois-Fontaines from the centralist policy Bernard followed even before 1130 with regard to the daughter monasteries of
Clairvaux[115] may explain another, hitherto unclear, matter. We have al-

113. Dimier, "Les fondations manquées de saint Bernard," 8. Also "Saint Bernard
and the Historians" (1977), 53, with note 104.
114. *Ep.* 273, c.2; SBO VIII, 184. For the succession of Abbot Hugh by Thorald,
cf. BdC, 169-170, and Knowles, *The Monastic Order,* 256.
115. Pacaut, "La filiation claravallienne" (1991), 135-147.

ready discussed how Guy, who had been abbot of Trois-Fontaines since 1127, was chosen abbot of Cîteaux in 1133 as successor of Stephen Harding, who had resigned from his office. The choice of Guy must at the time have met with Bernard's approval. This we deduce from a letter in which he comforted the monks of Trois-Fontaines with the departure of their abbot.[116]

It seems likely that his predecessor, Stephen Harding, also had some say in the choice of Guy as the abbot of Cîteaux. If that was indeed the case, it is possible that one of the reasons for this choice was that Guy had succeeded in maintaining a larger degree of independence as the abbot of Trois-Fontaines within the family of monasteries so centrally directed by Clairvaux. The monks of Cîteaux would hardly have wanted to be completely dominated by Clairvaux, the more so since they already knew that not everything that was undertaken or supported by their community met with Bernard's approval. This reconstruction — for which we have no solid evidence — would in turn explain why some months later, after the death of Stephen Harding, Guy was again released from this position.

For if Guy as the abbot of Cîteaux lived up to the expectation on which his choice in 1133 was based, it is very well possible that Bernard, who at the time was in Italy, may in retrospect have had second thoughts about this choice, and — in the same manner in which he at times succeeded in having some episcopal choices he disagreed with annulled — he may also have seen to it that Guy had to make room for another abbot of Cîteaux. Moreover, if indeed Bernard had in the meantime experienced that Guy would not be as submissive as he had initially expected, he would have to count on some resistance from Guy with regard to the policies he pursued for the order as a whole. Such a perspective would have had little appeal for him at that moment.

A few of those policies, in particular regarding the liturgy, were put into practice by Bernard soon after this episode;[117] while it is also clear that already in 1134 he had demanded that Cîteaux more closely conform to his wishes with respect to the illumination of manuscripts. He must have demanded from the scriptorium a much larger degree of simplicity than was customary during the

116. *Ep.* 71; SBO VII, 174. It has been suggested that this letter dates from 1127 and was written after Roger's death. This view is no longer held, due to the work of Dimier; cf. Gastaldelli, *Opere* VI-1, 322, note 1.

117. Already in 1134, Bernard charged the general chapter with the reform of the gradual and the antiphonary that were in use in the monasteries of the Cistercian Order. See Bouton, "La réforme du Chant," 158-165, as well as the *Prologus in antiphonarium quod cistercienses canunt ecclesiae*, SBO III, 511-516.

abbacy of Stephen Harding. All this would explain why at the time of Stephen Harding's death, Guy had to make place for Rainald de Bar as the abbot of Cîteaux. For Bernard could expect more docility from him than his short-term predecessor had manifested.

But it remains an open question to what extent this explanation of the change in abbots after Stephen Harding's death is correct. Those who want to summarily reject it as inadequately founded must remember, however, that we have no other plausible reason for Guy's replacment by Rainald de Bar, unless we want to proceed with the suggestion, for which we have no proof whatsoever, that from the very beginning this abbot, who had been appreciated in Trois-Fontaines, proved to be totally inept in his new position. But whatever the case, since Guy was replaced as abbot of Cîteaux by a monk from Clairvaux, it is unthinkable that this change took place without some involvement on Bernard's part.[118]

With further regard to the policies of affiliation in Bernard's days, the difference between these and those pursued at Cîteaux and other mother monasteries reflects another important fact. These policies were fully compatible with the unique nature and content of the *summa cartae caritatis,* the text of which, as was already mentioned, originated in Clairvaux. For this text is missing the stipulation (which does appear in the *carta caritatis et unanimitatis prior),* prohibiting the Cistercian abbeys from having an annual chapter meeting with the monasteries belonging to their own affiliation. With this rule Stephen Harding had wanted to prevent the unity of the order from being disturbed when one of the affiliate monasteries developed into a separate order, as had happened in Molesme.

Considering the fact that in Bernard's days Clairvaux maintained its direct authority even over filiations that once had been founded or acquired by one of its daughter monasteries, the absence of the stipulation in the *summa carta caritatis* against convening their own monastic chapters must be understood as an attempt to retain the possibility of forming a separate order through its filiations. This particular version must have been of importance in the period before 1134, when Bernard had not yet succeeded in fully putting his own stamp on the policies of

---

118. We know but little about the cooperation between Bernard and Rainald. It does seem clear, however, that the letter they collectively addressed to Innocent II in 1141 (*Ep.* 348; SBO VIII, 291-293), requesting that he approve the choice of Arnulf of Séez as the bishop of Lisieux, was not written at Rainald's initiative, since this intervention concurs with a letter Peter the Venerable sent to the pope about the same subject; *Ep.* 101; *Letters* I, 261-262. We also know that subsequent to the Council of Sens, Rainald, at the request of Peter, mediated in a reconciliation between Bernard and Abelard.

Cîteaux. This initial distancing itself from Cîteaux by Clairvaux may also be apparent in the different ways in which the two texts describe the status of the *novum monasterium* in the order. The *carta caritatis* calls this monastery the "mother of our churches," while the *summa carta caritatis* does not refer to Cîteaux as such, but only speaks of the abbot of Cîteaux as the "chief of all abbots."[119]

Although the further expansion of Clairvaux indicates that, particularly in later years, Bernard strongly clung to this direct authority over the most recent filiations, this version which Clairvaux introduced of the *carta caritatis prior* did not become accepted in the order. The *carta caritatis posterior*, which — it is generally assumed — was issued shortly after 1165, agrees fully in content with the *carta caritatis prior*, and thus contains the rule that none of the monasteries was allowed to convene an annual chapter with its filiations.[120] This may point to the fact that after 1134, through its domination, Clairvaux had acquired a status in the order that no longer required punctual insistence upon a version of its own. On the other hand, it seems reasonable to conclude that after the death of Bernard, this dominance of Clairvaux was no longer accepted at face value.

B. The Indirect Role of Bernard in This Expansion

The diplomatic role Bernard played in the expansion of Clairvaux and, in fact, of the Cistercian Order as a whole, also deserves attention, even though we know but few details about the way in which these monasteries were founded or acquired and must usually content ourselves with legendary or apocryphal stories. The available documents do indicate, however, that there is little evidence of direct involvement of Bernard in this expansion.

Initially, when Bernard was still relatively unknown outside his order, the founding of daughter monasteries must have been quite important to him; for each founding or acquisition required material and legal arrangements if the venture was to be a success. But the charters that have been preserved show that Bernard seldom involved himself directly in such foundings or acquisitions. From what he writes

119. Auberger (1986), 335. Cf. above, 215.

120. In the *carta caritatis prior*, art. VIII, this precept reads: "Ipsi vero cum his quos genuerint, annum capitulum non habebunt"; Auberger (1986), 333. In the *carta caritatis posterior*, art. XIV, 2: ". . . excepto quod annuum inter se capitulum non habebunt," ibid., 332.

in his own letters, we gain the impression that he did so only when there were unforeseen difficulties. A side remark from Bernard on the occasion of one of those difficulties shows, however, that Bernard was intimately acquainted with the material preparations for the various foundings and acquisitions.[121]

But we should not detach Bernard's role in the expansion of Clairvaux from his significance for the expansion experienced by the Cistercian Order as a whole. If we look at the expansion during the years from 1112/13 to 1153, subdivided in five-year periods, we see that in 1118 it consisted already of 7 monasteries, and that by 1123 another 12 had been added to this total, by 1128 another 12, and by 1133 no fewer than 38. In the five-years periods that ended in 1138, 1143, and 1148, the new acquisitions numbered 62, 66, and 99 respectively. This last figure included the incorporation, in 1147, of the Order of Savigny with 27, and of Obazine with 2 filiations. In the final period (1148-1153), during which the failure of the Second Crusade occurred, the order was further enriched with 54 monasteries, in spite of the directive from the general chapter in 1152 that prohibited the founding of additional monasteries. This directive was apparently not closely adhered to.[122]

Since this growth stagnated to a large degree after Bernard's death — that is, if we disregard the beginning emergence of the female Cistercians that took place just at that time — this tempestuous expansion has been viewed as mainly due to his influence. This was indeed true to a significant degree, as René Locatelli has clarified in a careful summary:

> In the midst of the numerous agents of this success, who are listed in the Cistercian annals, the name of Bernard himself immediately jumps to the front. As already indicated, his active working life coincided with the emergence of the white monks. Historians have often emphasized his role: by his many interventions, and his constant travels in the Christian part of the world; by his charismatic personality and his writings; by his ties with the Burgundian nobility and the network

---

121. *Ep.* 299; SBO VIII. In this letter, addressed to the Duke of Angoulême, about the founding of the abbey of Charente, Bernard wrote: "We have founded many abbeys, but none of them have been liable to such exactions." Transl. James, 436. Dimier, "Les fondations manquées," 9.

122. These figures are given by Locatelli, "L'expansion de l'ordre cistercien au temps de saint Bernard," 106-107. Contrary to Father Dimier (above, 250, note 111), Locatelli arrives at a total of 352 monasteries.

of relationships he wove around himself, he did much to give high visibility to the Cistercian cause.

Prior to 1153, the growth of fruitful branches and their seedlings throughout Europe owes much to Bernard. Comparing his itinerary with the foundings of the branch of Clairvaux, is enough to convince us of this fact. His sojourns in the Champagne, his travels to the North of the Burgundian kingdom, his business trips to Italy, his preaching of the Second Crusade, his relationships with the kings of France and England everywhere elicited monastic vocations, which resulted in the founding of additional monasteries, as well as the incorporation of already existing houses in the Cistercian Order.[123]

This expansion was determined both by circumstances and by persons. Among these persons were bishops who were sympathetic toward the Cistercian Order, and Cistercian monks who had been chosen as bishops. Sometimes worldly founders could be inspired to make donations because of the economic importance of a new monastery for a specific region. But there may also have been moments of repentance, when feelings of contrition and a desire for reconciliation with God motivated them. And repeatedly the order profited from the impasse in which already existing monasteries at times found themselves, through divisions or the absence of new entrants.

With regard to Bernard himself, our questions touch his motivation as much as they do the visible results of his involvements. Did his political activities afford him the opportunity to found and acquire new monasteries, or did he actively pursue possibilities that would allow him to leave his monastery, and which would then give him the chance to seek possibilities for the founding or acquisition of monasteries? Our knowledge is too limited to give a final answer to this question. So much, however, is clear: that his judgment of where additional monasteries could possibly be founded or acquired was sharpened by his activities. As a result, his opinion as to what was and was not feasible with regard to the founding of new monasteries changed over the years.

A well-known and somewhat extraordinary example of this shift in perspective is the founding of the Moreruela monastery in Leon, Spain, which was undertaken from Clairvaux in 1130/31. The plans for this venture dated from about the same time as the founding of a monastery in England

123. Ibid., 117-119.

was first envisioned. Nonetheless, there seems to have been a degree of duplicity in the founding of Moreruela, unless we acknowledge a change of policy. For only a few years earlier Bernard had counseled his fellow-brother Artald — who had made his vows in Cîteaux together with him and had since 1119 been the abbot of the Preuilly abbey, which had been founded from there — not to proceed with such a founding:

> I have heard that you are thinking of making a foundation in Spain from your monastery. I cannot possibly understand why you should want to do this, what point, what advantage there can be in exiling your sons to such a distant region, where the expense of finding a site and erecting a building will be very great, when you have quite near you a place already built and ready for you.[124]

As already mentioned, we do not know the precise details as to how Bernard utilized the opportunities for the founding of monasteries that he encountered during his travels. Usually his involvement was largely dictated by the circumstances. But a comparison of his itinerary and the list of dates when new filiations were founded from Clairvaux shows that, from about 1135, Bernard returned from his journeys not only with new candidate-monks, but also with newly acquired monasteries.

For instance, in 1135 his journey to Aquitaine brought him la Grâce-Dieu (diocese of Saintes) and Buzay (diocese of Nantes). His journey to Germany led to the transfer of Eberbach (diocese of Mainz); and that to Italy, to the founding of Chiaravalle near Milan. In addition, on his way to and fro, he succeeded in arranging the affiliation with Clairvaux of three former daughter monasteries of Molesme that had gained their independence: Hautecombe and Aulps (both in the diocese of Geneva) and Balerne (diocese of Besançon); while his next journey to Italy in 1137 led to the founding of the abbey of Chiaravalle di Colomba. During his travels of 1145, he acquired the abbey of Grandselve in the diocese of Toulouse; and during his preaching of the Crusade in 1147/48, he procured Villers and Aulne (both in the diocese of Liège). During this journey to Germany, Bernard may also have visited Afflighem, but without the result he had possibly hoped for.

On the other hand, Bernard also succeeded in obtaining filiations for Clairvaux through political channels and by seizing the opportune mo-

---

124. *Ep.* 75; SBO VII, 182. Transl. James, 108-109. The letter dates from 1127. Cocheril, "L'implantation des abbayes cisterciennes dans la péninsule ibérique," 230.

ments. Gilbert de la Porrée apparently refused to facilitate the entry of the Cistercians into his diocese of Poitiers. This was hardly unexpected considering the aversion Bernard had manifested toward Gilbert's scholastic theology. Nevertheless, in 1152 Bernard did succeed in acquiring the monastery of Moureilles, which was situated in that bishopric. This can only be explained by the intervention of Eleonora of Poitou, who had recently been divorced from Louis VII and, possibly with the intent of enhancing her image, felt the urge to make a major donation to the monastery of Fontevrault. In view of the excellent relationship between Bernard and Eleonora, we have reason to suppose that she may also have mediated in the acquisition of Moureilles.[125] It is also clear, however, that Bernard knew how to utilize moments of contrition on the part of some of the powerful of the world.

In any case, this method must have been employed to acquire La Grâce-Dieu with the assistance of William of Aquitaine after Bernard had brusquely and publicly urged William to repent.[126] Of special note also is the founding of the abbey of Boxley, in the archdiocese of Canterbury, which took place in 1143, from Clairvaux, and was made possible by William of Ieper, the count of Kent. Subsequently, this William of Ieper apparently wanted to reaffirm his bad reputation by burning a nunnery, with its inhabitants, to the ground, and by demanding a large bribe from the abbot of St. Albans, who thereby could prevent his abbey from suffering the same fate. Most intriguing also are the donations received in 1144 by the abbey of Longpoint from Raoul de Vermandois; as a result of these, he was later considered as one its secular founders. Raoul made these donations even though he was excommunicated because of his adulterous relationship with Adelaide of Aquitaine. Most remarkably, he even succeeded in 1148 during the Council of Reims — where Bernard played an important role — in having this illegal relationship legitimized.[127]

At times Bernard was also able to clear up the difficulties in dioceses where the Cistercians were unwelcome. We already saw this in the case of Poitiers. But for a long time the Cistercians were also impeded from coming to the bishopric of Limoges. The change that Bernard undoubtedly wanted failed to materialize during the *sedis vacatio* in 1137. Innocent intended to appoint Alberic, the abbot of Vézelay and a friend

125. "St. Bernard and the Historians" (1977), 56, with note 115.
126. Vp II, c. VI, 37-38; P.L., CLXXXV, 289-290.
127. Hill (1968), 54. Also "St. Bernard and the Historians" (1977), 55-56.

of Bernard; but Peter the Venerable, under whose authority the Cluniac abbey of Vézelay fell, succeeded in preventing this. He argued that Alberic was irreplaceable, considering the difficult situation in which the abbey found itself. However, he did not object when in 1138 the pope chose Alberic as the cardinal-archbishop of Ostia.[128]

So nothing changed in Limoges, where finally, in 1142, a cousin of Eustorge, the bishop who had died in 1137, was appointed. The Cistercians did not gain a foothold until 1147, when Obazine, which had two daughters in that diocese, became a filiation of Cîteaux. But prior to this, in 1146, the Cistercian monastery La Colombe had been founded from Preuilly, near the border between the dioceses of Limoges and Bourges. This founding could be realized with the support of Pierre de la Châtre, who in 1142, with the backing of Bernard, had become archbishop of Bourges. Earlier — in 1145 — the monastery of La Prée had been founded from Clairvaux in this bishopric, which at that time already had seven Cistercian abbeys. It was situated near the border with the bishopric of Nevers, where the Cistercians had also been prevented from founding monasteries.[129]

It seems that in 1140 Bernard took a remarkable initiative in connection with his monastic expansion policy, when he saw the chance of playing off Roger II of Sicily against Pope Innocent II. In 1139 the pope had seriously upset Bernard. During the Second Lateran Council, in which Bernard strangely enough did not participate, he had unseated all supporters of Anacletus, the anti-pope who in the meantime had died. Among these was also Cardinal Peter of Pisa, whom Bernard — at the request of Innocent II before the end of the schism — had convinced to distance himself from the anti-pope and to choose the side of Innocent.[130]

Roger II had also been among the supporters of Anacletus, who already in 1130 had recognized him as the king of Sicily, Calabria, and Apulia. When the schism ended, Innocent II wanted to take this title from him. When Roger did not surrender his royal claims, the pope decided to fight him. But the papal army suffered bitter defeat, and Innocent II himself was among those taken captive. Three days later (July 22, 1139), he concluded the Peace of Mignano with Roger, whose claims were now

128. Manselli, "Alberico, cardinale vescovo d'Ostia e la sue attivita di legato pontifico," 28-29.

129. "St. Bernard and the Historians" (1977), 55-56.

130. *Ep.* 213; SBO VIII, 73.

officially recognized. Bernard also reconciled himself with Roger, in spite of all the negative things he had earlier written and said about him.

A year later Innocent risked a new conflict with Roger, this time about his holdings in Southern Italy. This coincided with the preparations for the wedding between Roger's son and a daughter of the count of Champagne, who was a close friend of Bernard. On her journey to the South of Italy, the bride was accompanied by twelve Cistercian monks, who upon their arrival were allowed to take charge of the Sambucino abbey as a filiation of Clairvaux. Simultaneously, Bernard fulfilled an order given to him by Innocent II to found a monastery in Sabine territory, northwest of Rome, with financial support that had been promised by the abbot of Farfa.[131]

To execute this order, a group of monks had come from Clairvaux. Bernard had appointed Paganelli as their abbot. But the transfer of the Sambucino abbey to Clairvaux caused Innocent to fear that Bernard had now chosen Roger's side. He therefore made another, more enticing proposal to tie Bernard more securely to his side. He offered him the abbey of Tre Fontane in Rome for his monks. This monastery had formerly been inhabited by Benedictines, who had been expelled from it after the schism had ended because they had supported Anacletus.[132]

⁂   ⁂

THIS PARTICULAR STORY about Bernard's sagacity in acquiring a daughter monastery for Clairvaux by manipulating the political situation is not supported by enough concrete evidence to be presented as the only interpretation. This view does not, of course, harmonize with the cultic image of Bernard that has long been common, but it fits remarkably well with the portrayal of Bernard that can be distilled from what we know about his role in the founding of monasteries.

However, this reconstruction lacks one essential element: the real reason why Bernard so frequently involved himself with political affairs and so often meddled in things that must have made him, a monk, controversial for many. Did he, in fact, have a split personality, or was he simply a human person who inevitably made mistakes in the realization of the multifaceted religious project he envisioned?

131. Dimier, "Les fondations manquées," 8.
132. "St. Bernard and the Historians" (1977), 58, note 120.

We have already posed the question regarding Bernard's motives: Did he found and acquire monasteries because his political activities presented him with the opportunity, or did he welcome activities that would bring him outside his monastery with the intent of discovering these possibilities? The only real answer must be: both. But such a response demands that we determine the relative weight of both aspects. Bernard's writings show that the monastery, more specifically Clairvaux, was the most important element in his life. Repeatedly he writes in his letters that he has decided not to leave his monastery and for that reason cannot accept an invitation to deal with matters outside. But when he put such intent in writing, he did so as an excuse when he found it opportune.[133] In any case, these excuses did not express any intention that he consistently practiced.

Elsewhere in his writings, Bernard dealt in more depth with the spiritual meaning that Clairvaux held for him as a monk. Therefore, if we want to answer the question regarding Bernard's motivation for his activities in the world, for the expansion of his abbey and his order, we must also study the metaphors he used in his statements about the spiritual meaning of Clairvaux.

C. Clairvaux as the Home of the Poor in Christ

The name of Clairvaux occurs 216 times in Bernard's letters, but only 12 times in all his other writings. Usually Bernard mentioned the name when he introduced himself as the abbot of this monastery. At times he referred in his letters to Clairvaux as a community, consisting of *pauperes Christi* — people who are poor for Christ's sake. In addition, he also referred to Clairvaux in a figurative sense at times. In a number of these instances, he compared his monastery with a fortress, which he sometimes identified as the heavenly Jerusalem. He included in this representation the other monasteries that were either filiations of this specific abbey, or belonged to the Cistercian Order as a whole.

Bernard described Clairvaux as a home for the poor in Christ, and as such he compared it at one time with the heavenly Jerusalem, a regular topic in his writings. The conflation of these two metaphors is found in a particular context: in a letter, written in early 1147, in which Bernard

---

133. *Epp.* 17; SBO VII, 65; 21, c. 1; VII, 71; 48, c. 3; VII, 139; 228, c. 2; VIII, 99; 245, VIII, 136. Diers (1991), 163-166.

informed Geoffrey of Staufen that the latter's brother had changed his plan to participate in the crusade preached by Bernard. Instead, this knight had made a better decision, to become poor for the sake of Christ. He had therefore opted for a life as a religious in the home for the poor in Christ, and had turned to the true Jerusalem "that does not kill its prophets, but is 'bound firmly together' in brotherhood" (Psalms 122:3).[134]

Bernard refers to Clairvaux as a community of the poor in Christ in only four of his letters. One of these letters, in which he gave the motives for this description, was mentioned above. In two other letters Bernard refers to himself in the introduction, without any further comment, as "the servant of the poor in Christ, who live in Clairvaux." In both instances he probably did so because of the topic of these letters. In one of these, written around 1125, he intervened with Geoffroy of Lèves, the bishop of Chartres, on behalf of an Eremite who had left his own monastery. He sent the other around 1129 to Thomas, the provost of the abbey of St. John the Baptist in Beverley, Yorkshire. Therein Bernard tried to convince Thomas to enter Clairvaux. Finally, in a fourth letter, which he and Abbot Hugh of Pontigny collectively addressed to Pope Honorius II, they both called themselves abbots of the poor in Christ, who resided in Clairvaux and Pontigny.[135]

Thus in three of Bernard's letters, this description "poor in Christ," which he used in his correspondence with reference to the monks of Clairvaux, had some connection with the content or with the intention of the letter. In the letter to Honorius II, this characterization was mainly used as a commonplace, as in a letter of commendation that he sent to Innocent II around 1141. He therein praised the one he recommended to the pope as "a friend of the poor in Christ and a servant of your servants." He did the same in a letter that he sent in 1147 to Dermond, the king of Ireland. He thanked the king for the way in which he had received in his country "the poor in Christ, or rather Christ through the poor." In this case also, this description was little more than a commonplace. The poor that Bernard was here referring to were the Cistercians of Mellifont, who had received material support from the king when they founded the monastery of Baltinglass, or Vallis Salutis.[136]

---

134. *Ep.* 459; SBO VIII, 437. Cf. Gastaldelli, *Opere* VI-2, 632, note 1.

135. *Epp.* 55, 411, and 46; SBO VII, 147; VIII, 392 and VII, 135.

136. *Epp.* 349 and 546; SBO VIII, 293. The other letters in which Bernard speaks of the *pauperes Christi* or the *pauperum Cristi*, are *Epp.* 7 (c. 8) and 235, c. 2; SBO VII, 37; VIII, 109. Cf. also *Ep.* 173 from 1138, in which he recommends the monks of Bénissons-Dieu, which he had founded himself, to Falco, the newly elected bishop of Lyon; SBO VII, 387.

Only once in his sermons does Bernard use the metaphors of poverty and the poor in connection with the monks. In that particular sermon he compares the poor who followed Christ with the hem of his robe. This lowest and most unworthy part of his robe was, however, able to support those who touched it with alms. Forsaking everything, they followed Christ as his poor. Bernard also applied this metaphor to "insignificant monks, since they help the people, when they see their humiliation and humility, to show remorse and to repent."[137]

On the other hand, life as a Cistercian monk is presented in the *vita prima* as a conscious choice for poverty for the sake of Christ:

> The site for the abbey of Clairvaux was in the Langres district, not far from the River Aube, and the place had for many years been used as a robbers' lair. Of old it was called the Vale of Absinth, either because wormwood grew there in great abundance, or because of the bitter sorrow experienced by those who fell into the hands of the robbers who lived there. Such was the place in which the men of God from Cîteaux settled. Formerly it had been a place in which fear and loneliness held sway, but they made this den of thieves into a temple of God and a house of prayer. They began to serve God in this place in poverty of spirit, in hunger and thirst, in coldness and nakedness, and in long vigils, following the example of the Apostle. Often their food was nothing but a stew of beech leaves. Their bread was of the roughest, being made of barley, millet and vetch, so that one day a monk who was staying in the guest house secretly took some of it away with him when it was served to him, and later he showed it to everyone as if it were a miracle that any man could live on this food, and especially men who lived such a hard life.[138]

With this metaphor for Clairvaux, William evoked associations with the cave of Subiaco, where Saint Benedict had lived for some time. It also fits with the characterization Bernard had given, around 1124/25, of the Cistercian way of life in his "Letter in the Rain" and in his *Apology*. But in the ensuing books of the *vita prima*, it is relegated somewhat to the background. It is true that Arnold of Bonneval also referred to the picture that Bernard had evoked in his polemics about the lifestyle of his brethren,

---

137. *Sententiae*, series tertia; SBO VI-2, 169, lines 1-9.
138. Vp I, c. V, 25; P.L., CLXXXV, 241-242; transl. Webb and Walker, 44-45. This passage is repeated verbatim in Vs, c. VI, 18; P.L., CLXXV, 480.

but from what this hagiographer wrote about the new constructions at Clairvaux that were necessary, and in his opinion very justifiable — and which were approved by Bernard — it is also apparent that these buildings that were erected in 1136 could no longer simply be regarded as a place where "the poor in Christ" lived.[139]

Likewise, from the report of Geoffrey of Auxerre, who entered only in 1140, it also becomes clear that this abandonment of the earliest designs for Clairvaux must have been a difficult decision for Bernard. Geoffrey tells in his *Fragmenta* how the choice of the terrain where the new buildings, which were needed because of the enormous influx of new monks, were to be constructed, was made in accordance with the instructions one of the novices received in a vision.[140] This story no longer appears in the *vita prima*. It no longer deals with the question of where the new monastery was to be built, but whether it ought to be built. We learn from two visions, which Geoffrey relates, that in Bernard's absence it was decided to build a much larger monastery. Bernard's approval came later through a vision:

> During the time when Bernard was near Rome, one of the brothers, named Robert, became seriously ill. In a vision he saw a young man, who looked like the infirmarian, and who commanded the brother to follow him. It seemed as if he followed the one who preceded him, until he came to a high mountain. There he met the Lord Jesus together with a group of angels, and he heard Him say to His guide, "Keep him safe for me." The Lord also put some words in the heart of the sick brother, by which He gave a command, through this brother, to Clairvaux, which belonged to Him. At dawn the person who was thought to be dying sat upright, and to the amazement of all he asked for lord Godefroy, who at the time was the prior and presently is the bishop of Langres. When Godefroy had arrived, he said to him among other things, "The Lord commands you to build large houses which can accommodate the multitudes, which He will send you in great numbers. Also tell the brothers of the granges that they behave in a virtuous way and serve as an example to the people in the world. For woe the person through whom someone might err along the path of evil."

139. Vp II, c. V, 29-31; P.L., CLXXXV, 284-285. For the textual changes in Redaction B, see *Etudes* (1960), 38.
140. *Fragmenta*, c. 35 and 37; A.B. 50, 107-109.

About twenty days later, while he was still suffering from this illness, without any hope of recovery, the admirable father Bernard, though physically absent, was in Clairvaux in the spirit. He visited the sick man, sang the hymns of the office of the night together with a large group of brothers, and stayed with him throughout the night. When the morning came, this same brother was healed, and he told the brothers how he had been delivered from his illness.[141]

This account of Geoffrey of Auxerre refers to the building of the new monastery of Clairvaux. The decision to go ahead with the construction was made in 1136, while Bernard was absent. In spite of Bernard's strong objections, his prior persisted in the execution of the construction plans. The story further illustrates why Clairvaux could from that time on no longer be considered as an eremitical community, and why it must have become difficult for Bernard to speak of a community of the poor in Christ when referring to the spiritual significance of his monastery and its immediate filiations.

It is therefore small wonder that the two other metaphors that Bernard used with regard to Clairvaux — "the heavenly Jerusalem" and "the fortress of God" — henceforth received more emphasis in his writings, even though infrequently he would still refer to that other image of Clairvaux as a home of the poor in Christ, who himself had chosen to be poor.[142]

D. Clairvaux as the Entrance to the Heavenly Jerusalem

The characterization of Clairvaux as the home of the poor in Christ suffered from yet another, more practical objection. This metaphor, regardless of whether it had become irrelevant, offered Bernard but few opportunities for allegorical elaborations, in contrast to the scriptural notion of the Jerusalem from above. Moreover, Bernard could easily link this latter metaphor for Clairvaux with that of a fortress for the Lord. Bernard's identification of the heavenly Jerusalem with a fortress is not so strange in view of the trying situation in which the earthly Jerusalem had gradually found itself again, after it had been conquered and "delivered" in 1099. He was also acquainted with this threat as a result of his close

---

141. Vp IV, c. I, 4; P.L., CLXXXV, 323-324. This incident is omitted in Redaction B and in a large number of the manuscripts of Redaction A; *Etudes* (1960), 44-45.

142. Diers (1991), 88-89.

ties with the Order of the Templars, whose task it was to defend this city, which had acquired the appearance of a fortress, and to protect the roads that led toward it.

But in actual fact, this comparison of the heavenly Jerusalem with a fortress is derived from a much older usage, already employed and elaborated upon by St. Augustine. He contrasted Jerusalem as the city of eternal peace with Babylon as the symbol of the eternal struggle between righteousness *(iustitia)* and unrighteousness *(malitia)*.[143] In combining the two images, Bernard could also utilize other, already current allegorical applications of Bible texts about the heavenly Jerusalem, particularly the metaphor of Jerusalem that must be "searched by the light of lamps" — an image Bernard elaborated upon three times in his writings.[144] Furthermore, Bernard repeatedly referred to the biblical metaphor of Jerusalem as a heavenly city, our mother who descends on the earth, as the royal city and the city of peace. This last description was further strengthened from the eighth century onward by an etymological explanation of the name Jerusalem. Earlier, in patristic commentaries, it had already become common to contrast the heavenly Jerusalem, as a city of peace, with Babylon, the earthly city of confusion.[145]

Bernard felt that the text from Isaiah, "O Jerusalem, I have set watchmen; all the day and all the night, they shall never be silent" (62:6), fitted perfectly with the image of Jerusalem as a fortress. This text repeatedly inspired him to speak of the heavenly Jerusalem as a fortress. In his explanation, these watchmen initially were the angels; but since the rebellion of Lucifer and his supporters, great breaches had been made in the walls. These walls were now to be rebuilt with living stones: the blessed people who through their entry into the heavenly Jerusalem became the stones that would strengthen this fortress.[146]

In addition, Bernard interpreted this text in yet another way, situating the heavenly Jerusalem also on earth. That is how he referred to

143. Timmermann (1982), 107-114. For Bernard's knowledge of the writings of St. Augustine, see Rigolot, "Bernard de Clairvaux, lecteur de saint Augustine," 132-144.

144. *In Super Canticum*, sermo 55, c.2 (cf. above, 191, with note 112), and also in *Sermo ad clericos De Conversione*, c. IX, 19, and *In vigilia Navitatis*, sermo 3, c. 6; SBO IV, 92, line 14, and 216, line 17.

145. *Christendom* (1994), 86-89. Raedts, "St. Bernard and Jerusalem" (1994), 169-182.

146. *In Psalmam qui habitat*, sermo 12, c. 5; SBO IV, 46, lines 9-10. *Super canticum*, sermo 77, c. 4; II, 263, line 17–264, line 11.

church buildings. In one of his dedication sermons, he called the church a holy building, since holy spirits guard it without ever getting tired. He gave the following explanation to his hearers:

> You may say: the things just mentioned we understand, but who can claim to have seen a guard of angels? But even when you do not see them, there is one who does: He who sent them. Who is He? He is the one who speaks through the prophet, "On your walls, Jerusalem, I have set watchmen." Now, above there is a Jerusalem that is free, our mother, but I can hardly assume that watchmen have been set on those walls. For the prophet sings her praise with these words: "He makes peace in your borders" (Psalms 147:14). If that is not convincing enough, continue to listen to the rest of the earlier testimony: "All the day and all the night, they shall never be silent" (Isaiah 62:6). From this you must conclude that this is not the Jerusalem about which you have read: "Its gates shall never be shut by day — and there shall be no night there" (Revelation 21:25). That Jerusalem will not suffer contingencies and does not need watchmen. Watchmen are needed because of our days and our nights. "Upon your walls, O Jerusalem, have I set watchmen."[147]

In this allegorical development he also fitted the last part of the text from the Song of Songs, where the bridegroom says to his bride: "You are beautiful . . . my love, comely as Jerusalem, terrible as an army with banners" (6:4). Bernard paraphrased this passage (*terribilis sicut castrorum acies ordinata;* Vulgate), which occurs elsewhere in the Song of Songs at least ten times (e.g., 6:10), though without this reference to Jerusalem. In those cases where he refers to Jerusalem, he associates this military terminology with the life of the monks, comparing their monastery with Jerusalem as a fortress besieged by Babylon. In one of his sermons, Bernard states that the power of a religious community is as intimidating as that of an army on the march; while elsewhere he put a sanctified soul on a par with an army, since such a soul is equipped with a multitude of well-arranged virtues and is also protected by angels.[148]

The parable in which Bernard sketched the activities of a young and inexperienced knight, who had been accepted into the army of King David and had received

---

147. *In dedicatione ecclesiae,* sermo 4, c. 1; V, 383, line 14–384, line 5.

148. *In circumcisione,* sermo 3, c. 6; SBO IV, 287, 11. *Super canticum,* sermo 39, c. II, 4; SBO II, 20, line 18.

from him his spiritual armory, became the best known of this kind of stories.[149] The army in which this knight served had to defend Jerusalem against the troops of Babylon, which, under the command of Nebuchadnezzar, consisted of only evil spirits and vices. Disobedient to the orders he had received, and ignoring the discipline of the encampment, the inexperienced knight got on a fiery horse: his own body. He failed to heed the warning David sent to him through Solomon: "Woe to him who is alone when he falls and has not another to lift him up" (Ecclesiastes 4:10). He left his fellow-soldiers (the virtues) behind and rode before the army to show his courage and to make a name for himself.

The adventure ended badly for this young knight. He was ambushed by pride and vain glory, which encouraged him in his audacity and caused him to fall in the hands of his "comrades." Gluttony and immorality overpowered his "horse," while he himself was beaten by hostility, jealousy, and other vices. Then immorality delivered him into the hands of the cook of Nebuchadnezzar, who made him participate in the most disgusting orgies. And so this knight became a prisoner of war of his enemies, who chained him to his evil habits and left him in the dungeon of despair.

The absence of the knight, whom we are then told had the name of Absalom, worried King David. He therefore sent his servants, Fear and Obedience, to make enquiries. The first resuscitated the unfortunate knight and succeeded in taking away his chains and delivering him. The knight then submitted himself to Obedience, who put the knight of Christ again on his horse, after he had subdued this animal, which had become obstinate, and led him along another road to Jerusalem. On their return trip they halted six times. The first stop was with Piety, which counterbalanced Fear; then they paused with Knowledge, where the knight found the equilibrium between Fear and Piety.

After this they interrupted their journey at Power, where the knight found the energy to continue his journey. The fourth stop was at Wise Counsel, to prevent the knight from withdrawing from the guidance of Obedience. The fifth stopover was at Insight, to learn more about God's will. In the company of these virtues the knight then reached his sixth stop, Wisdom, where he began to consider the divine promises. "From there he arrived in Jerusalem, in the kingdom and the city of David, where peace can be found, and where the blessed and peace loving sons of God, who have come to experience peace both internally and externally, share in the joy of their Lord and celebrate the eternal Sabbath."

Bernard uses the various Jerusalem metaphors in his many sermons, regardless of the occasions of his preaching and the subject: in his sermons on the Song of Songs, in preaching at feasts during the ecclesiastical year

---

149. *Parabolae* III; SBO VI-1, 274-276. Timmermann (1982), 119-123, and Diers (1991), 85-88.

or on saints' days, and in his talks about sundry topics. Sometimes it is a mere allusion, but at times Bernard begins a sermon with an extended metaphor about the heavenly Jerusalem, which must have been inspired by the various ways in which people prepared for, and made, their journey to the terrestrial city. An example of such a use is in his sermon "About the fourfold duty":

> Brethren, you are travelling along the road that leads toward life, the straight and undefiled way to that holy city Jerusalem, which is free, which is situated in a high place, and which is also our mother. The way to enter it is steep, for it is hewn in the top of the mountain itself, but a shorter way reduces, or even prevents, the burden of your efforts. For you not only travel along this road with an ease that is as fortuitous, as your fortune is easy, but you also travel fast. For you are without luggage and well equipped, without carrying burdens on your back. Some do not travel in this manner. For they take along a four-in-hand, and the outfitting for a four-in-hand, and therefore decide to take a route that leads them around the mountain. But descending sideroads lead them to the foot of the mountain and allow them to just barely reach their destination.[150]

Sometimes the topic of the sermon determines the manner in which Bernard touches the Jerusalem theme. In his first sermon for Palm Sunday, for instance, he encourages the religious who listen to him or read his writings to understand the entry into Jerusalem as an image of the glory of the heavenly fatherland. He exhorts them to long for that day when the Lord will receive his triumphant welcome into heavenly Jerusalem. And in his third sermon for that Sunday, Bernard compares the contemplative life of the brethren with the experience of those who were closest to the Lord when he entered Jerusalem.[151] But in his first sermon at the beginning of Septuagesima, he presents a totally different comparison about Jerusalem to the brethren. In that sermon he contrasts the dearth of our earthly existence with the abundance of heaven, and then ends this part of his sermon with the following exclamation:

> O Jerusalem, city of the great king, "He fills you with the finest of the wheat" (Psalms 147:14), and gladdens you with its fast flowing river;

---

150. *De diversis,* sermo 22, c. 1; SBO VI-1, 170.
151. *In ramis palmarum,* sermo I, c. 2; SBO V, 43; sermo III, c. 1; V, 52.

in you there is no weight nor measure, but fullness and rich abundance. You know of no numbers, for everything in you is a perfect unity (Psalms 121:3).[152]

In the sermon already referred to above, at the occasion of the dedication of the church at Clairvaux, Bernard refers to his own monastery as the city of the eternal king, which is besieged by enemies. He calls this fortified city Zion, with reference to Isaiah 26:1. He not only speaks of the enemies who attack this fortress from the outside, but also mentions the possibility of traitors from within. Among these he counts those who strive for a softening of discipline, and who destroy the zeal, disturb the peace, and hurt the love toward others. Then he asks his monks to realize what they put at risk by their vanity and lukewarmness:

> You undoubtedly rob Christ of a mighty fortress, when you deliver Clairvaux into the hands of his enemies. Year after year He [Christ] receives from there the best, and in his eyes the most costly, income. He regularly brings a substantial booty, which He has seized from the enemy, to this, his fortified place, and great is the confidence He has in its might. Just look at the many He has saved from the power of the enemy and has assembled here from all sides, from the rising of the sun to its setting, from the North and from overseas.[153]

In this sermon Bernard compares Clairvaux with Jerusalem as the fortified stronghold of the Lord. Elsewhere he omitted this specific identification, but applied the term more generally to the Cistercian monasteries. But Clairvaux served as a role model in the order. Bernard's writings contain other indications that this was the case. For instance, in a letter that he wrote around 1129 to Alexander, the bishop of Lincoln, he identified Clairvaux directly with the heavenly Jerusalem. In this letter he reported to the bishop that one of the latter's religious, named Philip, who *en route* to Jerusalem had stayed in his monastery, had decided not to continue his journey, but to stay in Clairvaux — a decision that needed the bishop's approval.

Bernard argued that in Clairvaux Philip had found the shorter path to Jerusalem, and in fact had already arrived there. He had become not a nosy observer, but a pious inhabitant and an officially registered citizen,

---

152. *In septuagesimo,* sermo I, c. 3; SBO V, 347, lines 6-9.
153. *In dedicatione ecclesiae,* sermo 4, c. 3; SBO V, 381.

not of the earthly, but of the free Jerusalem that is from above: our mother. Bernard further explained:

> And this, if you want to know, is Clairvaux. She truly is Jerusalem, united to the one in heaven by whole-hearted devotion, by conformity of life, and by a certain spiritual affinity. Here, he himself promises, will be his rest for ever and ever. He has chosen to dwell here, because here he has found, not yet, to be sure, the fullness of vision, but certainly the hope of that true peace, "the peace which surpasses all our thinking" (Philippians 4:7).[154]

There are other indications that Bernard wanted Clairvaux to function as a role model for all the monasteries of its immediate network and for all other Cistercian monasteries, but these are not as obvious as those that point to his view of his abbey as the gate of entrance to the heavenly Jerusalem. The first evidence in that direction is the close ties between Clairvaux and its daughter institutions. We detect this close relationship with these monasteries in several letters that Bernard addressed to abbots of these filiations or wrote on behalf of one of them to some third party.

We find a much more important indication, however, in the manner in which Bernard involved Clairvaux in his mystical experience of God. This has been discovered and analyzed by the late Jean Deroy in his study of the influence of Origen on the terminology Bernard used in his sermons on the Song of Songs.

In the concluding chapter of this study, Deroy dealt with a problem of a mystical nature, which Bernard addressed anew in some of these sermons, building on what Origen had earlier said: "the coming and departing of the beloved"; that is, the mystical interaction between the Word of God and the soul that receives the Word. In this context Deroy discusses, for instance, the seventy-fourth sermon Bernard preached on the Song of Songs. This sermon contains a passage in which Bernard describes such an experience of the divine. The passage consists of a number of short, staccato-like sentences in which Bernard declares that his sight, hearing, smell, taste, and feelings — in short, all of his senses — are unable to reach the Word.[155]

Deroy also counted the number of syllables of this passage in the Latin text of the sermon, as he did with some other parts of Bernard's

---

154. *Ep.* 64, c. 2; SBO VII, 158. Transl. James, 91.
155. Deroy (1963), 149-154.

writings. He found a total of ninety-nine. In Roman numerals this would be written as *IC,* which stands for *Jesus Christus.* Deroy had discovered this same phenomenon in another text by Bernard: a similar cryptogram, also with ninety-nine syllables, but with a different content. The cryptogram that Deroy detected in this seventy-fourth sermon on the Song of Songs describes, as we have just stated, the inability of the human senses to reach God. The passage in which Bernard expresses this inability may be translated as follows:

> "Thy footprints were unseen" (Psalms 77:19).
> Certainly, the Word did not enter through my eyes,
> because It does not have color.
> Neither through my ears,
> since It does not make any sound.
> And not through my nose,
> as It does not mix with air,
> but with the spirit.
> It did not influence the air,
> but It was its maker.
> It does not pass through my throat,
> since It has no permanency and is not swallowed.
> And It cannot be found by touching,
> because It is untouchable.[156]

Bernard discusses this human inability at more length than Origen, who only stated that the Word could not be touched. In fact, Bernard here complements the description this early Christian author gave of his experience of a mystical encounter with the divine and then testifies, as Origen does, after his description of the inability of his senses to experience the Word, of his utter ignorance about the way in which the Word came to him. Once again, Deroy argues, Bernard has woven a cryptic game of syllables into his testimony. This passage also contains a series of short, staccato-like sentences. The translation reads as follows:

> Along what path did the Word in fact enter?
> Or did It perhaps not enter,
> since It did not come from outside?
> For It is not a something

---

156. *Super canticum,* sermo 74, c. 5; SBO II, 242, lines 23-27.

that belongs to things that are external.
On the other hand, It did not originate inside me,
because It is good;
and I know that there is no good within me.
I also did ascend above myself,
and, lo, the Word was higher than I was.
I also descended into the depths of my inner self
as a curious explorer,
but It was below where I was.
Looking outside,
It was further away from me
than anything that was outside me;
looking inwardly,
This was even more inward.[157]

Bernard concludes this description about the mystical entry and departure of the Word in him with these words: "And I understood how true it was what I had read: 'In Him we live, and move, and have our being' (Acts 17:28)."

This final quotation from Acts gives this text a very special meaning if we realize that the original Latin version consists of exactly 159 syllables. Written with Roman numerals, this number is CLIX. Since X is usually equated with S, the number 159 leads to the letters CLIS, a common contraction for the word *CLARAVALLIS*. All this tells us that Bernard linked his mystical encounter with God, which he described in this passage, very closely with the place where he lived. There he had been given the opportunity to live, move, and be in God.

Returning to our point of departure, we may conclude that this symbolism, which Bernard at times links to the name of Clairvaux, points to his belief that the monastic life of the Cistercians was the shortest route for a human being to the heavenly Jerusalem as his final destination. The link that Bernard concealed in this passage (and possibly in other of his writings) between the mystical encounter with God and the name Clairvaux makes it clear that this abbey held a mystical meaning for him, similar to that of the heavenly Jerusalem. Those who entered Clairvaux — or other Cistercian monasteries, since this mystical meaning was not limited to Clairvaux — embarked on their journey toward the heavenly city.

157. Ibid., 242, line 27–243, line 6.

4. EPILOGUE: RACHEL AND LEAH

IN CONTRAST TO the earlier editions of Bernard's letters, the edition prepared by Jean Leclercq and H. Rochais does not contain a selection from the letters Bernard received from others. But these authors made an exception for three letters, probably because Bernard himself had made sure that those letters were included in the register of his letters. None of the other letters addressed to Bernard received the same honor. No mention is made of the reason these letters were included in the letter register, but there is a ready explanation for the presence of each. Two of these letters have been referred to earlier: one written by Peter the Venerable, the other by Pope Innocent II.[158]

The letter in which Bernard received lavish praise was written by Peter the Venerable in the autumn of 1150, in part to assure Bernard's assistance in the reforms of his own Cluniac order. We may assume that the letter was added to Bernard's letter register either by himself or, after his death, by Geoffrey of Auxerre, in order to disguise the breach in the relationship between the two abbots that occurred in 1152.[159]

Innocent's letter, which was addressed to the archbishops of Reims and Sens and their suffragan bishops, but also to Bernard, dates from 1140. As has already been mentioned, this letter contained the papal confirmation of the condemnation by the Council of Sens of the theological views of Abelard. In the letter Abelard was also personally branded a heretic. The inclusion of this letter in the register, in which as a rule Bernard did not include letters from others, may be explained by the fact that subsequently Bernard was often criticized for his actions against Abelard. This letter would make clear that such criticisms were invalid.

The third letter addressed to him, which Bernard had included in this register, was sent to him between 1125 and 1130, when he had not yet reached the age of forty. It was un unsolicited letter from a much older man, Hildebert of Lavardin (1056-1133), the former bishop of Le Mans, who had been elected archbishop of Tours in 1125. Hildebert enjoyed great

---

158. *Epp.* 264 and 194; SBO VIII, 174-175 and 46-48. See above, 243 and 247. This does not take into account any letters Bernard wrote on behalf of others, such as *Ep.* 45, which Stephen Harding, together with all Cistercians, sent in 1129 to King Louis VI; SBO VII, 133f. This letter was not addressed to him; moreover, the letter is found only in the register of Stephen's letters, which provides another reason to assume that Bernard was responsible for its redaction. Cf. Teubner (1993), 258.

159. *Ep.* 264 = *Ep.* 175; *Letters* I, 416-417. See above, 243, note 100.

fame as a literary, humanist author.[160] There is no immediate explanation for the insertion of this letter in the register. Reading the response that Bernard sent to the archbishop, we cannot but wonder why this letter became part of the collection, since Bernard appears to distance himself somewhat not only from the praise that was bestowed upon him, but also from the manner in which Hildebert expressed his appreciation for Bernard's words and actions.[161]

What Bernard possibly liked in this letter was Hildebert's positive approach to the apparent paradox, which Bernard's contemporaries may have detected in him and which must have raised some eyebrows on the part of those who did not know him intimately. This seeming paradox concerned the way in which action and contemplation were combined in Bernard's person. In his writings, Hildebert had already dealt with these different aspects earlier. He did not regard them as necessarily contradictory,[162] and, using a metaphor that had long been used in the allegorical Bible exegesis typical of those days, he had compared Bernard with the patriarch Jacob, who had two wives: Leah and Rachel:

> There are only few people who do not realize that you know a balm from its scent and a tree from its fruits. Similarly we, dear brother, have learned from what is current knowledge about you, how much you are focused on virtue and how impeccable you are in doctrine. For, although we are separated from you by too great a distance, we have heard what delightful nights you pass with your Rachel, and what abundant posterity is born to you from Leah, and how in all respects you live as one who pursues virtue and hates the flesh. None of those who have told us about you, has spoken of you in any other way.[163]

Bernard himself seldom used this image for the convergence of the *vita activa* and the *vita contemplativa* that was rather common in his days, and never with reference to himself. He saw this convergence as normal, in contrast to others who did not know him intimately, and who, as William of Saint-Thierry expressed it, had not received the grace to live according to the Spirit, as Bernard himself did.[164] Although Hildebert of Lavardin

160. Von Moos (1965).
161. *Ep.* 123; SBO VII, 304.
162. Von Moos (1965), 130-138.
163. *Ep.* 122, c. 1; SBO VII, 302.
164. See above, 84, note 45.

did not know Bernard personally, he did not belong to those others, possibly because he had more often given ample thought to the convergence of these two approaches to life.

Later in his letter, Hildebert mentions that he sent this epistle to Bernard because of his intense desire to be allowed to share in his friendship. But he also remarks that the reputation of saints cannot be damaged by false rumors. This could be an indication that Hildebert wrote to Bernard to encourage him with regard to the criticism the latter must have experienced. On the other hand, we know nothing of a friendship between those two; and most likely this did not develop. For after the schism that began in 1130, Hildebert refused to speak out in favor of the legitimacy of one of the two papal candidates, in spite of an exhortation from Bernard to acknowledge Innocent as the legitimate pope.[165]

But all this does not help to explain the exceptional presence of Hildebert's letter in Bernard's letter register. It seems to me that we are left with only one explanation: the endorsement by this archbishop of the convergence in Bernard of a contemplative and an active life. This was expressed in the metaphor of the dual marriage the abbot had entered into, following the example of the patriarch Jacob; in this union Rachel at last gave him his sons, Joseph and Benjamin, after he had sired a number of sons with Leah. Even though Bernard did not refer to this passage in his response to this letter, he must have been so pleased that Hildebert applied this metaphor to him that he decided to include this letter in the register.

The possible objections of his contemporaries against the dualism in Bernard's life *(vita biformis)* were, as has been shown earlier in this book, cleverly concealed in the *vita prima*. After Bernard's death, this problem required no further attention since it played no role in his cult. He was venerated as a perfect saint, having been predestined for that status in all

---

165. *Ep.* 124; SBO VII, 305-307. Since Hildebert made no choice, after his death in 1133 one of his candidate-successors turned, when he was passed over, to Anacletus in a belated effort to gain the episcopal see. *Ep.* 151; SBO VII, 357-358. Hildebert's reluctance no doubt was influenced by the good relationship that had existed between him and Pons of Melgueil, the former abbot of Cluny. For at Pons's request he wrote after the canonization of Abbot Hugh — that is, after January 1120 — a *vita Hugonis;* see "La canonisation de Saint Hughes" (1990). This is another indication that one of the differences of opinion that must have played a role in the schism of 1130 had to do with the condemnation of Pons of Melgueil in 1126 by Honorius II. For a summary of the causes of this schism, see Stroll (1991), XVII-XXIII.

respects from before his birth. And as long as there was no need for a different kind of life story than had been provided by his contemporary hagiographers, the problem of his contradictory double life would not emerge, the more so since it was not encountered in his writings. And often knowledge about Bernard was exclusively based on his writings, as was still apparent during the important international congress organized by the Cistercians in 1990 to commemorate the ninth centennial of Bernard's birth.[166]

However, since historical research has established a number of human shortcomings in Bernard's activities — as discussed at length in an earlier chapter — an alternative portrait of Bernard has emerged that in many ways differs from the traditional cultic portrayal by his contemporary hagiographers. As a result, this duality in Bernard's life has reemerged as a historiographical problem.

Those who have met Bernard only in his writings and thus have to some extent shared in the experience of some of his "nights with Rachel" find it difficult, of course, to come to terms with those facts that disagree with the cultic life story of this abbot. Some believe that this information about Bernard's activities in society are only of secondary importance, that they are of a lower order since they take away from Bernard's role in the divine plan of salvation. This, however, is a method of reasoning that allows cultic-theological arguments to determine the outcome of scientific historical research.

In the meantime, in order to evaluate this rediscovered duality in Bernard's life, a compromise has been invented that supposedly would do justice to both views regarding Bernard's personality. This would enable us to recognize him as a saint, while viewing him as a charlatan in his manipulation of his contemporaries. This compromise is based on the presupposition that Bernard must have been internally torn in different directions. It has been argued that proof for this theory may be found in a characterization Bernard once gave of himself — to which we have earlier referred — of a chimera or the monstrous dual being of his times.

In this presentation of Bernard, the contradiction between the pious content of his mystical writings and the excesses in his public actions grow into totally unacceptable paradoxes. And the proponents of this view seem to find it unnecessary to investigate whether Bernard was able to integrate

---

166. *La dottrina della vita spirituale nelle opere di san Bernardo di Clairvaux.* Atti del convengo internazionale, 11-15 September 1990, Rome 1991. AnCi 66 (1990).

these contradictory elements, which arose from the differences between an active and a contemplative life, in a harmonious way within himself. Because of this integration, as Hildebert also testified, he was, in the eyes of many, an acceptable person with great significance. But this quality of Bernard will never be discovered if attention is not paid to a harmonious convergence of his search for contemplation on the one hand, and his desire, on the other hand, to realize in contemporary society the ideals that he cherished in his contemplation — or, to use Hildebert's words, if any possible relationship is denied between the nights Bernard passed with Rachel and his fertility with Leah.

This relationship must above all be sought in that particular domain where these conflicting ambitions of Bernard clearly touched each other. It seems to me that the route in that direction has been shown in the vision, earlier referred to, and which William of Saint-Thierry may or may not have invented *a posteriori,* but, in any event, described in the first book of the *vita prima.* In that vision, Bernard saw how the valley of Clairvaux was filled by all kinds of people who came from everywhere. For his conflicting ambitions meet in his choice for the monastic life, since this choice affected not only himself but also many others. From the moment he left the world, he tried to take the world with him into the monastery. Such endeavors inevitably led to inner conflicts that gradually developed further. For in the realization of the two ambitions, he traveled along different roads, with the intent of finding as broad and as deep an interest in monastic life as possible — on the one hand by urging as many as possible to opt for this state of life, and on the other hand by giving this state of life more depth in a mystical sense.

When he experienced abundant success in the recruitment of monks, Bernard decided to found or acquire as many monasteries as possible. In so doing he used all available means, at every opportune moment, and excluded and resisted anything and everything in society that could pose a threat to monasticism. This part of his zeal in favor of the monastic world came from what Hildebert of Lavardin referred to as Bernard's fertile relationship with Leah. Historical research has, in the meantime, traced a number of clear examples of his blunt defiance of those who posed a threat to his efforts or were perceived by him as such.

The other road along which Bernard traveled was to lead him in providing a new depth to the monastic life, to which he gave a new spiritual direction. On this mystical path he met Rachel, with whom he spent enjoyable nights; that is, in contemplating divine and heavenly things.

This road also he did not travel by himself, but he leveled it for those who followed him then and later to his monasteries. Those who pay attention only to what Bernard has written about the summits of his mystical experiences, or to his often very controversial actions to create the material space where his followers would be able to share in these experiences, cannot but view these matters as utterly contradictory.

Those who focus only on the two extremes and want to judge Bernard on that basis will do him great injustice, for they ignore the identical point of departure from which Bernard could move to these extremes. This injustice can be avoided if, in our study of Bernard, we begin with his constant involvement with Cistercian monasticism, and then balance our attention between the two inherently conflicting aspects of his active and contemplative life. Thus we begin to understand the intrinsic affinity of these two aspects of Bernard, which Hildebert of Lavardin, using the imagery that was current in his days, once described as his dual marriage with the two wives of the the patriarch Jacob. For those who are convinced that the blending of cult and history in Bernard must be a thing of the past, this approach to the duality in Bernard's life may open possibilities that bring new life to the historical study of his person, which has been at an impasse for a considerable time. This has been the rationale for this final chapter, in which I have tried to take a first step in that direction.

Appendix 1

Chronological Summary (1075-1174)

⤳ ⤳

1075: Abbot Robert founds Molesme.

1086: Stephen Harding enters Molesme.

1091: Bernard is born in Fontaines-lès-Dijon.

1098: Founding of Cîteaux.

1098-1099: Bernard attends the chapter school of St.-Vorles in Châtillon-sur-Seine.

1099: Conquest of Jerusalem.

1100: Abbot Robert returns to Molesme; Alberic abbot in Cîteaux.

1108: Stephen Harding succeeds Alberic as abbot of Cîteaux.

c. 1110: The scriptorium of Cîteaux produces and illustrates the "Bible of Stephen Harding" and the "Moralia of Gregory the Great."

1112: Together with friends and relatives, Bernard establishes a monastic community in his parental home — Preparations are made in Cîteaux to found the first daughter institution: the monastery of La Ferté-sur-Grosne.

1113: Bernard enters Cîteaux — Founding of La Ferté.

1114: Founding of Pontigny — First version of *Carta caritas*.

1115: (June 25): Founding of Morimond and Clairvaux — Bernard confirmed as abbot by William of Champeaux, bishop of Châlons-sur-Seine.

1117: Founding of Trois Fontaines, first filiation of Clairvaux.

1119: Archbishop of Vienne in Cluny elected as Pope Calixtus II — Founding of Fontenay, second filiation of Clairvaux — Bernard is absent during meeting of general chapter for health reasons — general chapter accepts *Carta caritas (prior)* — William of Champeaux receives permission to place Bernard outside Clairvaux for a year — William becomes the abbot of Saint-Thierry, and, possibly at the instigation of Bishop William of Champeaux, begins to visit Bernard in Clémentinpré — Calixtus II ratifies the *Carta caritas* — the *Exordium parvum* written in Cîteaux — Abbot Hugh is canonized by Calixtus II at the request of his predecessor Pons of Melgueil, the abbot of Cluny.

1120: Hildebert of Lavardin writes a *vita Hugonis,* at the request of Abbot Pons.

1121: In Rome Abbot Pons abdicates from his position in Cluny after the complaint against him by Matthew, the prior of St. Martin des Camps in Paris — Pons makes a pilgrimage to Jerusalem — Peter the Venerable becomes the abbot in Cluny and prior Matthew becomes its grand prior — Founding of Foigny, the third monastery affiliated with Clairvaux.

1122: Grand prior Matthew entices the young monk Robert of Châtillon to leave Clairvaux for Cluny.

c. 1123: Editing at Clairvaux of the *Exordium cisterciense.*

1124/25 Pons of Melgueil returns from Jerusalem — Bernard intervenes in the crisis at Morimond — Pope Calixtus II dies (December 1124) and is succeeded by Honorius II — This election follows an attack on the conclave, arranged by Chancellor-cardinal Haimeric — Honorius forbids the Cluniac monks from contacting Pons — At the instigation of William of Saint-Thierry, Bernard attempts to intervene in the internal conflict that divides Cluny; he also writes his "Letter in the Rain."

1125: William urges Bernard to repeat his attempt; Bernard writes his *Apologia* — Abbot Pons returns to Cluny, where his supporters temporarily succeed in evicting his opponents.

1126: Bernard avoids contact with the papal legate who inquires after his role in the events in Cluny — Pons is condemned in Rome and imprisoned — Matthew, his chief accuser, becomes cardinal-bishop of Albano, and subsequently papal legate in France.

1127: Bernard discourages the abbot of Preuilly from establishing a monastery in Spain — Peter the Venerable defends the Cluniac customs in a circular letter to the priors of these monasteries; he addresses this to Bernard as a reply to his *Apology.*

1128: Godefroy de la Roche Vanneau prior in Clairvaux — Matthew invites Bernard to participate in the Council of Troyes about the Templars — Bernard writes the "Praise to the new militia," but refuses to establish an abbey in the Holy Land — Founding of Reigny, the fifth filiation of Clairvaux.

1129: Chancellor-cardinal Haimeric initiates a friendly correspondence with Bernard — Abbey of Ourscamp to be the sixth filiation.

c. 1130: *Summa cartae caritatis* replaces the *Carta caritatis* in Clairvaux — Death of Honorius II — Cardinals deadlocked in election of new pope — Haimeric and Matthew support the choice of Innocent II, who is crowned in great haste — Majority of cardinals chooses Anacletus II — Innocent II flees to France — En route, he appoints Baldwin, a monk from Clairvaux, as cardinal — Bernard defends the claims of Innocent II during a synod in Etampes.

1130/38: Bernard fights for the recognition of Innocent II; for that reason travels to France, Germany, and Italy.

1131: From the northwestern part of France, Bernard brings with him to Clairvaux thirty new monks — Innocent II visits Clairvaux and grants a privilege to the Cistercians, exempting them from the duty to pay tithes from the income, which others used to receive from estates donated to the Cistercians.

1132: Acquisition of monasteries in England (Rievaulx), Spain (Moreruela), and Belgium (Orval) — Bernard absent from the chapter of reform-minded Benedictine abbots in the church province of Reims, chaired by William of Saint-Thierry — Matthew of Albano disapproves of these reform plans and tries to block them — Bernard combats the supporters of Anacletus in Aquitaine — Bernard begins his series of sermons on the Song of Songs after returning to Clairvaux.

1133: Hildebert of Lavardin dies — First journey of Bernard to Italy to accompany Innocent II — Stephen Harding abdicates as abbot of Cîteaux and is succeeded by Guy, the abbot of Trois-Fontaines.

1134: Stephen Harding dies — Guy, his successor in Cîteaux, is deposed and succeeded by Rainald de Bar, a monk from Clairvaux.

1135: Bernard attends the Diet in Bamberg; he urges Emperor Lotharius to begin a campaign against Roger II of Sicily — He travels on to Italy, where he meets Peter the Venerable at a synod in Pisa — Prior Godefroy of Clairvaux develops plans for new buildings in Clairvaux — Bernard confronted with these plans in December upon returning from Rome — Signy, near Reims, incorporated in the Cistercian Order through Igny's initiative — William of Saint-Thierry abdicates as abbot and becomes monk in Signy.

1136: Matthew, cardinal-bishop of Albano, dies — Construction of Clairvaux II — In December Bernard again leaves for Italy.

1137: Bernard remains a full year in Italy — He is instrumental in persuading Petrus, the cardinal-bishop of Pisa, belatedly to join the party of Innocent II — The episcopal see of Langres is vacant — General chapter about the difficulties resulting from le Miroir's refusal to pay tithes to Gigny.

1138: Death of Anacletus II leads to end of the schism — During his return journey, Bernard protests against the election and consecration of the new bishop of Langres — Peter the Venerable criticizes Bernard's attitude in this matter — Bernard Paganelli, vidame of the chapter of Pisa, enters Clairvaux.

1139: Godefroy de la Roche Vanneau elected and consecrated as bishop of Langres — Bernard continues his sermons on the Song of Songs — Acquisition of Ter Duinen as the 28th filiation of Claivaux — Robert of Brughes, who entered Clairvaux in 1130, becomes abbot of Ter Duinen — The scriptorium of the chapter of St. Donatian in Brughes now produces manuscripts for Ter Duinen — Peter of Pisa is demoted during the Second Lateran Council — Bernard protests against this in a letter to Innocent II — Innocent II begins a crusade against Roger of Sicily, a supporter of Anacletus; Innocent is taken prisoner and makes peace.

1140: Sambucino abbey in Calabria transferred to Clairvaux by Roger of Sicily — The Tre-Fontane abbey in Rome transferred to Clairvaux by Innocent II — William of Saint-Thierry warns Bernard regarding Abelard's theology — Bernard preaches about "the conversion" for a group of Parisian students — Geoffrey of Auxerre, until then a student of Abelard, follows Bernard to Clairvaux.

1141: Bernard accuses Abelard of heresy during the Council of Sens; the attending bishops condemn Abelard's theology — Abelard finds refuge in Cluny on his way to Rome — Peter the Venerable succeeds in reconciling Bernard and Abelard — Alanus of Lille, monk in Clairvaux since 1131, becomes abbot of l'Arrivour — Death of Thurstan, archbishop of York — Pierre de la Châtre chosen as archbishop of Bourges, against the will of Louis VII; this results in a protracted struggle between the king and Thibaut, the count of Champagne.

1142: Death of Abelard — The chapter of York elects William FitzHerbert as the successor of Thurstan — Bernard counsels Innocent II not to accept this choice, which had the approval of the papal legate, but allegedly was irregular.

1143: Death of Innocent II — Peter the Venerable begins to seek support from Bernard for his reforms in Cluny — Bernard accuses William FitzHerbert of simony in letters to Celestine II and the Curia.

1144: Death of Richard, the abbot of Fountains — Henri Murdach, the abbot of Vauclair, succeeds Richard — Death of Celestine II — Lucius II elected pope, but dies soon afterward.

1145: Henri de France, the brother of Louis VII, becomes a monk in Clairvaux — Nicholas, a monk from Montiéramy, enters Clairvaux to assist Bernard as secretary — Bernard Paganelli, the abbot of Tre Fontane, is elected as pope: Eugenius III — Geoffrey of Auxerre begins collecting materials for a *vita Bernardi* and organizes Bernard's letter register — Bernard preaches in the Languedoc against Henry of Lausanne — Geoffrey reports on this journey — Eugenius travels to France because of unrest in Rome; Bernard acts as his advisor until Eugenius returns.

1146: Following the pope's orders, Bernard begins the preaching of the Second Crusade in Vézelay — His preaching in Germany is reported, with emphasis on the miracles he performed.

1147: Bernard returns from Rhineland and receives Eugenius III in Clairvaux — William FitzHerbert deposed as archbishop of York and succeeded by Henri Murdach, the abbot of Fountains — Departure of armies recruited by Bernard for the crusade — William of Saint-Thierry writes the first book of the *Vita prima* — Bernard resumes his sermons on the Song of Songs in Clairvaux.

1148: Council of Reims — Under pressure from Bernard, the council decides to condemn the teachings on the Trinity by Gilbert de la Porrée — Eugenius III returns to Rome — Bernard writes the first book of the *De consideratione* — Death of William of Saint-Thierry — Arnold, abbot of Bonneval, is asked to write the second book of the *vita prima* — Malachias, abbot of Armagh, dies in Clairvaux.

1149: Bernard defends himself with regard to the failed crusade — He writes the second book of the *De consideratione* — Henri de France leaves Clairvaux to become bishop of Beauvais — Peter the Venerable solicits the support of Bernard for reforms in his order through Nicholas of Montéramy as intermediary — In letter 250, addressed to the prior of Portes, Bernard calls himself the "chimera of his century."

1150: Bernard writes the *vita Malachiae* — Death of Reinoud de Bar — The Council of Chartres charges Bernard with the responsibility for another crusade — The Cistercians arrange for nullification of this command.

1151/52: Escalation of the conflict between Gigny and Le Miroir, in spite of the consultations of Bernard with Peter the Venerable — Nicholas of Montiéramy expelled from Clairvaux because of his falsification of letters of Bernard — This leads to a lasting breach in the relationship between Bernard and Peter the Venerable — Alain of Lille, until then the abbot of Arrivour, is elected bishop of Auxerre after intervention by Bernard.

1152: Bernard completes the *De consideratione* — Eskil, archbishop of Lund, visits him in Clairvaux.

1153: Bernard, restored from an illness, travels to Metz, where he intercedes in a conflict between the bishop and the duke of Lorraine — Pope Eugenius III dies on July 8 — Bernard dies on August 20, after an illness of several months — Robert, abbot of Ter Duinen, succeeds him in Clairvaux — Geoffrey of Auxerre sends an account of the last year and death of Bernard to archbishop Eskil.

1154: Henri Murdach dies — William FitzHerbert succeeds him as archbishop of York.

1154/55: Geoffrey of Auxerre writes the last three books of the *vita prima*, using the account sent to Eskil as the basis for the fifth book.

1155/56: A group of Cistercian abbots and bishops who had been favorably disposed toward Bernard meet in Clairvaux to evaluate the text of the *vita prima* (redaction A) — They add miracle stories and focus primarily on the text that would be submitted to the pope together with the canonization request.

1157: Death of Abbot Robert — He is succeeded by Fastredus, coming from Hainault, who had been abbot of Cambron since 1148.

1159: The general chapter authorizes the Clairvaux community to initiate a liturgical commemoration of Bernard — The election of Alexander III as pope causes a schism — The Cistercians immediately take the side of Alexander and promote his recognition — Geoffrey of Auxerre becomes the abbot of Igny.

1162: Fastredus becomes the abbot of Cîteaux — Geoffrey abbot of Clairvaux.

1163: Council of Tours, chaired by Alexander III — The pope does not act upon the request for Bernard's canonization — The *vita* manuscript that had been submitted is returned to Geoffrey.

1163/65 Geoffrey of Auxerre revises the text of the *vita prima* (redaction B) — Godefroy de la Roche Vanneau, back in Clairvaux, attempts to write a new *vita*.

1165: Geoffrey of Auxerre objects against a stay of Thomas Becket in Pontigny — Alexander III and Louis VII demand his abdication as abbot of Clairvaux — He moves to Cîteaux — Pons of Auvergne becomes the abbot of Clairvaux.

1167: Alain of Lille, bishop of Auxerre, abdicates and returns to Clairvaux.

1167/70 Alain continues the endeavor of Godefroy de la Roche Vanneau and writes the *vita secunda*.

1169: Geoffrey of Auxerre mediates in the conflict between Thomas Becket and Henry II of England — At Cîteaux he prepares a manuscript of the *vita prima* to support a new request for Bernard's canonization.

1170: Pons of Auvergne becomes bishop of Clermont — Girald, abbot of Fossa Nova, becomes abbot of Clairvaux — Geoffrey of Auxerre becomes abbot of Fossa Nova.

1171: Thomas Becket, back in England, is murdered in the cathedral of Canterbury.

1173: Alexander III canonizes Thomas Becket — Girald, abbot of Clairvaux, submits a request for the canonization of Bernard.

1174: Bernard canonized (January 18) — Elevation of his mortal remains in the abbatial church of Clairvaux (October 13).

Appendix 2

Summary of Some of the Textual Problems Discussed in This Book

ə❦   ə❦

I. As far as we know, two manuscripts of the *Vita prima* (Vp) were lost during World War II. Presently 129 manuscripts of this text, complete or in part, are extant. Some follow redaction A, others redaction B, while some offer an inter-- mediary phase: A-B.[1]

	Red. A	Red. B	Red. A-B	Total
12th century	7	6	1	14
12th-13th century	10	12	1	23
13th century	13	15	1	29
13th-14th century	2	4		6
14th century	4	8	1	13
15th century	23	19	1	43
16th century	1			1
Total	60	64	5	129

II. Two of the fourteen manuscripts from the 12th century were written in 1154/55 and 1165 respectively. The ms from 1154/55 (Paris, BNL 7561) is a working copy,

1. For the complete list of manuscripts see *Etudes* (1960), 15-28.

originating in Clairvaux. It can in part be considered as an autograph by Geoffrey of Auxerre. This ms contains his revision of his account to Eskil into a first draft of book V, partly in his own handwriting.[2]

III. The ms from 1165 originated in the scriptorium of the Benedictine monastery of Anchin (Douai, Bibl. mun. 372, vol. II). It was copied from a ms presented by Geoffrey of Auxerre in Paris in 1163 to Alexander III, in support of his request for Bernard's canonization, prior to the Council of Tours. It was returned to him when the request was not acted upon. This ms must have been easy to read because of its wide margins and ample spacing between the lines, and it was therefore very suitable for a text revision. When this revision was almost completed, it was given by Geoffrey to the then famous scriptorium of Anchin, where at the time Bernard's complete oeuvre was copied. Consequently, the ms of the *Vita prima* that was produced in Anchin presents an intermediate stage (A-B), which also contains the peculiarities of the canonization ms, redaction A.

IV. Four of the remaining 12th-century manuscripts originated in Cistercian monasteries; two follow redaction A and two redaction B. They all date from the end of the 12th century. One ms, redaction A (Düsseldorf, Stadt und Landesbibl. B 26), has the original text of Geoffrey's account to Eskil. There are no evidences that any of these mss dates from before the canonization of Bernard. This seems to indicate that the *Vita prima* began to stir interest in the Cistercian Order only with the next generation of monks, who had no personal memory of Bernard as abbot.

V. With regard to the 23 manuscripts from the 12th-13th centuries, 6 of the 10 mss that follow redaction A originated in Cistercian monasteries. The same number out of a total of 11 mss, redaction B, also stem from these monasteries. One of these latter 6 (Dijon, Bibl. mun. 659) is from Cîteaux. It contains a passage which Geoffrey of Auxerre must have added to the fifth book, redaction B, when he stayed in Cîteaux in 1169. The only other instance where this passage is found is in two later mss, in Châlons-sur-Sâone (Bibl. mun. 6), written in 1290 in Clairvaux, and Genua (U.B. A IV 33), end 13th–beginning 14th century. This passage reiterates a characterization of Bernard found more extensively in redaction A, but later eliminated from redaction B. In view of the content of this passage and of the time when it was added, we may deduce that at that time Geoffrey had already made arrangements for a special ms in support of the request for Bernard's canonization. It would seem that this ms was a copy of that particular codex. This would also mean that a critical redaction of the *Vita prima* ought to opt for the ms Dijon 659 as its basis.

2. Cf. "Un Brouillon du XIIe siècle" (1959), 27-60; especially 47.

VI. This same ms, Dijon 659, mentions (folio 19-recto) that Bernard entered Cîteaux in the year of the Lord MCXII: 1112. This date is also found in the above-mentioned ms from Genua. There is, however, one difference: In the ms from Cîteaux, it is clearly visible that the original reading was MCXIII; thus, the year 1113 was changed into 1112 at some later date. The reason may be that the founding of La Ferté took place as early as 1113. The story in the first book about the resuscitation of this seemingly moribund monastery as a result of the arrival of Bernard and his companions might not have been very credible if Bernard had not entered Cîteaux until sometime during 1113. The ms in Châlons-sur-Sâone (end of 13th century), originating from Clairvaux and donated in 1390 to La Ferté, lacks the first section of the first book, including this particular passage and this earlier date.

Bibliography

1. COLLECTIONS

Aus Kirche und Reich. Festschrift für Friedrich Kempf, publ. H. Mordak. Sigmaringen, 1983.

Bernard de Clairvaux, 1953: Commission d'Histoire de l'ordre de Cîteaux. Paris, 1953 (BdC).

Bernard de Clairvaux: histoire-mentalités-spiritualité. Actes du colloque de Lyon-Cîteaux-Dijon, juin 1990, Oeuvres Complètes, I: Introduction générale, Paris, 1992, Sources Chrétiennes, n⁰ 380. Paris, 1992.

Bernardus Magister. Papers Presented at the Nonacentenary Celebration of the Birth of Saint Bernard, ed. J. R. Sommerfeldt; *Cistercian Publications.* Kalamazoo, Mich., 1993 (C.S.S. 135) and *Cîteaux: Commentarii Cistercienses* 42 (1992).

Bernard of Clairvaux. Studies Presented to Dom Jean Leclercq. Washington, D.C., 1973 (C.S.S. 23).

Bernhard von Clairvaux. Rezeption und Wirkung im Mittelalter und in der Neuzeit, publ. K. Elm. Akten des Wolfenbütteler Symposions, Oktober 23-27, 1990. Wiesbaden, 1994 (Wolfenbütteler Mittelalter-Studien, B. 6).

Bijdragen. Tijdschrift voor filosofie en theologie.

Councils and Assemblees. SCH, Subsidia 7, ed. G. J. Cuming and D. Baker. London, 1971.

291

Die Chimäre seines Jahrhunderts, publ. J. Spörl. Würzburg, 1954.

Die Zisterzienser. Ordensleben zwischen Ideal und Wirklichkeit, publ. K. Elm, Ergänzungsband. Cologne, 1982.

Fälschungen im Mittelalter. Internationaler Kongreß der MGH, Munich, 16-19 September 1986, vol. V, Fingierte Brieven. Hannover, 1988 (MGH Schriften B. 33, V).

Festschrift zum 800-Jahresgedächtnis Bernhards von Clairvaux. Vienna-Munich, 1953.

Histoire de Clairvaux. Association Renaissance de l'Abbaye de Clairvaux. Actes du Colloque de Bar-sur-Aube/Clairvaux, 22 et 23 juin, 1990. Bar-sur-Aube, 1991.

Hommes et structures du moyen âge. Un recueil d'articles, éd. G. Duby. Paris, 1973.

La dottrina della vita spirituale nelle opere di san Bernardo di Clairvaux. Atti del convegno internazionale, Roma, 11-15 settembre 1990. Rome, 1991.

L'économie cistercienne. Géographie, Mutations, du Moyen Age aux Temps modernes (Troisièmes Journées internationales d'histoire, 1981). Auch, 1983.

Le gouvernement d'Hugues de Semur à Cluny. Actes du colloque scientifique international, Cluny, September 1988. Cluny, 1990.

Maisons de Dieu et hommes d'Église. Florilège en l'honneur de Pierre-Roger Gaussin. Saint-Étienne, 1992.

Mélanges à la mémoire du père Anselme Dimier, présentés par Benoît Chauvin, I, 2, Travaux inédits et rééditions. Puppelin, 1987.

Mélanges saint Bernard. XXIVe congrès de l'association Bourguignonne des société savantes. Dijon, 1953.

Medieval Women, ed. D. Baker. SCH, Subsidia 1. Oxford, 1978.

Monachisme et technologie dans la société du Xe au XIIIe siècle. Actes du colloque international, Cluny, septembre 4-6, 1991. Cluny, 1994.

Papauté, monachisme et théories politiques. Mélanges en honneur de Marcel Pacaut. 2 tomes, Lyon, 1994.

Pascua Medievalia. Studies voor Prof. J.-M. De Smet, Medievalia Lovaniensia, Series 1, Studia X. Louvain, 1983.

Petrus Venerabilis (1156-1956). Studies and Texts commemorating the Eighth Centenary of his Death, ed. G. Constable and J. Kritzeck. Rome, 1956 (Studia Anselmiana, fasc. 40).

Prophecy and Eschatology, ed. M. Wilks, SCH Subsidia 10. Oxford, 1994.

Recueil d'études sur saint Bernard et ses écrits, éd. J. Leclercq, 5 tomes. Rome, 1962-1992.

Renaissance and Renewal in the Twelfth Century, publ. R. L. Benson and G. Constable. Oxford, 1982.

Saint Bernard et la philosophie, sous la direction de R. Brague. Paris, 1993.

Saint Bernard et la recherche de Dieu. Actes du colloque organisé par l'Institut catholique de Toulouse (25-29 janvier 1991), *Bulletin de Littérature Ecclésiastique* 93 (1992), fasc. 1.

Saint Bernard et son temps. Association Bourguignonne des sociétés savantes, congrès de 1927, 2dln. Dijon, 1928-1929.

Saint Bernard of Clairvaux. Studies Commemorating the Eighth Centenary of His Canonization, ed. B. Pennington. Kalamazoo, 1977. (C.S.S 28).

Saint Bernard théologien. Actes du congrès de Dijon, 15-19 septembre 1953. AnCi IX, fasc. 3-4, 1953.

Saint-Thierry, une abbaye du VIe au XXe siècle. Actes du colloque international d'histoire monastique, Reims-Saint-Thierry, 11-14 octobre 1976, ed. M. Bur. Saint-Thierry, 1979.

San Bernardo. Pubblicazione commemorativa nell'VIII centenario della sua morte. Milan, 1954.

Studi su San Bernardo di Chiaravalle nell'ottavo centenario della canonizazione. Convengo internazionale, Certoza di Firenze (November 6-9, 1974). Rome, 1975.

Texte und Textkritik. Eine Aufsatzsammlung, publ. J. Dümmer. Berlin, 1987.

The Second Crusade and the Cistercians, publ. M. Gervers. New York, 1992.

Thomas Becket. Actes du colloque international de Sédières, August 19-24, 1974, publ. by R. Foreville. Paris, 1975.

Vies et légendes de saint Bernard, création, diffusion, réception. Actes des rencontres de Dijon, June 7-8, 1991, publ. J. Berlioz, P. Arabeyre, and P. Poirrier. Subsides *Cîteaux, Commentarii Cistercienses,* 1993.

William, Abbot of St. Thierry. A Colloquium at the Abbey of St. Thierry. Kalamazoo, 1987 (C.S.S. 94).

Zisterziensische Spiritualität. Theologische Grundlagen, funktionale Voraussetzungen und Bildhafte Ausprägungen im Mittelalter, publ. C. Kaspar and K. Schreiner, SMBO 34. Ergänzungsband. St. Ottilien, 1994.

2. SOURCES

"*Acta primi capituli provincialis ordinis S. Benedicti, Remis* A.D. *1131 habiti,*" in *Saint-Thierry,* 312-350.

Alain of Auxerre, *Vita secunda s. Bernardi,* P.L., CLXXXV, 469-524.

Barlow, Fr., ed., *The Letters of Arnulf of Lisieux.* London, 1939 (Camden Third Series, 61).

Bernardus, *Sancti Bernardi Opera,* éd. J. Leclercq et H. Rochais (abbr. SBO). rééditions: *Bernhard von Clairvaux. Sämtliche Werke* in 10 Bänden (Latin-German), publ. G. B. Winkler. Innsbruck-Vienne, 1990–; *Opere di San Bernardo,* a cura di F. Gastaldelli (Latin-Italian), 7 vols. Rome, 1984– S.C.ⁿ 367, 380 (introduction), 390, 393 . . . (Latin-French).

Bouthillier, D., ed., *Petri Cluniacensis abbatis de Miraculis,* libri duo. Turnhout, 1988. (CC cont. med. 83).

————, and J. B. Van Damme (1974), *Les plus anciens textes de Cîteaux.* Achel, 1974.

Bullarium sacri ordinis cluniacensis, ed. Simons. Lyon, 1680.

Canivez, J.-M., *Statuta capitulorum generalium Ordinis Cisterciensis,* vol. I. Louvain, 1933.

Chibnall, M., ed., *The "Historica Pontificalis" of John of Salisbury.* Edinburgh, 1956 (repr.: Oxford, 1965).

————, *The Ecclesiastical History of Orderic Vitalis,* 6 tomes. Oxford, 1969-1980.

Chartres et documents concernant l'abbaye de Cîteaux, éd. J. Marilier. Rome, 1961.

Chronicon Sigeberti, continuatio premonstratensis, MGH SS VI, 447-456.

Constable, G., ed., *The Letters of Peter the Venerable,* 2 tomes. Cambridge, Mass., 1967.

————, ed., "Statuta Petri Venerabili," CC Mon. VI, 19-106.

Davy, M. M., éd., *Guillaume de Saint-Thierry: Meditativae Orationes,* texte et traduction. Paris, 1934.

Dialogus duorum monachorum. See Huygens, R. B. C., *Le moine Idung.*

Exordium magnum. See B. Griesser.

Gastaldelli, F., éd., *Goffredo di Auxerre, Expositio in Cantica Canticorum* I. Rome, 1974.

————, ed., *Opere di San Bernardo* VI 1/2 (Lettere). Milan, 1986/87.

Griesser, B., éd., *Exordium magnum Cisterciense, auctore Conrado.* Rome, 1961 (BHL 1235).

Guizot, M., éd., *Vie de Saint Bernard* (transl.), in *Collection des Mémoires rélatifs à l'histoire de France*. Paris, 1825, 145-479.

Heinzer, F. "Zwei unbekannte Briefe Bernhards von Clairvaux in einer Handschrift der Zisterzienserabtei Lichtental," *Scriptorium* 41 (1987), 97-105.

Huygens, *Le moine Idung et ses deux ouvrages:* "Argumentum super quatuor questionibus" et "Dialogus duorum monachorum." Spoleto, 1980.

James, B. C., transl. *The Letters of St. Bernard of Clairvaux*. London, 1953.

Lechat, R., ed., "Les *Fragmenta de Vita et Miraculis S. Bernardi* par Geoffroy d'Auxerre," AnBoll 50 (1932), 83-122 (BHL 1207).

Ottonis et Rahewenini Gesta Friderici I imperatoris, ed. G. Waitz and B. Simson. Hannover, 1912 (SRG B. 46).

Poncelet, A., ed., "Vie ancienne de Guillaume de Saint-Thierry," in *Mélanges Godefroid Kurth* I. Liège, 1908, 85-96.

Rau, R., *Bonifatii Epistulae: Willibaldi Vita Bonifatii*. Darmstadt, 1968.

Vita prima sancti Bernardi. See William of St. Thierry.

Vita secunda sancti Bernardi. See Alain d'Auxerre.

Waquet, J., *Recueil des chartres de l'abbaye de Clairvaux*, fasc. 1. Troyes, 1950.

Webb, G., and A. Walker, *Saint Bernard of Clairvaux: The Story of His Life as Recorded in the Vita prima*. London, 1952.

William of St. Thierry, Arnald of Bonneval, and Geoffrey of Auxerre, *Vita prima sancti Bernardi* (Libri V), P.L. 185, 225-368.

Willeumier-Schalij, J. M., ed., *Willlem van St. Thierry's Epistel totten Bruederen van den Berghe Godes*. Leiden, 1950.

Ysengrimus. Text with Translation, Commentary, and Introduction, ed. Jill Mann.

3. BOOKS, MONOGRAPHS, ARTICLES

Aigrain, R., *L'hagiographie: ses sources, ses méthodes, son histoire*. Paris, 1953.

Auberger, J.-B., *L'unanimité cistercienne primitive: mythe ou réalité*. Cîteaux-Achel, 1986.

————, "La législation cistercienne primitive et sa relecture claravallienne," in *Bernard de Clairvaux: histoire*, 181-207.

Baker, D., "*Viri religiosi* and the York Election Dispute," in *Councils and Assemblees* (SCH 7), 87-100.

————, "San Bernardo e l'elezione di York," *Studi su san Bernardo*, 115-180.

Barlow, Fr., "The Canonization and Early Lives of Hugh I, Abbot of Cluny," AnBoll 98 (1980), 297-334.

Barrière, B., "L'économie cistercienne du sud-ouest de la France," in *L'économie cistercienne*, 75-99.

Bartlett, R., *Gerald of Wales*, 1982.

Bell, D. N. (1984), *The Image and Likeness. The Augustinian Spirituality of William of Saint-Thierry*. Kalamazoo, 1984 (C.S.S. 78).

————, *The Librairies of the Cistercians, Gilbertines and Premonstatensians*. London, 1992 (*The Corpus of British Medieval Library Catalogues*, vol 3).

Bell, T., *Divus Bernhardus. Bernhard von Clairvaux in Martin Luthers Schriften*. Mainz, 1993.

————, "Pater Bernardus: Bernard de Clairvaux vu par Martin Luther," *Cîteaux* 41 (1991), 233-255.

Berger, D., "The Attitude of St. Bernard towards the Jews," *Proceedings of the American Academy for Jewish Research* 40 (1972-1973), 89-108.

Berlioz, J., "Saint Bernard dans la littérature satirique de l'Ysengrinys aux Balivernes des courtisans de Gautier Map (XIIe-XIIIe siècles)," in *Vie et légendes*, 211-228.

———— a.o., "Saint Bernard dans les *exempla* (XIIIe-XVe siècles)," in *Vie et Légendes*, 116-140.

Berman, C. H., "Origins of the Filiation of Morimond in Southern France," *Cîteaux* 41 (1990), 256-277.

————, "Les cisterciens et le tournant économique de XIIe siècle," in *Bernard de Clairvaux: histoire*, 155-177.

————, "The Development of Cistercian Economic Practice during the Lifetime of Bernard of Clairvaux: The Historical Perspective and Innocent's 1132 Privilege," in *Bernardus magister*, 303-313.

Bertrand, D., "Littérature et vérité. *Aux clercs, sur la conversion* et textes paralleles," in *Maisons de Dieu*, 11-27.

Bethel, D, "The Foundation of Fountains Abbey and the State of St. Mary-York," JEH 17 (1966), 11-27.

————, *English Cistercian Monasteries and Their Patrons in the Twelfth Century*. Chicago, 1968.

Billy, D. J., "The *Ysengrimus* and the Cistercian-Cluniac Controversy," *ABR* 43 (1992), 301-328.

Bledniak, S., "L'hagiographie de saint Bernard au XVIe siècle," in *Vie et légendes*, 91-115.

Bligny, B., *L'Eglise et les ordres réligieux dans le royaume de Bourgogne au XIe et XIIe siècles*. Paris, 1960.

————, "Les chartreux dans la société occidentale du XIIe siècle," *Cahiers d'Histoire* 20 (1975).

Bolton, B. M. "The Cistercians and the Aftermath of the Second Crusade," in *The Second Crusade*, 131-140.

Botteril, Steven, *Dante and the Mystical Tradition:* "Bernard of Clairvaux in the *Commedia*." Cambridge, 1994 (Cambridge Studies in Medieval Literature 22).

Bouchard, C. H,, "*Holy Entrepreneurs. Cistercians, Knights and Economic Exchange in Twelfth Century Burgundy.* Cornell U.P., 1991.

Bouhot, J.-P., "La bibliothèque de Clairvaux," in *Bernard de Clairvaux: histoire*, 141-153.

Boureau, A., "La présence de saint Bernard dans les légendiers dominicains du XIIIᵉ siècle," in *Vie et légendes*, 84-90.

Bouton, J. de la Croix, *Bibliographie bernardine (1891-1957)*. Paris, 1958.

————, "Bernard et l'ordre de Cluny," BdC, 193-217.

————, "Bernard et les monastères bénédictins non clunisiens," BdC, 219-249.

————, "Bernard et les ermites et groupements érémitiques," BdC, 251-262.

————, "Bernard et les Chanoines réguliers," BdC, 263-288.

————, "Saint Bernard et les moniales," in *Mélanges saint Bernard*, 225-247.

————, "La réforme du chant *(Negotia Ordinis),*" BdC, 158-166.

Brague, M., "L'anthropologie de l'humilité," in *Saint Bernard et la philosophie*, 129-152.

Bredero, A. H. (1956), "The Controversy between Peter the Venerable and Saint Bernard of Clairvaux," in *Petrus Venerabilis*, 53-71.

———— (1958), "Studien zu den Kreuzzugsbriefen Bernhards von Clairvaux und seiner Reise nach Deutschland im Jahre 1146," M.I.ö.G. 66, 331-343.

———— (1959), "Un Brouillon du XIIe siècle: L'autographe de Geoffroy d'Auxerre," *Scriptorium* 13, 27-60.

———— (1960), *Etudes sur la "Vita Prima" de saint Bernard*. Rome, reprinted in AnCi 17 (1961), 3-72; 215-260 et 18 (1962), 3-59.

———— (1962), "De paus uit het Ghetto. Achtergronden en betekenis van het schisma van 1130," *Annalen van het Thijmgenootschap* 51, 51-70.

———— (1966), *Bernhard von Clairvaux im Widerstreit der Historie*. Wiesbaden (Mainzer Vorträge nr. 44).

———— (1974), "La canonisation de saint Bernard sous un nouvel aspect," *Cîteaux* 25, 185-196.

———— (1975), "S. Bernardo di Chiaravalle: Correlazione tra fenomeno cultico e storico," in *Studi su san Bernardo,* 23-48.

———— (1975*), "Thomas Becket et la canonisation de saint Bernard," in *Thomas Becket,* 55-62.

———— (1977), "Saint Bernard and the Historians," in *Saint Bernard of Clairvaux,* 27-62.

———— (1977), "The Canonization of Bernard of Clairvaux," in *Saint Bernard of Clairvaux,* 63-100.

———— (1980), "The Conflicting Interpretations of the Relevance of Bernard of Clairvaux to the History of His Own Time," *Cîteaux,* 31, 53-81.

———— (1983), "Henri de Lausanne: un réformateur devenue hérétique," in *Pascua Medievalia,* 108-123.

———— (1985), *Cluny et Cîteaux au douzième siècle.* L'histoire d'une controverse monastique. Amsterdam-Maarssen et Lille.

———— (1987/88), "De toegankelijkheid van het historische leven van Sint Bernard," *Sacris Erudiri* 30, 293-328.

———— (1988), "Der Brief des heiligen Bernhards auf dem Sterbebett: eine authentische Fälschung," in *Fälschungen im Mittelalter* V, 201-224.

———— (1990), "La canonisation de saint Hugues et celle de ses devanciers," in *Le gouvernement d'Hugues de Semur à Cluny,* 149-171.

———— (1992), "La vie et la *Vita prima,*" in *Bernard de Clairvaux: histoire,* 53-81.

———— (1992), "L'intérêt historique de la première Vie de Saint Bernard," in *Maisons de Dieu,* 83-93.

———— (1992), "Saint Bernard in His Relations to Peter the Venerable," in *Bernardus magister,* 315-347.

———— (1994), *Christendom and Christianity in the Middle Ages: The Relations between Religion, Church and Society.* Grand Rapids, Mich.

———— (1994), "Saint Bernard, est il né en 1090 ou en 1091," in *Papauté* I, 229-241.

———— (1994), "Le rôle de l'agriculture dans la crise de Cluny en 1122," in *Monachisme et technologie,* 109-122.

———— (1994), "Bernhard von Clairvaux zwischen Kult und Historie. Das Heiligkeitsbild in der Zisterzienserhistoriographie des 12. Jahrhundert," in *Zisterziensische Spiritualität,* 135-151.

————— (1994), "Der Heilige Bernhard von Clairvaux im Mittelalter: von der historischen Person zum Kultgestalt," in *Bernhard von Clairvaux: Rezeption*, 141-159.

Brezzi, P., "San Bernardo e Roma," in *Studi Romani* I (1953), 496-509.

Bur, M., "Le monachisme en Champagne méridionale et dans le nord du diocèse de Langres à l'arrivée de Saint Bernard à Clairvaux en 1115," in *Histoire de Clairvaux*, 3-19.

Burckhardt, J., *Weltgeschichtliche Betrachtungen*, ed. W. Kaegi. Bern, 1947.

Cantarella, "Cluny, Lione, Roma (1119-1140)," RBen 90 (1980), 263-287.

Carbonell, Ch.-O., *Histoire et historiens: Une mutation idéologique des historiens français, 1865-1885*. Toulouse, 1976.

Casey, M., "Le spirituel: les grands thèmes bernardins," in *Bernard de Clairvaux: histoire*, 605-635.

—————, "Towards a Methodology for the *Vita prima:* Translating the First Life into Biography," in *Bernardus magister*, 55-70.

Ceglar, S., "William of Saint-Thierry and His Leading Role at the First Chapters of the Benedictine Abbots," in *William Abbot*, 34-49.

Chaume, A., "Les origines familiales de Saint Bernard," in *Saint Bernard et son temps*, I, 75-112.

Chauvin, B., "Réalités et évolution de l'économie cistercienne dans les duché et comté de Bourgogne au Moyen Age. Essai de synthèse," in *L'économie cistercienne*, 13-52.

—————, "Un disciple méconnu de saint Bernard: Burchard de Balerne puis de Bellevaux," *Cîteaux* 40 (1989), 5-66.

Chomton (l'abbé), *Saint Bernard et le château de Fontaines-lès-Dijon*. Étude historique et archéologique, 3 vols. Dijon, 1891-1895.

Claude, H., "Autour du schisme d'Anaclet: Saint Bernard et Girard d'Angoulême," in *Mélanges saint Bernard*, 80-94.

Clémencet, Ch., *Histoire littéraire de S. Bernard, abbé de Clairvaux, et de Pierre Vénérable, abbé de Cluni*. Paris, 1773.

Cocheril, "L'atlas de l'ordre cistercien," *Cîteaux* 20 (1969), 119-144.

—————, "L'implantation des abbayes cisterciennes dans la péninsule ibérique," *Anuario des estudios medievales* I (1964), 217-287.

—————, "Quelques remarques sur 'Saint Bernard, l'art cistercien'," COCR 43 (1981), 377-388.

Constable, G. "The Disputed Election at Langres in 1138," *Traditio* 13 (1957), 119-152.

—————, "Cluniac Tithes and the Controversy between Gigny and le Miroir," RBen 70 (1960), 591-624.

————, *Monastic Tithes, from Their Origins to the Twelfth Century.* Cambridge, Mass., 1964.

————, "The Popularity of Twelfth-Century Spiritual Writers in the Late Middle Ages," *Studies in Honor of Hans Baron.* Florence, 1977, 5-28.

————, "Twelfth-Century Spirituality and the Late Middle Ages," M.R.S. 5 (1971), 27-60.

————, *Letters and Letter-Collections. Typologie des sources* 17. Turnhout, 1976.

————, *Cluniac Studies.* London, 1980 (Variorum Reprints).

————, "Forged Letters in the Middle Ages," in *Fälschungen im Mittelalter* V (1988), 11-37.

Cousin, P., "Les débuts de l'ordre des Templiers et saint Bernard," in *Mélanges saint Bernard,* 41-52.

Cowdrey, H. E. J., *The Cluniacs and the Gregorian Reform.* Oxford, 1970.

————, "Abbot Pontius of Cluny," *Studi Gregoriani* 11 (1978), 177-298.

Dahan, G., "Saint Bernard et les Juifs," *Sens* année 43 (1991), 163-170.

Dal Prà, L., *Iconografia di San Bernardo in Italia* II, 1. Rome, 1991.

d'Eberbach, Conrad, *Exordium magnum.* See B. Griesser.

De Jong, M. B., *In Samuel's Image: Child Oblation in the Early Medieval West.* Leiden, 1996.

Delehaye, H., *Les Légendes hagiographiques.* Bruxelles, 1954 (4th ed.).

Dempf, A. "Die geistige Stellung Bernhards von Clairvaux gegen die kluniazensische Kunst," in *Die Chimäre seines Jahrhunderts,* 29-53.

Den Boer, P. *History as a Profession: The Study of History in France (1818-1914).* Princeton U.P., 1995.

De Place, Fr., "Bibliographie raisonnée des premiers documents cisterciens (1098-1200)," *Cîteaux* 34 (1984), 7-54.

Deroy, J. P. Th., *Bernardus en Origenes.* Haarlem, 1963.

Dessi, R. M., en M. Lamy, "Saint Bernard et les controverses mariales au moyen âge," in *Vies et légendes,* 229-260.

De Vooght, P., "De *De consideratione* de saint Bernard au *De potestate* de Wycliff," *Irenikon* 25 (1953), 114-132.

Diers, M., *Bernhard von Clairvaux: Elitäre Frömmigkeit und begnadetes Wirken.* Münster, 1991.

Dimier, A., *Saint Bernard "pêcheur de Dieu."* Paris, 1953.

————, "Le monde claravallien à la mort de saint Bernard," in *Mélanges saint Bernard,* 248-253; rewritten in *Mélanges Anselme Dimier,* I, 2, 595-598.

————, "Les fondations manquées de saint Bernard," *Cîteaux* 20 (1969), 5-13.

————, "Saint Bernard et les abbayes-filles," AnCi 25 (1969), 245-268.

Dinzelbacher, P. "Zum Konzept persönlicher Heiligkeit bei Bernhard von Clairvaux und den frühen Zisterziensern," in *Zisterziensische Spiritualität*, 101-133.

Donkin, R. A., *The Cistercians: Studies in the Geography of Mediaeval England and Wales.* Toronto, 1978.

Duby, G., "Le budget de l'abbaye de Cluny entre 1080 et 1155," AnnESC 7 (1952), 155-171; republished in *Hommes et structures*, 61-82.

————, "Un inventaire des profits de la seigneurie clunisienne à la mort de Pierre le Vénérable," in *Petrus Venerabilis* (1956), 129-140; republished in *Hommes et Structures*, 87-101.

————, "Les 'jeunes' dans la société aristocratique dans la France du Nord-Ouest au XIIe siècle," AnnESC 19 (1964), 835-846; republished in *Hommes et structures*, 1973, 213-225.

————, *Guerriers et paysans*. VIIe-XIIe siècle, premier essor de l'économie européenne. Paris, 1973.

————, *Saint Bernard, L'art cistercien.* Paris, 1976.

Evans, G. R., "The *De consideratione* of Bernard of Clairvaux: A Preliminary Letter," *Cîteaux* 35 (1984), 129-134.

Evans, J., *Cluniac Art of the Romanesque Period.* Cambridge, 1950.

Farkasfalvy, D., "The Authenticity of Saint Bernard's Letter from His Deathbed," AnCi 34 (1987), 263-268.

Fechner, H., *Die politische Tätigkeit des Abtes Bernhard von Clairvaux in seinen Briefen.* Bonn and Cologne, 1933.

Feiss, H., "*Bernardus scholasticus:* The Correspondence of Bernard of Clairvaux and Hugh of Saint Victor on Baptism," in *Bernardus magister*, 349-378.

Figuet, J., "La Bible et Bernard: données et ouvertures," in *Bernard de Clairvaux: histoire*, 237-269.

Flasche, H. "Bernhard von Clairvaux als Geistesahne Pascals," *Sacris Erudiri* 5 (1953), 333-337.

Folz, R., "Die Gründung von Cîteaux," in *Die Chimäre seines Jahrhunderts*, 9-28.

Fossier, R., "Le plateau de Langres et la fondation de Clairvaux," BdC, 67-75.

————, "L'installation et les premiers années de Clairvaux," BdC, 77-93.

————, "L'essor économique de Clairvaux," BdC, 95-114.

————, "La fondation de Clairvaux et la famille de saint Bernard," in *Mélanges saint Bernard,* 19-27.

————, "L'économie cistercienne dans les plaines du nord-ouest de l'Europe," in *L'économie cistercienne,* 53-74.

Gastaldelli, F., "I primi venti anni di san Bernardo. Problemi e interpretazioni," AnCi 43 (1987), 111-148.

————, "Le piu antiche testimonianze biografiche su San Bernardo. Studio storico-critico sui *Fragmenta Gaufridi,*" AnCi 45 (1989), 3-80.

————, "Le tre ultime lettere dell' Epistolario di San Bernardo," AnCi 50 (1994), 251-292.

————, "*Optimus praedicator.* L'opera oratoria di San Bernardo," AnCi 51 (1995), 321-418.

Gaussin, P. R., *L'abbaye de la Chaise-Dieu.* Paris, 1962.

Genest, J.-F., "La bibliothèque de Clairvaux de Saint Bernard à l'humanisme," in *Histoire de Clairvaux,* 113-133.

Ghellinck, J. de, *L'essor de la littérature latine au XIIe siècle.* Bruxelles-Bruges, 1955 (2nd ed.).

Gilson, E. *La théologie mystique de Saint Bernard.* Paris, 1934 (repr. 1947, 1969). English transl. *The Mystical Theology of Saint Bernard.* London-New York, 1940; repr. 1955.

Gimpel, J., *The Medieval Machine: The Industrial Revolution of the Middle Ages.* London, 1977 (transl. from the French).

Goetz, H. W., "Bernard et Norbert: eschatologie et réforme," in *Bernard de Clairvaux: histoire,* 505-525.

————, "Eschatologische Vorstellungen und Reformziele bei Bernhard von Clairvaux und Norbert von Xanten," in *Zisterziensische Spiritualität,* 153-169.

Goodrich, W. E., "The Reliability of the *Vita S. Bernardi: The Image of Bernard in Book I of the Vita prima* and His Own Letters: A Comparison," AnCi 43 (1987), 153-180.

Graboïs, A., "Le schisme de 1130 et la France," R.H.E. 76 (1981), 593-612.

————, "*Militia and Malitia:* The Bernardine View of Chivalry," in *The Second Crusade,* 49-56.

Grill, L., "Der heilige Bernhard von Clairvaux und Morimond, die Mutterabtei der österreichischen Zisterzienserklöster," in *Festschrift,* 31-118.

————, "Morimond, soeur jumelle de Clairvaux," BdC, 118-125.

————, "*Epistola de Charitate.* Des älteste St. Bernardsbrief," *Cîteaux* 15 (1964), 26-51.

Grivot, D., "Saint Bernard et Pierre le Vénérable," in *Saint Bernard et la recherche de Dieu*, 85-99.

Grotz, H., "Kriterien auf dem Prüfstand: Bernhard von Clairvaux angesichts zweier kanonisch strittiger Wahlen," in *Aus Kirche und Reich*, 1983, 237-263.

Grundmann, H., "Der Typus des Ketzers im Mittelalter," *Ausgewählte Aufsätze* I. Stuttgart, 1976, 311-327.

Guardini, R., "Bernhard von Clairvaux in Dantes göttlicher Kommödie," in *Die Chimäre seines Jahrhunderts*, 54-70.

Häring, N., "A Latin Dialogue on the Doctrine of Gilbert of Poitiers," M.S. 15 (1953), 243-289.

———, "The Writings against Gilbert of Poitiers by Geoffrey of Auxerre," AnCi 22 (1966), 3-83.

———, "Saint Bernard and the *litterati* of His Days," AnCi 25 (1974), 199-222.

Heathcote, S. J., "The Letter Collections attributed to Master Transmundus," AnCi 21 (1965), 35-109, 167-238.

Haskins, C. H., *Renaissance of the Twelfth Century*. Cambridge, Mass., 1927.

Heer, Fr., *Aufgangs Europa*. Eine Studie zu den Zusammenhängen zwischen politischer Religiosität, Frömmigkeitsstil und den Werden Europas im 12. Jahrhundert. Vienna-Zürich, 1949.

Heller, D., *Schriftauslegung und geistliche Erfahrung bei Bernhard von Clairvaux*. Würzburg, 1990.

Hendrix, G., *Bibliotheca auctorum traductorum et scriptorum Ordinis Cisterciensis*. Louvain, 1992.

Higounet, C., "Essai sur les granges cisterciennes," in *L'économie cistercienne*, 157-180.

Hill, B. D., *English Cistercian Monasteries and Their Patrons in the Twelfth Century*. Chicago-London, 1968.

Hoffmann, H, "Die beiden Schwerter im hohen Mittelalter," D.A. 20 (1964), 78-114.

Holdsworth, C., "The Reception of St Bernard in England," in *Bernhard von Clairvaux: Rezeption*, 161-177.

———, "The Early Writings of Bernard of Clairvaux," *Cîteaux* 45 (1994), 21-60.

———, "Sanctity and Secularity in Bernard of Clairvaux," NAKG 75 (1995), 149-164.

Hüffer, G., "Handschriftliche Studien," H.J. 5 (1884), 576-624 en 6 (1885), 31-91 en 232-270.

————, *Der heilige Bernard von Clairvaux*. Eine Darstellung seines Lebens und Wirkens. Münster, 1886 (Erster Band: *Vorstudien*).

Hümpfner, T., "Archivum et bibliotheca Cistercii et quatuor filiarum eius," AnCi 2 (1946), 119-145.

Jacqueline, B., *Épiscopat et papauté chez saint Bernard de Clairvaux*. Sainte-Marguerite d'Elle, 1975.

James, B. S., "The Personality of St. Bernard as Revealed in His Letters," COCR 14 (1952), 30-34.

————, *Saint Bernard of Clairvaux: An Essay in Biography*. London, 1957.

Janauschek, L., *Bibliographia Bernardina*. Vienna, 1891 (repr. Hildesheim, 1959).

————, *Originum Cisterciensium*. Vienna, 1877.

Jelsma, A., *De blaffende hond. Aspecten uit het leven van Wynfreth Bonifatius*. The Hague, 1973.

Kahl, H. D., "Crusade Eschatology as Seen by St. Bernard in the Years 1146 to 1148," in *The Second Crusade*, 35-48.

Kemp, E. W., *Canonization and Authority in the Western Church*. Oxford, 1948.

Kennan, E., "The *De Consideratione* of Saint Bernard of Clairvaux and the Papacy in the Mid-Twelfth Century: A Review of Scholarship," *Traditio* 33 (1967), 73-115.

————, "Antithese and Argument in *De Consideratione*," in *Bernard of Clairvaux*, 91-109.

Kienzle, B. M., "*Verbum Dei et verba Bernardi:* The Function of Language in Bernard's *Second Sermo for Peter and Paul*," in *Bernardus magister*, 149-159.

Kinder, T. N., "Les églises de Clairvaux. Probabilités et fiction," in *Histoire de Clairvaux*, 205-229.

Klauser, R., *Der Heinrichs- und Kunigunde-Kult im mittelalterlichen Bistum Bamberg*. Bamberg, 1957.

Knowles, D., *The Monastic Order in England*. Cambridge, 1963.

————, *Great Historical Enterprises and Problems in Monastic History*. London, 1963.

————, "Saint Bernard of Clairvaux (1090-1153)," in *The Historians and Character and Other Essays*. Cambridge, 1964, 30-49.

————, "Cistercians and Cluniacs: The Controversy between St. Bernard and Peter the Venerable," in *The Historians*, 50-75.

Koch, E. "Die Bernhard-Reception im Luthertum des 16. und 17. Jahrhundert," in *Bernhard von Clairvaux: Rezeption*, 333-351.

Köpf, U., *Religiöse Erfahrung in der Theologie Bernhards von Clairvaux.* Tübingen, 1980.

————, "Bernhard von Clairvaux — ein Mystiker," in *Zisterziensische Spiritualität,* 15-32.

————, "Die Rolle der Erfahrung im religiösen Leben nach dem heiligen Bernhard," in *La dottrina,* 307-319.

————, "Die Rezeptions- und Wirkungsgeschichte Bernhards von Clairvaux. Forschungsstand und Forschungsaufgaben," dans *Bernhard von Clairvaux: Rezeption,* 5-65.

Lackner, B. K., *The Eleventh-Century Background of Cîteaux.* Washington, D.C., 1972 (C.S.S. 8).

Lane, A. S. N., *Calvin's Use of Bernard of Clairvaux.* Hilary Hill, 1982.

————, "Bernard of Clairvaux: A Forerunner of John Calvin?" in *Bernardus magister,* 533-545.

————, "Calvin's Use of Bernard von Clairvaux," in *Bernhard von Clairvaux: Rezeption,* 303-332.

Lang, A. P., "The Friendship between Peter the Venerable and Bernard of Clairvaux," in *Bernard of Clairvaux,* 35-53.

Langer, O. "Affekt und Ratio. Rationalitätskritische Aspekte in der Mystik Bernhards von Clairvaux," in *Zisterziensische Spiritualität,* 33-52.

Lardreau, G., "Amour philosophique et amour spirituel," in *Saint Bernard et la philosophie,* 27-48.

Leclercq, J., *Saint Bernard mystique.* Brughes-Paris, 1948.

————, *Études sur saint Bernard et le texte de ses écrits.* Rome, 1953 (AnCi 9, fasc. 1).

————, *L'amour des lettres et désir de Dieu.* Paris, 1957; 2nd ed. 1963. Eng. ed. *The Love of Learning and the Desire for God.* New York, 1961 (paperback ed. 1962).

————, *Nouveau visage de Bernard de Clairvaux.* Paris, 1976.

————, *Monks and Love in the Twelfth Century.* Oxford, 1979.

————, *La femme et les femmes dans l'oeuvre de saint Bernard.* Paris, 1982.

————, "S. Bernard et la théologie monastique du XIIᵉ siècle," in *Saint Bernard théologien,* 7-23.

————, "The Renewal of Theology," in *Renaissance and Renewal* (1982), 68-87.

————, *Bernard de Clairvaux.* Paris, 1989.

————, "Lettres de saint Bernard, retrouvés depuis les Mauristes," in *Texte und Textkritik,* 311-324.

————, "Notes sur la tradition des épitres de saint Bernard," *Recueil* III, 307-322.

————, "Lettres de s. Bernard: Histoire ou littérature?" *Recueil* IV, 125-225.

————, "Agressivité et répression chez saint Bernard de Clairvaux," R.H.S. 52 (1976), 155-172.

————, "Le portrait de saint Bernard dans la littérature des 'exempla' du das Moyen Age," COCR 50 (1988), 256-267.

————, "Aspects littéraires de l'oeuvre de saint Bernard," *Recueil* III, 13-210.

————, "L'écrivain," in *Bernard de Clairvaux: histoire,* 529-556.

————, "Towards a Sociological Interpretation of the Various Bernards," in *Bernardus magister,* 19-33.

————, "La paternité de saint Bernard et les débuts de l'ordre cistercien," RBen 103 (1993), 451-469.

————, "Saint Bernard and the Beginnings of the Cistercian Order," Cist. St. 29 (1994), 379-393.

Le Goff, J., *La civilisation de l'Occident médiéval.* Paris, 1964.

Lekai, L. J., *The Cistercians: Ideal and Reality.* Kent State U.P., 1977.

Leonardi, C., "Bernard de Clairvaux entre mystique et cléricalisation," in *Bernard de Clairvaux: histoire,* 703-711.

Leyser, H., *Hermits and the New Monasticism: A Study of Religious Communities in Western Europe,* 1000-1150. London, 1984.

Little, E., "Bernard et Abelard at the Council of Sens, 1140," in *Bernard of Clairvaux,* 55-71.

Lobrichon, G., "Représentations de Clairvaux dans la *Vita prima sancti Bernardi,*" in *Histoire de Clairvaux,* 245-255.

————, "La Bible des maîtres du XIIe siècle," in *Bernard de Clairvaux: histoire,* 209-236.

Locatelli, R., "L'implantation cistercienne dans le comté de Bourgogne jusqu'au milieu du XIIe siècle," *Cahiers d'Histoire* 20 (1975), 167-225.

————, "L'expansion de l'ordre cistercien," in *Bernard de Clairvaux: histoire,* 103-139.

Lohse, B., "Luther und Bernhard von Clairvaux," in *Bernhard von Clairvaux: Rezeption,* 271-301.

Louf, A., "Bernard, abbé," in *Bernard de Clairvaux: histoire,* 349-379.

————, "Saint Bernard, fut-il un iconoclaste?" in *Saint Bernard et la recherche de Dieu,* 49-64.

Lubac, H. *Exégèse médiévale. Les quatre sens de l'Ecriture,* 4 tomes. Paris, 1959-1964.

Luchaire, A., *Les premiers Capétiens.* Paris, 1911 (*Histoire de la France des origines à la révolution,* éd. E. Lavisse); réimpr., Paris, 1980.

Luscombe, D., *The School of Abélard.* Cambridge, 1970.

Magnard, P., "Image et ressemblance," in *Saint Bernard et la philosophie,* 73-85.

Mann, Jill, ed., *Ysengrimus.* Text with Translation, Commentary and Introduction. Leyden, 1987.

Manselli, R., "Alberico, cardinale vescovo d'Ostia et la sua attività di legato pontifico," *Archivio della società romana di Storia patria* 78 (1955), 56-59.

Marilier, J., éd., *Chartes et documents concernant l'abbaye de Cîteaux.* Rome, 1961.

Marion, J.-L., "L'image et la liberté," in *Saint Bernard et la philosophie,* 49-72.

Maseron, A., *Dante et saint Bernard.* Paris, 1953.

McGinn, B., "St Bernard and Eschatology," in *Bernard of Clairvaux,* 161-185.

————, "*Alter Moyses:* The Role of Bernard in the Thought of Joachim of Fiore," in *Bernardus magister,* 429-448.

McGuire, B. P., "A Lost Clairvaux *Exemplum* Found: The *liber visionum et miraculorum* Compiled under Prior John of Clairvaux (1117-1179)," AnCi 39 (1983), 27-60.

————, "The First Cistercian Renewal and a Changing Image of St Bernard," Cist. St. 24 (1989), 25-49.

————, "La présence de saint Bernard dans l'*Exordium Magnum Cisterciense*," in *Vie et légendes,* 63-83.

————, "A Saint's Afterlife: Bernard in the Golden Legend and Other Medieval Collections," in *Bernhard von Clairvaux: Rezeption,* 179-211.

Mellinghoff-Bourgerie, V., "Bernhard von Clairvaux in der französischen Frommigkeitsliteratur des 17. Jahrhunderts: François de Sales," in *Bernhard von Clairvaux: Rezeption,* 389-420.

Mellot, P., "Saint Bernard et la guérison des malades," in *Mélanges saint Bernard,* 181-186.

Merton, T., "Saint Bernard, moine et apôtre," BdC (1953), VII-XII.

————, *The Last of the Fathers.* London, 1954.

Mesnard, J., "Pascal et Bernard de Clairvaux," in *Bernhard von Clairvaux: Rezeption,* 375-387.

Michel, B., "La philosophie: le cas du *De Consideratione*," in *Bernard de Clairvaux: histoire,* 579-603.

————, "La considération et l'*unitas spiritus*," in *Saint Bernard et la philosophie*, 109-127.

Milis, L., "William of Saint-Thierry, His Birth, His Formation and His First Monastic Experiences," in *William Abbot*, 9-33.

Mortet, V., "Hugues de Fouilloi, Pierre le Chantre, Alexander Neckam et les critiques dirigées au douzième siècle contre le luxe de construction," in *Mélanges offerts à M. Charles Bémont*. Paris, 1913, 105-137.

Murray, A., *Reason and Society in the Middle Ages*. Oxford, 1978.

Nilgen, U., "Historischer Schriftsinn und ironische Weltbetrachtung. Buchmalerei im frühen Cîteaux und der Stein des Anstoßes," in *Bernhard von Clairvaux: Rezeption*, 67-140.

Ochsenbein, P., "Bernhard von Clairvaux in spätmittelalterlichen Gebets büchern," in *Bernhard von Clairvaux: Rezeption*, 213-232.

Oury, G.-M., "La vie monastique dans l'oeuvre d'Ernaud, abbé de Bonneval," R.H.S. 51 (1975), 267-280.

————, "Recherches sur Ernaud, abbé de Bonneval, historien de saint Bernard," RMab 49 (1977), 97-127.

Pacaut, M., *Louis VII et les élections épiscopales dans le royaume de France*. Paris, 1957.

————, *La théocratie. L'église et le pouvoir au moyen âge*. Paris, 1989.

————, "La filiation claravallienne dans la génèse et l'essor de l'ordre cistercien," in *Histoire de Clairvaux*, 135-147.

————, "Une fille stérile de Cîteaux: le Miroir," in *Maisons de Dieu*, 95-105.

————, "Saint Bernard dans l'historiographie française du dix-neuvième siècle," in *Bernhard von Clairvaux: Rezeption*, 421-430.

Packard, S. R., *12th Century Europe: An Interpretive Essay*. Amherst, 1973.

Palumbo, F. P., *Lo scisma del MCXXX*. I precedenti, la vicenda romana e le ripercussioni europee della lotta tra Anacleto e Innocenzo II. Rome, 1942.

Passerat, G., "La venue de Saint Bernard à Toulouse et les débuts de l'abbaye de Grandselve," in *Saint Bernard et la recherche de Dieu*, 27-37.

Paul, J., "Les débuts de Clairvaux. Histoire et théologie," in *Vie et légendes*, 19-35.

Philips, P., "The Presence — and the Absence — of Bernard of Clairvaux in the Twelfth-century Chronicles," in *Bernardus magister*, 35-53.

Philips, W. E., "The Plight of the Song of Songs," *Journal of the Academy of Religion* 42 (1974), 82-100.

Piazzoni, A. M., *Guglielmo di Saint-Thierry: il declino dell'ideale monastico nel secolo XII*. Rome, 1988.

————, "La première biographie de saint Bernard. Guillaume de Saint-Thierry. La première partie de la *Vita prima* comme oeuvre théologique et spirituelle," in *Vie et légendes,* 3-18.

Picard, A., et P. Boglioni, "Miracle et thaumaturgie dans la vie de saint Bernard," in *Vie et légendes,* 36-59.

Plongeron, B., "Lumières contre l'époque mystique," in *Vie et légendes,* 306-327.

Posset, F., "*Divus Bernardus:* Saint Bernard as Spiritual and Theological Leader of the Reformer Martin Luther," in *Bernardus magister,* 517-532.

Pranger, M. B., *Bernard of Clairvaux and the Shape of Monastic Thought: Broken Dreams,* Leyden, 1994.

————, "The Virgin Mary and the Love-Language in the Works of Bernhard of Clairvaux," *Cîteaux* 40 (1989), 112-137.

————, "The Rhetorical Epistemology in Saint Bernard's *Super Cantica,*" in *Bernardus magister,* 95-128.

Preiss, M., *Die politische Tätigkeit und Stellung der Zisterzienser im Schisma von 1159-1177.* Berlin, 1934, repr. Vaduz, 1965).

Presse, A., "Un manuscrit des *Fragmenta Gaufridi,*" in *Saint Bernard et son temps* I, 1-7.

————, "Saint Etienne Harding," COCR 1 (1934), 21-30 en 85-94.

Prinz, Fr., *Askese und Kultur.* Vor- und frühbenediktinisches Mönchtum an der Wiege Europas. München, 1980.

Radecke, Fr., *Die eschatologischen Anschauungen Bernhards von Clairvaux.* Ein Beitrag zur historischen Interpretation aus den Zeitanschauungen. Langensalza, 1915.

Raedts, P., "St Bernard of Clairvaux and Jerusalem," in *Prophecy and Eschatology,* 169-192.

Reiter, J., "Bernard de Clairvaux, philosophe malgré lui entre coeur et raison?" in *Saint Bernard et la philosophie,* 11-25.

Richard, J., "Dans l'Europe du XIIe siècle," dans *Bernard de Clairvaux: histoire,* 83-102.

Riché, P., "La connaissance concrète de la chrétienté," in *Bernard de Clairvaux: histoire,* 381-399.

————, "Saint Bernard à Clairvaux," in *Histoire de Clairvaux,* 21-30.

————, "Saint Bernard et l'hérésie," in *Saint Bernard et la recherche de Dieu,* 17-25.

Rigolot, I., "Bernard de Clairvaux, lecteur de saint Augustin," COCR 54 (1992), 132-144.

Rosenwein, B. H., *Rinoceros Bound: Cluny in the Tenth Century.* Philadelphia, 1982.

————, *To Be the Neighbor of Saint Peter: The Social Meaning of Cluny's Property, 909-1049.* Ithaca and London, 1989.

Rousseau, O, "S. Bernard, «le dernier des Pères»," in *Saint Bernard théologien,* 300-308.

Rowe, J. G., "The Origins of the Second Crusade: Pope Eugenius III, Bernard of Clairvaux and Louis VII of France," in *The Second Crusade,* 79-90.

Rudolph, C., *The "Things of Greater Importance:"* Bernard of Clairvaux's *Apologia* and the Medieval Attitude towards Art. Philadelphia, 1990.

————, "The Scholarship on Bernard of Clairvaux's *Apologia,*" *Cîteaux* 40 (1989), 69-110.

Runciman, S. *A History of the Crusades,* II. Cambridge, 1952.

Schindele, P., "Rectitudo und Puritas. Die bedeutung beider Begriffe in den Gründungsdokumenten von Cîteaux und ihre Auswirkungen in der Lehre des hl. Bernhards von Clairvaux," in *Zisterziensische Spiritualität,* 53-73.

Schmale, F.-J., *Studien zum Schisma des Jahres 1130.* Cologne-Graz, 1962.

Schönfelder, *Isengrimus. Das flämische Tierenepos aus dem Lateinischen verdeutscht.* Münster, 1955.

Schonsgaard, A., "Un ami de saint Bernard, l'archevêque Eskil, de Lund," in *Saint Bernard et son temps,* II, 231-247.

Schreiner, K. "Puritas Regulae, Caritas und Necessitas. Leitbegriffe in der monastischen Theologie Bernhards von Clairvaux," in *Zisterziensische Spiritualität,* 75-100.

Séjourné, P., "Les inédits bernardins du manuscrit d'Anchin," in *Saint Bernard et son temps,* II, 248-69.

Sicard, G., "Le moine et les princes," in *Saint Bernard et la Recherche de Dieu,* 7-16.

Sigal, P.-A., *L'homme et le miracle dans la France médiévale* (XI-XIIe siècle). Paris, 1985.

Sinz, P., "Bernhard von Clairvaux. Vollmensch oder Chimäre?" *Cistercienser Chronik* 60 (1953), 16-38.

Smith, U. R., "Arnold of Bonneval, Bernard of Clairvaux and Bernard's Epistle 310," AnCi 49 (1993), 273-318.

Sommerfeldt, J. R., "The Chimaera Revisited," AnCi 38 (1987), 5-13.

————, "Bernard as Contemplative," in *Bernardus magister,* 73-84.

Sommerville, R., *Pope Alexander III and the Council of Tours* (1163). Berkeley, 1977.

Spijker, I. van 't, *Als door een speciaal stempel. Traditie en vernieuwing in heiligenlevens uit Noordwest-Frankrijk (1050-1150)*. Hilversum, 1990.

Spörl, J., "Bernhard von Clairvaux oder das Problem historischer Größe," in *Die Chimäre seines Jahrhunderts*, 71-95.

Stiegman, E., "A Tradition of Aesthetics in Saint Bernard," in *Bernardus magister*, 129-147.

Stratford, N., "A Romanesque Marble Altar-Front in Beaune and Some Cîteaux Manuscripts," in *Studies in Medieval Art, Liturgy and Metrology Presented to Christopher Holher*, ed. A. Borg and A. Martindale. Oxford, 1984, 125-157.

Stroll, M., *The Jewish Pope: Ideology and Politics in the Papal Schism of 1130*. Leyden, 1987.

———, *Symbols as Power: The Papacy following the Investiture Conquest*. Leyden, 1991.

Swietek, F. R., "The Role of Bernard of Clairvaux in the Union of Savigny with Cîteaux: A Reconsideration," in *Bernardus magister*, 289-302.

Talbot, C. H., "San Bernardo nelle sue lettere," in *San Bernardo*, 151-165.

Teubner-Schoebel, S., *Bernhard von Clairvaux als Vermittler an der Kurie. Eine Auswertung seiner Briefsammlung*. Bonn, 1993.

Thesaurus sancti Bernardi Claraevallensis, series A — Formae, curante Cetedox. Turnhout, 1987.

Thomson, R. M., "The Satirical Works of Berengar of Poitiers: An Edition with Introduction," M.S. 42 (1980), 89-138.

Thompson, S., "The Problems of the Cistercian Nuns in the Twelfth and the Early Thirteenth Centuries," in *Medieval Women*, 227-252.

Tierney, B., *The Crisis of Church & State, 1050-1300*. Englewood Cliffs (N.J.), 1964.

Timmermann, W., *Studien zur allegorischen Bildlichkeit in den Parabolae Bernhards von Clairvaux*. Frankfurt a.M., 1983.

Torre, Juan Maria de la, "Experiencia Cristiana y Expressión Estetica en los Sermones sobre El Cantar de los Cantares," in *Obras Completa de San Bernardo*, V. Madrid, 1988, 3-75.

Torrell, J.-P., *Pierre le Vénérable, abbé de Cluny. Le courage de la mesure*. Cambray-les-Tours, 1988.

———, and D. Bouthillier, *Pierre le Vénérable et sa vision du monde. Sa vie, son oeuvre, l'homme et le démon*. Louvain, 1986 (S.S.L. fasc. 42).

Türk, E., *Nugae curialium. Le règne d'Henri II Plantagenêt (1145-1189) et l'éthique politique,* Genève, 1977.

Turrini, C, "San Bernardo e l'allegoria delle due spade," *Rivista cisterciense* I (1984), 5-41.

Vacandard, E., *Vie de Saint Bernard,* 2 tomes. Paris, 1895.

————, "L'histoire de Saint Bernard. Critique des sources," R.Q.H., t. 43 (1888), 337-389.

————, "La vie de saint Bernard et ses critiques," R.Q.H., t. 62 (1897), 198-211.

Van Damme, J.-B., "La *summa cartae caritatis,* source de constitutions canonicales," *Cîteaux* 23 (1972), 5-54.

————, "*Novum monasterium.* Die Zisterzienserreform und die Regel des hl. Benedikt," in *Die Zisterzienser,* 39-45.

Van den Eynde, D., "Les premiers écrits de S. Bernard," *Recueil* III, 343-422.

Van der Meer, F., *Atlas de l'ordre cistercien.* Amsterdam-Bruxelles, 1965.

Van Engen, J., "The 'Crisis of Cenobitism' Reconsidered: Benedictine Monasticism in the Years 1050-1150," *Speculum* 61 (1986), 269-304.

Van Hecke, L., *Le désir dans l'expérience religieuse. L'homme réunifié. Relecture de saint Bernard.* Paris, 1990.

Van Mierlo, J., *Het vroegste dierenepos in de letterkunde der Nederlanden.* Antwerpen, 1943.

Van 't Spijker, I., *Als door een speciaal stempel. Traditie en vernieuwing in heiligenlevens uit Noordwest-Frankrijk (1050-1150).* Hilversum, 1950.

Van Moolenbroek, J. J., *Vital l'ermite, prédicateur itinérant, fondateur de l'abbaye normande de Savigny.* Assen-Maastricht, 1990.

Van Velzen, A., "Het misformulier op het feest van St. Bernardus," COCR 6 (1936), 110-112.

Vauchez, A., *La sainteté en Occident aux derniers siècles du moyen âge d'après les procès de canonisation et les documents hagiographiques,* Rome. 1981.

Verdeyen, P., "Un théologien de l'expérience," in *Bernard de Clairvaux: histoire,* 557-578.

Verger, J., "Le cloître et les écoles," in *Bernard de Clairvaux: histoire,* 459-475.

————, "Saint Bernard vu par Abélard et quelques autres maîtres des écoles urbaines," in *Histoire de Clairvaux,* 161-175.

————, "Saint Bernard et les scolastiques," in *Vie et légendes,* 201-210.

————, et J. Jolivet, *Bernard-Abélard ou le cloître et l'école.* Paris, 1982.

Vicaire, M.-H., *Histoire de saint Dominique*. Paris, 1982.

Villevorde, Mons. de, *La vie de Saint Bernard, premier abbé de Clairvaux*. Paris, 1723.

Vitri, G., and L. Dal Prà, ed., *Vita et miracula divi Bernardi Clarevallensis abbatis*. Florence, 1987. A reprint of the edition of 1587.

Volpini, R., "A proposito dell'anno del concilio di Sens (1141)," *Aevum 66* (1992).

Von Moos, P. L., *Hildebert von Lavardin (1056-1133). Humanitas an der Schwelle des höfischen Zeitalters*. Stuttgart, 1965.

———, "Le dialogue latin au moyen âge: l'exemple d'Evrard d'Ipres," AnnESC 44 (1989), 939-1028.

Waddell, "Chant cistercien et liturgie," in *Bernard de Clairvaux: histoire*, 271-285.

Ward, B., *Miracles and Medieval Mind*. London, 1982.

Werckmeister, O. K., "Cluny III and the Pilgrimage to Santiago de Compostella," *Gesta 27* (1988), 103-111.

Werner, E. et M. Erbstösser, *Ketzer und Heilige. Das religiöse Leben im Hochmittelalter*. Berlin, 1986.

Williams, W., *Saint Bernard of Clairvaux*. Manchester, 1935 (2nd ed. 1952).

Wilmart, S.,"La série et la date des ouvrages de Guillaume de Saint-Thierry," RMab 14 (1924), 157-167.

Winandy, J., "Les origines de Cîteaux et les travaux de M. Lefèvre," RBen 67 (1957), 49-67.

Zaluska, Y., *L'enluminure et le Scriptorium de Cîteaux au XIIe siècle*. Cîteaux, 1989 (*Studia et documenta IV*).

———, "L'enluminure cistercienne au XIIe siècle," in *Bernard de Clairvaux: histoire*, 271-285.

Zerbi, P., "I rapporti di S. Bernardo di Chiaravalle con I vescovi e le diocesi d'Italia," in idem, *Tra Milano e Cluny. Momenti di vita e cultura ecclesiastica nel secolo XII*. Roma, 1978, 3-109.

———, "Intorno allo scisma di Ponzio, abate di Cluny (122-1126)," *Tra Milano e Cluny*, 309-371.

———, "S. Bernardo di Chiaravalle e il concilio di Sens," in *Studi su S. Bernardo*, 49-73.

———, "Les différends doctrinaux," in *Bernard de Clairvaux: histoire*, 429-458.

Index

Abelard, Peter, 2, 15, 21, 31, 40, 47, 73, 79, 85, 93, 98, 113, 119, 127, 133, 175, 177, 181, 187, 196, 228, 235-36, 239-40, 276
Adam of Morimond, 213
Adrian IV, 43, 103
Afflighem, 259
agriculture, 9
Aigran, R., 173n.70
Alain of Auxerre, 53-54, 168
Alberic, 202, 211, 260-61
Albi, 25, 76
Albigenses, 76
Albinus, 100
Aleth (mother of Bernard), 29-30, 32, 58, 79-80
Alexander III, 33, 43-44, 49-50, 53, 55, 56, 67, 71-76, 138n.108
Alexander of Lincoln, 272
allegorical interpretation, 174, 267-69, 277
Anacletus II, 21, 34, 47, 112-13, 114-15, 117-18, 130, 146, 154, 232, 261, 262
Anastasius IV, 43, 156n.34, 233
Anchin, 48-49, 50-51, 62, 66-67, 68, 105
Anselm of Canterbury, 119
Anselm, bishop of Havelberg, 195

Apology (Bernard), 78, 103, 111, 129, 144, 204, 217, 221-26, 228, 238, 265
Aquitaine, 113, 114, 259
Archenfridus, 25
Armagh, 251
Arnold of Bonneval, 28, 34, 38, 78, 92, 97, 98-99, 102-18, 128, 265
Arnold of Brescia, 146, 152, 175, 187
Arnold of Morimond, 216-17
Arnulf of Séez, 115, 255n.118
Arrivour, 53
Artald, 108, 206n.26, 259
asceticism, 74, 119, 128, 174, 214, 222
Auberger, Jean-Baptiste, 215
Augustine, 268
Aulne, 259
Aulps, 259
Auvergne, 119

Babylon, 268-70
Baldwin, Cardinal, 115, 130, 146
Balerne, 259
Baltinglass, 264
barking dog vision, 29-30, 79-80, 133
Baruch Judaeus, 130n.93
Basil, 227
Battle of Blénau, 176